THE KGB

THE KGB

Police and Politics in the Soviet Union

AMY W. KNIGHT

Boston
UNWIN HYMAN
London   Sydney   Wellington

Allen & Unwin, Inc.,
8 Winchester Place, Winchester, MA 01890, USA.

Published by the Academic Division of
Unwin Hyman Ltd,
15/17 Broadwick Street, London W1V 1FP, UK

Allen & Unwin Australia Pty Ltd,
8 Napier Street, North Sydney, NSW 2060, Australia

Allen & Unwin (New Zealand) Ltd, in association with the
Port Nicholson Press Ltd
60 Cambridge Terrace, Wellington, New Zealand

Library of Congress Cataloguing-in-Publication Data

Knight, Amy W., 1946–
   The KGB, police and politics in the Soviet Union.
Bibliography: p.
Includes index.
1. Soviet Union. Komitet gosudarstvennoĭ bezopansnosti—
History.   2. Police—Soviet Union—History.   3. Soviet Union—
Politics and government—1945–
I. Title.
HV8224.K57   1988   363.2'83'0947   87–19533
ISBN 0–04–445035–4

British Library Cataloguing in Publication Data

Knight, Amy W.
   The KGB: police and politics in the Soviet Union.
1. Union of Soviet Socialist Republics.
Komitet gosudarstvenno i bezopasnosti
I. Title
327.1'2'0947   HV8224
ISBN 0–04–445035–4

Set in 10 on 12 point Palatino by Computape (Pickering) Ltd
and printed in Great Britain by Biddles of Guildford

To my parents

Contents

[ix]

Abbreviations

BSE	*Bol'shaia sovetskaia entsiklopediia*
FBIS	*Foreign Broadcast Information Service*
CCE	*Chronicle of Current Events*
JPRS	*Joint Publications Research Service*
KZ	*Krasnaia zvezda*
POC	*Problems of Communism*
RLRB	*Radio Liberty Research Bulletin*
SVE	*Sovetskaia voennaia entsiklopediia*
SZ	*Sotsialisticheskaia zakonnost'*

Acknowledgments

I am deeply indebted to a number of persons whose generous help has made this study possible. I particularly want to thank Robert Slusser and George Leggett. Their own excellent scholarship on the Soviet political police served as an inspiration to my work; both painstakingly read my manuscript in its entirety and provided invaluable source materials. I am also grateful to my former teacher at the London School of Economics, Peter Reddaway, who read and commented on the manuscript and whose work on the dissident movement stimulated my initial interest in the KGB. Harry Rigby, Graeme Gill, Werner Hahn, George Breslaver, Robert Sharlet, and Robert Stephan were also kind enough to read and comment upon portions of the manuscript.

A number of other scholars have given advice, expertise, and help. Special thanks are due to Barbara Chotiner, Martin Dewhirst, Rose Gottemoeller, Thane Gustafson, Eugene Huskey, Ellen Jones, Bruce Parrott, and Elisabeth Ropeson.

My colleagues at the Library of Congress have provided much support. Albert Graham, David Kraus, and George Bugounoff were especially helpful in my efforts to locate sources. I am also grateful to the staff at Radio Liberty in Munich, in particular Keith Bush, Elizabeth Teague, Peter Kruzhin, Herwig Kraus, and Peter Dornin, and to the Centre for International Studies at the London School of Economics for assistance when I served there as a Visiting Fellow. My editor, Lisa Freeman, and her assistant, Peggy McMahon, efficiently and enthusiastically coordinated the production of this book.

Finally, I owe deepest gratitude to my husband, Malcolm, and my daughters, Molly, Diana, and Alexandra for their unfailing support and patience.

Introduction

THEY HAVE SOME ROOM FOR MANOEUVRE, WITHOUT
FUNDAMENTALLY CHANGING THE SYSTEM. THEY CAN
RELEASE POLITICAL PRISONERS. THEY CAN EVEN
PUBLISH THE *GULAG ARCHIPELAGO*. BUT THEY CAN'T DO
IT FOR LONG.

—VLADIMIR BUKOVSKY (1987)

With the decline of the Brezhnev regime in the early 1980s the Soviet Union entered a period of political upheaval unequaled except by that which followed Stalin's death. In fewer than three years three successive general secretaries took power; unprecedented turnover occurred in party and state cadres; and now, amid signs of heated Kremlin debate, what could be substantial political and economic reforms are being introduced. These developments, which are in sharp contrast to the conservatism and stagnation of Soviet politics in the 1970s, have prompted Western scholars to look anew at the Soviet system and to reassess assumptions about the nature of Kremlin politics, just as they did during what seemed to be a turning point in Soviet history after Stalin died. Much of the scholarly debate has centered on the role of Soviet institutions in the political process and on the question of how Soviet leaders gain power and authority. Did Gorbachev, for example, rely on support from a specific group of party cadres to consolidate his power, or did he appeal to institutions outside the party? Where have the various interests lined up over key issues, such as economic reform and relations with the West, and how do they exert their influence?

[xv]

The Soviet security police, or KGB, looms as an uncertain variable for scholars examining these issues, mainly because we have no commonly accepted conceptual framework to explain its role in the system. The KGB has never received much scholarly attention in West. Although several Western publications on the KGB's foreign espionage and intelligence operations have appeared in recent years, scholars have devoted little effort to the KGB's internal political role. Unlike the Soviet military, which has been the subject of numerous institutional studies and analyses, the KGB has been virtually ignored by Western experts. The dearth of serious scholarly research on the KGB has left a deep gap in our knowledge of how the Soviet system works and what factors influence Soviet decision making.

The apparent reason for this absence of research lies in the fact that the security police has long been identified with the totalitarian aspects of the Soviet system. During the past two and a half decades Western scholars have abandoned the totalitarian model of Soviet politics that was developed in the 1950s and have turned to other explanations of how the Soviet system works. Instead of focusing on power struggles and personalities in the Kremlin, they have studied other phenomena—interest groups, local party politics, economic managers, nationality problems, and so on—in order to understand the dynamics of the system. Underlying this change of emphasis has been an effort to stress the more rational aspects of Soviet society and the ways in which it resembles Western societies. Not surprisingly, the Soviet security police lost its appeal as a subject of research after these new approaches began to take hold.

It is ironic that at the very time Western analysts were looking for new models to replace totalitarian theories of Soviet politics, the security police was gaining political prominence in the Soviet Union. The Brezhnev era witnessed a concerted effort to rehabilitate the police and restore its credibility and image in the eyes of the Soviet public. Since that time a plethora of Soviet publications on the history and current operations of the security police has emerged. Some Western scholars have recently availed themselves of these sources and have produced excellent studies of earlier Soviet police organizations—the Cheka, OGPU and NKVD. But as yet these sources have not been exploited for research on the KGB.

This book represents an attempt to redress the balance and fill a significant gap in Western Sovietology by describing and analyzing the KGB as a political institution. While by implication to embark on a study of any such institution is to assume its importance in the political

[xvi]

process, this study does not aim to rehabilitate the totalitarian model, a task that would be formidable with the reformist Gorbachev leadership in full swing. Rather, it considers the usefulness of different models to explain how the Soviet system—and the role of the political police as an integral part of this system—has evolved over time. An underlying premise is that the mixture of continuity and change evident in the development of the political police sheds light on the nature of the regime as a whole. Probably the best description of the theoretical approach used here is to call it a functional one. The study examines the tasks carried out by the KGB on behalf of the regime and its relationship with other Soviet political institutions—the party, the military, and the regular police—with the underlying purpose of assessing the relative power and authority of the KGB. The approach is at the same time an evolutionary one, since the study presumes that the KGB as it functions today cannot be properly understood without considering what historical factors have influenced its development and the extent to which the Soviet regime has discarded its Stalinist features by reforming its police and legal systems.

The book begins by examining the KGB's historical predecessors, going back to the tsarist period and then tracing the development of the political police from 1917 to 1954, when the KGB was established. The following two chapters describe the subsequent evolution of the KGB as an actor in the political process during the Khrushchev, Brezhnev, and post-Brezhnev periods. The focus here is on the KGB's role in Kremlin politics and how the different regimes have approached the problem of integrating the political police into a system that no longer relies on physical terror and violence. One persistent theme that emerges from these chapters is that Russia's leaders, from the nineteenth century to the present have, with the exception of Stalin, grappled with a similar problem. They have all encountered a conflict between the desire to reform and rationalize the system by creating a normative legal order and the necessity of relying on a strong political police to preserve their power.

A general trend throughout this period has been the continued failure of efforts to establish institutionalized limitations on police powers. While Khrushchev downgraded the status of the political police and put an end to widespread police violence, he did not close the legal loopholes that enabled the KGB to infringe on individual rights. Nor did he establish formal regulations to order the relationship between police and party. As a result there have been fluctuating periods of relaxation and repression with regard to political dissent, and the relationship between police and party itself has been subject to change.

Chapters 4 and 5 discuss the organizational structure of the KGB, its formal tasks as portrayed in official publications and the mechanisms through which the party implements control over the KGB, including recruitment and promotion of KGB personnel. We see from this discussion that the KGB's powers and prerogatives are vaguely defined at best and that the party's authority over this institution, while generally effective, is carried out more on an ad hoc, informal basis than through a system of established procedures. In exercising personnel policy, which is a key means of controlling the KGB, the party appears to be guided above all by the goal of maintaining an effective police institution.

The last four chapters of the book explain and analyze the various functions that the KGB carries out for the Soviet regime. These include internal security (the suppression and prevention of political dissent), border security, political surveillance of the Soviet armed forces, and, finally the implementation of various Soviet foreign policy goals. Again, the book uses a historical approach here by describing these functions as they have evolved during the Soviet period. What emerges is a general trend toward increasingly sophisticated methods and, until recently, greater scope in implementing these tasks. The KGB's role of ensuring the regime's internal political security and protecting it from threats by foreign enemies has expanded from the early sixties onward to include a broad range of tasks that extend beyond those generally ascribed to a police or intelligence agency. Furthermore, there is evidence to indicate that the KGB has not only implemented policy but has also influenced decision making.

The central thesis of this book is that the political police has continued to this day to be an essential institution for the Soviet regime, despite the disavowal of terror after Stalin died and the substantial political reforms that have been promoted by leaders such as Khrushchev and Gorbachev. There are two important reasons for this phenomenon. First, although violence ceased to be used as a weapon in Kremlin power struggles after Stalin's death, police coercion has continued to be relied upon (albeit to a limited extent) as one means of ordering regime-societal relations and ensuring public support for the leadership. To be sure, the powers of the political police were restricted considerably when the KGB was established in 1954, but they still encompassed extralegal methods. Harry Rigby, in discussing the basis for political legitimacy of Soviet-type systems, has noted that authority is legitimated in "goal-rational terms" rather than in "legal-rational terms." The "higher legitimacy of task-achievement criteria over rule-compliance criteria" helps to explain why the KGB has been allowed to circumvent the law in protecting the Soviet regime.[1]

The second point is that to the extent that the Soviet regime has shifted to a greater reliance on normative rather than coercive power, the KGB has been a key element in this process. This organization has taken an increasing role in what Alexander Dallin and George Breslauer have described as the "pervasive machinery of political persuasion, the many instrumentalities of political socialization and the sustained efforts to inculcate official values and attitudes in the citizenry."[2] In resorting to these more sophisticated and persuasive means of ensuring political stability, the KGB has been drawn closer to the party in terms of functions and goals, and its officials have been participating more and more in the policy process. At the same time—and this became particularly noticeable toward the end of the Brezhnev era with the anticorruption campaign—the KGB has been drawn into Kremlin power struggles not as a purveyor of violence but as the one organization having enough information on party and state officials to damage or destroy their careers. Although Soviet leaders no longer seek political support on the sole basis of power consolidation but rely more on their abilities to carry through with effective policies, power considerations come to the fore during periods of political succession, and the political police become more predominant. Thus we see a complex picture of the KGB as a bureaucratic actor contributing at times to leadership conflict while also becoming integrated into the policy process and sharing common goals with the party leadership.

The significance of the book's subject and its overall purpose is intended to go beyond that of the political police and police-party relations. It is hoped that light will be shed on deeper questions about the Soviet political system. This is particularly important now, when the Gorbachev leadership is attempting to introduce economic and political changes. By pushing the policy of openness in the press so far that even the KGB has been criticized, by attempting to curtail extralegal actions against Soviet citizens, and above all by taking the political process beyond the confines of the Kremlin and seeking to establish a broad public consensus for his leadership, Gorbachev may be reversing the trend of a more influential and authoritative political police than we have seen over the past three decades. Gorbachev's efforts have raised anew the question Soviet experts have been asking since Stalin's death: Is it possible for the Soviet Union to evolve into a state that allows some freedom of opinion, some form of pluralism, and a decentralized economic system? Or are we seeing under Gorbachev simply a phase in the cycle of repression and relaxation that we have witnessed before? By explaining the role played by the KGB and discussing the factors that influence its power and authority, this book will, it is hoped, help scholars to answer this question.

The main source of information used here is the Soviet press. The increased publicity accorded to the KGB in recent years has yielded numerous books and articles about the KGB and its forerunners. National and regional Soviet newspapers regularly publish reports of appointments and dismissals of KGB officials, their attendance at public functions, and their speeches and articles. This has made it possible to follow career patterns of security police personnel and to analyze their policy views. Obituaries of KGB officials, a rich source of biographical data, appear on a regular basis, and the Soviets issue general biographical publications on prominent party and state figures, including representatives of the KGB. Soviet legal textbooks and journals also offer valuable information on the formal structure and functions of the security police, as well as on its investigatory role in cases of political crime.

In addition to the official Soviet press, underground (*samizdat*) literature published in the Soviet Union is an important source of information on how the KGB deals with dissent. Writings by Soviet émigrés, especially those who have had firsthand experience with the KGB have also proved to be extremely valuable. As a supplement to these primary sources, this analysis has drawn upon Western studies of the Soviet political police, as well as upon general writings on the Soviet political process.

Throughout this book I have used the terms "political police" and "security police" interchangeably to refer to the KGB (Committee of State Security) and its various predecessors. The Soviets themselves generally employ the term "security organs" when discussing the KGB, avoiding the coercive connotation of the word "police." But as this book demonstrates, the KGB is clearly a police apparatus in every sense of the word.

Notes

1. T. H. Rigby, "Political Legitimacy, Weber and Communist Mono-organisational Systems," in T. H. Rigby and Ferenc Feher, eds., *Political Legitimation in Communist States* (New York: St. Martin's Press, 1982), pp. 1–26 (quotation, p. 13).

2. Alexander Dallin and George W. Breslauer, *Political Terror in Communist Systems* (Stanford, Calif.: Stanford University Press, 1970), p. 97.

I
Origins and Evolution

1
The Origins of the KGB

The Traditional "Police State" of Tsarist Russia

Perhaps the most noticeable feature of Soviet political propaganda is its continual reference to the Bolshevik foundations of the Soviet regime. In stressing their Leninist origins, Soviet leaders attempt to confer legitimacy on themselves, demonstrating that they are carrying on with the goals and purposes of a revolutionary leader who has been revered and sanctified in the minds of the population. Most governments, to be sure, invoke their historical predecessors to arouse feelings of loyalty and patriotism from their citizenry. In the Soviet Union, however, the cult of Lenin and the Bolshevik Revolution is carried much further. In a sense this is appropriate, given how the Soviet regime has evolved since 1917. Political leaders have come and gone; the system has survived the purges and a world war; and great industrial and technological advancements have been made. But the way in which Soviet leaders perform their functions and the institutional foundations upon which the regime rests show strong continuity with the past.

The Soviet political police, known since 1954 as the Committee of State Security (KGB), offers a clear example of this historical continuity. First created in 1917 as the Vecheka, this institution has undergone numerous changes in organization and method, but its underlying purpose—protecting the Soviet state against political subversion—has remained the same. Although Soviet propaganda skirts the period of

[3]

Stalin's terror, when the political police exceeded the bounds of party authority and turned against the system itself, the public is constantly reminded that the KGB is continuing the hallowed traditions of the Vecheka in defending the interests of the state.

In focusing on the historical roots of the KGB, Soviet spokesmen prefer to ignore two important facts. First, when the Vecheka was created in 1917 it was intended only as a temporary institution, to be dissolved when the new regime had defeated its enemies and secured its power. Second, the historical antecedents of the KGB extend back much further than 1917—to the early nineteenth century, when a permanent political police system was first established in Russia.[1] Although the tsarist political police was markedly different from its Soviet counterpart, its traditions had a lasting impact. According to one study of Western European police systems, "not only are police systems unique nationally, their distinctive features are relatively impermeable in the face of wars, revolutions and major social and economic transformations. The distinctive characteristics of these police systems have shown remarkable stability over time."[2] This statement is equally applicable to the Soviet Union; its current political police system cannot be properly understood without considering the evolution of the tsarist police, particularly as it related to Russia's political culture and governmental institutions.

By the middle of the nineteenth century Russia was, by all accounts, a "police state," not in the modern sense of the term, which connotes all the evils of Nazi Germany and Stalinism, but in the more traditional sense as it applied to certain European states in the eighteenth and early nineteenth centuries. The term "police state" (a translation of the German word *polizeistaat*) was first used to describe such regimes as Prussia under Frederick II (1712–1786), Austria under Joseph II (1741–1790), and postrevolutionary France (1789–1848). These traditional European police states developed at a time when police functions encompassed not only law and order but a whole range of administrative and welfare tasks. Their rule was by no means arbitrary; it rested upon normalized bureaucratic standards and operated according to well-defined rules and principles. As one scholar expressed it, "the traditional police state was based on a rational division of labour within society and within administration, and its bureaucratic values of order, form and discipline extended from the offices to the citizen in his private as well as his public life."[3] Such states, which incorporated secret political police, spying, and continual encroachments on individual rights in conjunction with both paternalism and enlightenment, were motivated not by evil aims but by a desire to reform and modernize.[4]

[4]

Russia's monarchical police state was similar in many respects to those that had developed in Western Europe, particularly in the broadly conceived paternalistic role of the police in society. What was different about the Russian model was that it lagged far behind Western Europe in terms of its political evolution and it was also much less efficient. By the middle of the nineteenth century the institutional and theoretical bases of the traditional police state in Western Europe were giving way to democratic influences, and the vast powers of the police were being dispersed. In Russia at this time the foundations of the tsarist police state had only recently been established.

In 1826, following the Decembrist uprising (a conspiracy involving members of Russia's nobility) Nicholas I formed the so-called Third Section (or Third Department) of the Imperial Chancellery, a political police whose purpose was to protect the state from internal subversion.[5] Although the staff of the Third Section was small, numbering from thirty to forty full-time employees, it had a wide net of informers and also controlled a Corps of Gendarmes, or military personnel. This institution was subsequently buttressed by a new criminal code, which appeared in 1845 and dealt extensively with crimes against the state. The codes established for the first time a legal basis through which the government could combat political dissent.

Like its earlier counterparts in Western Europe, the tsarist police state distinguished between the ordinary or "lower" police, whose responsibility, along with numerous administrative and economic tasks, was the enforcement of public order, and the political or "higher" police.[6] Despite its greater importance in the eyes of the monarchy, the political police was also burdened with information-gathering and welfare functions that extended well beyond the realm of political surveillance. As a result its role was vague and ill-defined, and its efforts to combat political dissent on the whole were ineffective. As one scholar noted,

> Constant interference by the Third Department in all kinds of activities must be considered the chief reason, not only for its unpopularity, but also for its inefficiency. Its officials were overworked, not because political subversion was rife throughout the empire, but because by Nicholas' wish so many non-political cases engaged their attention.[7]

The struggle against internal dissent was further constrained by the 1864 reform of the judiciary system, initiated by Alexander II as part of a broad effort to transform Russia into a *Rechtsstaat*, or a state based on the rule of law. This reform set up a modern system of courts with judges appointed for life, an independent bar to defend the accused, and public trials by jury for all criminal cases, including those involving political crimes. Taking advantage of the new judiciary system, young radicals and revolutionaries began to use the courtrooms as forums for espousing their political views and often gained enough sympathy from judges and jurors to be treated leniently.[8]

The last straw for the government was the acquittal of Vera Zasulich, a young female revolutionary who shot (but did not manage to kill) General Trepov, the police chief of St. Petersburg, in March 1878.[9] In response to this incident a government committee was set up to deal with the growing threat of revolutionary activities, and special laws were enacted to allow punishment for political crimes without judicial proceedings.[10] In August 1880, as part of an effort to improve the effectiveness of the political police, the much discredited Third Section was abolished and replaced by a central Department of State Police under the Ministry of Interior. Its chief responsibility was political crimes, and although its staff consisted of only 161 full-time employees, it had at its disposal the Corps of Gendarmes, numbering several thousand. In addition, the notorious "security sections" (*okhrannye otdeleniia*) were established in St. Petersburg, Warsaw, and Moscow in 1881, following the assassination of Alexander II. The Okhrana, as it was known collectively, was to uncover revolutionary groups and to collect evidence against their participants, while formal inquiries were left to the gendarmes. The Okhrana's operations were largely covert, utilizing nonuniformed agents and informers. The latter penetrated revolutionary organizations under the guise of being radicals while secretly being paid by the police.[11]

The creation of the Okhrana was accompanied by a government measure that went further than any other to destroy the spirit of the 1864 reform. On 14 August 1881 a decree was issued allowing the minister of interior and governors general to place certain areas of Russia under a state of emergency (called "reinforced safeguard" or "extraordinary safeguard"), giving the police wide latitude in dealing with political dissent by virtually suspending civil rights in the regions under emergency rule.[12] The introduction of such extralegal measures, designed not only to persecute those who had broken the law but also to suppress any type of potentially threatening political behavior, was to become common practice in the Soviet period.

However lofty and democratic were the ultimate goals of the revolutionaries, their activities had the effect of strengthening the reactionary tendencies in the government, which rejected the rule of law in favor of stronger political controls. At the same time, government measures to curb the revolutionary movement served only to fuel the fires of radicalism by stimulating the bitterness of those who sought to bring about political change. To be sure, the tsarist political police, particularly in the period after 1905, enjoyed considerable success in using secret agents to penetrate revolutionary parties and groups, where widespread arrests wrought havoc.[13] Despite their formidable powers, however, in the end the Russian political police proved incapable of stemming the tide of the revolutionary movement, which by 1905 had reduced the government to a state of paralysis and by 1917 helped to bring it down completely.

The tsarist government took broad steps to strengthen the authority of the political police after the assassination of Alexander II, but this institution was unable to defend the monarchy, for several reasons. First, police operations continued to be inefficient throughout the period up to 1917. As Jacob Walkin points out in his study of political and social institutions under the last three tsars, bureaucratic rivalries and confusion over responsibilities, particularly between the Corps of Gendarmes and the Department of Police, impeded police efforts.[14] According to the memoirs of General A. I. Spiridonovich, a former gendarme officer who later (from 1906 to 1916) served in the Okhrana:

> The dual subordination of the Corps [of Gendarmes] was very harmful and had a negative effect on its work. The staff was always at war with the [Police] Department and this affected the officers. . . . Dependent on both the Department and the Staff, officers had to be diplomatic and manoeuver so that work for one institution was not fouled up by the other.[15]

Police operations were further hampered by the low quality of personnel and the grave deficiencies in their training. Spiridonovich noted bitterly that although there were numerous institutions for training military personnel, there were no corresponding institutions for training gendarmes despite the crucial role these men played in protecting the regime. "This deficiency was scandalous," he wrote, "and we [the newly recruited gendarme personnel] were astonished."[16] The consequences of this situation could be foreseen by A. A. Lopukhin, chief of the Department of Police from 1902 to 1905. Citing the gendarmes' complete lack of understanding of the political movements they were dealing with, Lopukhin noted that any societal phenomenon was viewed by them as a threat to the state: "As a result, the protection of the state by the Corps of Gendarmes becomes a struggle with all of society, in the end leading to the destruction of the state, whose inviolability can be preserved only by uniting with society."[17]

In addition to inefficiencies within the police apparatus itself, there were also numerous loopholes in the system that inadvertently fostered the radical movement. Political dissidents were able to travel abroad in order to avoid arrest and many of them did, often making European cities the headquarters of their groups. Finland, for example, was a popular haven for revolutionaries. Another loophole, as Richard Pipes notes, was the institution of private property. It provided radicals with a source of funds and also enabled them to find jobs with private employers who were not concerned about their political views. Furthermore, prison or exile by no means meant an end to a revolutionary career. Conditions in tsarist prisons, though far from comfortable, were remarkably free. Books, mail, and writing supplies were openly available; political prisoners were segregated from common criminals and enjoyed better living conditions. As numerous memoirs attest, prisons became a breeding ground for radical ideas. Exile also offered the leisure time to engage in developing radical ideas and programs. (Lenin, for example, wrote *The Development of Capitalism in Russia* while in prison and later in Siberian exile.)[18]

One of the greatest impediments to the suppression of Russia's radical movement was the general reluctance on the part of the state to use violence. Whether it stemmed from a fear of being censored by more civilized Western societies or from an endemic cultural inhibition, the idea of violence or terror was repugnant to the monarchy (and to most Russians, save the small minority of terrorists). Despite the introduction of the emergency statute of 1881, transferring political cases to military tribunals, which could order capital punishment, executions for political crimes were rare until 1905, when acts of terrorism reached such a peak that the government saw no other alternative. As Walkin notes, "the Czarist government neither was organized to rule by terror nor prepared to do so."[19] Herein lies one of the crucial differences between the monarchical police state of tsarist Russia and the Soviet regime, which from the outset used violence to preserve its rule.

Underlying all these factors was the social foundation of the Russian radical movement. Because the tsarist government tended to view any form of public expression as a threat to its security, making no distinction between real subversives and mere progressive thinkers, privileged, well-educated individuals not necessarily prone to radicalism were pushed in that direction. Thus far from being outcasts who came from the lowest rungs of society, Russian revolutionaries were often sons and daughters of the gentry, the intelligentsia, and the merchant class.[20] Permeating the highest echelons of society, the radical movement evoked sympathy—or at least understanding—from influential segments of the population. This circumstance no doubt accounts to a great extent for the ambivalence demonstrated by the monarchy in dealing with revolutionaries, as well as for the difficulties encountered by the police as they sought cooperation from the public.

Although Russia in the nineteenth and early twentieth centuries was a traditional monarchical police state, its political police, unlike those in Western Europe, were unable to protect and defend the state they had been created to serve. Instead of making a peaceful transition to a state based on the rule of law and some form of participatory democracy, Russia underwent a violent revolution. There are, of course, deeper and more complex social and economic reasons for Russia's failure to follow in the path of its Western European counterparts. The absence in Russia of a politically conscious urban middle class or a strong independent nobility, with its own economic wealth and political power, to serve as a check on the monarch were no doubt important factors.[21] This left the political arena open to radicals and terrorists, who pushed the tsarist state into a fatal cycle of repression and reaction, with both the monarchy and the police itself on the defensive. In the final analysis, the authority of the police in any system of government is always proportionate to the strength of the ruler. The tsarist government by 1917 had lost the support of even the more moderate elements of the intelligentsia and had aroused deep dissatisfaction among workers and peasants. Thus as the powers of the monarchy began to erode in the face of widespread opposition, those of its political police did likewise. Engaged as they were in a war against Russian society, the political police were bound to fail.[22]

The Bolshevik regime created a political police system that proved to be far more effective than the tsarist version.[23] The loopholes that had existed before 1917, which enabled political dissidents to evade police repression, were closed, and the Soviet state showed no reluctance to use the ultimate weapon of violence against its perceived opponents. Above all, the monarchy's conflict between the desire to create a *Rechtsstaat* and its fear of relinquishing domination over political and legal functions was not faced by the Bolsheviks, who viewed bourgeois concepts of legality with disdain.

Nevertheless several of the features that characterized the tsarist police state have persisted to this day. The bureaucratic rivalries and confusion over responsibility within the police and legal apparatus

[9]

remain a constant theme in Soviet official life. Furthermore the state has continued to view the role of the police as extending far beyond that of law enforcement. The idea that the police are to act as moral guardians, reformers, and agents of social transformation has found full expression under the Soviets, particularly in regard to the political police. Finally, although political authoritarianism has prevailed over efforts to create an autonomous legal order, the Soviets have tried to establish a system of legal norms that preclude arbitrary or irrational police repression and validate their claims to being a democratic state. Even this rather modest goal has come into conflict with the regime's desire for complete political control, creating tensions reminiscent of the tsarist period that have had important implications for the role of the political police.

The Political Police and Bolshevism: The Police as Revolutionary Expedient

The Bolshevik Revolution and the ensuing years of civil war precluded any possibilities for Russia to evolve from a monarchical police state to a democracy. The tsarist police, so despised by Russians of all political persuasions, was swept away along with other tsarist institutions. But it was replaced by a political police of considerably greater dimensions, both in the scope of its authority and in the severity of its methods. Just as the French revolutionaries of 1789 vowed to destroy the police of the ancien régime but ended up with a more repressive police system, the Bolsheviks had lofty goals of a free stateless society, one with no coercive police apparatus. These goals, however, were gradually lost to the demands of political reality.

To be sure, Lenin and his followers had always accepted the need for a "machinery of repression" in the phase of consolidation of the proletarian victory over its bourgeois foes, just as they foresaw that a state authority would be necessary during this transitional period. Nor had the Bolsheviks opposed the use of terror under certain circumstances. They had always disavowed isolated terrorist acts on the ground of inexpediency, but they condoned terror as a weapon of the proletariat against the bourgeoisie in the class struggle.[24] Moreover the repression was to be that of a worker-peasant majority over a minority of capitalist exploiters, which would make it more democratic. What Lenin did not foresee was that the transition to the socialist order could not be achieved immediately. The expected support of the Russian peasantry and the European proletariat for the Russian revolution did not emerge. Without this support the new Bolshevik regime was isolated, surrounded by enemies, and a dictatorship of not a majority but a minority. Not only did the Bolsheviks have to build and retain a strong state bureaucracy to replace the "bourgeois state machine" they had destroyed, they also had to establish a powerful police apparatus to preserve their own rule.

The first Soviet political police, created in December 1917 under the name Vecheka (All-Russian Extraordinary Commission for Combating Counterrevolution and Sabotage),[25] was very much an ad hoc organization, whose powers gradually accrued in response to various emergencies and threats to Soviet rule. No formal legislation establishing the Vecheka was ever enacted, and the resolution of the Sovnarkom (Council of People's Commissars), passed on 20 December 1917, by which the Vecheka was founded, was not even published until 1922.[26] The resolution specified that the commission was "to investigate and liquidate all counterrevolutionary and sabotage attempts and activities throughout Russia," and was then to turn over the culprits to revolutionary tribunals for trial. The Vecheka was thus established as an organ of preliminary investigation, though the resolution did allow it the option of applying certain minor punitive measures by administrative means.

From the outset the powers of the Vecheka were ill-defined. There were no written definitions of the crimes it was to uncover, no procedures were established to determine whether the Vecheka should handle cases administratively or send them to revolutionary tribunals, and the Vecheka's relationship with the latter (which were under the jurisdiction of the People's Commissariat of Justice) was vague. The first formal statute on the Vecheka, enacted on 28 October 1918, did little to clarify these issues. This situation was the result of the extralegal character of the Vecheka, which was conceived not as a permanent state institution but as a temporary organ for waging war against "class enemies." As E. H. Carr noted, "its operations had as little to do with law as the operations of an army: *inter arma silent leges.*"[27]

Given its militant role and supralegal status, it is not surprising that the Vecheka acquired powers of summary justice as the threat of counterrevolution and foreign intervention grew. When the Germans denounced the armistice and resumed their advance against Russia, the new Soviet regime issued the famous proclamation of 22 February 1918, declaring the "Socialist Fatherland in Danger." This was followed by a Vecheka announcement that it would mercilessly annihilate on the spot enemy agents, counterrevolutionaries, and speculators.[28] These two proclamations paved the way for the introduction of mass terror, which began in earnest after several acts of violence against the Bolshevik regime, including an attempt on Lenin's life and the assassination of the Petrograd Cheka chief, Uritskii, on 30 August. On 2 September 1918 the All-Russian Central Executive Committee (VTsIK) passed a resolution on "mass red terror against the bourgeoisie and its agents." Then, on 5 September, after hearing a situation report from Feliks Dzerzhinskii, chairman of the Vecheka, the Sovnarkom enacted the Decree on the Red Terror, affirming that "it is absolutely essential to safeguard the rear by means of terror."[29] From this point onward the terror gained momentum and continued unabated throughout the years of civil war, which lasted until the end of 1920. The Vecheka directed its terror not only against those who had committed specific offenses but also against all members of the bourgeoisie, whose crime was ideological rather than legal.

It is important to note that the Red Terror was not unleashed without considerable opposition from within the government and the party. The Vecheka's growing powers and ruthless methods were challenged from several quarters. The People's Commissariat of Justice deeply resented the Chekas' practice of exercising summary justice rather than turning over offenders to the Revolutionary Tribunals, while the People's Commissariat of Internal Affairs (NKVD) was hostile toward the Chekas because of their continual encroachments on its prerogatives in the districts and provinces away from Moscow.[30] There were also idealists within the party who objected to the Vecheka on moral and ethical grounds. They voiced vigorous protests against the Vecheka, demanding restrictions on its powers and, by 1919, calling for its dissolution altogether.[31] Responding to the widespread criticisms, Lenin and other party leaders took steps to resolve the problem, but in the end they came up with only halfhearted measures, which did little to curb the Chekas' excesses.[32]

In the final analysis no attempts to curb the powers of the political police were likely to succeed as long as Russia was in the throes of civil war. The ambivalence expressed by party leaders toward the Vecheka reflected the fundamental dilemma they faced. However repugnant were its methods, however much dissention it caused within the party, the Vecheka's existence was seen as crucial to the very survival of the regime. "The government of the workers," stated Lenin, "cannot exist without such an organization as long as exploiters remain in the world."[33]

This was the basic moral defense of the political police put forth by the Bolsheviks. But they soon went beyond mere justification of the

Vecheka's excesses and arbitrary terror, seeking to elevate the Vecheka to heroic status. Thus "Chekists" were portrayed as militant, self-sacrificing defenders of the revolution, who might in their revolutionary zeal commit excesses but who were motivated by the highest Communist goals. Dzerzhinskii stated in 1922:

> The Vecheka has stood on guard of the revolution and with honor has fulfilled the difficult task it was entrusted with. At the very height of the civil war, when we were caught in the fiery grip of the blockade, when we suffered from hunger, cold and devastation, when the white guards at home and the imperialists abroad approached the heart of the republic, the Vecheka and its local organs carried out self-sacrificing, heroic work. . . . The Vecheka is proud of its heroes and martyrs, who perished in the struggle.[34]

This image of the Vecheka, embodied in the person of Feliks Dzerzhinskii, has been embellished by Soviet historians ever since. It was the elevation of Chekists into an elite vanguard and the special revolutionary mission ascribed to them that set them off so clearly from their tsarist predecessors. Although the tsarist police enjoyed many supralegal powers, they were not glorified as heroes or portrayed as having a lofty mission. Of course most of the romantic myths about Chekists' heroism and moral purity were generated after the Vecheka had ceased to exist.[35] It would have been difficult at the time for the Bolsheviks to apotheosize an organization whose reputation was so unsavory and whose rank-and-file personnel were known to be uneducated, unscrupulous, and, in some cases, sadistic. But the Bolsheviks set the stage for a process by which the political police would be transformed into an institutional pillar of the Soviet state.

The Police as an Institution of State

The end of the civil war, the demobilization of the Soviet Army, and the introduction of the New Economic Policy (NEP) brought about a changed atmosphere in 1921 that seemed incompatible with the existence of a terrorist political police. Along with the partial restoration of a free market system in Soviet Russia went a distinct relaxation of tension marked by renewed calls for the establishment of a regime based on legality and for the dissolution of the Vecheka. Many influential party members believed that as a wartime emergency organization, the

[13]

Vecheka had fulfilled its mission and was no longer necessary. Lenin himself acknowledged the need for a reform of the political police in a speech to the Ninth All-Russian Congress of Soviets on 23 December 1921 and participated actively in working out the details. On 8 February 1922, a decree of the VTsIK announced the abolition of the Vecheka and its local commissions, whose functions were transferred to a State Political Administration (GPU).[36]

On paper it appeared that the powers of the political police had been reduced significantly. The GPU did not have the emergency special status of the Vecheka but was a regular branch of the state, incorporated into the NKVD. (Dzerzhinskii, however, had been people's commissar for internal affairs since March 1919, so the political police were not in new hands.) The GPU's jurisdiction was curtailed in that it was to be responsible only for overt threats to the state's security—counterrevolutionary activity, banditry, espionage, and smuggling—as well as for defense of Soviet borders and protection of railways and waterways. All other offenses previously handled by the Vecheka (such as speculation and bribery) were to be dealt with by Revolutionary Tribunals or courts. Moreover the GPU was to be subject to definite procedural requirements regarding arrests and was to perform only investigative functions, without the powers of summary justice that the Vecheka had enjoyed.

But the Bolsheviks made it clear that their vision of a society without a political police was still far in the future. Whereas the Vecheka had been portrayed as a temporary extraordinary organization for defending the revolution, the GPU was established as a formal part of the state apparatus with no pretense of being temporary. When the USSR was formed in 1923, the GPU was raised to the level of a federal agency, designated the OGPU (Unified State Political Administration) and attached to the USSR Council of People's Commissars.[37]

Soviet historians portray the creation of the GPU/OGPU as a genuine attempt by the party to reform the political police and restrict its powers.[38] Indeed, police operations during NEP were considerably more restrained in terms of violence, and widespread terror such as that inflicted by the Vecheka did not occur. In addition, the staff and budget of the political police were reduced significantly after the Vecheka was disbanded.[39] But the legal constraints on police operations were so swiftly removed that it is difficult to accept that the party leadership ever seriously intended to curtail the powers of the security police. Two decrees, issued in August and October 1922, gave the GPU broad powers to exile, imprison, and in some cases execute persons accused of various crimes.[40] Even more ominous was the creation of a "judicial

[14]

collegium," attached to the OGPU, for carrying out summary justice against counterrevolutionaries, spies, and terrorists. Although there was no mention of this collegium in the statute of the OGPU adopted by the VTsIK on 15 November 1923, an official Soviet source later claimed that the statute had in fact served as the basis for granting these judicial powers to the OGPU.[41]

A key factor in the growing power of the political police was the enactment of the RSFSR Criminal Code in 1922 (revised and expanded in 1926) and the RSFSR Code of Criminal Procedure in 1923.[42] These codes provided a legal basis for the political police to persecute Soviet citizens with impunity and served as the theoretical foundation for the development of the Soviet police state. The changes enacted in the codes during the 1920s and '30s reflected the expanding role of the political police in the legal and judicial processes.

Although the jurists who drafted the criminal codes relied to some extent on prerevolutionary Russian and Western models, there were essential differences that reflected the influence of Leninist thought and the experience of the Bolshevik Revolution. As Harold Berman points out, the strong emphasis on protecting the political order led to a highly differentiated approach toward political and nonpolitical crimes. Political offenses were dealt with extremely harshly, whereas nonpolitical crimes were treated with leniency.[43] The legal codes, however, defined political, or state, crimes very broadly, to include a wide range of offenses normally considered to be nonpolitical, such as violation of foreign exchange regulations, smuggling, and others. Nonpolitical crimes were restricted mainly to crimes against individuals. This feature reflected the highly ideological nature of the newly created Soviet state, whereby political considerations dominated attitudes toward crime and criminal responsibility. As Stephen Schafer put it, "the more pronounced the ideology of a political-social power, and the less possible the participation of ordinary men and social groups in the decision-making processes, then the easier it is to see that all crimes are of a political nature."[44]

Because Soviet criminal law was designed to protect the state and defend its ideology, the degree of responsibility was determined more by the criminal's personality and how it deviated from the ideological and political norms than by any concrete criminal act. Thus punishment could be inflicted not only against those who had committed specific crimes but also against those who represented a so-called social danger, though they had not violated any provisions of the Criminal Code.[45] The RSFSR Criminal Code also incorporated the doctrine of analogy, according to which a person could be subject to criminal responsibility for an act not specifically provided for but analogous to an act prohibited in the code.[46]

It is doubtful that Lenin and his colleagues were so politically naïve that they could not see the consequences of the concept of crime embodied in the 1922 Criminal Code. Lenin himself was deeply involved in its preparation and issued numerous detailed instructions to D. I. Kurskii, the People's Commissar for Justice, who was charged with formulating the code. Indeed, Lenin is credited with setting forth its basic principles and insisting on its severity.[47] That he intended to use the Criminal Code as a weapon against political opposition became clear when the trial of twenty-two Socialist Revolutionaries opened in Moscow on 8 June 1922, just a week after the code came into force. A few months previously, shortly before the trial was announced, Lenin had written to Kurskii on the need for organizing a number of "model trials" of political opponents for the purpose of "educating" the public.[48] The trial contained many of the elements of the Stalinist show trials in the 1930s—in particular its large-scale use for propaganda purposes—and thus served as a prototype for these later trials.

It is important to note that the definition of "counterrevolutionary crimes" (which fell under the investigative purview of the security police) was steadily broadened during the 1920s and the criminal codes were amended accordingly.[49] In 1927 a new all-union law on counterrevolutionary crimes was incorporated into the 1926 RSFSR Code (Article 58). It expanded the concept of counterrevolutionary crime to include actions directed against "the external security of the USSR and other workers' states" and made numerous additional changes.[50] A Soviet source makes it clear that the changes in the code were designed to strengthen the powers of the security police: "The law on state crimes proved to be an effective weapon in the hands of the Soviet organs of justice. With the help of the norms of this act, the organs of state security and the courts successfully struggled with counterrevolutionary elements."[51]

The 1923 RSFSR Code of Criminal Procedure provided few restraints to offset the broad application of police powers encouraged by the Criminal Code. As Berman has noted, it permitted prosecution of political crimes to be carried out secretly and swiftly, while at the same time creating the potential for serious abuse of individual rights.[52] Although Article 107 of the code stipulated that the Procuracy, or State Prosecutor's Office, was to exercise supervision over criminal investigation by "agencies of inquiry" (the OGPU and the militia), an amendment was added to this article in 1924 providing that supervision of inquiries by the state security organs "shall be regulated by a special statute." Article 104 of the code stated that arrests carried out by state security organs were also "determined by special rules;" finally, a 1929 amendment stipulated that "special rules" governed the types of cases subject to preliminary investigation by the security organs.[53] Thus by means of these special regulations, which were never published, the Procuracy was deprived of any control over the investigative activities of the political police.

The code included no provisions making it illegal for nonjudicial agencies such as the OGPU to apply criminal sanctions, which it did through its judicial collegium. Nor was any code published either at the republic or all-union level to govern administrative procedure. This meant that various "administrative means" of punishment employed by the political police were subjected to no regulations beyond what was set forth in the OGPU's founding statutes. Significantly, it was primarily by means of administrative action that the OGPU and its successor organizations carried out their repressive policies.

The increasingly broad interpretation of political crime on the part of the Soviet regime was reflected in the fact that the OGPU gradually extended its competence to a widening sphere of Soviet life, including the economy. The onset of NEP, which encouraged commercial interests and capitalist enterprise, created widespread graft and corruption, particularly among the so-called Nepmen, or small urban capitalists. Not surprisingly, this was viewed as a threat to the political order. Thus with the aid of its highly specialized Economic Administration (EKU), the GPU/OGPU was given the task of destroying these "economic counterrevolutionaries" as well as handling numerous other economic problems associated with NEP. The appointment in early 1924 of Dzerzhinskii as chairman of the Supreme Council of the National Economy (VSNKh), the state organ responsible for supervising Soviet industry, facilitated the OGPU's involvement in the country's economic life. Dzerzhinskii placed several trusted police comrades in top VSNKh posts and gave the OGPU additional responsibilities in enforcing government economic policy.[54] Such interference in economic affairs and ordinary criminal justice by the OGPU resulted in dilution of the authority of other elements of the state bureaucracy, such as the NKVD, which controlled the regular police, or militia.[55]

[17]

The Police as Vanguards of Socialism

As formal powers gradually accrued to the OGPU a distinct change occurred in its overall purpose and goals. By the mid-1920s nearly all opposition to the Bolshevik regime from leftist parties and former tsarist groups had been defeated. Henceforth the only major threats faced by Soviet leaders came from dissent within the party itself. There was indeed considerable dissatisfaction with the policies of the leadership, and this was voiced loudly by party members. Sensitive and insecure, the ruling group viewed this opposition with increasing intolerance and began to enlist the OGPU in a struggle against it. As Carr points out, "it was becoming more and more difficult to distinguish between disloyalty to the party and treason against the state."[56] By 1924 there were several reports of routine OGPU surveillance of opposition party members, and when the Fourteenth Party Congress met in December 1925, these opposition elements protested against the growing practice of party members informing on their comrades.[57]

Adding to these ominous developments was a Central Committee directive, issued in May 1926, that prohibited local party officials from making changes in OGPU personnel above the rank of ordinary agent without permission from OGPU headquarters in Moscow. This step in effect removed the security police from party control at all levels below the national one, thereby placing the police in a position to attack dissident party members. Then, in July 1926, the Central Committee passed a resolution of censure against party oppositionists, which made them vulnerable to the attention of the OGPU.[58] These measures coincided with the emergence in the spring of 1926 of the so-called United Opposition—a merger of groups opposed to Stalin's policies under the leadership of Trotsky and Zinoviev.

As the United, or Left, Opposition became increasingly vociferous in 1926–1927, the OGPU was drawn further into the struggle, acting on behalf of Stalin and his supporters. By August 1927 many lower-level party oppositionists had been arrested and exiled by the OGPU under Article 58 of the RSFSR Criminal Code. Using its covert agents, the OGPU penetrated the opposition's organization and waged a campaign to discredit its actions. The culmination of the struggle against the opposition came in the autumn of 1927, when the OGPU, on the basis of information provided by one of its agents, seized an underground press used to print the opposition's platform and arrested those involved in its operations. Just a few weeks later, at a joint meeting of the Central

Committee and the Control Commission, Trotsky and Zinoviev were expelled from the Central Committee.[59]

Among the party leaders who defended police tactics against the oppositionists was Stalin's erstwhile ally, Nikolai Bukharin, who would himself become a victim of police repression. Bukharin, a strong advocate of NEP and other "rightist" polices, showed himself to be an enthusiastic supporter of the OGPU when the tenth anniversary of the Soviet political police was celebrated with unprecedented publicity in December 1927. Writing in *Izvestiia* on 20 December, Bukharin hailed the police in the most laudatory terms, idealizing and romanticizing them as representatives of the new Soviet man.[60] It is difficult to understand why a man of Bukharin's intellect and stature would go to such lengths to encourage the cult of the security police. It has been suggested that in addition to gratitude for police help in defeating the Left Opposition, Bukharin may have been making a bid for OGPU support in his upcoming struggle with Stalin.[61] If so, events would prove that his advocacy of the political police would eventually contribute to his own ignominious death.

There is little evidence that the OGPU, headed by V. R. Menzhinskii after Dzerzhinskii's death in 1926, played an important role in the struggle between Bukharin and Stalin that took place during 1928–1929. Although Stalin was able to have Bukharin placed under OGPU surveillance by mid-1928, it appears that certain police officials, including two OGPU deputy chiefs, G. G. Iagoda and M. A. Trilisser, were sympathetic toward Bukharin.[62] In any case Stalin was able to defeat Bukharin and the rightists largely through his adept manipulation of party factions, his control over the Secretariat, and, most important, his ability to take advantage of the rightists' desire to preserve party unity. Right leaders enjoyed considerable support among the party's rank and file, but they were reluctant to appeal to this support for fear that it would trigger outside opposition and threaten the party's rule. As Stephen Cohen points out in his biography of Bukharin, conflict within the leadership, which had been largely a matter of public record until Trotsky's defeat in 1927, grew increasingly covert by 1928–1929 and was confined to select, unpublicized meetings.[63] This "fetishism of party unity" not only gave Stalin an advantage over the rightists; it also created a situation in which party leaders would silently acquiesce to police persecution of party members.

Stalin's victory over the rightists, who had been the strongest proponents of NEP, paved the way for the abandonment of NEP and the introduction of his "revolution from above," or the so-called Third Revolution, launched in 1929. This was a twofold process of rapid industrialization and forced collectivization of agriculture. The OGPU played a key role in Stalin's drive to collectivize the countryside by participating, along with local party and state officials, in the confiscation of the property of the kulaks, or middle-class peasants, and banishing them to far-off regions. According to Leonard Schapiro,

> party members could not always be relied upon to stomach the task that was now imposed upon them under the guise of "war against the kulaks," which turned out to be a war against the whole peasantry. The brunt of the operation fell on the OGPU, whose officials participated in every one of its grim phases.[64]

The OGPU's participation in the collectivization drive meant that the political police had assumed a new, offensive role—that of social and economic transformation of the countryside. In taking up this mission they were encroaching upon the functions of other elements of the state apparatus and, to a certain extent, of the party itself.

The war against the peasantry also signified a movement toward harsher and more brutal police methods. In 1928, as Bukharin and "right deviationism" came increasingly under attack for posing an obstacle to forced industrialization, both Soviet legal theory and practice underwent substantial changes. Law, it was stressed, was to be an instrument of change and a tool of economic planning. Far from withering away, it was to be a key weapon in the struggle against such class enemies as the kulaks and the bourgeoisie. Humanitarian idealism and equality before the law were dismissed as bourgeois notions associated with NEP, and more repressive penalties for both ordinary and political criminals were called for.[65] As a result of several decrees passed in 1928 and 1929, sentences for all types of crimes became longer and confinement in labor camps more common. The distinction between ordinary and political criminals was further weakened by a decree of 6 November 1929, which transferred all prisoners serving sentences of more than three years to the jurisdiction of the OGPU, even if the crimes involved were not political. Thus in the interests of state security the remedial view of penal policy gradually was replaced by a policy of maximum sentences and extensive use of forced labor, all of which paved the way for the establishment of the OGPU's massive network of forced labor camps in the 1930s.[66]

As the legal structure and jurisprudence of NEP collapsed, the OGPU stepped in to fill the void with what Robert Sharlet has termed the "jurisprudence of terror."[67] By June 1930 RSFSR Procurator Krylenko complained to the party leadership that "extralegal authorities" (i.e.,

[20]

the OGPU) were usurping the role of legal institutions in the country-side.[68] The OGPU had already dealt a significant blow to the legal system and the economic apparatus in 1928 with the "Shakhty Trial"—a highly publicized show trial of old-regime engineers which resulted in several executions on charges of "wrecking or economic subversion." This trial (as well as several other economic trials that followed in 1930–1933) was intended to divert public attention from the mounting economic hardships and to provide the regime with scapegoats for its disastrous economic policies. But it also resulted in a victory, at the expense of other institutions, for the political police, which was credited with uncovering the "conspiracy" and saving the country from an economic disaster.[69] Increasingly the criminal process was politicized and the security police were emerging as the prime defenders of the economic and political order.

Not surprisingly, both the People's Commissariat of Justice (NKIu) and the People's Commissariat of Internal Affairs (NKVD), which were closely associated with NEP and the bourgeois legal order, suffered a deterioration in their positions. Both came under heavy criticism in 1928–1929, and in 1930 the republic commissariats of internal affairs were abolished. The militia, which had been under the NKVD's jurisdiction, survived as a separate republic administration until 1932, when it was absorbed by the OGPU. Thus by 1932 the OGPU had gained total dominance over the state's punitive apparatus.

While party leaders tolerated the executions of nonparty specialists on trumped-up charges of economic sabotage, they were as yet unwilling to allow Stalin to use the police for terrorizing the party itself. This was demonstrated when an opposition group led by a former secretary of the Moscow Party Committee, M. N. Riutin, was discovered by the OGPU in 1932. Stalin demanded that the leaders of the group be shot, but his colleagues in the Politburo refused.[70] Thus at this point Stalin and the OGPU were still subject to restraints in acting against internal party opposition. Faced with this obstacle and with growing dissatisfaction over his policies on the part of the party leadership, Stalin sought to strengthen his position by turning to other sources of support.

According to the available evidence, one approach was to promote his own personal agents into key positions of party control over the police. Probably the most important of these men was N. I. Ezhov, who became chief of the Cadres Department of the Secretariat in 1930 and by early 1935 was CC secretary responsible for supervising the security police.[71] Another such official was A. N. Poskrebyshev, who by about 1931 became head of Stalin's personal secretariat, which maintained a close liaison with the security police.[72] Stalin also moved some allies in the security police into important party posts outside Moscow. L. P. Beria, a fellow Georgian and chief of the political police for Georgia and the Transcaucasus, was made first secretary there in 1931. Beria launched a massive turnover of party cadres, replacing the first secretaries of thirty-two districts (*raions*) with police officials.[73] In addition, M. D. Bagirov, who had served as head of the security organs in Azerbaidzhan since the early 1920s, was made first secretary of that republic's Communist party in 1933.[74] Although this may not have been Stalin's intention at the time, these moves were eventually to prove crucial in his use of the security police for an onslaught against the party.

The Stalinist Police State: Theoretical Framework

The theoretical concepts used by Western historians to describe the Soviet state in the Stalin period have not fully elucidated the role of the political police. Although most proponents of the totalitarian model have considered the political police to be one of its essential components, they have not defined the precise relationship of this institution to other actors. The terms "police" and "terror" have been used interchangeably, thus fusing the methods with the organization employing these methods, and scholars have not explained how the role of a political police in an autocratic state can be distinguished from that of the police in a totalitarian state.[75]

One of the early proponents of the totalitarian thesis, Hannah Arendt, did in fact deal extensively with the political police and its relationship to other institutions.[76] Arendt distinguished between the roles of the political police under despotism and totalitarianism by stressing that in the latter stage, when political opposition had been defeated, the police were seeking "objective" enemies rather than actual opponents of the regime. One problem with her interpretation as it applied to Stalinism, however, was that she set 1930 as the point when the stage of totalitarianism was reached in Soviet Russia. In fact by the mid-1920s dissent from even the most loyal supporters of the Bolshevik regime was seen to be as threatening as the anti-Bolshevik opposition. Thus when most real opponents of Bolshevism had been defeated, the police turned its attention to opposition from within the party and began hunting what Arendt would term "objective enemies." Although this marked a distinct change in the role of the police, not until after 1934, when it was empowered to use violence against important party leaders, did the real turning point come. Furthermore Arendt considered the position of the totalitarian political police to be much weaker than that of the police under despotism. According to Arendt, the former are "totally subject to the will of Leader" and have "lost all the prerogatives which they held under despotic bureaucracies."[77] The example of Stalinist Russia casts doubt upon this view.

In their famous six-point definition of totalitarianism, Friedrich and Brzezinski listed a "system of terror effected through party and secret police control." Later they noted that as the purge became violent, "it ceased being merely a party operation and the secret police became the prime agent."[78] But the mechanisms of this process and the relationship of the police to the party and the leader in the totalitarian system remain unclear. Similarly, Dallin and Breslauer's study of political terror provides an excellent theoretical framework for analyzing the functions of terror under Stalin but does not address itself specifically to the role of the political police.[79]

In his book *Totalitarianism*, while drawing on certain aspects of the "six-point" theory, Leonard Schapiro did much to clarify the question of interrelationships by distinguishing between "instruments of rule"—party, police, and ideology—and characteristic features, or "contours"—the Leader, subjugation of the legal order, control over private morality, continuous mobilization, and legitimacy based on mass support.[80] Schapiro pointed out that under Stalin the regular machinery of party and government gave way to the role of Stalin's "personal agents and agencies." He noted that the party was not allowed to maintain control over the security organs, but he did not consider specifically how the police related to other "instruments of rule" or to the "contours" of the regime except to say that it remained under Stalin's control.

The reduction in the police powers and changes in the Soviet system in the years after Stalin's death led some Western scholars to question the validity of the totalitarian model, not merely as it applied to the post-1953 period but also in relation to the Stalin era. Even such a leading proponent of the totalitarian model as Carl Friedrich modified his views. Criticizing Arendt for overestimating the role of the secret police as an aspect of totalitarianism, Friedrich noted that "it has been made clear by historical studies that terror and secret police cannot be taken by themselves as the decisive trait of totalitarian role. In all autocracies, the secret police and its terror have played their role and there is no need to review this material here."[81]

[23]

Unfortunately, few of the theories and models that have been offered as alternatives to the totalitarian interpretation of the Stalin period have shed light on the role of the political police. Recent efforts to explain the purges and the police terror as a logical process that was motivated by rational administrative concerns, for example, have been unconvincing. To view the "Ezhovshchina" as "a fulfillment of the 'democratic' principles of the October Revolution" because it displaced the entrenched Soviet establishment, or to call Stalin a "populist muck-raker" and Ezhov a "puritan" and an "antibureaucrat" who carried out the purges in order to fight corrupt local officials, does little to enhance our understanding of the role of the police in the Stalin period.[82]

Not all of the "revisionist" scholarship has downplayed the role of the political police under Stalin, however. Scholars such as Stephen Cohen and Moshe Lewin, in objecting to the "determinist" approach of the totalitarian theory and stressing instead the uniqueness of the Stalin period, have pointed to a distinct change that took place in the relationship between the police and party during the 1930s. Cohen, who argues that Stalinism represented an aberration from Bolshevism rather than an evolution, discusses how the role of the party degenerated significantly under Stalin. Furthermore—and this is the crucial point for our analysis—Cohen states that "even in its new Stalinist form, the party's political importance fell below that of the police."[83] Lewin goes further and speaks of an alliance between the dictator and the police: "the building up of the secret police as a partner in the 'alliance' consisted in elevating them above the party."[84]

It may be difficult to accept the thesis of Cohen and Lewin that this development was not inevitable, particularly in view of the fact that police powers had already begun to expand significantly in the 1920s. Moreover, given Lenin's intolerance toward any kind of political dissent outside the party, it is not surprising that dissent within the party would eventually be treated as treasonous and that party members would be persecuted by the police.[85] Nevertheless, as these scholars stress, the Leninist political police remained under the party's control despite their awesome powers. The most distinctive feature of "full-blown Stalinism" was the fact that the police gained political importance that was greater than that of the party, establishing what is termed here a "Stalinist police state."

Two key developments in 1934 were indicative of this process. The first related to the organization and powers of the political police. In July 1934, after the death of Menzhinskii, the OGPU, now headed by Iagoda, was transformed into a Main Administration of State Security (GUGB)

[24]

and integrated into a newly formed All-Union NKVD (People's Commissariat for Internal Affairs).[86] The functions of the security police and the internal affairs apparatus were united in one body. This included not only the militia, which had been under OGPU control since 1932, but also the criminal investigation organs and other services of the regular police. It might have appeared initially that the powers of the security police were circumscribed by this reorganization, but in fact just the opposite happened. Iagoda, Menzhinskii's former deputy in the OGPU, became head of the NKVD, and the security police in effect gained dominance over the entire NKVD apparatus.

In addition to the security and regular police, the NKVD was in charge of border and internal troops, fire brigades, convoy troops, and, after October 1934, the entire penal system, which included regular prisons and forced labor camps (GULAG). During the period from 1934 to 1940 the NKVD took charge of numerous economic enterprises that employed forced labor, such as gold mining, major construction projects, and other industrial activity.[87] An internal passport system, which had been introduced in 1932 and was administered by the NKVD, provided the police with an effective means of watching over Soviet citizens. In addition, a so-called Special Board was attached to the NKVD, which operated outside the legal codes and was empowered to impose on persons deemed "socially dangerous" sentences of exile, deportation, and confinement in labor camps for up to five years. This Special Board, the successor to the OGPU's judicial collegium, soon became one of the chief instruments of the Stalinist purges.[88] As was stressed earlier, there were no procedural restraints governing bodies that inflicted punishments by "administrative means."

With the formation of the NKVD and its Special Board, the police apparatus had acquired vast powers. It had amalgamated under its authority the ordinary police and criminal investigation organs. The judiciary system had in effect been neutralized by the official disavowal of bourgeois legality and by the NKVD's power to circumvent the state organs of justice entirely by inflicting its own extralegal punishments. The political police had also emerged as a key actor in the regime's social and economic mobilization programs, displacing other elements of the state apparatus. Even the Soviet Army, which might have posed a challenge to Stalin's rule, was safely constrained by an extensive network of political police agents throughout its ranks.[89]

The second development in the process of Russia's transformation into a Stalinist police state concerned the party and its relationship with the police. The Seventeenth Party Congress, held in early 1934, was a strong indication of how much political authority the police had achieved. It was represented by no less than twenty-five delegates while Iagoda and V. A. Balitskii, head of the security police in the Ukraine, became full members of the Central Committee and two other police officials became candidate members.[90] As far as Stalin was concerned, however, his domination over the party was not absolute. Dissatisfaction with his policies continued to be manifested by some party members, and elements existed within the leadership that might have been expected to oppose any attempt to use police terror against the party. According to the available evidence, the most prominent of these potential challengers was Sergei Kirov, chief of the Leningrad party apparatus.[91]

The story of Kirov's murder on 1 December 1934 has been told before. Stalin's responsibility for this act has not been conclusively established, but it is clear that Kirov's death provided Stalin with the pretext for launching an assault against the party.[92] Immediately following the assassination, arrests of former party oppositionists began, and the announcement of the trial of G. E. Zinoviev, L. B. Kamenev, and others was made the next month. Although Stalin proceeded cautiously in his moves against the party and another year would pass before large-scale arrests and executions would occur, the turning point had been reached.[93] The terror machinery was in place and the party's subjugation to the police was only a matter of time.

The Convergence of Ideology and Terror

As Robert Sharlet pointed out, Stalin used legal forms to legitimize and rationalize the terror he imposed on the Soviet people: "The jurisprudence of terror institutionalized and routinized political terror within the context of formal legalism. In effect, terror was 'legalized,' and the criminal process 'politicized.'"[94] An amendment to the RSFSR Code of Criminal Procedure introduced on 1 December 1934 immediately following Kirov's assassination typified this phenomenon. This amendment established a special procedure for crimes involving terrorism (Article 58-8 of the Criminal Code): the time of preliminary investigation was shortened to a maximum of ten days; the accused was to receive the indictment only twenty-four hours prior to trial; neither the defendant nor his counsel was permitted in the courtroom; no appeals were allowed; and the sentence (usually death) was to be carried out immediately.[95] A similar procedural amendment for cases of wrecking and sabotage was introduced by a law of 14 September 1937, though here the defense was permitted in the courtroom.[96]

The continued adherence to these quasi-legal norms that supposedly governed the prosecution of "real criminals" by the NKVD provided a facade for the indiscrimate application of terror, just as the state machinery—the courts, soviets, commissariats—continued to exist formally, while the real authority was exercised by Stalin and the political police. As Leonard Schapiro put it, "it was not the state which increasingly absorbed society. It was the Leader and the apparatus of control which he created, or which operated under him, which progressively, like some evil cancer, ate their way into the fabric of both state and society."[97] Stalin's so-called revival of legality, exemplified in the 1936 Soviet Constitution, the purges of the "legal nihilists," and steps to centralize control over the justice system, did indeed stabilize the law, but it did little to protect citizens from the "jurisprudence of terror." USSR Procurator A. I. Vyshinskii, who led the movement, epitomized the dualism between law and terror. While campaigning publicly for a restoration of rule by law, he actively encouraged the abuse of procedural norms by the state security agencies and prosecuted members of the Procuracy who drew attention to these abuses.[98]

As the institution chiefly responsible for uncovering ideological enemies of the regime, the NKVD became in effect the guardian of the regime's ideology. Whereas previously the party itself had exercised this function, the presence of so many "ideological subversives" within its ranks discredited the party, so that the police gradually took on the role of ideological arbitrator. Brian Chapman describes this process:

> When the party is undermined, the way is open for the police to move up to become the leading apparat of the state, assuming the party's role of ultimate guardian of ideological purity. The police apparat takes on itself the responsibility for mobilizing society, but, with the intellectual limitations of the police, the weapon most likely to be used is terror, and the terror, in the first instance, is turned against the party.[99]

Theorists of both the totalitarian and antitotalitarian schools have stressed the importance of ideology for a regime of the Stalinist type.[100] It legitimizes the regime and its policies while at the same time serving as an instrument of mobilization. By continually postulating new goals, which the society is consistently to strive for, the ideology justifies all deviations from accepted concepts of morality in the name of the greater good, laid claim to by the ideology. The experience of collectivization and forced industrialization illustrated how effective Soviet ideology could be for the successful mobilization of society. But the full extent of the powers of this ideology was not realized until the political police gained a monopoly over it.

Of course the ultimate custodian of the official truth was the Leader, Stalin, and the ideology served above all to deify him. By the 1930s the myth of Stalin's omnipotence and his special role as the bearer of Lenin's Truth was well established. As Margaret Mead described it in a study of Soviet attitudes toward authority:

> In the approved poetry of the new folklore, as in the continued repetition of the names of Lenin and Stalin in the phrase Leninism-Stalinism, the halo around the figure of Lenin is made to embrace Stalin also, and he, like Lenin in obedience to Lenin, sharing Lenin's knowledge of the Truth, leads the people, will "give happiness to all the people."[101]

Yet as Stalin forged his alliance with the political police, he inevitably imparted sanctity to them as well. According to the dissident Soviet historian Antonov-Ovseyenko, "under Stalin, who abolished religion and destroyed the church, the function of spiritual shepherd passed to the investigators of the secret police."[102]

The NKVD's unique status and special claim to the Truth is amply illustrated in the memoir literature. Thus Nadezhda Mandelstam described the NKVD official who interrogated her husband, the poet Osip Mandelstam, in 1934: "Both M and I had the same general impression that, as M put it, 'this Christophorovich has turned everything upside down and inside out!' The Chekists were the avant-garde of the 'new people' and they had indeed basically revised, in the manner of superman, all ordinary human values."[103] Solzhenitsyn wrote of the NKVD:

> Your name, like that of a jealously guarded deity, cannot even be mentioned. You are there; everyone feels your presence; but it's as though you didn't exist. From the moment you don that heavenly blue service cap, you stand higher than the publicly acknowledged power. . . . For you, of course, you are the one—and no one else—who knows about the *special considerations*. And therefore you are always right.[104]

The alliance between Stalin and the NKVD was at best uneasy, fraught with tension and intrigue. Despite the slavish devotion and loyalty displayed to him by the police, Stalin apparently was always

[28]

fearful that its leaders would turn against him, just as he was constantly suspicious of his party colleagues. For their part, top members of the police apparatus and their followers had placed their fate in Stalin's hands, and any day could bring their political and physical destruction. Nevertheless the alliance remained intact, and though many of its officials were destroyed in these years and its authority was challenged by other bodies, the political police as an institution survived and prospered. The cult of the security police grew side by side with the cult of Stalin.

The NKVD's first big task was preparation of the first Moscow trial, in which Zinoviev and Kamenev were the principal defendants. The trial, which did not take place until August 1936, was an important political event for Stalin. Months were spent in efforts to get the accused to confess to their alleged crimes, which included organizing a terrorist center in collusion with Trotsky and plotting the murder of Kirov.[105] Iagoda, as Stalin's henchman, devoted all his energy to this and other tasks. He became the "eyes and ears" of Stalin, tirelessly gathering secret information on all Stalin's potential political rivals and ruthlessly persecuting Stalin's victims. According to one source, if Stalin became suspicious of a colleague in the leadership, he would have one of Iagoda's men appointed to be his deputy.[106]

Apparently Iagoda and his associates failed to understand the inexorable logic of their relationship with the ruler: having organized the liquidation of Lenin's former colleagues and imprisoned countless innocent victims on Stalin's behalf, they themselves were now prey to the executioner's axe. It could be that after Iagoda's apparent reluctance to side with Stalin in his earlier struggle with the right opposition, Stalin never fully trusted him. There were also reports that members of the Politburo, L. M. Kaganovich in particular, did their best to discredit Iagoda in Stalin's eyes and to arouse the latter's suspicions about Iagoda's loyalty.[107] Whatever was the case, Iagoda and his deputies knew all the grim secrets behind the assassination of Kirov and the Moscow trials, which was probably enough, from Stalin's point of view, to make their elimination essential.

Perhaps fearing that they would conspire against him, Stalin gave Iagoda and his men no hint of their impending doom. On the contrary, he is said to have heaped praise and honors on Iagoda right to the end. In the spring of 1936 Iagoda received the title of General Commissar of State Security and was invited by Stalin to take up residence in the Kremlin—an honor reserved only for Stalin's inner circle. Stalin also reportedly promised Iagoda that he would become a candidate member of the Politburo at the next party congress.[108] By this time, however, Stalin had already designated Iagoda's successor: N. I. Ezhov. As a Central Committee secretary and head of the Party Control Commission, Ezhov had been supervising NKVD activities on Stalin's behalf for some time. Impatient to get the trial of Zinoviev and Kamenev under way, Stalin had assigned Ezhov to participate in the preparation of the trial and to help in obtaining the necessary confessions of the victims. Ezhov's performance evidently pleased Stalin; on 27 September 1936 *Pravda* announced that he had been appointed People's Commissar for Internal Affairs, and Iagoda was named People's Commissar of Posts and Telegraph.[109]

Iagoda languished in this post for six months, until he was finally arrested in April 1937. Meanwhile Ezhov had brought with him several men from the Central Committee apparatus to serve as assistants to NKVD department heads in Moscow and to provincial chiefs, who were allowed to remain in their posts temporarily. This enabled the new deputies to learn their trade while their bosses prepared the second big show trial—that of Piatakov, Radek, and others, which took place in January 1937. In March 1937, with this trial out of the way, Ezhov had the majority of Iagoda's associates in NKVD arrested and shot.[110]

Despite the purge of many of its leading cadres, the NKVD itself continued to thrive. According to Roy Medvedev, the Central Committee had passed a resolution in summer 1936 granting the NKVD extraordinary powers for one year to destroy all "enemies of the people." These powers were reportedly extended indefinitely at a June 1937 CC plenum.[111] In October 1937 NKVD Chief Ezhov was made a candidate member of the Politburo, which gave the police some form of representation on the party's leading policy-making body. On the occasion of the twentieth anniversary of the founding of the political police (20 December 1937), awards and honors were bestowed upon Ezhov and his organization. A plethora of articles, books, poems, and songs appeared in praise of the political police, and at a triumphal celebration in the Bolshoi Theater Ezhov received a gold star with white wings. Anastas Mikoian, who gave a speech for the occasion, went into raptures over the NKVD's achievements, calling upon those present to "study the Stalin-style of work by the model of Comrade Ezhov, for he has studied and studied the model of Comrade Stalin."[112]

Under Ezhov's leadership the NKVD raised the purges and terror to a scale that had not been approached by his predecessor, Iagoda. In the period from the spring of 1937 to the end of 1938 the purges were extended from former party oppositionists to the broader party apparatus, the Komsomol, the army, and the population at large. The culmination of the terror came in March 1938 with the last great show trial, that of Bukharin, A. I. Rykov, Iagoda, and eighteen others. As before, the defendants were accused of conspiring with Trotsky to bring about the overthrow of the Soviet regime. Iagoda in particular was charged with responsibility for the assassination of Kirov, the medical murder of several other important personages, and an attempt on the life of Ezhov.[113] After this Stalin seemed to abandon the tactic of the show trial; henceforth executions of prominent figures were carried out without the formalities of a courtroom.

The Police State Stabilized

By late 1938 the purges began to wind down, arrests were curtailed considerably, and there were even some rehabilitations. These developments coincided with a change in the leadership of the NKVD. This change had apparently been planned by Stalin for some time; there were several indications that Ezhov was in trouble well before he actually lost his post. The appointment of L. P. Beria to First Deputy Chief of the NKVD on 20 July 1938 was the first sign of Ezhov's decline. Beria, at the time head of the Transcaucasian party organization, was from Stalin's point of view an ideal successor to Ezhov. A fellow Georgian, he had long been a faithful follower of Stalin and had already demonstrated, by his bloody purges in the Transcaucasus, a capacity for extreme ruthlessness. A further bad omen for Ezhov was his own appointment, on 21 August 1938, as People's Commissar for Water Transport, a post to be held concurrently with his NKVD post.[114]

Even more ominous was the establishment, in the autumn of 1938, of a special Central Committee subcommittee to check on NKVD activities. Beria was included as a member, along with Vyshinskii and party leaders V. M. Molotov and G. M. Malenkov. On the recommendations of the subcommittee, two resolutions were subsequently issued by the Central Committee: one on strengthening procuratorial oversight of the NKVD's procedures of arrest and investigation, and the other on recruiting "honest people" into the state security organs.[115] On 8 December, only a few weeks after these resolutions were passed, Ezhov was removed as head of the NKVD.[116]

It is possible that Stalin removed Ezhov because he was dissatisfied with Ezhov's performance as NKVD chief, but the most probable reason for Ezhov's demise was the leadership's need for a scapegoat for the purges. As Conquest notes,

> Ezhov's removal was a simple piece of Stalinist expediency. . . . In fact, throughout the Purge, Stalin had largely avoided public responsibility. And now, when the Terror had gone as far as it conceivably could, he could profitably sacrifice the man who had overtly carried out his secret orders, the man the party and public then blamed most—and still, to some degree, do.[117]

Stalin and his colleagues promoted an idea that the Soviet public was only too anxious to grasp—namely, that the 1936–1938 terror was not their responsibility but was the fault of evil men like Ezhov and his associates, who had "wormed their way into the NKVD" and misguided the party leadership. This idea was conveyed in the term "Ezhovsh-china" (the Ezhov thing), used to this day to describe the terror. As Medvedev notes, "the sudden disappearance of Ezhov seemed to confirm this story, which was only a new version of the common people's faith in a good tsar surrounded by lying and wicked minis-ters."[118]

Although they were manipulated by Stalin into the role of scape-goats, Ezhov and his men had not been mere "puppets" in Stalin's hands, as some have suggested.[119] Stalin, after all, depended on the security apparatus for his own survival as leader, and he had to maintain a precarious balance between promoting the cult of the security police while ensuring that his own predominance was not threatened. As long as they had control of the means of coercion, combined with a virtual monopoly of information on party and state figures as well as on individual citizens, the police wielded incredible powers of life and death over Soviet society. Accounts by survivors of the purges on the extreme brutality and inhumanity employed by NKVD men, including Ezhov, as they went about their tasks of interrogation hardly bespeaks any unwillingness on their part.

Isolated from the rest of society and imbued with a sense of privilege and superiority, many of these officials may have believed that the arrests and killings were somehow justified. Because almost every act in Stalinist Russia was viewed as a political one, the ordinary citizen was faced with a high level of accountability, and even the most insignif-icant mistake could be construed as a crime against the state. Thus as Margaret Mead suggested, the police could with some justification believe that every citizen was to some degree guilty and see nothing wrong in their arbitrary arrests.[120] The sheer magnitude of the arrests served to confirm the view that Soviet society was filled with political subversives.

By mid-1938, however, the level of arrests had reached such a height that it became impractical to continue the pace. There is evidence that the NKVD, particularly at lower levels, shared the views of the party on the necessity of stemming the tide of the purges.[121] But they did not foresee that such an abrupt reversal of the regime's policy called for some sort of renunciation of past action and for someone upon whom to inflict the blame. Ezhov and his NKVD associates were the logical candidates. Robert Conquest, in his book *The Politics of the NKVD*, concluded that the post-Ezhov purge of the NKVD was far more radical than what occurred after the ouster of Iagoda. Of the top 122 NKVD officers identified by Conquest as serving under Ezhov, only 21 survived to appear in a list of leading NKVD officers decorated in April 1940.[122]

At the Eighteenth Party Congress in January 1939, when Beria announced that "the NKVD had cleansed its ranks of the hostile elements which had worked their way into it and strengthened its ranks with verified cadres," the general assumption was that this signified a reassertion of party control over the police. Indeed, this view seemed reasonable given the fact that the Congress added two paragraphs to the party statutes which were intended to protect party members from indiscriminate purges.[123] A closer look at these developments, however, reveals that it is not accurate to portray Ezhov's demise and the concomitant winding down of the purges as a victory for the party over the police. After all, Ezhov himself was a "party man" until his appointment to the NKVD in 1936, and many of his subordinates had also come straight from the party apparatus. Several leading party figures, including Malenkov, Kaganovich, and Mikoian (not to mention Stalin himself), had participated enthusiastically in the purges, working closely with Ezhov. Some, such as Mikoian and Malenkov, were ardent promoters of the cult of the security police and went out of their way to praise Ezhov in the most extravagant terms.[124] Moreover the police were not the only scapegoats for the purges. Although members of the central party leadership escaped responsibility and portrayed themselves as indignant over the excesses, many local party committees were accused of having arbitrarily persecuted loyal party members.

It is important to note that the majority of NKVD cadres brought in by Beria, himself a former police official, had extensive background in the political police. Some came straight from police posts while others, including the new First Deputy People's Commissar, V. N. Merkulov, had served in the political police for long periods.[125] Because their party

[33]

and government experience was of only recent vintage, their basic orientation and loyalties probably lay with the police. The majority of these men were to enjoy an unprecedented security of tenure, remaining in their posts until the early 1950s, when Beria's machine began to collapse. Furthermore, they swiftly acquired even more power, prestige, and perquisites than their predecessors had enjoyed. At the Eighteenth Party Congress Beria and Merkulov were elected into full membership in the Central Committee, while Beria himself was promoted to candidate membership on the Politburo. No fewer than eight leading NKVD officials were elected candidate members of the Central Committee, and a total of fifty-seven NKVD officers were among the delegates, as compared with twenty-five delegates at the previous congress.[126]

By appointing as police chief a man who had a power base of his own, built up in the Transcaucasian republics, Stalin changed the relationship between himself and the police and, as Robert Slusser noted, created a problem of control that would eventually pose a serious threat. Using the group of protégés that he brought to Moscow, Beria was able to convert the police apparatus into his own fiefdom. Thus unlike his predecessors, who had no power beyond that conferred by their positions, Beria enjoyed a measure of independence from Stalin in his dominance over the security police.[127]

By 1939 all the best buildings in Moscow and Leningrad were reportedly occupied by NKVD employees, who continued to be awarded prestigious honors and to be glorified extravagantly in the press. As Antonov-Ovseyenko observed, the security police official became the symbol of the new era, "guarding the people's total happiness. To this glorious, epoch-making hero, songs, odes, verses and plays were dedicated."[128] In a sense the fact that the police no longer relied on the highly destabilizing technique of mass terror made them even more powerful. Because the potential to use violence was still in their hands, the police inspired fear and submission among the population. Yet they were not faced with the probability that mass terror would suddenly spill over into their ranks.

The war years brought further opportunities for the political police to expand its authority. According to one Soviet source, a number of additional economic functions were entrusted to the NKVD during the war, including the construction of military installations, hydroelectric projects, and canals.[129] The NKVD also established several scientific research institutes, using professional engineers and scientists who had been imprisoned. In the initial period of the war Marxist-Leninist party slogans were abandoned in favor of appeals to patriotism and there was some relaxation of party controls, but the fascist threat was used to justify the most extreme police repression. Soon after the outbreak of the war Stalin ordered the immediate execution of anyone suspected of espionage. Mass NKVD deportations of "anti-Soviet elements" were carried out in the newly occupied territories of eastern Poland and the Baltic states, contributing to the steady growth of forced labor camps. NKVD presence in the Red Army, through its so-called Special Departments, was expanded considerably because of the great increase in the size of the armed forces and the influx of so many inexperienced men as well as non-Russian nationalities. Toward the end of the war the political police moved into areas formerly under German occupation to cleanse the population of the effects of German rule and to arrest those suspected of sympathy for the Nazis. They also took on the responsibility of repressing nationalist movements in the Baltic states and the Western Ukraine.[130]

A rise in the authority of Beria, as head of the police, reflected the growing importance of his institution in the war years. He was promoted to the rank of General Commissar of State Security (equivalent to the military rank of Marshal of the Soviet Union) in January 1941. When the State Defense Committee was established in June 1941, it consisted originally of only five men: Stalin, Molotov, Voroshilov, Malenkov, and Beria. The latter was given overall responsibility for domestic policy and was also placed in charge of armaments and munitions, including research on atomic weapons. Beria's promotion to this all-powerful central policymaking body over the heads of several full Politburo members was a clear sign of the importance of the NKVD. Furthermore he was made a deputy chairman of the State Defense Committee in May 1944. After the Soviets gained the offensive, the state security organs were removed from the NKVD, and a separate NKGB, People's Commissariat of State Security, was formed in April 1943. (Such a reorganization had in fact been effected earlier, in February 1941, but had been reversed when the war broke out.) Beria retained his position as chief of the NKVD and was able to exert control over the NKGB through his trusted ally, Merkulov, who was appointed chief of that organization. Thus Beria remained tsar of the entire police apparatus throughout the war years.[131]

In early 1946, when Beria was made a full member of the Politburo and a deputy chairman of the Council of Ministers, he relinquished his NKVD post to his former first deputy, S. N. Kruglov. Some months later Merkulov was replaced as chief of security police by the former head of military counterintelligence, V. S. Abakumov. (In March 1946 the com-

missariats were renamed ministries, and the NKVD and NKGB became·
the MVD and MGB, respectively.) It has been suggested that these
changes did not bode well for Beria because neither Kruglov nor Abakumov was part of Beria's Caucasian *khvost*, which had dominated the
police under his leadership. Furthermore there was evidence that Leningrad Party chief A. A. Zhdanov was campaigning to restrict Beria's
power.[132] Beria's setback was temporary, however, and with the aid of
Malenkov, he intrigued successfully against Zhdanov. After the latter's
death in August 1948, Beria managed to fabricate the so-called Leningrad
Case, which resulted in a bloody purge of most of Zhdanov's associates.
In carrying out his vendetta against the Leningrad group, Beria relied
heavily on the services of Abakumov and the MGB, which indicates that
he had made Abakumov an ally.[133]

The postwar years saw the expansion of political police responsibilities as the Soviet regime sought to establish its control in Eastern
Europe. The military counterintelligence services of the MGB were
heavily represented among Soviet armed forces stationed in these countries, and they frequently extended their political surveillance to the local
population. Furthermore the MGB supervised the creation of political
police apparatuses in Eastern Europe in order to ensure conformity with
Moscow's operations. Satellite security organs were permeated with
security officials from Moscow, who helped them in adopting Soviet
techniques. The same terrorist methods used by the NKVD in the 1930s
were employed in Eastern Europe during the wave of purges and trials
following Yugoslavia's expulsion from the Comintern in 1948.[134]

From 1948 to 1952 not a single Central Committee plenum was
held, and political decision making was restricted to a small coterie of
men around Stalin. As one of these men, Beria played a key role in both
internal and foreign policy, relying heavily on the MGB until late 1951,
when Abakumov was suddenly removed as MGB chief and arrested. His
replacement, S. D. Ignat'ev, was associated with the Zhdanov group,
while Ignat'ev's deputy, A. A. Epishev, was a protégé of Khrushchev.
These changes, along with a massive purge of Beria's allies in the Georgian party organization in early 1952, indicated that Beria was being
attacked by Stalin. The threat became more ominous when the new MGB
leadership began an investigation of the so-called Doctors Plot in late
1952. Public criticism of the state security organs for failing to discover
the plot earlier was a blow to Beria because his protégés were blamed.[135]
Significantly, although the police was well represented among the new
Central Committee members elected at the Nineteenth Party Congress in
October 1952 (three full and five candidate members), the majority was

from the MVD, whose chief and deputy chief, Kruglov and I. A. Serov, respectively, were to prove key figures in Beria's subsequent demise.[136]

Had Stalin not died suddenly in March 1953 Beria might have suffered the fate of Iagoda and Ezhov. Indeed, it appeared that once again Stalin was preparing to move against that organization upon which he had relied so heavily to maintain his power. In the case of Beria, however, Stalin faced a political threat that he had not faced with earlier police chiefs, so his removal would have been more than a simple matter of expediency. Stalin's death was fortuitous for Beria, to say the least, and he was to see in it the opportunity to achieve his own bid for the Kremlin leadership on the basis of the security police. The fact that Beria came close to succeeding was evidence of the power achieved by the security police during the Stalin era.

Notes

1. There had been earlier attempts to create a political police in Russia (the Oprichnina of Ivan the Terrible and Peter the Great's Preobrazhenskii prikaz), but these were short-lived institutions and were later dismantled. See Ronald Hingley, *The Russian Police. Muscovite, Imperial Russian and Soviet Security Operations, 1565–1970* (London: Hutchinson, 1970), pp. 1–27.

2. David H. Bayley, "The Police and Political Development in Europe," in Charles Tilly, ed., *The Formation of National States in Western Europe* (Princeton, N.J.: Princeton University Press, 1975), p. 377.

3. Brian Chapman, *Police State* (London: Pall Mall, 1970), p. 31. This interesting study sets forth a theoretical basis for defining the relationship between police and political cultures, providing useful models of different types of police states that have emerged in modern times.

4. As Marc Raeff notes, "at the core of the system there was a profound contradiction between its fundamental aims and purposes, on the one hand, and the means it resorted to, on the other." Raeff, "The Well-Ordered Police State and the Development of Modernity in Seventeenth- and Eighteenth-Century Europe: An Attempt at a Comparative Approach," *American Historical Review* 80, no. 5 (December 1975):1221–1243 (quotation, p. 1228). Also see Raeff's more recent study, *The Well-Ordered Police State: Social and Institutional Change Through Law in the Germanies and Russia, 1600–1800* (New Haven and London: Yale University Press, 1983).

5. There are two good English-language studies of the Third Section: Sidney Monas, *The Third Section* (Cambridge, Mass.: Harvard University Press, 1961), and P. S. Squire, *The Third Department. The Establishment and Practices of the Political Police in the Russia of Nicholas I* (Cambridge: Cambridge University Press, 1968). Also see Ernest V. Hollis's unsubmitted Ph.D. dissertation, "Police Systems of Imperial and Soviet Russia," Archive of Russian and East European History and Culture, Columbia University, 1957.

6. Although they do not use the terminology of "higher" and "lower" police, the Soviets still distinguish very clearly between the ordinary and the political police, giving the latter clear priority. See chapter 3. The lower police in nineteenth-century Russia were part of the Ministry of Interior. For an excellent study of this institution, see Daniel T. Orlovsky, *The Limits of Reform: The Ministry of Internal Affairs in Imperial Russia, 1802–1881* (Cambridge, Mass., and London: Harvard University Press, 1981).

7. Squire, *The Third Department*, p. 197.

8. See Samuel Kucherov, *Courts, Lawyers and Trials under the Last Three Tsars* (New York: Praeger, 1953), and Richard Pipes, *Russia under the Old Regime* (New York: Scribner's, 1974), pp. 295–297.

9. So despised were Russia's police officials that Zasulich's acquittal (by a jury composed mainly of government bureaucrats and merchants) was greeted with widespread approval by large segments of Russian society. See P. A. Zaionchkovskii, *Krizis samoderzhaviia na rubezhe 1870–1880-x godov* (Moscow: Izdatel'stvo Moskovskogo Universiteta, 1964), p. 59.

10. Ibid., pp. 59–88.

11. On the Okhrana, see Hingley, *The Russian Secret Police*, pp. 69–116; and Hollis, "Police Systems of Imperial and Soviet Russia." Also see Edward Ellis Smith, *"The Okhrana": The Russian Department of Police: A Bibliography* (Stanford: Stanford University Press, 1967).

12. See V. M. Gessen, *Iskliuchitel'noe polozhenie* (St. Petersburg, 1908); and Pipes, *Russia under the Old Regime*, pp. 305–309.

13. As Hollis notes, "the gendarmerie managed to keep the revolutionaries infiltrated, frustrated, divided and heavily populating the prisons and points of exile, not to mention the many who found it necessary to flee abroad. However, in view of the fact that the sweepingly inclusive criteria employed in respect of political phenomena resulted in rounding up of persons of many shades of nonconformist opinion, revolutionaries among them, it is not justified to call this accomplishment a mark of efficiency." Hollis, "Police Systems of Imperial and Soviet Russia," p. 383.

14. Jacob Walkin, *The Rise of Democracy in Pre-Revolutionary Russia: Political and Social Institutions under the Last Three Czars* (New York: Praeger, 1962), pp. 59–60.

15. A. I. Spiridonovich, "Pri tsarskom rezhime," *Arkhiv russkoi revoliutsii*, vol. 15 (Berlin, 1924), pp. 85–208 (quotation, p. 116).

16. Ibid., p. 115.

17. A. A. Lopukhin, *Nastoiashchee i budushchee russkoi politsii*, (Moscow: V. M. Sablin, 1907), p. 33.

18. See Pipes, *Russia under the Old Regime*, pp. 313–314; Walkin, *Rise of Democracy*, pp. 67–68; and R. V. Ivanov-Razumnik, *The Memoirs of Ivanov-Razumnik*, trans. and annot. P. S. Squire (London: Oxford University Press, 1965). Ivanov-Razumnik, a well-known Russian literary critic, experienced both tsarist and Stalinist prisons. The former, as he described it, were far from a hardship; he and fellow university students who were in prison with him received unlimited parcels, walked about freely, played cards, staged plays, and so on. This marked a sharp contrast with his later experiences in prisons during the 1920s and 1930s.

19. Walkin, *Rise of Democracy*, p. 62. Rural unrest and strikes were in fact put down by armed force, but the government did not espouse violence against individual political dissenters.

20. This was particularly true of the most extreme element of the movement, the Socialist Revolutionaries. See Amy Knight, "Female Terrorists in the Russian Socialist Revolutionary Party," *Russian Review* 38, no. 1 (1979):139–159.

21. Raeff makes an important point about the evolution of Russia as a police state and its failure to follow in the path of Western European states. Although Russian tsars as far back as Peter the Great sought to create a "well-ordered police state" on the German model, which would promote modernization and economic growth, they did not have the social resources to do this successfully: "It is precisely the corporate bodies and autonomous social institutions—Montesquieu's famous *corps intermediaires*—that provided the essential framework for cameralism and police in Central and Western Europe and that were most conspicuously absent in Russia." Raeff, "The Well-Ordered Police State," p. 1237. Also see Raeff's book, *The Well-Ordered Police State*, pp. 237–250.

22. As Hollis expressed it, "it was a counter-fight against society's war upon the existing system that the gendarmerie is seen eventually to have been carrying on, a battle

that could not possibly be won by the only means available to a tiny security police—action against leading individuals and particularly active groups—because disaffection had also deeply infected the masses. The gendarmerie, as such, was simply incapable of dealing with violent mass phenomena, nor did the government depend on it to do so." Hollis, "Police Systems of Imperial and Soviet Russia," p. 381.

23. For a general discussion of the differences between the two police systems, see Jacob Walkin, "Some Contrasts between the Tsarist and Communist Political Systems," *New Review of Soviet and East European History* 15 (March 1976):55–66.

24. As long ago as 1901 Lenin wrote: "In principle, we have never renounced terror and cannot renounce it." V. I. Lenin, *Sochinenia*, 5th ed. (Moscow: Gosizdat, 1959), 5:7. On Lenin and terror, see G. H. Leggett, "Lenin, Terror and the Political Police," *Survey* 21, no. 4(97) (Autumn 1975):157–187.

25. *Vserossiiskaia chrezvychainaia komissiia po borbe s kontrrevoliutsii i sabotazhem.* This referred to the central organization. The term "Cheka" was applied to subordinate commissions under the Vecheka in the various localities, but the Soviets often used "Cheka" when referring to the overall organization. For an excellent comprehensive English-language study of the Vecheka, see George Leggett, *The Cheka: Lenin's Political Police* (Oxford: Clarendon Press, 1981). Also see Lennard D. Gerson, *The Secret Police in Lenin's Russia* (Philadelphia: Temple University Press, 1976). Among the more useful Soviet publications on the Cheka are G. A. Belov et al., eds., *Iz istorii vserossiiskoi chrezvychainoi kommissii, 1917–21 gg. Sbornik dokumentov* (Moscow: Politizdat, 1958); and S. K. Tsvigun et al., eds., *V. I. Lenin i VchK: Sbornik dokumentov* (Moscow: Politizdat, 1975). Also see note 35.

26. This date was 7 December, according to the Julian Calendar. For the text of the decree, see Belov et al., *Iz istorii*, pp. 78–79. Also see Leggett, *The Cheka*, pp. 29, 371, n. 159; and E. H. Carr, "The Origin and Status of the Cheka," *Soviet Studies* 10, no. 1 (July 1958): 1–11.

27. Carr, "Origin and Status of the Cheka," p. 4. On the Vecheka statute, see Leggett, *The Cheka*, pp. 129; 131–132.

28. See E. H. Carr, *The Bolshevik Revolution, 1917–23*, vol. I (London: Macmillan, 1950), pp. 165–167; and Leggett, *The Cheka*, pp. 56–58.

29. The 2 September resolution is reprinted in Belov et al., *Iz istorii*, pp. 179–180. The 5 September decree appeared in *Izvestiia* on 10 September 1918 and is cited here from Leggett, *The Cheka*, p. 110.

30. Leggett, *The Cheka*, pp. 121–137; Samuel Kucherov, *The Organs of Soviet Administration of Justice: Their History and Operation* (Leiden, The Netherlands: E. J. Brill, 1970), pp. 62–64.

31. Leggett, *The Cheka*, pp. 117–120; Carr, *Bolshevik Revolution*, I:179–180.

32. On these measures and how they failed, see Leggett, *The Cheka*, pp. 137–138; 145–146; Kucherov, *Organs of Soviet Administration of Justice*, pp. 65–66.

33. Quoted in *Kommunist*, no. 18 (1977):62.

34. Quoted in Belov, *Iz istorii*, pp. 474–475. Also see Gary Richard Waxmonsky, "Police and Politics in Soviet Society, 1921–29" (unpublished Ph.D. diss., Princeton University, 1982), pp. 31–32, 54–58.

35. A vast body of literature glorifying the Vecheka has emerged since the early sixties. See a Soviet bibliography: N. S. Aksenova and M. V. Vasil'eva, *Soldaty Dzerzhinskogo soiuza beregut. Rekomendatel'nyi ukazatel' literatury o chekistakh* (Moscow: "Kniga" 1972); and *Soviet Intelligence and Security Services: A Selected Bibliography of Soviet Publications*, prepared by the Congressional Research Service, Library of Congress, vol. I, covering 1964–1970 (Washington, D.C.: U.S. Government Printing Office, 1972) and vol. II, covering 1971–1972 (Washington, D.C.: U.S. Government Printing Office, 1975). Also see a recent discussion of the historiography of the Vecheka, which includes references to numerous sources: A. L. Litvin (Kazan'), "VChK v sovetskoi istoricheskoi literature," *Voprosy istorii*, no. 5 (May 1986):96–102. For a bibliography of literature on Dzerzhinskii, see I. A. Doroshenko et al., eds., *Feliks Edmundovich Dzerzhinskii, Biografiia*, 2d ed. (Moscow: Politizdat, 1983). In contrast to the official portrayals of Chekists as selfless

humanitarians and dedicated revolutionaries, contemporary observers had a different view. According to the Communist Viktor Serge, "the only temperaments that devoted themselves willingly and tenaciously to this task of 'internal defence' were those characterized by suspicion, embitterment, harshness and sadism. Long-standing inferiority complexes and memories of humiliation and sufferings in the Tsar's jails rendered them intractable, and since professional degeneration has rapid effects, the Chekas inevitably consisted of perverted men tending to see conspiracy everywhere and to live in the midst of perpetual conspiracy themselves." Quoted in Leggett, *The Cheka*, p. 189.

36. See Appendix A for a chart of the organizational history of the security police. The decree on the GPU was published in *Izvestiia*, 8 February 1922, p. 10. It was reprinted in Belov et al., *Iz istorii*, pp. 471–474. For a discussion of the events leading up to the dissolution of the Cheka, see Leggett, *The Cheka*, pp. 339–344.

37. Gerson, *The Secret Police*, pp. 229–230; E. A. Skripilev, ed., *Istoriia sovetskogo gosudarstva i prava*, vol. 2: *Sovetskoe gosudarstvo v periode stroitel'stva sotsializma (1921–1935 gg.)* (Moscow: Gosizdat, 1968), p. 402.

38. See, for example, Skripilev, *Istoriia sovetskogo gosudarstva i prava*, pp. 401–403; and K. A. Sofronenko, ed., *Istoriia gosudarstva i prava SSSR.*, pt. 2: *Istoriia sovetskogo gosudarstva i prava* (Moscow: Gosizdat, 1962), p. 158. Also see Waxmonsky, "Police and Politics," pp. 87–91.

39. See Gerson, *The Secret Police*, p. 228, and Robert Slusser, "The Budget of the OGPU and Special Troops from 1923–4 to 1928–9," *Soviet Studies* 10, no. 4 (April 1959): 375–382.

40. Leggett, *The Cheka*, p. 348; Ger P. Van Den Berg, *The Soviet System of Justice: Figures and Policy* (Dordrecht, Boston, Lancaster: Martinus Nijhoff, 1985), p. 18.

41. See A. A. Gertsenzon, et al., eds., *Ugolovnoe pravo. osobennaia chast'. Gosudarstvennye prestupleniia* (Moscow: Iuridicheskoe izdatel'stvo, 1938), p. 66. Other Soviet sources also refer to a judicial collegium of the OGPU. See Sofronenko, *Istoriia gosudarstva i prava*, p. 243; Skripilev, *Istoriia sovetskogo gosudarstva i prava*, p. 407; and S. S. Studenikin et al., eds., *Sovetskoe administrativnoe pravo* (Moscow: Gosizdat, 1950), p. 273.

42. *Sobranie Uzakonenii RSFSR*, 1922, no. 15, art. 153; 1923, no. 7, art. 106; 1926, no. 80, art. 600.

43. Harold J. Berman, *Soviet Criminal Law and Procedure: The RSFSR Codes*, 2d ed. (Cambridge, Mass.: Harvard University Press, 1972), p. 25.

44. Stephen Schafer, *The Political Criminal* (New York: Free Press, 1974), p. 22.

45. See Article 7 of the 1922 and 1926 Criminal Code. The wording is somewhat different in the two codes but the basic concept is the same.

46. See Article 10 of the 1922 Criminal Code and Article 16 of the 1926 Criminal Code. Not surprisingly, these elastic concepts of crime formed the basis for criminal law in the Third Reich, where, as Schafer points out, the law "ideologized the interpretation of all crime so extensively that the criminal act and its definition were no more than aids to the political evaluation of crimes." Schafer, *The Political Criminal*, p. 23.

47. See G. Shvekov, "Iz istorii bor'by s melkoburzhuaznoi ideologiei levykh eserov pri sozdanii pervogo sovetskogo Ugolovnogo Kodeksa," *Vestnik Moskovskogo Universiteta. Seriia 11, Pravo.*, no. 3 (1967):26–35; N. Durmanov, "Ugolovnyi Kodeks RSFSR 1922 goda," *Sovetskaia iustitsiia*, no. 16 (1972):23–25.

48. See Marc Jansen, *A Show Trial under Lenin: The Trial of Socialist Revolutionaries, Moscow 1922*, trans. Jean Sanders (The Hague, Boston, London: Martinus Nijhoff, 1982), p. 27.

49. See Gertsenzon, *Ugolovnoe pravo*, pp. 12–14; V. I. Kurliandskii and M. P. Mikhailov, eds., *Osobo opasnye gosudarstvennye prestupleniia* (Moscow: Gosiurizdat, 1963), pp. 54–55.

50. See Gertsenzon, *Ugolovnoe*, pp. 14–15; Kurlianskii and Mikhailov, *Osobo opasnye*, pp. 55–58; Berman, *Soviet Criminal Law*, pp. 23–24; and E. H. Carr, *Foundations of a Planned Economy 1926–29*, vol. 2 (London: Macmillan, 1971), pp. 348–353.

51. Kurliandskii and Mikhailov, *Osobo opasnye*, p. 58. Solzhenitsyn's remarks about Article 58 are illustrative of its broad application: "Paradoxically enough, every act of the all-penetrating, eternally wakeful *Organs*, over a span of many years, was based solely on

one article of the 140 articles of the nongeneral division of the Criminal Code of 1926. . . . Who among us has not experienced its all-encompassing embrace? In all truth, there is no step, thought, action, or lack of action under the heavens which could not be punished by the heavy hand of article 58." Alexander Solzhenitsyn, *The Gulag Archipelago 1918–1956*, trans. Thomas P. Whitney (New York: Harper & Row, 1974), p. 60.

52. Berman, *Soviet Criminal Law*, p. 48.

53. Ibid., pp. 48–49. Also see *Sovetskaia prokuratura v vazhneishikh dokumentakh* (Moscow: Gosizdat Iuridecheskoi Literatury, 1956), pp. 310, 357.

54. Gerson, *The Secret Police*, pp. 243–246; Waxmonsky, "Police and Politics," pp. 142–148.

55. Waxmonsky, "Police and Politics," pp. 152–159. According to Waxmonsky, there was even a movement in the spring of 1924 to abolish the republic NKVDs and place the militia and criminal investigation under the OGPU, but the proposals were defeated and the NKVDs survived until 1930.

56. Carr, *The Bolshevik Revolution*, I:212.

57. Waxmonsky, "Police and Politics," pp. 170–171, 175, citing the report from the Fourteenth Party Congress. Actually the Cheka was intercepting the mail of the veteran Communist and member of the "Workers' Group," G. I. Miasnikov, as early as November 1921. He was expelled from the party in February 1922 and arrested by the GPU two months later. See Paul Avrich, "Bolshevik Opposition to Lenin: G. T. Miasnikov and his Workers' Group," *Russian Review* 43, no. 1 (January 1984):1–29. Another indication that the security police was being drawn into intraparty struggles actually came when, with the cooperation of the OGPU, Stalin obtained evidence to arrest a party member, Sultan-Galiev, in 1923 on charges of disobeying the party's nationality policy. See Leonard Schapiro, *The Communist Party of the Soviet Union* (New York: Vintage Books, 1971), pp. 353–354.

58. Waxmonsky, "Police and Politics," pp. 177–179; Schapiro, *The Communist Party*, p. 334. While not having formal rights to arrest party oppositionists, the OGPU cooperated closely with the party in building up cases against them.

59. For accounts of the defeat of Trotsky and the Left Opposition, see Schopiro, *The Communist Party*, pp. 290–312; Carr, *Foundations*, II:34–53. For a Soviet version of these events, see B. A. Abramov, "Razgrom trotskistskogo-zinov'evskogo antipartiinogo bloka," *Voprosy istorii KPSS*, no. 6 (1959):25–47. Abramov (p. 40) states that OGPU chief Menzhinskii produced evidence at the October 1927 CC plenum proving that the opposition had planned to overthrow the Bolshevik regime.

60. See Waxmonsky, "Police and Politics," pp. 213–214. It is significant that the representation of the political police among delegates to the Fifteenth Party Congress that same month showed a marked increase. According to Waxmonsky (p. 207), there were no less than eight OGPU delegates, as compared with two to four delegates at previous congresses.

61. Ibid., p. 218.

62. Apparently Iagoda, Trilisser, and certain other OGPU officials did not approve of Stalin's plans for forced collectivization because they feared it would have dangerous political consequences. See Simon Wolin and Robert Slusser, eds., *The Soviet Secret Police* (New York: Praeger, 1957), pp. 43–46, and an unpublished paper by Robert Slusser, "Stalinism and the Secret Police" (April 1979) for a discussion of the OGPU's relations with the Right.

63. Stephen Cohen, *Bukharin and the Bolshevik Revolution: A Political Biography 1888–1938* (New York: Alfred A. Knopf, 1973), pp. 276–277, 322–327.

64. Schapiro, *The Communist Party*, p. 388. The extent to which the OGPU actually controlled the "de-kulakization" program is still unclear. For a discussion of this question, see Lynne Viola, "The Campaign to Eliminate the Kulak as a Class, Winter 1929–1930: A Review of the Legislation," *Slavic Review* (Fall 1986):518–519. Robert Conquest has estimated that 14.5 million peasants lost their lives as a direct result of the collectivization drive and the subsequent famine. See his recent study, *The Harvest of Sorrow: Soviet Collectivization*

and the Terror-Famine (New York: Oxford University Press, 1986), esp. p. 301. Also see Roy Medvedev, *Let History Judge: The Origins and Consequences of Stalinism*, trans. Collen Taylor, ed. David Joravsky and Georges Haupt (New York: Alfred A. Knopf, 1971), pp. 71–109.

65. See Carr, *Foundations*, II:373–376. This attitude was expressed clearly by Yanson, the newly appointed People's Commissar for Justice, who wrote in *Pravda* on 20 February 1929, "The task of the Procuracy and the courts is to struggle against and to punish with the greatest severity any kind of attempt to restrain or prejudice the tempo of industrialization" (quoted in ibid., p. 369).

66. See ibid., pp. 358–373; Skripilev, *Sovetskoe gosudarstvo*, p. 404. On the establishment of forced labor camps, see David J. Dallin and Boris I. Nicolaevsky, *Forced Labor in Soviet Russia* (London: Hollis and Carter, 1947).

67. Sharlet notes, "this development entailed the expansion of the prerogative state at the expense of the normative state. As Stalin launched his 'revolution from above,' the sphere of politically deviant activity was greatly enlarged. The use of political terror grew apace with the prerogative state. The most dramatic expression of prerogative action overriding heretofore normative regulation was epitomized in the process of 'de-kulakization' in the course of the initial phase of the forced collectivization campaign during the winter of 1929–30." Robert Sharlet, "Stalinism and Soviet Legal Culture," in Robert C. Tucker, ed., *Stalinism: Essays in Historical Interpretation* (New York: W. W. Norton, 1977), pp. 155–179 (quotation, p. 163).

68. Ibid., p. 163.

69. As *Izvestiia*, 14 April 1928, p. 2, pointedly noted, the plot was uncovered "not by Communist economic officials, not by the local party or professional organizations, but by the organs of the OGPU." As quoted in Waxmonsky, "Police and Politics," p. 232. For a discussion of the Shakhty and other economic trials, see Medvedev, *Let History Judge*, pp. 110–139.

70. Schapiro, *The Communist Party*, pp. 396–397. Slusser, in "Stalinism and the Secret Police," p. 13, claims that it was Iagoda who insisted on confirmation of Stalin's order to execute Riutin.

71. On Ezhov's background see Medvedev, *Let History Judge*, pp. 171–172, and Abdurakhman Avtorkhanov, *Stalin and the Soviet Communist Party: A Study in the Technology of Power* (Munich: Institute for the Study of the USSR, 1959), p. 218. Also see chapter 4 for further details on his role in controlling the police.

72. On Poskrebyshev and Stalin's personal secretariat, see Leonard Schapiro, "The General Department of the CC of the CPSU," *Survey* 21, no. 3 (Summer 1975):53–65; and a detailed study by Neils Erik Rosenfeldt, *Knowledge and Power: The Role of Stalin's Secret Chancellery in the Soviet System of Government* (Copenhagen: Rosenkilde and Bagger, 1978).

73. See Medvedev, *Let History Judge*, p. 243. Medvedev refers to NKVD officials, but he probably means OGPU, given that the NKVD at the republic level had been abolished in 1931.

74. Bagirov survived the purges and became the first communist of Turkic and Moslem origin to achieve status in the leading party body, the Presidium, to which he was appointed a candidate in 1953. He was shot in 1956 for his crimes during the Stalin era and his association with Beria. See Merle Fainsod, *How Russia Is Ruled*, rev. ed. (Cambridge, Mass.: Harvard University Press, 1967), pp. 163–164, 326.

75. The literature on the theory of totalitarianism is vast. For an excellent survey of some the writings on the subject and a discussion of the various alternative models of the Soviet system, see Daniel Tarschys, *The Soviet Political Agenda: Problems and Priorities, 1950–1970* (White Plains, N.Y.: M. E. Sharpe, 1979), pp. 10–40. Also see a recent article by Pierre Hassner, "Communist Totalitarianism: The Transatlantic Vagaries of a Concept," *Washington Quarterly* 8, no. 4 (Fall 1985):17–29.

76. Hannah Arendt, *The Origins of Totalitarianism* (New York: Harcourt Brace and World, 1966), esp. pp. 419–437.

77. Ibid., p. 425.

78. Carl J. Friedrich and Zbigniew Brzezinski, *Totalitarian Dictatorship and Autocracy*, rev. ed. (New York: Praeger, 1967), pp. 22, 76.

79. Alexander Dallin and George W. Breslauer, *Political Terror in Communist Systems* (Stanford: Stanford University Press, 1970).

80. Leonard Schapiro, *Totalitarianism* (New York: Praeger, 1972).

81. Carl J. Friedrich, "The Evolving Theory and Practice of Totalitarianism," in Benjamin Barber, ed., *Totalitarianism in Perspective: Three Views* (New York: Praeger, 1969), p. 144.

82. For these interpretations see, respectively, Marshall Shatz, "Stalin, The Great Purge and Russian History: A New Look at the New Class," *The Carl Beck Papers in Russian and East European Studies*, no. 305, p. 30; and J. Arch Getty, *Origins of the Great Purges: The Soviet Communist Party Reconsidered, 1933–1938* (Cambridge: Cambridge University Press, 1985), pp. 196–206.

83. Stephen F. Cohen, "Bolshevism and Stalinism," in Tucker, *Stalinism*, p. 18.

84. Moshe Lewin, "The Social Background of Stalinism," in Tucker, *Stalinism*, pp. 111–136 (quotation, p. 131). Tucker himself leaves open the question of "whether Stalinism signified the eclipse of the communist party-state by an *oprichnina*-state under the Soviet secret police." Ibid., p. xx.

85. As Sidney Hook observed, "the logic of political experience shows that, where public expression of differences is not tolerated outside the party, it is soon suppressed within the party, lest a split develop." Hook, "The Case of Comrade Bukharin," *Encounter* 43, no. 6 (December 1974):81–92 (quotation, p. 88).

86. For the legislation establishing the NKVD and subsequent decrees defining its composition and functions, see Wolin and Slusser, *The Soviet Secret Police*, pp. 46–47 (notes 68–70).

87. Some of these projects were directly under the GULAG; others, such as Dalstroi (for gold mining), highway construction, and hydroelectric construction, were established as independent NKVD administrations. For details see Wolin and Slusser, *The Soviet Secret Police*, pp. 46–47, and Robert Conquest, *The Soviet Police System* (New York: Praeger, 1968), pp. 84–87. Also see Stanislaw Swianiewicz, *Forced Labor and Economic Development: An Enquiry into the Experience of Soviet Industrialization* (Westport, Conn.: Greenwood Press, 1985), esp. pp. 290–303.

88. See *Sobranie zakonov i rasporiazhenii SSSR*, 1934, no. 36, item 283; 1935, no. 11, item 84; Wolin and Slusser, *The Soviet Secret Police*, pp. 15, 48 (note 71); Berman, *Soviet Criminal Law*, pp. 49–50; Sharlet, "Stalinism and Soviet Legal Culture," pp. 165–166. Also see N. V. Zhogin, "Ob izvrascheniiakh Vyshinskogo v teorii sovetskogo prava i praktike," *Sovetskoe gosudarstvo i pravo*, no. 3 (March 1965):22–31. At first the Special Board was limited to handing out five-year sentences, but its powers were gradually increased to ten- and then twenty-five-year sentences. In addition to the Special Board, from 1934 to 1938 special judicial collegia existed within the regular court system from the *oblast* level upward to hear certain crimes investigated by the NKVD, while the more serious cases (espionage, terror, and diversion) were handled by military tribunals. After 1938 the special collegia no longer existed, but Soviet sources claim that the regular courts continued to handle some political cases. See D. S. Karev, *Sovetskoe sudoustroistvo* (Moscow: Gosiurizdat, 1951), pp. 90–92. Also see Van Den Berg, *The Soviet System of Justice*, pp. 18–19; and Harold J. Berman and Miroslav Kerner, *Soviet Military Law and Administration* (Cambridge, Mass.: Harvard University Press, 1955), pp. 106–111.

89. For a discussion of the NKVD's network in the Soviet army, see chapter 8.

90. The two candidate members were T. D. Deriabas and G. I. Blagonravov. See Robert Conquest, *Inside Stalin's Secret Police: NKVD Politics 1936–1939* (Stanford, Calif.: Hoover Institution Press, 1985), p. 111.

91. See Schapiro, *The Communist Party*, pp. 400–402. Tibor Szamuely gives a different interpretation, claiming that all opposition to Stalin had been defeated by the time of the Seventeenth Party Congress. See Szamuely, "The Elimination of the Opposition between the Sixteenth and Seventeenth Congresses of the CPSU," *Soviet Studies* XVII, no. 3 (January 1966):318–338. Schapiro's interpretation, however, seems more convincing.

92. This has long been the accepted interpretation of the Kirov affair among

Western scholars, although some dispute has arisen over the issue in recent years. For details see a discussion among J. Arch Getty, Robert C. Tucker, and Neils Erik Rosenfelt in the *Slavic Review* 42, no. 1 (Spring 1983):60–96.

93. Dallin and Breslauer characterize the stages that terror goes through in communist systems: "The typical pattern is a sequence of victimization beginning with active enemies and moving to erstwhile partners in the ruling party, to quasi-legal opponents from the 'bourgeois' and 'petty-bourgeois' camp and finally to members of the Communist Party, state, military and police hierarchies. At the mobilization stage, these last groups join the list of victims." Dallin and Breslauer, *Political Terror in Communist Systems*, p. 28.

94. Sharlet, "Stalinism and Soviet Legal Culture," p. 164. Solzhenitsyn, *The Gulag*, pp. 60–67.

95. See M. S. Strogovich, *Ugolovnyi protsess* (Moscow: Iuridicheskoe Izdatel'stvo, 1946), p. 66. Strogovich and other Soviet sources make it clear that this amendment was a direct response to Kirov's murder.

96. Ibid. For a discussion of other laws passed during 1929–1936 which increased the repressive features of Soviet criminal jurisprudence and further broadened the concept of political crime, see Berman, *Soviet Criminal Law*, pp. 28–32.

97. Schapiro, *Totalitarianism*, p. 69.

98. See Zhogin, "Ob izvrascheniiakh Vyshinskogo." The revival of legality in the late 1930s involved mainly cosmetic reforms. While the doctrine of analogy, for example, was given a restricted interpretation and was excluded from a 1939 draft of a new criminal code, one scholar points out that this was only a theoretical distinction. Definitions of crimes in the Soviet legal code were so vague that it was not necessary for courts to cite the analogy clause in order to convict persons. See Hiroshi Oda, "Criminal Law Reform in the 1930's" (Paper delivered at the III World Congress for Soviet and East European Studies, Washington D.C., 30 October–4 November, 1984), p. 24. For a different interpretation of Vyshinskii and the legality campaign, see Peter Solomon, "Local Political Power and Soviet Criminal Justice, 1922–41," *Soviet Studies* 37, no. 3 (July 1985):305–329.

99. Chapman, *Police State*, p. 114.

100. See, for example, Zbigniew K. Brzezinski, *The Permanent Purge: Politics in Soviet Totalitarianism* (Cambridge: Harvard University Press, 1956), pp. 173–174: "The roots of totalitarian power are to be found in the system's ability to generate the enthusiasm of the masses through a constant process of inventing new goals and new objectives. It is this drive towards the millennium which is the real source of totalitarian power and the justification for its coercion." According to Moshe Lewin, the cult of the leader, his alliance with the secret police, and the ideological justification for this alliance are the "three essential ingredients of the Stalinist trademark." Lewin, "The Social Background of Stalinism," p. 131.

101. Margaret Mead, *Soviet Attitudes toward Authority: An Interdisciplinary Approach to Problems of Soviet Character* (New York: Schocken Books, 1966), p. 60.

102. Anton Antonov-Ovseyenko, *The Time of Stalin: Portrait of a Tyranny*, trans. George Saunders (New York: Harper & Row, 1981), p. 149.

103. Nadezhda Mandelstam, *Hope against Hope*, trans. Max Hayward (Harmondsworth: Penguin, 1975), p. 93.

104. Solzhenitsyn, *The Gulag*, pp. 148–149.

105. See Robert Conquest, *The Great Terror: Stalin's Purge of the Thirties*, rev. ed. (New York: Collier Books, 1973), pp. 133–144.

106. Alexander Orlov, *The Secret History of Stalin's Crimes* (New York: Random House, 1953), p. 252.

107. Ibid., p. 256. Also see Antonov-Ovseyenko, *The Time of Stalin*, pp. 122–123. Slusser, "Stalinism and the Secret Police," pp. 13–17, claims that Iagoda demonstrated insubordination to Stalin on numerous occasions and in fact had never been Stalin's choice to head the NKVD.

108. Orlov, *The Secret History of Stalin's Crimes*, p. 257.

109. Conquest, *The Great Terror*, pp. 217–219.

110. Conquest estimates that about three thousand NKVD men were shot. See Conquest, *Inside Stalin's Secret Police*, p. 30. Also see Medvedev, *Let History Judge*, p. 172.

111. Medvedev, *Let History Judge*, p. 392. Medvedev also claims that in 1937 the pay of NKVD employees was "approximately quadrupled" and that "in the latter half of the thirties, their numbers were so swollen as to become a whole army, with divisions and regiments, with hundreds of thousands of security workers and tens of thousands of officers" (p. 392).

112. His speech, along with that of Ezhov and others, appeared in a special book that was published to commemorate the NKVD anniversary: *20 let VChK-OGPU-NKVD* (Moscow: Gosizdat, 1938).

113. On this trial see Conquest, *The Great Terror*, pp. 496–573; and Robert C. Tucker and Stephen F. Cohen, eds., *The Great Purge Trial* (New York: Grosset & Dunlop, 1965).

114. Conquest, *The Great Terror*, pp. 607–609; Medvedev, *Let History Judge*, p. 244.

115. Roy Medvedev, "New Pages from the Political Biography of Stalin," in Tucker, *Stalinism*, pp. 217–218; Antonov-Ovseyenko, *The Time of Stalin*, p. 124.

116. Ezhov retained his post as People's Commissar for Water Transport for the next few months and then disappeared. See Conquest, *The Great Terror*, pp. 622–623.

117. Ibid., p. 624.

118. Medvedev, *Let History Judge*, p. 290. As Medvedev points out, many people actually believed this version of the purges and blamed Ezhov rather than Stalin.

119. See, for example, Robert Payne, *The Rise and Fall of Stalin* (London: Pan Books, 1968), p. 438.

120. Mead goes on to make a religious parallel that seems apt in view of the sanctimonious nature of Soviet ideological propaganda at the time: "Within many Christian communities it would not seem inappropriate to select at random someone to play Judas, for all are believed to have, to some degree, betrayed their savior in their hearts." Mead, *Soviet Attitudes toward Authority*, p. 92.

121. Conquest, *The Great Terror*, p. 624.

122. Conquest, *Inside Stalin's Secret Police*, p. 103.

123. See Brzezinski, *Permanent Purge*, pp. 128–129. Brzezinski notes: "It is clear that the leadership of the party had decided to seize the initiative from the secret police . . . the police could not resist."

124. The journal *Partiinoe stroitel'stvo*, for example, which was edited by Malenkov, frequently expressed extravagant flattery for Ezhov in 1937–1938. See Roy Medvedev, *All Stalin's Men*, trans. Harold Shukman (Oxford: Basil Blackwell, 1983), p. 144; and Avtorkhanov, *Stalin and the Communist Party*, pp. 303–304.

125. On the background of these men see Conquest, *Inside Stalin's Secret Police*, pp. 88–89.

126. Ibid., pp. 93–94.

127. Slusser, "Stalinism and the Secret Police," pp. 26–27.

128. Antonov-Ovseyenko, *Time of Stalin*, p. 219.

129. M. I. Eropkin and L. L. Popov, *Administrativno-pravovaia okhrana obshchestvennogo poriadka* (Leningrad: Lenizdat, 1973), p. 86.

130. See V. V. Korovin, "Uchastie organov gosudarstvennoi bezopasnosti v osushchestvlenii funktsii oborony strany," *Sovetskoe gosudarstvo i pravo*, no. 5 (May 1975):53–60; "Sovetskie organy gosudarstvennoi bezopasnosti v gody velikoi otechestvennoi voiny," *Voprosy istorii*, no. 5 (1965):20–39; Boris Levytsky, *The Uses of Terror: The Soviet Secret Police 1917–1970*, trans. H. A. Piehler (New York: Coward, McCann and Geoghegan, 1972), pp. 156–175; Wolin and Slusser, *The Soviet Secret Police*, pp. 18–20. Antonov-Ovseyenko, *Time of Stalin*, pp. 275. Also see chapters 7 and 8.

131. Levytsky, *The Uses of Terror*, pp. 156–184; Wolin and Slusser, *The Soviet Secret Police*, p. 21. Also see Vladimir and Evdokia Petrov, *Empire of Fear* (New York: Praeger, 1956), pp. 83–84. Beria did lose formal control over military counterintelligence when the NKVD was split up in 1943. At this time a separate military counterintelligence agency, known as SMERSH, was created and placed under the control of the People's Commissariat of Defense. In 1946 military CI was again placed under the security police.

132. See William McCagg, *Stalin Embattled 1943–48* (Detroit: Wayne State University Press, 1978), p. 85.

133. On these events see Werner Hahn, *Postwar Soviet Politics: The Fall of Zhdanov and the Defeat of Moderation, 1946–53* (Ithaca and London: Cornell University Press, 1982), pp. 104–113.

134. See Ferenc Vali, "Hungarian Secret Police: The Early Years," and Condolleza Rice, "Czechoslovakia's Secret Police," in Jonathan R. Adelman, ed., *Terror and Communist Politics: The Role of the Secret Police in Communist States* (Boulder and London: Westview Press, 1984), pp. 155–194; Conquest, *The Soviet Police System*, pp. 91–92; and Z. B. Brzezinski, *The Soviet Bloc: Unity and Conflict*, rev. and enlarged edition (Cambridge, Mass., and London: Harvard University Press, 1967), pp. 120–121.

135. Hahn, *Postwar Soviet Politics*, pp. 141–148.

136. Conquest, *Inside Stalin's Secret Police*, p. 154.

2

The KGB:
Reform and Rehabilitation, 1954–1967

The Party Asserts Control

The political police played a key role in the events that followed Stalin's death, mainly because Beria's efforts to consolidate his power centered on this organization. On 6 March 1953, the day after Stalin died, it was announced that the MVD and MGB had been amalgamated into one organization, a united MVD, under the leadership of Beria. Beria moved swiftly to get rid of those police officials who were hostile toward him and to reinstate his supporters in the central police apparatus in Moscow. This involved putting a halt to the prosecution of those accused in the "Doctors Plot."[1] Beria also appointed his men as MVD ministers in several republics, including Georgia, where he carried out a wholesale purge of the party and government apparatus and, according to Khrushchev, he began using the MVD to collect evidence against the Ukrainian party leadership.[2] Beria seized the initiative in a general program to "liberalize" both Soviet domestic and foreign policy by repudiating the Russification campaign, calling for a halt in the program of amalgamating collective farms and advocating a relaxation of aggressive Soviet policies abroad.[3]

Beria's reforming zeal and his efforts to gain popularity no doubt alarmed his colleagues in the Kremlin, though the policies he advocated were in tune with their own sentiments. Above all it was his control of the vast police apparatus and the evident signs that he was using it to gain predominance in the leadership that provided the catalyst for them to unite in opposition against him. One source notes that after Beria brought MVD troops into Moscow on the pretext of a widespread outbreak of burglaries, there was serious danger of a coup d'état in his name.[4] Numerous charges were laid against Beria when *Pravda* announced his overthrow on 10 July 1953, but the accusation that he had "tried to place the MVD above the party and the government and to misuse the MVD organs against the party and the government of the USSR" was emphasized above the others.[5]

The "Beria affair" and the shake-up in the Kremlin leadership that followed his arrest had far-reaching consequences both within the Soviet Union and abroad. But the greatest impact of this episode in Soviet history was on the relationship between the political police and the party. Henceforth although "collective leadership" would not always be observed and new leadership cults would arise, the party would not allow the political police to reemerge as the dominant institution in the Soviet system. The party leadership not only arrested and later executed Beria and several of his allies in the MVD, but it also took measures to place the security police under its firm control to prevent any future threats to the party's preeminence. Some key decisions in this regard appear to have been reached at the Central Committee plenum that took place from 2 to 7 July 1953. The decree adopted at the plenum was never published within the Soviet Union, though a version of it reportedly appeared in the West in the early 1960s, and the Soviets themselves have offered summary accounts.[6] According to a 1959 party history, the plenum, in addition to condemning Beria and his associates, "took measures to strengthen party leadership of all branches of the state apparatus, ensuring effective control over the work of all organs and agencies, including the organs of state security."[7]

The precise nature of the measures to strengthen party control over the security police have never been made clear. Presumably steps were taken to prevent individual leaders from bypassing normal party channels in overseeing the security police. In addition, the position of party bodies charged with oversight for the security police—in particular the CPSU Department of Administrative Organs—was strengthened. The most crucial decision, however, was the disavowal of terror as a means of settling conflict with the leadership. Dallin and Breslauer point out that "terror as an instrument of purposive policy does not erode or wither 'on its own,' even as a consequence of systemic changes. The decline in its use requires active or passive, explicit, or tacit, decision-making."[8] Why did the new leaders take this course? Above all, it seems, they wanted stability and security in their public and private lives.[9]

The decision to abolish terror had a far-reaching impact on Soviet leadership politics. First, it resulted in a shift from one-man rule to a more oligarchic form of leadership within the party. As Grey Hodnett observed,

> the primary and uneradicable source of weakness of one-man rule under Khrushchev was unquestionably the dissipation of terror as a credible means of dealing with real or perceived opposition within the leadership. Failure to take account of the qualitative change this factor introduced in intraleadership relations is a root cause of the overestimation of Khrushchev's power.[10]

Hodnett goes on to point out that a concomitant effect of the elimination of terror was the opening up of communications among the leadership. The fact that disagreements could no longer be suppressed by police violence, as they were under Stalin, placed a distinct limit upon the leader's power because he was subject to criticism from other members of the elite. Furthermore the party leader could no longer rely solely on the traditional means of gaining political support: through patronage or the appointment of allies to key positions. As George Breslauer demonstrated, the post-Stalin leader had to "build authority" by legitimizing his policies and demonstrating his ability to solve problems.[11]

The quest for legitimacy was not confined to the political elite. Terror was also disavowed as a means of subduing the masses, which meant that other, more persuasive methods—such as material incentives, consumer satisfaction, and broader public participation—were introduced to help ensure obedience. The biggest problem facing Khrushchev and subsequent leaders was to achieve these reforms without undermining the party's dominant role and the elitist nature of the system. Thus while the new leadership sought to break with the past, it would retain certain traditional Stalinist elements. The tension between these two conflicting goals was reflected in the regime's policies toward the political police and the legal system.

One indication of the regime's commitment to a reversal of Stalinist methods had in fact been demonstrated before Beria's fall, in late March 1953, with the announced amnesty for many types of ordinary and political prisoners. Further amnesties followed in the next four years.[12] Equally significant was the abolition, in September 1953, of the MVD's notorious Special Board. This deprived the political police of their main

[49]

vehicle for imposing punishments by extrajudicial means.[13] At the same time, the military tribunals of the MVD troops were eliminated, and for a brief period in 1953–1954 corrective labor camps were placed under the jurisdiction of the Ministry of Justice.[14]

A key reform that the new leadership introduced—and one upon which there was probably fairly strong consensus—was the reorganization of the police apparatus. On 13 March 1954 a decree of the Presidium of the USSR Supreme Soviet established a new Committee of State Security attached to the USSR Council of Ministers (Komitet Gosudarstvennoi Bezopasnosti pri Sovete Ministrov SSSR).[15] The establishment of a state security apparatus separate from that of the regular police was designed to diminish the formidable powers that the police had wielded when its activities were concentrated in one organization. Henceforth the functions of ensuring the political security of the USSR would be ascribed to a special police agency, whose powers were substantially less than what they were under Stalin.

It might be added that the MVD had lost important economic functions by the time the KGB was established. In 1953 control of key enterprises run by the MVD's Main Administration of Corrective Labor Camps (GULAG), including Dalstroi, highway construction, and hydroelectric construction, had been transferred to newly established economic ministries, while some time in 1954 nuclear weapons production was reportedly turned over to the Ministry of Medium Machine-building.[16] In addition, although corrective labor camps were returned to the MVD by 1954, the amnesties had begun to deplete the MVD's large pool of forced labor.[17]

The road to socialist legality was not without diversions, however. First, the party leadership in 1953 did not go beyond the denunciation of Beria and his cohorts to condemn Stalin's role in the purges or to admit publicly that the security police had terrorized Soviet society on his behalf. Several members of the post-Stalin leadership, including Malenkov, Molotov, and Kaganovich, were themselves deeply implicated in Stalin's crimes. To disavow Stalinist practices openly would entail casting the net of accusations much further than Beria and possibly threaten the stability of the new leadership. The trial of Beria, reportedly held in December 1953, and four subsequent trials of his associates that took place from 1954 to 1956 were another sign that the regime was moving slowly in eradicating Stalinist practices. The cases were conducted under the draconian procedural laws that stipulated summary justice for cases of terrorism, wrecking, or sabotage. It was not until April 1956 that these laws were repealed.[18]

The police and legal reforms were diminished further by the appointment of a long-time police official, Ivan Aleksandrovich Serov, to head the KGB. Serov's past was heavily tainted by his participation in Stalinist police repression.[19] Born in 1905, Serov joined the Red Army at the age of twenty. He graduated from the Frunze Military Academy in 1939, whereupon he entered the ranks of the NKVD. After directing the brutal campaign for Sovietization of the Baltic republics, Serov was appointed chief of the NKVD for the Ukraine, working closely with Ukrainian Party First Secretary Khrushchev in the process of incorporating the Polish Ukraine into the Soviet Union. Serov was promoted to Deputy People's Commissar of State Security in 1941 and later, in 1943–1944, supervised the mass deportations of Chechens, Ingushes, Kalmyks, and Crimean Tartars from the North Caucasus.[20]

In 1945 Serov became deputy chief of SMERSH (military counterintelligence) in the Soviet Zone of Germany, after which he served from 1946 to 1953 as First Deputy Minister of the MVD under Kruglov. During this period Serov apparently retained close ties with military counterintelligence officials but kept his distance from the Beria group, including former SMERSH chief Abakumov, which dominated the MGB. When Khrushchev made his move against Beria in June 1953, Serov and Kruglov, both deputy ministers of the MVD, proved to be valuable supporters. This probably explains why Khrushchev gave Serov the top security post in 1954 and retained Kruglov as head of the MVD. Kruglov, who also joined the NKVD in 1939 and served in SMERSH during the war, had a reputation that was equally as ruthless as Serov's.[21] In addition, another former SMERSH colleague, Petr Ivashutin, whose NKVD career dated from the same period, became one of Serov's deputies, rising to First Deputy Chairman of the USSR KGB by the early 1960s.[22]

Although Khrushchev and the party leadership wanted to demonstrate that they were "cleansing the ranks" of the security police, other considerations—namely personal loyalty and professional experience—prevailed in the case of the top police posts. Khrushchev himself, well aware of Serov's tainted past, sought to justify the appointment when he later wrote his memoirs:

> I hardly knew Kruglov, but I knew Serov well, and I trusted him. I thought, and still think, Serov is an honest man. If there are a few dubious things about him, as there are about all Chekists, then let's just say he was a victim of Stalin's general policy.[23]

Khrushchev also managed to move at least two of his protégés from the party apparatus into top KGB posts. K. F. Lunev, who had worked under Khrushchev in the Moscow City Party Committee, was made a deputy chairman of the KGB in 1954. (He had actually been appointed deputy chief of the MVD in 1953 and had served on the special tribunal that condemned Beria and his colleagues in December 1953.) Another Moscow *Gorkom* official, V. I. Ustinov, also became a KGB deputy chairman in 1954. He served simultaneously as chief of the Ninth Directorate of the KGB, which encompasses the highly important Kremlin guards.[24]

At the republic level the majority of KGB appointees were long-time security police officials. Of the fourteen republic KGB chairmen appointed in 1954, at least nine were police professionals, some with careers dating from the OGPU in the 1920s.[25] More detailed career information on KGB officials offered in chapter 5 confirms that the initial post-Stalin purges of the state security organs did not extend much further than Beria and his allies, leaving the majority of officials untouched. Indeed, it was openly acknowledged that a large number of Stalinist security officials were allowed to remain in their posts after 1953. In a speech marking the fortieth anniversary of the state security organs in December 1957, KGB chief Serov stressed that the "newcomers" were working together with "old experienced workers to whom the Central Committee and the party accorded their complete trust and support."[26]

De-Stalinization and the Appointment of Shelepin

Khrushchev's Secret Speech, delivered at the Twentieth Party Congress in February 1956, was an important step in the process of de-Stalinization and had potentially great significance for the role of the post-Stalin security police.[27] His revelations of the crimes committed by the security police under Stalin inevitably weakened the prestige of the KGB and may well have demoralized its cadres, many of whom had participated actively in the purges. Significantly, only five identifiable KGB officials were represented among the delegates to the congress—a considerably lower number than at past congresses.[28] Another blow to the police establishment was the fact that only one KGB official, Serov, was elected a full member of the Central Committee, while his deputy, Lunev, was elected a candidate member. Moreover Kruglov was removed from his post as MVD chief only a few days before the congress and replaced by a former Moscow *Gorkom* official, N. P. Dudorov.[29]

In his published report to the congress, however, Khrushchev was careful not to go too far in damaging the image of the state security organs. He stressed that it was "incorrect and very harmful" for party members to distrust state security workers. "We know," he continued, "that the overwhelming majority of our Chekists consists of honest officials devoted to our common cause and we trust them." Noting that the enemy camp was sending many spies and saboteurs into the Soviet Union, Khrushchev added: "Therefore, we must raise the revolutionary vigilance of our people and strengthen the organs of state security."[30]

This emphasis on vigilance was echoed in speeches delivered on the occasion of the fortieth anniversary of the security police on 20 December 1957. Serov conceded that "there are no domestic reasons to keep the apparatus of the state security organs on alert, as was the case in the first years of the Soviet regime." But, he went on, "it would be naive to suppose that our enemies will now give up their efforts to harm us in every way. . . . We must therefore do everything to raise the revolutionary vigilance of the Soviet people and strengthen the state security organs."[31] Speeches on this occasion by other KGB officials also emphasized the growing threat of outside subversion as a justification for a strong state security apparatus.[32]

A leading party journal, *Partiinaia zhizn'*, took up the campaign for vigilance in late 1958 with an article by V. Moskovskii, head of the Propaganda and Agitation Department of the RSFSR Central Committee, on the need to raise party awareness of the dangers of enemy efforts to gain access to secret information. After urging party members to guard state secrets more carefully, Moskovskii quoted Khrushchev in a speech to construction workers: "The enemy hopes that we will weaken our vigilance and weaken our organs of state security. No, this will never happen!"[33] Khrushchev himself reasserted this position at the Twenty-First Party Congress in 1959:

> Our enemies are expending vast resources on subversive work against socialist countries. How could we ever liquidate the organs that are charged with protecting the security of the Soviet state! It would be stupid and criminal.[34]

It is not difficult to understand why the party leadership would be anxious to persuade the Soviet public that the security police could be fully trusted and should be strengthened. As long as the regime continued to rely on the security organs to ensure domestic stability and protect the Soviet state from spies, it was inadvisable to downgrade these organs, particularly in view of the fact that the party was simultaneously carrying out a program of de-Stalinization and legal reforms that restricted the KGB's prerogatives. The situation abroad may have been another factor. The uprisings and unrest in Eastern Europe had made Khrushchev and other party leaders aware of the consequences of going too far in their efforts to de-Stalinize. Furthermore Khrushchev was pursuing an active policy of détente with the West by the late 1950s, and he may have considered it necessary to assure both his party colleagues and his Western counterparts that this policy did not mean a decrease in vigilance against perceived Western efforts to subvert the Soviet state.

The removal of Serov and the appointment of Central Committee official Aleksandr Shelepin to the post of KGB chairman in December 1958 lent credence to the claims that the security police had been success-fully reined in. The fact that the KGB was no longer under the direction of a security police professional, but rather a party *apparatchik*, signified a reassertion of party control over the police. It is not entirely clear what precipitated Serov's sudden removal. He had again demonstrated his support for Khrushchev during the latter's threatened ouster by the so-called anti-party group in June 1957, and there seemed to be no question of his loyalties to the First Secretary. Shelepin, on the other hand, had no apparent career or personal connections with Khrushchev. Roy Medvedev claims that a scandal involving past illegalities precipi-tated Serov's removal, but the fact that he was transferred to the post of chief of the GRU (military intelligence) indicates that he was not in serious disgrace at this time.[35] Most probably Serov's reputation was seen as a hindrance to party efforts to give the KGB a new, more legitimate image.

Shelepin's untainted record did much to raise the stature of the KGB. His entire career, with the exception of a few months as chief of the CC Party Organs Department in 1958, had been in the Komsomol, or Communist Youth League. After obtaining a higher degree at the Moscow Institute of History, Philosophy and Literature, Shelepin fought in the Russo-Finnish War and served as an organizer of the partisan movement near Moscow in World War II. From 1943 to 1958 he had worked in the Secretariat of the All-Union Komsomol, rising to First Secretary in 1952.[36] With his higher education in humanities and his "clean" record, Shelepin marked a sharp contrast with his predecessors. As later developments were to show, however, Shelepin was not without aspirations to power. Medvedev notes, "As for Shelepin, he was an unprincipled careerist with immense political ambition. When he was still a twenty-year-old student at the Moscow Institute of Philosophy and Literature, friends asked him what he wanted to become. He replied without hesitation: 'a chief.'"[37] Michael Voslensky presents a similar portrayal of Shelepin as one who had set his sights on the general secretaryship and "spent years building up his following and using his influence on their behalf."[38]

As head of the Komsomol Shelepin had supervised key appointments within this organization throughout the country and had gained many supporters among the group of young up-and-coming Komsomol officials. He brought several of these men into the KGB with him. In addition to V. S. Tikunov, appointed a deputy chairman of the USSR KGB in 1959, at least two of the seven new republic KGB chairmen appointed in 1959–1960 and the new chief of the Leningrad KGB had served under Shelepin in the Komsomol.[39] Although there are scant data on lower-level KGB appointments, Medvedev claims that Shelepin's arrival precipitated significant changes, with several regional Komsomol first secretaries transferred to head regional KGB admininstrations.[40]

In a speech delivered to the Twenty-First Party Congress in February 1959, less than two months after he took on his new job, Shelepin indicated that the KGB had been reduced in size and that further reductions were planned: "We shall continue our measures to improve the quality of state security personnel, to perfect their work, to simplify the structure and reduce the apparatus."[41] Some months later, writing in the legal affairs journal *Sovetskoe gosudarstvo i pravo*, KGB Deputy Chairman Tikunov referred to the changes being implemented in the KGB:

> The party has appointed to leading posts in the central apparatus of the state security committee, the republic state security committees and the regional admininstrations, responsible party officials who have gained wisdom from experience in the struggle to realize the goals set by the Communist Party.[42]

Tikunov stressed that the laws set forth in the 1958 Fundamentals of Criminal Procedure were applicable without exception to all KGB employees, and he also made the remarkable claim that only those with higher legal education and practical experience could become KGB investigators.[43]

The overwhelming impression conveyed in the official Soviet press from 1958 onward was that the state security organs had been completely transformed from what they were in the days of Stalin. Underlying the official statements was a discernible effort to legitimize the KGB and raise its prestige in the eyes of the public. Tikunov and others attempted to illustrate by means of examples that the KGB was prepared to show mercy by reeducating persons who had committed crimes rather than arresting them. Reflecting the populist spirit of Khrushchev, KGB officials were reported to be in close contact with the population, going to factories, workshops, and student organizations in order to explain their functions and convince people to participate in safeguarding state security.[44]

Thus while Shelepin's appointment did indeed signify greater party involvement in the activities of the security police, it also brought a new legitimacy and effectiveness to this organization. Far from declining in stature as an institution, the security police embarked on an era of prestige and stabilization. The KGB was now acting on behalf of the party, which had set down rules to guide KGB operations and sanctioned it as a legitimate and necessary organization of the Soviet state. It should be noted, however, that this new approach was not connected with Shelepin alone. His appointment was followed, in 1959, by the transfer of N. R. Mironov from the post of Leningrad KGB chief to the head of the Central Committee's Administrative Organs Department. As will be discussed later, Mironov was a very authoritative figure who played a role in party efforts to legitimate the KGB.

It is significant that improvement in the security police's image began at the very time that Khrushchev was heightening his efforts to de-Stalinize. Shelepin's participation in the de-Stalinization campaign was indicative of how the Khrushchev leadership managed to discuss the Stalinist terror publicly without drawing attention to the specific role of the police. The Twenty-Second Party Congress in October 1961 marked the high point of de-Stalinization. Aside from Khrushchev himself, who took the lead by giving what Michel Tatu noted was a public version of the 1956 secret speech, Shelepin emerged as one of the most outspoken de-Stalinizers at the congress.[45] In his speech he gave a dramatic and graphic account of the murders of innocent party, state, and military figures, offering revelations of the sinister role of Molotov, Kaganovich, Malenkov, and Voroshilov.[46] Although he condemned Stalin and the anti-party group, however, Shelepin made no mention of the role of the security police or the criminal actions of police leaders, aside from a passing reference to Beria. Indeed the focus was entirely on individual party leaders, who personally had ordered repressions against specific persons. The fact that the police apparatus itself had carried out mass illegal arrests and executions among the population at large was omitted in Shelepin's speech.

Shelepin was careful to stress that "violations of socialist legality have been completely eliminated" in the work of the state security agencies and noted that "the Chekists can look the party and the Soviet people in the eye with a clear conscience."[47] All in all, Shelepin's speech was, as Robert Slusser put it, "a masterpiece of dissimulation."[48] Shelepin even equivocated on the question of criminal sanctions for the anti-party group. Rather than supporting the idea or advocating the group's expulsion from the party, he simply stated that the Party Control Committee should "consider calling the members of the anti-party group to the strictest account."[49] It is thus not surprising that Khrushchev remarked in his concluding speech that Shelepin had "told by no means all that has now come to light."[50]

In the final analysis Khrushchev's de-Stalinization efforts proved a failure. The real mechanisms of Stalin's purges and details about such episodes as the Kirov murder were never revealed and the guilty were not punished. Part of the problem was that Khrushchev, though perhaps genuinely motivated by a desire to prevent a recurrence of the Stalinist terror, was also using de-Stalinization as a means of settling political scores and getting back at enemies. Hence the congress failed to consider the real causes of the Stalinist terror and focused instead on only a few culprits. Many party officials, reluctant to trample on vested interests or to turn the de-Stalinization process into a witch hunt, opted for shelving the issue altogether. The Twenty-Second Party Congress marked the end of Khrushchev's de-Stalinization drive and closed the curtain on the underlying question of police repression in the Stalin era. In short, de-Stalinization ended with a whitewash of the security police, leaving the question of its future role in Soviet society and government unanswered.

Legal Reforms: 1955–1961

Although the party leadership took only half measures with regard to de-Stalinization, it did introduce significant legal reforms after the KGB was established to protect Soviet citizens from police persecution. On 24 May 1955 a new statute on procuratorial supervision was enacted by the Presidium of the Supreme Soviet. This statute provided procedural guarantees of procuratorial power to protest illegalities committed by state agencies and to make proposals for their elimination.[51] For the specific purpose of supervising the investigative agencies of the KGB, a Special Department of Supervision of Investigations by the State Security Organs was established within the USSR Procuracy in April 1956.[52] The pre-1953 Procuracy had likewise been charged formally with the supervision of the observance of legality by investigative agencies of the state security organs, but no instructions had been published on how this supervision was to be exercised; rather, such procuratorial oversight was governed by a "special statute." In practice procurators in the Stalin era, with the possible exception of Vyshinskii, had little control over the actions of the security organs. Thus the 1955 Statute on the Procuracy represented an attempt to regulate the investigative activities of the state security organs.

Another reform that restricted the powers of the security police and protected Soviet citizens from police persecution was the enactment in December 1958 of the Fundamental Principles of Criminal Procedure, which were later incorporated into the 1960 RSFSR Code of Criminal Procedure and are still in effect today, although they have been amended numerous times.[53] Article 13 of the RSFSR CCP stated unequivocally that justice in criminal cases was to be administered only by the courts and that no one could be subjected to criminal punishment except by judgment of a court. This meant that the state security organs were no longer empowered to administer criminal punishment but had to submit all cases investigated by them to judicial bodies.[54] Article 97 of the RSFSR CCP eliminated the powers previously exercised by the police of indefinite confinement of accused persons by limiting confinement of those being investigated to two months with a possibility of an extension to six months and, in exceptional cases, with the permission of the USSR procurator-general, to nine months.

The organs of state security were subjected, on paper at least, to the same procedural rules to which other investigative agencies were subject. Under Article 122 the officer making an arrest had to inform the procurator within twenty-four hours and obtain authorization within the next forty-eight hours in order to detain the suspect further. Other legal protections were the requirement that searches could be carried out only with the permission of the procurator, although this could be obtained up to twenty-four hours after the search (Article 168 of the CCP), and the establishment of the right to defense counsel after the first stage of the preliminary investigation had been completed and the investigator was ready to submit his "conclusion to indict" to the procurator for approval (Article 47).

Article 126, paragraph 3, specified precisely the type of crimes under the investigative purview of the state security organs. As originally enacted, the RSFSR Code of Criminal Procedure authorized the Procuracy alone to conduct investigations in all cases except those arising under the following articles of the 1960 RSFSR Criminal Code, where the security police had concurrent jurisdiction: 64 (treason), 65 (espionage), 66 (terrorism), 67 (terrorism against a representative of a foreign government), 68 (sabotage), 69 (wrecking), 70 (anti-Soviet agitation and propaganda), 72 (organizing activity directed toward the commission of especially dangerous crimes), 73 (especially dangerous crimes committed against another workers' state), and 79 (mass disorders). In comparison with the broad powers of the state security organs under Stalin, the KGB's purview in investigating crimes was restricted significantly.

A new law on state crimes, enacted on 25 December 1958 and incorporated into the 1960 RSFSR Criminal Code, introduced several changes in the legislation that limited the vagueness and broad applicability of the codes on state crimes that had been in effect since 1927, and also made criminal sanctions less severe. The term "counter-revolutionary crime" was dropped as a description of state crimes and replaced by the term "especially dangerous crimes against the state" (which applied to Articles 64 through 73 of the RSFSR Criminal Code). Although this new category encompassed most of the crimes previously listed in the infamous Article 58, there were significant changes.[55] On balance, the new laws on crimes against the state narrowed the concepts of political crimes that were embodied in the earlier codes, rendering them less susceptible to the sweeping interpretations applied in the Stalin era.

The 1960 RSFSR Criminal Code, which was based on the 1958 Fundamental Principles of Criminal Legislation, introduced other important reforms reflecting a reaction against the abuses of the legal system under Stalin.[56] Article 3 stated that no person may be subjected to criminal prosecution without having committed a crime, thus eliminating the possibility that had existed under the 1926 code of prosecuting someone merely for representing a "social danger." Furthermore according to Article 7, a punishable crime could only be one specifically laid down in the codes, which meant that the infamous doctrine of analogy could no longer be applied, and Article 6 denied retroactive application of the law.[57]

Despite the progress made by the legal reforms, the new laws still reflected the traditional Soviet position that legality exists primarily to protect the state rather than the individual, and they did not close all the loopholes that made possible the grave abuse of human rights under Stalin. Furthermore, as numerous Western experts have stressed, the legal norms and procedural guarantees set forth in the post-Stalin legislation have frequently been bypassed in political cases. The party, as the ultimate arbiter of legal practices, has consistently resorted to what has been termed "ad hoc legal policy" in order to achieve its political objectives.[58] Thus the prerogative sphere, which dominated Stalinist legal practice, was narrowed considerably after Stalin died, but it continued to exist alongside the normative sphere. As before, the political police have been the dominant actors in the prerogative sphere. Finally, although Khrushchev can be credited with the initial restrictions on the powers of the political police, it was under his leadership that this process began to reverse itself. Not only were efforts stepped up to rehabilitate the public image of the KGB, but also changes in the legal codes from 1961 onward enlarged its jurisdiction in investigating crimes.

In June 1961 the KGB's investigatory powers were expanded significantly. Article 126 of the RSFSR Code of Criminal Procedure was amended to give the KGB concurrent jurisdiction with the Procuracy in investigating several additional crimes specified in articles of the RSFSR Criminal Code: 75 (disclosure of a state secret), 76 (loss of documents containing state secrets), 78 (smuggling), 83 (unlawful departure abroad and unlawful entry into the USSR), 84 (violations of the rules of international flights), 88 (violations of rules for currency transactions), 259 (a, b, c) (divulgence of a military secret or loss of documents containing military secrets), and 189 (concealment of a crime) and 190 (failure to report a crime), where they related to crimes against the state under the purview of the KGB.[59]

These amendments to the CCP enhanced the authority of the KGB in investigating crimes. Henceforth, for example, the KGB was empowered by law to protect state and military secrets. The list of information considered secret was narrower than that of the Stalin period; nevertheless it covered a wide range of military and economic data[60]: military mobilization plans, location and content of military supplies and weapons, defense installations, civil defense plans, information on military industry and technology, plans for dislocation of industry during wartime, supply and production of rare and precious metals and radioactive materials, information on currency reserves and Soviet balance of payments, state ciphers, and so on. In addition to information specifically cited, state secrets also included "other information" determined to be secret by the Ministry of Defense or other state or government agencies. As one authoritative Soviet source points out, the determination of whether or not information is secret often depends on the circumstances at the time, such as the international climate or economic conditions.[61]

Prior to 1961 there had been increasing emphasis in the official press on the need to raise vigilance in protecting state secrets.[62] Thus presumably the conferment upon the KGB of the task of investigating criminal acts involving divulgence of state secrets signified a further strengthening of these efforts. In view of the fact that the KGB was already responsible under the law on treason for crimes involving the deliberate transmission of state secrets to foreign governments, it was not surprising that these two additional crimes were added to KGB responsibilities. As a result of these changes the KGB now had formal grounds for placing its employees in government ministries and agencies (in particular the Ministry of Defense) to investigate violations of security procedures, and was presumably given access to all secret information circulated in these bodies.

The extension of the KGB's investigative purview to include the crimes specified in Articles 78, 83, 84, and 88 formalized powers already conferred on the KGB as a result of its responsibilities for border protection. The crimes described in the aforementioned articles—smuggling contraband across the border, illegal border crossing, violation of rules for internal flights, and violation of currency rules—all involved contravention of border regulations as set forth in the 1960 Statute on the USSR State Border.[63] According to this statute (Article 32), the KGB border guards had the authority, in cases of violations of these regulations, to act as agents of inquiry and "in essential cases to carry out operative-search measures and conduct urgent investigatory activity." The 1961 changes in the CCP simply gave the KGB more direct investigative authority over these crimes. In addition, presumably such investigations would not be restricted to employees in the border guard but would include regular KGB investigators. Given the fact that such crimes as currency speculation often are committed and uncovered not at the border but well within the country, it seems reasonable that the services of regular KGB investigators would be enlisted. Indeed this seems to have been the situation in several cases of currency speculators' rings that were publicized in the press shortly before the changes in the RSFSR CCP were enacted.[64]

The June 1961 decree coincided with the beginning of a highly publicized anticrime campaign initiated by Khrushchev to deal with a phenomenon that was viewed as a serious threat to Soviet society. Special legislation was enacted in 1961–1962 amending the criminal codes to create harsher penalties (including death) for certain economic crimes, and the KGB began to bring numerous cases to trial. These cases concerned mainly embezzlement of state property and other types of economic crime not under the KGB's purview, but the fact that they also involved currency speculation gave the KBG the formal right to intervene.[65]

The Political Police Rehabilitated

A noticeable feature of the gradual improvement in the KGB's status was how it contrasted with the position of the regular police, under the Ministry of Internal Affairs (MVD).[66] It soon became clear that the new emphasis on socialist legality was more to the detriment of the MVD than to the KGB. The KGB, for example, had been authorized by the new codes of criminal procedure to conduct preliminary investigations of crimes, whereas the MVD was permitted only to conduct inquiries. Local and regional administrations of internal affairs were subordinated in 1956 to local and regional soviets while at the same time being under the authority of the MVD hierarchy. By contrast, the KGB was not subjected to such dual subordination: its local organs were made responsible only to the KGB chain of command. In June 1957 the MVD relinquished control of the border guards to the KGB, though it retained authority over labor camps.[67] Then, in 1960, the USSR Ministry of Internal Affairs was abolished and its functions assumed by republic ministries of internal affairs. Such decentralization was unfavorable to interests of the MVD because it detracted from its ability to defend its prerogatives at the center. A further blow to the status of the MVD came in 1962, when it was redesignated the Ministry for the Protection of Public Order (MOOP). This name change implied a break with the all-powerful MVD created by Beria, as well as a narrower range of functions. Finally, Khrushchev's campaign of popular justice, aimed at enlisting the public in the maintenance of law and order by means of comrades' courts and people's voluntary patrols, was another incursion on the powers of the regular police. These developments were curiously reminiscent of the infringement of regular police prerogatives by the political police in the early Soviet period.

In April 1963 the internal affairs apparatus was granted investigatory powers concurrent with the Procuracy over certain types of crimes, including some economic crimes. This change enhanced the MVD's authority at the expense of the Procuracy and marked the beginning of a continued controversy between these two organizations over jurisdiction in the criminal process.[68] While it also created some competition with the KGB, reports in the press soon made clear that the KGB would prevail in important economic cases that the regular police appeared to be mishandling. A good example was the much-publicized case of Shakerman and Roifman, who allegedly confiscated millions of rubles' worth of state property and were engaged in large-scale illegal currency transactions. According to a press report in October 1963, "the thieves were active for quite a long time before the matter came to the attention of the state security committee." Not only had MOOP's Division for Combatting the Theft of Socialist Property failed to uncover the crime, but two of its officials were actually in collusion with the criminals.[69]

MVD/MOOP came under increasing fire in the Soviet press for its shortcomings in combating crime. Continued dicussions on the need for improvements in the operations of the militia and other internal affairs organs revealed serious problems: poorly educated, untrained personnel whose operations were fraught with inefficiency and corruption.[70] Yet the image of the security police in the press continued to improve. Why did the Khrushchev leadership favor the KGB over the MVD/MOOP? The measures to downgrade the regular police accommodated Khrushchev's utopian visions of socialist legality and his efforts to make the system less coercive. The security police, who defended the USSR against outside subversion, were tied more directly to the prestige and legitimacy of the Soviet state. As Darrell Hammer expressed it,

> it was possible to cloak the KGB in a certain romanticism. The targets of the regular police, on the other hand, were murderers, thieves and hooligans—products of Soviet society rather than foreign imports. Hence the very existence of the regular police establishment cast a certain shadow on the idea that Khrushchev had brought a new era to Soviet society.[71]

The KGB was drawn into the campaign to transform Soviet society and achieve communism. Since it was no longer to play a strictly coercive role but rather a persuasive, reforming one, its image had to be changed from that of policeman to moral guardian.

Beginning in the mid-1950s there was a marked increase in the number of Soviet works on the history of the security police. Initially the concentration was on the early period, with biographies of Dzherzhinskii, along with editions of his writings and laudatory histories of the Vecheka. Soon afterward a new genre of writings appeared: fictionalized histories about the activities of police officials that were not restricted to the period of the Cheka but covered more recent periods as well.[72] Typical of these literary works was a novel serialized in *Zvezda* whose hero, an MGB *oblast* chief, was portrayed as exceptionally honest and kind. Living a frugal, ascetic life, he opposed any violation of legality and released, in 1938, persons accused of political offenses.[73] Another such work was *Chekisty*, written in 1964 by Ivan Golovchenko, a veteran of the state security organs and a member of the Ukrainian Writers' Union.[74] Golovchenko depicted "Chekists" (the term used to describe all Soviet security officials, including those in the KGB) as kind, fearless defenders of justice. Golovchenko was the first of several security policemen who turned their talents to creative writing.[75]

Numerous other publications glorifying the KGB appeared in the late Khrushchev era and were aptly described by one Western expert:

> The police officials in all the works we have discussed have much in common; they are selfless and democratically-minded, spent their youth fighting enemies of the Soviet regime, are of pure working-class origin, are considerate husbands and fathers. Of course, such men must have existed in the Soviet police, but they were certainly a rarity and by no means typical of their colleagues as the authors of the above works would have the reader believe.[76]

The public was frequently reminded that the purges were not the fault of the majority of security personnel but rather of a few provocateurs who had "wormed their way into NKVD agencies," and there were even stories and letters praising the courage and humanity of the security police under Stalin.[77] Current activities of the KGB were increasingly publicized in a favorable light. In late 1962 *Nedeliia*, the Sunday supplement of *Izvestiia*, presented an interview with KGB official N. F. Chistiakov, who made a point of stressing how much the security organs had changed. KGB investigators were portrayed as humane, even compassionate individuals whose cares and concerns were shared by ordinary citizens and whose methods were kind and well-meaning. "We are like doctors," one Chekist was quoted as saying. "For us both treatment and prevention are important. A criminal is for us first a man and only then a criminal."[78]

It has been suggested that Shelepin was largely responsible for the campaign to rehabilitate the police.[79] Shelepin himself left his post as head of the KGB in December 1961, but it is widely thought that he continued to oversee the security police in his capacity as CC secretary.[80] His successor, Vladimir Semichastnyi, was by all accounts hand-picked by Shelepin, though he had ties with Khrushchev as well.[81] Semichastnyi, a Ukrainian, had risen in the Ukrainian Komsomol to become First Secretary of that organization in 1947, when Khrushchev was party first secretary of the Ukraine. In 1950 Semichastnyi moved to Moscow, where he became a secretary of the All-Union Komsomol, serving with Shelepin. When the latter left his post as Komsomol chief in 1958, Semichastnyi replaced him. In 1959 Semichastnyi moved into Shelepin's former position as head of the CC Department of Party Organs for the Union Republics and later that year was appointed second secretary of the Azerbaidzhan party, where he remained until becoming head of the KGB.[82]

At age thirty-seven Semichastnyi did not display particularly remarkable qualifications for his new post as KGB chief. Indeed the appointment of such a young man with relatively little political status was probably seen as a slight to the KGB. Unlike Shelepin, he had only a middle-level education and no experience that made him especially suited to his new job. He did, however, have a hard-line reputation as an ardent opponent of both détente with the West and cultural liberalism. In 1958 he reportedly denounced Boris Pasternak at a Komsomol CC plenum, comparing him unfavorably with a pig and noting that his departure would purify the air inside Russia.[83]

Shake-up in the Kremlin

Although Semichastnyi's connection with both Khrushchev and Shelepin seems to have prompted his appointment to the KGB, whatever loyalty he had to Khrushchev was short-lived; both Semichastnyi and Shelepin appear to have joined the ranks of the opposition to Khrushchev sometime before his ouster in October 1964. According to Roy Medvedev and others, they were actively involved in the plot to overthrow the party leader. Semichastnyi actually met Khrushchev at the Moscow airport on his return from the Crimea to face the members of the leadership.[84] The fact that he was coopted into full membership in the Central Committee at the November 1964 CC plenum while Shelepin climbed straight to full membership in the Presidium confirms the impression that they played important roles in Khrushchev's demise.

There are several explanations for the fact that the KGB leadership backed Khrushchev's ouster. De-Stalinization, legal reforms, and various other measures to curtail the activities of the security police had no doubt created resentment within its ranks. To be sure, it was the regular police, MVD/MOOP, that had borne the brunt of Khrushchev's reforms.[85] The KGB's stature, in terms of both public image and legal prerogatives, had risen considerably by the early 1960s. But Khrushchev's stress on innovation, public participation, and cultural liberalization was incompatible with a strong and effective political police. The abandonment of terror called for more consistency and caution in policymaking than Khrushchev was able to offer. As Brzezinski pointed out, "the elimination of violence as the decisive instrumentality of political competition . . . meant that Khrushchev, unlike Stalin, could not achieve both social dynamism and stability of his power. Stalin magnified his power as he strove to change society; to change society Khrushchev had to risk his power."[86]

Another possible reason for the KGB's disavowal of Khrushchev might have been connected with signs of opposition to its rising public stature shortly before Khrushchev fell. This opposition may have been a reaction to the publicity surrounding the Oleg Penkovskiy spy case, which was first brought to light in late 1962. Penkovskiy, who was caught passing Soviet military secrets to a British businessman, worked for the GRU. The scandal devastated the career of GRU chief Serov, who lost his post early in 1963. It also embarrassed Khrushchev. Not only had Khrushchev been on close terms with Serov for many years, but he had also been making renewed efforts at détente with the West. The KGB itself, however, gained considerable prestige for uncovering the case and benefited from calls in the press for increased vigilance against the efforts of Western intelligence services to subvert Soviet citizens.[87]

This type of publicity apparently gave rise to alarm in some circles about the emergence of a Stalinist-type "spy mania." An article in *Izvestiia* noted: "God forbid that everything the newspapers write about imperialist intelligence services and their agents should cause general suspicion among people. The story of P is a highly exceptional story."[88] Some time later, in September 1964, another *Izvestiia* article inveighed against the idea expressed by a Procurator that an individual could be considered guilty before being proven so:

> In the years of the cult of personality, when they would come for a man in the night, by morning he would already be called an enemy of the people. . . . Times are now different and different people have been employed in the investigatory agencies for a long time now. But this is not a question of whether someone working in the justice system is good or bad. An investigator can be Praiseworthy in the extreme—intelligent, educated, talented and humane. But still, no one should ever give him the right to decide the question of guilt.[89]

It is possible that Khrushchev encouraged these expressions of concern and hence aroused the displeasure of the KGB. It is also possible, as Slusser claims, that the KGB was at odds with Khrushchev over his foreign policy. According to Slusser, Shelepin and Semichastnyi were part of a group led by CC secretaries Mikhail Suslov and Frol Kozlov (the latter until his illness in 1963) which opposed Khrushchev's efforts toward rapprochement with the West. A bizarre mustard-gas attack on a West German diplomat in September 1964, which was attributed to the KGB, is one piece of evidence cited by Slusser to show that the KGB attempted to hinder better East-West relations.[90] Whatever the case may be, Shelepin and Semichastnyi gained political advancement by supporting Khrushchev's ouster. Indeed, Shelepin in particular achieved such a strong position in the post-Khrushchev leadership that he was seen by some as a potential successor to Brezhnev.[91]

The KGB also enjoyed greater prestige and good fortune under the new regime. Its investigative powers, along with those of the internal affairs apparatus, were extended further by a decree of December 1965.[92] According to revisions made in Article 126 of the RSFSR CCP, crimes specified in Articles 88 (currency speculation), 92 (misappropriation of state property by misuse of official position) and 93-1 (misappropriation of state property on an especially large scale) of the RSFSR Criminal Code were now to be investigated by the agency that instigated the case—either MOOP (renamed MVD in 1968), the KGB, or the Procuracy. If in the course of these investigations official crimes (Articles 170–175 of the RSFSR Criminal Code) were established, they were to be investigated by the agency that initiated the original case. These changes broadened the authority of both the MVD and the KGB but were particularly significant for the KGB, as they moved this agency further from the realm of strictly "political" cases into the area of economic crime by adding Articles 92 and 93-1 to its investigative purview. As before, the KGB appeared to retain the right to involve itself in the cases of its own choosing regardless of the MVD's new investigatory powers.[93]

Brezhnev did much to raise the status of both the regular police and the KGB. In 1966, after replacing MOOP chief Tikunov with a trusted protégé, N. A. Shchelokov, Brezhnev reinstated MOOP as a union-republic ministry. Two years later MOOP was renamed the MVD, an apparent symbol of its increased authority. Efforts were made to raise the effectiveness of the MVD by recruiting better-qualified personnel and upgrading equipment and training. In addition, Brezhnev reversed the trend of popular participation in the administration of justice by restricting the scope of comrades' courts. Nevertheless the MVD continued to be plagued with problems arising from inadequate financial and manpower resources. One 1970 Soviet publication noted, for

[67]

example, that MVD investigators were vastly overworked and had neither cars nor personal telephones at their disposal.[94]

While the Soviet press discussed the MVD's problems and the need to raise its effectiveness, the media image of the KGB and its predecessors continued to be one of courage, valor, and perfection. Shortly after Khrushchev fell a number of articles depicting the security police in these glowing terms appeared in the press. *Komsomolskaia pravda*, for example, published a series of gripping articles on the KGB and espionage.[95] This was followed by the airing of espionage films on Moscow television with KGB officers as the heroes. Significantly, the press began to glorify KGB spy Rudolf Abel (convicted in the United States in 1957) by publishing a piece on his career in May 1965 and later a full-length biography.[96] The admission that the Soviet security police engaged in peacetime spying abroad was seen as something of a milestone by Western observers.

The arrest by the KGB of writers Andrei Sinyavsky and Iulii Daniel in 1965 and the ensuing publicity surrounding the case were further signs that the KGB's influence was making itself felt in Kremlin circles. Again cries for greater vigilance were raised. An article in *Partiinaia zhizn'* in March 1966 signified strong party support for more stringent internal security policies.[97] The article, coauthored by KGB Deputy Chairman A. N. Malygin and an unidentified official, presented a graphic account of the sinister activities of Western intelligence agencies (which, the authors noted pointedly, occupied a privileged position in Western society). The authors discussed the expensive technologically advanced equipment used by spies for these agencies in their efforts to obtain secret military and economic information from the Soviet Union and to subvert weak Soviet citizens. They also described how the enemies of the Soviet Union exploited "anti-Soviet slander" of the type produced by Sinyavsky and Daniel. Accordingly the party's task was to step up the ideological struggle against the West and campaign for greater vigilance. Although not stated specifically in the article, this implied a greater role for the KGB.

Although these developments were favorable to the KGB, there were indications at about this time that its chairman, Semichastnyi, and his mentor, Shelepin, were facing some opposition. It would seem that the memory of Beria's attempt to achieve power via the police apparatus had not faded in the Kremlin. Shelepin's ambitions and his strong connections with the KGB may well have caused other party leaders to fear another such attempt and thus to block his further advancement. Signs that Shelepin's advance was being challenged appeared in 1966 as

Suslov sought to deprive him of his influential role in the Secretariat.[98] Then in May 1967 Semichastnyi was removed as KGB Chairman and replaced by Iurii Andropov. Finally, with Shelepin's dismissal from the Secretariat in November of that year, which deprived him of any remaining oversight for the police, the possibility that he would use the KGB as a means of gaining power was eliminated.[99] Significantly, it was Suslov who represented the party leadership at ceremonies marking the fiftieth anniversary of the KGB in December 1967.

Although the party leadership had managed to neutralize the Shelepin faction, the KGB was left with its authority and prestige as an institution intact. Brezhnev had realized the importance of the security police to the survival and successful functioning of the Soviet regime. To be sure, all members of the party leadership saw the necessity of preventing the KGB from becoming powerful enough to pose a threat to the party's predominance. But this institution was too important for its interests to be ignored and its operations downgraded.

Could the Soviet Union in 1967 still be described as a "police state"? Clearly not in the Stalinist sense of the term. The Kremlin's self-imposed taboo on the use of terror had deprived the political police of its most potent weapon while at the same time causing an essential change in Soviet elite politics. Without the threat of violent reprisals, party leaders could disagree among themselves and even reveal these disagreements—in veiled forms—in the press. This opening up of communications meant that there was little opportunity for an individual leader to use the police apparatus to achieve the kind of power wielded by Stalin. Also, of course, because terror was no longer a means available to the political police in ordering regime-societal relations, Soviet citizens, while still subjected to enormous constraints, could express politically unorthodox views without facing death.

Insofar as the party leadership at this time continued to depend on the political police to maintain its rule, however, the term "police state" was not an inaccurate description. The problem, as in the past, was to achieve a correct balance between an effective political police and the existence of safeguards against the abuse of police power. The introduction of legal reforms had achieved much toward protecting Soviet citizens from police persecution, but the institutional role of the KGB remained ill-defined, and the possibility that it would assert itself as an actor in the political process had not been eliminated. As events would later show, a political challenge based in part on the support of the security police would emerge again toward the end of Brezhnev's reign and would not be successfully defeated.

Notes

1. On 4 April 1953 *Pravda* announced that the plot had been fabricated and two days later placed the main responsibility on former MGB Deputy Chief M. D. Riumin, who was arrested, and former MGB Chief Ignat'ev was attacked for his "political blindness." See Wolfgang Leonhard, *The Kremlin since Stalin*, trans. Elizabeth Wiskemann and Marian Jackson (London: Oxford University Press, 1962), pp. 63–68.

2. *Khrushchev Remembers*, intro. Edward Crankshaw, trans. and ed. Strobe Talbot (London: Andre Deutsch, 1971), pp. 328–330; Boris Levytsky, *The Uses of Terror: The Soviet Secret Police 1917–70*, trans. H. A. Piehler (New York: Coward, McCann, & Geoghegan, 1972), pp. 217–218; Zbigniew K. Brzezinski, *The Permanent Purge: Politics in Soviet Totalitarianism* (Cambridge: Harvard University Press, 1956), pp. 158–160.

3. According to Brzezinski, *The Permanent Purge*, pp. 158–160, Beria's offensive was so successful that by late May 1953 Communist leaders in Soviet satellite countries were predicting a Beriá dictatorship. Interestingly, such reformist tendencies and "liberal" leanings were later displayed in a similar manner by Iurii Andropov when, as chief of the political police, he began his campaign to gain the party leadership post in 1982.

4. R. J. Service, "The Road to the Twentieth Party Congress: An Analysis of the Events Surrounding the Central Committee Plenum of July 1953," *Soviet Studies* 33, no. 2 (April 1981):232–245.

5. Ibid.; and Leonhard, *Kremlin since Stalin*, pp. 68–73. Also see Boris Nicolaevsky, *Power and the Soviet Elite* (New York: Praeger, 1965), pp. 130–147.

6. The version that appeared in the West was obtained through high-ranking members of the Italian Communist party. For details see Service, "The Road to the Twentieth Party Congress."

7. B. N. Ponomarev et al., eds., *Istoriia kommunisticheskoi partii sovetskogo soiuza* (Moscow: Gosizdat, 1959), p. 629.

8. Alexander Dallin and George W. Breslauer, *Political Terror in Communist Systems* (Stanford: Stanford University Press, 1970), p. 83.

9. As Seweryn Bialer notes, "this in the deepest sense was the key reason why the system of mature Stalinism could not survive its creator. The leadership *as a whole* and the elites *as a whole* wanted a new deal." *Stalin's Successors: Leadership, Stability and Change in the Soviet Union* (Cambridge: Cambridge University Press, 1980), p. 46.

10. Grey Hodnett, "The Pattern of Leadership Politics," in *The Domestic Context of Soviet Foreign Policy*, ed. Seweryn Bialer (Boulder, Colo.: Westview Press, 1981), p. 89.

11. George Breslauer, *Khrushchev and Brezhnev as Leaders: Building Authority in Soviet Politics* (London: Allen & Unwin, 1982).

12. See *Vedomosti Verkhovnogo Soveta SSSR* [hereafter *Vedomosti VS SSSR*], no. 4, 1953, reprinted in *Pravda*, 28 March 1953. On the further amnesties see Robert Conquest, *The Soviet Police System* (New York: Praeger, 1968), p. 82.

13. The edict abolishing the Special Board was never published. The first official Soviet reference to its abolition appeared in *Sovetskoe gosudarstvo i pravo*, no. 1 (January 1956):3. See Harold Berman, "Soviet Law Reform—Dateline Moscow 1957," *Yale Law Journal*, no. 8 (1957):1192.

14. See George Ginsburgs, "The Reform of Soviet Military Justice: 1953–58," *Soviet Law after Stalin: Part III. Soviet Institutions and the Administration of Law*, ed. Donald B. Barry, F. J. M. Feldbrugge, George Ginsburgs, and Peter B. Maggs (Leiden: Sijthoff and Noordhoff, 1979), pp. 34–35; and Berman, "Soviet Law Reform," p. 1198.

15. This decree was ratified as a law by the USSR Supreme Soviet and published in *Pravda*, 28 April 1954, p. 2.

16. See Conquest, *The Soviet Police System*, pp. 23; 78–79; 87; and Stephen M. Meyer, "Soviet Nuclear Operations," in *Managing Nuclear Operations*, ed. Aston B. Carter, John D. Steinbruner, and Charles A. Zraket (Washington, D.C.: Brookings Institution, 1987), p. 487.

17. According to Berman, "Soviet Law Reform," p. 1195, 85 percent of those

serving sentences in March 1953 were no longer in detention by 1957. For a further discussion of figures on camp inmates, see Ger P. Van Den Berg, *The Soviet System of Justice: Figures and Policy* (Dordrecht, Boston, Lancaster: Martinus Nijhoff, 1985), chap. 6.

18. Vladimir Gsovski and Kazimierz Grzybowski, eds., *Government, Law and Courts in the Soviet Union and Eastern Europe* (London and the Hague: Stevens & Sons, 1959), I:580. For a detailed examination of the circumstances surrounding Beria's arrest and death, see Vladimir Tolz, "The Death and 'Second Life' of Lavrentii Beria," *Radio Liberty Research Bulletin* [hereafter *RLRB*], RL 479/83, 23 December 1983. Khrushchev actually gave several conflicting accounts of how Beria died, including a claim that he was immediately executed after his arrest in July. So it is possible that Beria's reported trial in December 1953 was a fiction. See Bertram Wolfe, *Khrushchev and Stalin's Ghost* (New York: Praeger, 1957), pp. 316–317. Also see a biography of Beria by Thaddeus Wittlin, *Commissar: The Life and Death of Lavrenty Pavlovich Beria* (New York: Macmillan, 1972). For details on the trials of Beria associates see Nicolaevsky, *Power and the Soviet Elite*, pp. 120–187. Interestingly the decree repealing the Stalinist procedural laws for cases of terrorism, wrecking, and sabotage was enacted on 19 April 1956 (see *Vedomosti VS SSSR*, no. 9, 29 April 1956, item 193), while one trial, that of M. D. Bagirov, former party chief in Azerbaidzhan, was heard from 12 to 26 April. Presumably the repeal did not apply to cases that were already in process.

19. For an official Soviet biography of Serov, see *Bolshaia sovetskaia entsiklopediia* [hereafter *BSE*], 2d ed. (Moscow: Sovetskaia Entsiklopediia, 1958), 51:268.

20. *Khrushchev Remembers*, pp. 115, 135–149.

21. Roy Medvedev, for example, in his biography of Khrushchev, describes Kruglov's "monstrous deeds" and claims that Kruglov later committed suicide rather than be punished for them. See Roy Medvedev, *Khrushchev*, trans. Brian Pearce (New York: Anchor Press, 1983), pp. 113–114.

22. In March 1963 Ivashutin became chief of the GRU, replacing Serov, who had moved to this post from the KGB in 1958. Ivashutin's official biographies (see *BSE*, 1972, X:21, and *Deputaty Verkhovnogo Soveta SSSR* [hereafter *Deputaty VS SSSR*], published from 1966 to 1984) do not mention his years of service in the state security organs. Earlier, however, he had been referred to publicly as a deputy KGB chairman (see, for example, *Pravda*, 27 June 1961). Ivashutin had an article published in *Izvestiia* on the occasion of the fortieth anniversary of the state security organs, 21 December 1957, p. 5. This would indicate that he was at least a deputy chairman of the USSR KGB by this time.

23. *Khrushchev Remembers*, p. 338.

24. Lunev rose to be first deputy chairman of the USSR KGB by 1959, at which time he was abruptly transferred to the post of KGB chairman in Kazakhstan and then was released "for reasons of health" a year later. See *Moskovskaia pravda*, 20 January 1955, p. 2; and *Kazakhstanskaia pravda*, 13 September 1960, p. 2. On his participation in the Beria trial, see Gsovski and Grzybowski, *Government, Law and Courts*, I:580. Ustinov served in the KGB until 1957, when he became first secretary of the Moscow *Gorkom*. See *Ezhegodnik BSE* 1958 (Moscow: Sovetskaia entsiklopediia 1958), p. 644; and Peter Deriabin, *Watchdogs of Terror: Russian Bodyguards from the Tsars to the Commissars* (New Rochelle, N.Y.: Arlington House, 1972), pp. 335, 338.

25. These nine police professionals were G. A. Badamiants (Armenia), A. M. Guskov (Azerbaidzhan), A. I. Perepelitsyn (Belorussia), A. P. Byzov (Uzbekistan), V. T. Vaskin (Turkmenistan), I. L. Mordovets (Moldavia), Ia. Ia. Vevers (Latvia), V. V. Gubin (Kazakhstan), and D. K. Vishnevskii (Tadzhikistan). No biographical data could be found on two of the new republic KGB chiefs (I. P. Karpov, chairman of KGB Estonia from 1954 to 1961, and A. V. Tereshchenko, chairman of KGB Kirgizia from 1954 to 1956), but it is possible that these men had similar backgrounds. Only two appointees, V. F. Nikitchenko, chairman of the Ukrainian KGB, and K. F. Liaudis, chairman of the Lithuanian KGB, had party backgrounds; one, A. N. Inauri, KGB chairman in Georgia, was transferred from the Soviet Army. (Nikitchenko, who had worked for several years with Khrushchev in the Ukrainian party apparatus, represented yet another ally for him in a key KGB post.) It

might be added that the two new chiefs of the Moscow and Leningrad KGB administrations, N. I. Krainov and S. S. Belchenko, respectively, were also security professionals rather than party men. Belchenko became a deputy chairman of the USSR KGB in 1957. For biographical sources on these and other KGB officials see chapter 5, note 1.

26. *Pravda*, 21 December 1957, p. 6.

27. For the full text of Khrushchev's speech and an accompanying analysis, see Wolfe, *Khrushchev and Stalin's Ghost.*

28. These officials were KGB Chairman Serov and republic KGB Chairmen A. P. Byzov, V. V. Gubin, I. N. Inauri, and V. F. Nikitchenko. Two former NKVD officials, A. I. Voronin and G. P. Dobrynin, were also among the delegates, but it is not clear that they were serving in the KGB at this time. Although Lunev was elected to candidate membership on the Central Committee, he was not listed as a delegate. By comparison, there were fifty-five NKVD delegates to the Eighteenth Party Congress in 1939.

29. Dudorov's biography appears in *BSE*, 2d ed. 1958, 51:108. Having worked under Khrushchev in Moscow, Dudorov was probably one of his supporters.

30. *XX s'ezd KPSS. Stenograficheskii otchet* (Moscow: Gosizdat, 1956), I:95.

31. *Pravda*, 21 December 1957, p. 6.

32. See, for example, the article by Ivashutin, cited in note 22, and articles by K. Liaudis in *Sovetskaia litva*, 22 December 1957 and by Ia. Vevers in *Sovetskaia latvia*, 20 December 1957. Vevers even went so far as to claim that the state security organs had "won the love and trust of the Soviet people."

33. V. Moskovskii, "O politicheskoi bditel'nosti i zorkosti," *Partiinaia zhizn'*, no. 21 (November 1958):20–25 (quotation, p. 25).

34. *Vneocherednoi XXI s'ezd KPSS. Stenograficheskii otchet* (Moscow: Gosizdat, 1959), I:105.

35. Medvedev, *Khrushchev*, pp. 132–133. It was not until 1963, when Serov was removed from his post as head of the GRU in connection with the Penkovskiy affair, that his demise occurred. In 1965 he was expelled from the party for his crimes in the Stalin era. See Michael Tatu, *Power in the Kremlin: From Khrushchev to Kosygin*, trans. Helen Katel (New York: Viking, 1970), pp. 325–326, for details on Serov's downfall. Khrushchev confirms in his memoirs that Serov was eventually punished. See *Khrushchev Remembers*, p. 115. It might be added that the USSR Supreme Soviet in April 1962 deprived Serov and other former NKVD officials of decorations awarded them in connection with the deportation of the Chechen-Inguishi in 1944. So Serov may already have been a marked man in 1962, protected only by Khrushchev. See *Vedomosti VS SSSR*, no. 14, item 149, 6 April 1962.

36. An official biography of Shelepin appears in *Deputaty VS SSSR, Shestoi sozyv* (Moscow: Izvestiia, 1962), p. 467. Also see a detailed sketch by Robert Slusser in George W. Simmonds, ed., *Soviet Leaders* (New York: Thomas Y. Crowell, 1967), pp. 87–95. On his participation in the partisan movement see S. V. Bilenko, *Istrebitel'nye batal'ony v velikoi otechestvennoi voine* (Moscow: Voenizdat, 1969), p. 99. Bilenko notes that Shelepin worked closely with local NKVD officials in carrying out his partisan activity. This gave him some experience with the state security organs that no doubt proved valuable when he assumed his KGB post. Interestingly, Andropov had similar wartime experiences.

37. Medvedev, *Khrushchev*, p. 133.

38. Michael Voslensky, *Nomenklatura: Anatomy of a Soviet Ruling Class*, trans. Eric Mosbacker (London: The Bodley Head, 1984), p. 257.

39. These were A. B. Randakiavichius, appointed KGB chairman in the Lithuanian republic in November 1959; A. V. Kardashev, appointed KGB chairman in Azerbaidzhan in September 1959; and V. T. Shumilov, appointed chief of the Leningrad KGB in January 1960.

40. Medvedev, *Khrushchev*, p. 133. Khrushchev also continued to bring his supporters into the KGB. I. T. Savchenko, for example, who was appointed KGB chairman in Moldavia in September 1959, had worked with Khrushchev in the Ukrainian CC apparatus.

41. *Vneocherednoi XXI s'ezd*, II:251–252. Shelepin asserted at the end of his speech

(p. 255), however, that the workers of the state security organs would be "the terror of all enemies of the Soviet state."

42. V. S. Tikunov, "Sotsialisticheskaia zakonnost—rukovodiashchii printsip v deiatel'nosti organov gosudarstvennoi bezopasnosti," *Sovetskoe gosudarstvo i pravo*, no. 8 (1959):13–26 (quotation, p. 23).

43. Ibid., p. 24. Also see an article by a high-ranking KGB official responsible for investigations: N. F. Chistiakov, "Sotsialisticheskaia zakonnost' i sviaz' s sovetskoi obshchestvennost'iu—osnovnye printsipy deiatel'nosti sledstvennogo apparata organov gosudarstvennoi bezopasnosti," *Sovetskoe gosudarstvo i pravo*, no. 11 (1960):34–41. Chistiakov, who was in charge of the Gary Powers case in 1960, wrote numerous articles and edited one book on KGB activities against foreign spies. By 1970 he was chairman of the Military Collegium of the USSR Supreme Court, which is responsible for hearing cases of espionage. As of 1985 Chistiakov was a senior associate of the prestigious Institute of State and Law of the USSR Academy of Sciences and a candidate of juridical science.

44. Tikunov, "Sotsialisticheskaia," pp. 24–26; Chistiakov, "Sotsialisticheskaia," pp. 39–41.

45. For a thorough analysis of the de-Stalinization issue at the Twenty-Second Party Congress, see Tatu, *Power in the Kremlin*, pp. 141–175; and Robert M. Slusser, *The Berlin Crisis of 1961* (Baltimore and London: Johns Hopkins University Press, 1973), pp. 316–459.

46. *XXII s'ezd KPSS. Stenograficheskii otchet* (Moscow: Gospolitizdat, 1962), II:399–409.

47. Ibid., II:407.

48. Slusser, *The Berlin Crisis*, p. 411.

49. *XXII s'ezd*, II:405.

50. Ibid., II:484–485.

51. The text is reprinted in *Sovetskaia prokuratura v vazhneishikh dokumentakh* (Moscow: Gosizdat, 1956), pp. 481–483. For a discussion of the statute see Harold J. Berman, *Soviet Criminal Law and Procedure: The RSFSR Codes*, 2d ed. (Cambridge, Mass.: Harvard University Press, 1972), pp. 99–105; and N. V. Zhogun, ed., *Kommentarii k polozheniiu o prokurorskom nadzore v SSSR* (Moscow: Iuridicheskaia Literatura, 1971).

52. *Sovetskaia prokuratura*, pp. 496–498. This was part of a general decree on the structure of the Procuracy issued by the Presidium of the USSR Supreme Soviet on 7 April 1956 (*Vedomosti VS SSSR*, no. 8, 1956, item 186).

53. The Fundamental Principles of Criminal Procedure of the USSR and Union Republics were confirmed by a law of the USSR Supreme Soviet on 25 December 1958. See *Vedomosti VS SSSR*, no. 1, 1959, item 15. The RSFSR Code of Criminal Procedure was confirmed by a law of the RSFSR Supreme Soviet on 27 October 1960 and went into effect on 1 January 1961. For a discussion of the changes in legal procedure established by the FPCP and RSFSR Code, see Berman, *Soviet Criminal Law*, pp. 47–70; and Christopher Osakwe, "Due Process of Law and Civil Rights Cases in the Soviet Union," in *Soviet Law after Stalin: Part I. The Citizen and the State in Contemporary Soviet Law*, ed. Donald D. Barry, George Ginsburgs, and Peter B. Maggs (Leiden: Sijthoff and Noordhoff, 1977), pp. 179–219 (esp. pp. 182–189). For an analysis of the debates over the FPCP in Soviet legal circles see Rudolph Schlesinger, "The Discussion on Criminal Law and Procedure," *Soviet Studies* 10, no. 3 (January 1959):293–306.

54. According to a statute on military tribunals, enacted as a law by the USSR Supreme Soviet on 25 December 1958, their jurisdiction over civilians was limited to cases of espionage. All other state crimes were to be heard by regular courts. See *Vedomosti VS SSSR*, no. 1, 1959, item 14.

55. The USSR Statute on Crimes against the State was adopted at the time the Fundamental Principles of Criminal Legislation were adopted. See Berman, *Soviet Criminal Law*, pp. 39–40, and *Vedomosti VS SSSR*, no. 1, 1959, item 8. For the full text of the law and a discussion of how it compared with that of the Stalin era, see appendix B. The one remaining crime that the state security organs were initially charged with investigating under the new Code of Criminal Procedure was described in Article 79 (mass disorders)

and placed in a second category called "other crimes against the state," which included a variety of slightly less serious crimes (stealing state property, smuggling, currency violations, etc.). Most of these crimes had been categorized in the earlier codes not as counterrevolutionary but as "crimes against socialist property" (Article 59-1) and "especially dangerous crimes against the administrative order" (Article 59-2).

56. For a translation of the code and a general discussion of these reforms, see Berman, *Soviet Criminal Law*, pp. 42–46.

57. Some aspects of these legal reforms had actually begun as far back as the 1930s as part of the campaign by Vyshinskii to stabilize the law. The requirements of specific intent to commit a crime, for example, were said to be emphasized by Soviet courts, and the doctrine of analogy was given a restrictive interpretation. In addition, the USSR Supreme Court declared in 1946 that Article 7 (social danger) had been repealed. But these changes actually had little practical meaning, and the new RSFSR Codes went significantly further in protecting the legal rights of Soviet citizens. See chapter 1, note 98 and ibid., pp. 32–39. It might be added that the death penalty for all crimes was repealed in 1947 but in 1950 was restored for treason, espionage, terror, subversion, and sabotage.

58. See Robert Sharlet, "Legal Policy under Khrushchev and Brezhnev: Continuity and Change," in *Soviet Law after Stalin: Part II. Social Engineering through Law*, ed. Donald D. Barry, George Ginsburgs, and Peter Maggs (Leiden: Sijthoff and Noordhoff, 1978), pp. 319–330.

59. See *Vedomosti VS SSSR*, no. 26, 29 June 1961, item 270, reprinted in *Pravda*, 4 July 1961, p. 2. In July 1962 two separate articles were introduced specifically covering the latter two crimes: Article 88-1 (failure to report a state crime) and Article 88-2 (concealment of a state crime). The KGB was given concurrent authority with the Procurator to investigate 88-1 (where it relates to Articles 64–69 and 72) and 88-2 (where it relates to Articles 64–69, 72, 78, and 88). See *Vedomosti VS RSFSR*, no. 29, 1962, item 449.

60. For a list of information considered secret see the decree of the USSR Council of Ministers dated 28 April 1956, reprinted in V. I. Kurliandskii and M. P. Karpushin, *Otvetstvennost'za gosudarstvennye prestupleniia*, pt. 2 (Moscow: Iuridicheskaia Literatura, 1965), pp. 101–102. For the earlier decree establishing a list of information considered secret see *Izvestiia*, 10 June 1947, reprinted in H. J. Berman and M. Kerner, *Documents on Soviet Military Law and Administration* (Cambridge, Mass.: Harvard University Press, 1955), pp. 102–103.

61. V. I. Kurliandskii and M. P. Mikhailov, eds., *Osobo opasnye gosudarstvennye prestupleniia* (Moscow: Gosivrizdat, 1963), p. 103. Interestingly as part of the current reassessment of the legal system, some experts have called for narrowing the definition of state secrets. See chapter 6.

62. See, for example, the article cited earlier by Moskovskii in *Partiinaia zhizn'*; and Kh. M. Akhmetshin, "O povyshenii politicheskoi bditel'nosti sovetskikh liudei i strogom khranenii gosudarstvennoi tainy," *Sovetskoe gosudearstvo i pravo*, nos. 2–3 (1953):83–94.

63. See chapter 7 for a detailed treatment of this statute.

64. See, for example, *Pravda*, 19 May 1961, p. 4, where the crimes of a ring of currency speculators in Moscow were described and it was noted that "the inveterate speculator vultures were unmasked and seized by our glorious Chekists."

65. Among these cases was that of a ring of embezzlers of state and public property in Kirgizia described in *Sovetskaia kirgizia*, 9 January 1962, pp. 2, 4. Also see "Economic Crimes in the Soviet Union," *Journal of the International Commission of Jurists* 5, no. 1 (Summer 1964):3–47.

66. Portions of the following discussion appear in Amy Knight, "Soviet Politics and the KGB-MVD Relationship," *Soviet Union* 11, pt. 2 (1984):157–181.

67. On the transfer of the border troops see P. A. Ivanchishin et al., eds., *Chasovye sovetskikh granits: Kratkii ocherk istorii pogranichnykh voisk SSSR* (Moscow: Politizdat, 1979), p. 161.

68. See *Vedomosti VS RSFSR*, no. 15, April 1963, item 288.

69. Iu. Feofanov, "Voram poshchady ne budet," *Izvestiia*, 20 October 1963, p. 5.

Also see reports on two similar cases: L. Bekhterev, "Krakh shaiki valiutchikov," *Sovetskaia Rossiia*, 30 August 1963, p. 4; and L. Torporkov, "Kak oni posmeli?" *Izvestiia*, 27 May 1964, p. 4.

70. See, for example, Iurii Klarov, "Arifmometr i pravosudie," *Izvestiia*, 15 July 1961, p. 4; S. Bunkov, "Za papinoi spinoi," *Izvestiia*, 22 May 1964, p. 3; and M. Sinitsa, "Posle togo kak vystupili 'Izvestiia,'" *Izvestiia*, 24 May 1964, p. 3. For a less critical and more constructive approach to the problems of the militia in particular, see Iu. V. Solopanov and S. V. Murashov, "Sovetskaia militsiia kak organ okhrany obshchestvennogo poriadka," *Sovetskoe gosudarstvo i pravo*, no. 12 (December 1962):111–119. The authors advocated giving the militia the right to conduct criminal investigations.

71. Darrell Hammer, *USSR: The Politics of Oligarchy* (Hinsdale, Ill.: Dryden Press, 1974), pp. 355–356.

72. For an excellent survey of publications on the police during the Khrushchev era see Robert M. Slusser, "Recent Soviet Books on the History of the Secret Police," *The Slavic Review* 24, no. 2 (March 1965):90–98. Also see A. L. Litvin (Kazan'), "VChK v sovetskoi istoricheskoi literature," *Voprosy istorii*, no. 5 (May 1986):96–102.

73. Iurii German, "Ia otvechaiu za vse," *Zvezda*, no. 10 (October 1964):18–120; no. 11 (November 1964):8–95.

74. Ivan Golovchenko, *Chekisty* (Kiev: Dnipro, 1964). Golovchenko served as chief of the MVD in the Ukraine from 1962 to 1982, when he was replaced by I. D. Gladush.

75. Another well-known KGB author was S. K. Tsvigun, first deputy chairman of the USSR KGB from 1967 to 1982, who was credited with having written and edited several literary works glamorizing Chekists, including one book, *V skhvatkakh s vragom* (Moscow: Moskovskii Rabochii, 1972), that contained a contribution by Golovchenko. See chapter 3.

76. A. Gayev, "The Noble Chekists," *Bulletin of the Institute for the Study of the USSR*, 22, no. 3 (March 1965):18–21 (quotation, p. 21).

77. One lengthy letter to *Izvestiia* that appeared shortly before Khrushchev's fall told of a kindly NKVD agent who, upon coming to arrest a woman, took her child on his lap and cried. See A. Levkovich, "Ob etom nel'zhia zabyvat," *Izvestiia*, 6 September 1964, p. 6.

78. "Vo imeni pravdy i spravedlivosti," *Nedelia*, 26 August–1 September 1962, pp. 4–5. Somewhat later Chistiakov also noted emphatically that the majority of Chekists under Stalin were honest men who "remained true sons of the party and strove honestly to fulfill their obligation to their country." N. Chistiakov, "Zakonnost' i spravedlivost'," *Moskovskaia pravda*, 13 May 1964, p. 3. Also see Iu. Feofanov, "Desiat i odna," *Izvestiia*, 3 February 1963, p. 2, where the author notes, "Chekists are humane, too; that is, if they have before them a person who has perhaps committed a crime but who is not lost to society. For many people, they have in fact reopened the doors to life."

79. See Gayev, "Noble Chekists," p. 21; and Slusser, "Recent Soviet Books," p. 94.

80. Shelepin continued to attend functions relating to legal and paramilitary issues. This suggests, as Michel Tatu points out, that he had overall responsibility for "administrative organs," which includes the police. See Tatu, *Power in the Kremlin*, p. 198.

81. For Semichastnyi's biography see *Deputaty VS SSSR*, 1962, p. 381; and *Ezhegodnik BSE*, 1962, p. 614. Also see Robert M. Slusser, "Vladimir Efimovich Semichastny," in Simmonds, *Soviet Leaders*, pp. 82–87.

82. Interestingly not only Shelepin and Semichastnyi but two others had worked in the CC Party Organs Department before becoming chief of the political police: N. I. Ezhov, NKVD chief from 1936 to 1938, and S. D. Ignat'ev, minister of state security from 1951 to 1953.

83. See Slusser, "Semichastnyi"; Medvedev, *Khrushchev*, p. 135; and Petr Deriabin, "Shelepin: Man to Watch in the Kremlin," *Chicago Daily News*, 25 November 1964, p. 9.

84. Medvedev, *Khrushchev*, pp. 235–236. Also see Robert Slusser, "America, China, and the Hydra-Headed Opposition," in *Soviet Policy-Making: Studies of Communism in Transition*, ed. Peter H. Juviler and Henry W. Morton (London: Pall Mall Press, 1967), pp. 183–269.

85. It was clear that his policies were deeply resented by internal affairs officials.

V. S. Tikunov, Shelepin's protégé who had moved from the KGB to head the MVD in 1961, voiced complaints about the inadequacies of resources for the regular police in the press. See *Izvestiia*, 21 July 1962, p. 1. The extent of his resentment came out more clearly after Khrushchev was ousted, when Tikunov wrote an article in *Partiinaia zhizn'*: "In the recent past the role of the militia was underestimated. This was manifested in an unjustified reduction of its staff, without consideration for the real potential and position of [the organs of] public order." V. S. Tikunov, "Na strazhe obshchestvennogo poriadka," *Partiinaia zhizn'*, no. 20 (October 1965):16.

86. Zbigniew Brzezinski, "The Soviet Political System: Transformation or Degeneration," *Problems of Communism* [hereafter *POC*] 15, no. 1 (January 1966):6.

87. "The trial of Penkovskiy and Wynne," noted the Chief Military Procurator, A. G. Gornyi, "reminds all Soviet people of the need for high revolutionary vigilance, the need to be irreconcilable toward loafing, idle chatter and carelessness, which make it possible for spies of foreign intelligence agencies to carry out their shady operations." See an interview with Gornyi in *Izvestiia*, 30 May 1963, p. 4.

88. Georgii Berezko, "Poedinok v temnote," *Izvestiia*, 12 March 1963, p. 4 and 13 March 1963, p. 4. (quotation, 13 March, p. 4).

89. O. Chaikovskaia, "Opasnoe nevezhestvo," *Izvestiia*, 10 September 1964, p. 3.

90. Slusser, "America, China and the Hydra-Headed Opposition." Slusser dates Shelepin's move into the opposition as far back as late 1959 or early 1960. Evidence supporting this contention might be the arrest and expulsion of Russell Langelle, an American Embassy employee in Moscow, in the autumn of 1959—a move that Shelepin no doubt sanctioned. Since this was at the time of the Camp David talks and improved U.S.-Soviet relations, it was a setback for Khrushchev. See chapter 9 for further discussion of this issue.

91. It is important to note that Shelepin retained a hand in KGB affairs after Khrushchev's fall. In April 1965, for example, he presided over a conference of "administrative organs" on problems of legality. See *Pravda*, 10 April 1965, p. 1.

92. *Vedomosti VS RSFSR*, no. 50, December 1965, item 1243.

93. See, for example, Arkadii Sakhnin, "Dengi," *Pravda* 10 February 1967, p. 6; 11 February, p. 4; and 12 February, p. 6. In a 1972 case the investigation was undertaken by the MVD but later was taken over by the KGB. See N. Sizov, "Konets 'zoloti firmy,'" *Moskva*, July 1972, pp. 176–177.

94. N. I. Porubov, *Nauchnaia organizatsiia truda sledovatelia* (Minsk: Vysshaia Shkola, 1970), pp. 38, 159–181. Also see Alexander Shtromas, "Crime, Law and Penal Practice in the USSR," *Review of Socialist Law*, no. 3 (1977):303. According to Shtromas, "it should be realized that lower-level law enforcement agencies in the USSR which deal with general delinquencies are themselves in a precarious situation. Party authorities press them very hard for good results in combating crime without bothering very much to allocate appropriate financial resources, manpower, and other necessary means. Instead, they demote, dismiss or otherwise reprimand members of law enforcement agencies if they do not produce good results with whatever resources are available."

95. See Ia. Golovanov, "Padenie 'Tseziura.' Istoriia odnogo prestupleniia," *Komsomolskaia pravda*, 8–20 December 1964.

96. See V. Drozhdov, "Tovarishch Abel—soldat nevidimogo fronta," *Nedeliia*, 2–8 May 1965, pp. 6–7; and Vadim Kozhevnikov, *Shchit i mech* (Moscow: Sovetskii Pisatel', 1965).

97. A. Malygin and K. Ushakov, "Byt' bditel'nymi," *Partiinaia zhizn'*, no. 3 (March 1966):52–58.

98. Roy Medvedev, *All Stalin's Men* (Oxford: Basil Blackwell, 1983), p. 74. Also see Tatu, *Power in the Kremlin*, pp. 503–508. The removal of Shelepin's ally Tikunov from his post as head of MOOP in 1966 was an early indication that Shelepin was losing control over the police.

99. While Shelepin remained in the Politburo until 1975, he was effectively neutralized as a potential threat to Brezhnev's predominance by 1967. Semichastnyi was

relegated to the post of a deputy minister in the Ukraine. Coincidentally on the very day that *Pravda* announced the removal of Semichastnyi (19 May 1967, p. 6), *Krasnaia zvezda* announced the "tragic death in the line of duty" of Maj. Gen. Vasilii Lukshin, a high-ranking KGB official. No connection between these two events could be established, however.

3

The KGB and
Party Politics, 1967–1987

Brezhnev and Andropov: Building Police Support

By 1967 Brezhnev had accomplished much toward consolidating his power, although he was by no means an absolute ruler and it would take him several more years to emerge as *primes inter pares* in the Politburo. Brezhnev's political strategy was based on building coalitions from different institutional groups rather than relying on the party apparatus alone. Unlike Khrushchev, who often offended established interests by attempting to introduce substantial changes in the system, Brezhnev took a consensus approach: he tried to preserve the status quo and avoid confrontation with key political groups.[1] Thus he sought to satisfy the demands of the KGB and ensure its prerogatives, just as he did with the military establishment.

The growing prestige and authority of the KGB accommodated those conservative neo-Stalinist trends that manifested themselves during the late 1960s and 1970s. Curbs on cultural freedom, the crackdown on dissent, and, above all, the process of re-Stalinization marked a victory for the pro-Stalinist elements in the leadership. By the late 1960s much had been done to restore Stalin's reputation as a political leader, and even the notorious purges were being justified in official circles. As Stephen Cohen wrote, "the policies of the Brezhnev government grew steadily into a wide-ranging conservative reaction to Khrushchev's reforms. The defense of the status quo required a usable Stalinist past."[2] The rehabilitation of Stalinism legitimized the past excesses of the political police and thus tempered those forces that sought to establish further limits on the KGB's authority. Although Iurii Andropov, who was appointed chairman of the USSR KGB on 19 May 1967, was a "party man" and did not appear to be a neo-Stalinist, he did much to encourage the revival of the security police as a force within the political system during his fifteen-year tenure in the KGB.

In terms of political stature and experience, Andropov surpassed his predecessors in the KGB. His early career was typical of the generation of party officials who rose to important posts in the Stalin era.[3] Born the son of a railway employee in 1914 in what is now the Stavropol District of the RSFSR, Andropov left school at the age of sixteen and held various menial jobs before becoming a sailor on the Volga, where his travels took him up to Rybinsk. There he attended the Water Transport School from 1932 to 1936 and became active in the Komsomol. Andropov was a direct beneficiary of the purges that were carried out in that organization in 1937–1938; by 1938, at the age of only twenty-four, he was first secretary of the Iaroslav *Oblast* Komsomol. In 1940 Andropov was promoted again; he became first secretary of the Komsomol Central Committee in the newly created Karelo-Finnish Republic, where he was to remain, serving in various posts, for the next eleven years.

Andropov took a leading role in organizing the partisan movement that developed in Karelia during World War II and worked closely with NKVD officials, who were deeply involved in partisan activities. In 1944 he was transferred to the party apparatus, rising to become Second Secretary of the Karelian party in 1947—a post of watchdog for the central leadership in Moscow. The next four years saw major purges in the Karelian party apparatus, which were closely connected with the intense power struggles going on in Moscow between Malenkov and Beria on the one hand and A. A. Zhdanov and the Leningrad group on the other. Andropov's survival throughout this upheaval was a testimony to his political acumen.

Andropov was transferred to Moscow in 1951 to work in the Central Committee apparatus, most probably in the Party Organs Department (where Ezhov, Ignat'ev, and later Shelepin and Semichastnyi served).[4] Shortly after Stalin's death Andropov was transferred to the Ministry of Foreign Affairs, where he worked briefly as head of the Fourth European Department before being sent to Budapest as a counselor in the Soviet embassy. Andropov was promoted in 1954 to the post of Soviet Ambassador to Hungary, and he held this position for three years. The experience of watching the tide of political unrest swell in Eastern Europe and the direct involvement in the suppression of the Hungarian Revolution in 1956 no doubt had a lasting effect on Andropov's outlook and policies. His performance in Budapest seems to have pleased the Kremlin leadership, for he received another promotion in May 1957 when he was returned to Moscow to head the CC Department for Liaison with Socialist Countries. He served there for ten years, rising to become a member of the CC Secretariat in 1962.

Andropov's experience in Hungary and in the Central Committee apparatus made him an excellent choice for the KGB chairmanship, particularly in view of developments in Eastern Europe at that time. Indeed, Jiri Valenta has suggested that it was Andropov's expertise on Eastern Europe that determined his appointment to the KGB.[5] As will be discussed later, the KGB plays an important role in maintaining the Soviet hold over Warsaw Pact countries. It should be added, however, that Andropov's lengthy tenure in the Komsomol and party apparatus in Karelia, where he helped to impose Soviet rule over newly acquired territory, also gave him valuable experience in domestic security problems and qualified him well for his new job. Finally, although he had worked closely with CC secretaries Mikhail Suslov and Boris Ponomarev in the Central Committee, Andropov was not linked to any particular coalition or faction within the leadership and therefore was a neutral figure upon whom members of the Politburo could agree. From Andropov's own point of view his new appointment was not a promotion. The post of KGB chairman ranked lower than that of a party secretary. But Andropov was compensated by being elected to the Politburo as a candidate member in June 1967, and he eventually brought such prestige and authority to his new post that he was able to use it as a stepping stone to the party leadership.

Brezhnev was not powerful enough to put one of his own men in as KGB chairman, but he did manage to bring in several protégés to serve directly below Andropov. The most important of these was Semen Tsvigun, who came to Moscow in June 1967 to become a deputy chairman of the USSR KGB and by December of that year was a first deputy chairman.[6] Tsvigun, a Ukrainian, had spent most of his career in the security police. Born in 1917, he graduated from the Odessa Pedagogic Institute and subsequently became a teacher before joining the NKVD in 1939. He first met Brezhnev while serving in the security police in Moldavia in the early 1950s and reportedly married a sister of Brezhnev's wife. Later Tsvigun served as KGB chairman in Tadzhikistan (1957–1963) and Azerbaidzhan (1963–1967). From his earliest days in the KGB Tsvigun consistently projected the image of a hard-liner. Thus in a speech delivered at the Thirteenth Party Congress in Tadzhikistan in 1961, at the height of Khrushchev's de-Stalinization drive, Tsvigun, railing against "politically immature" Soviet citizens who succumbed to evil Western influences, raised a cry of alarm about the dangers of subversion. He attested to the efficiency of KGB operations under his authority by noting that KGB personnel had delivered four hundred lectures at factories and *kolkhozes* in Tadzhikistan that year in an effort to combat subversive ideas, particularly those of religious sects.[7]

Tsvigun, who lived up to his hard-line reputation after moving to Moscow, was not shy of publicity. He wrote numerous articles for Soviet newspapers and journals, appeared on television frequently, and edited several books on the history of the police. He even had two novels glorifying the Chekisty published under his name, though it was claimed in the West that they were actually ghostwritten by Soviet novelist Iulian Semenov.[8] Tsvigun's main concern in articles and speeches on the contemporary state security organs centered on the "battle of ideas" with the West.[9] His high public visibility indicated that he was a figure of considerable authority in the KGB.

Viktor Chebrikov was another figure with links to Brezhnev who was brought to Moscow to serve in the KGB.[10] Born in 1923, Chebrikov attended Brezhnev's alma mater, the Dnepropetrovsk Metallurgical Institute. After graduating in 1950, he worked briefly as an engineer and then embarked on a party career in Brezhnev's former bailiwick of Dnepropetrovsk. By 1958 he had become second secretary, and by 1961 first secretary, of the Dnepropetrovsk *Gorkom*. Chebrikov then moved to the Dnepropetrovsk *Obkom*, where he served as a secretary and then second secretary from 1964 to 1967. Although Chebrikov had never worked directly under Brezhnev, his connections with the Dnepropetrovsk "mafia" (which included party officials Andrei Kirilenko and Vladimir Shcherbitskii, under whom Chebrikov had served) placed him in the Brezhnev camp. Chebrikov was head of the KGB Personnel Department from 1967 to 1968, after which he was promoted to deputy chairman of the USSR KGB. He apparently retained his responsibilities for KGB cadres for several years.[11]

Yet another Brezhnev ally in the KGB was Georgii Tsinev, who had attended the Dnepropetrovsk Metallurgical Institute with Brezhnev in the early 1930s. Tsinev had served as an army political officer during the war and in 1953 joined the Special Departments of the security police (for counterintelligence in the Soviet Army). Around 1959 he apparently became chief of the KGB Third Directorate (which oversees the Special Departments), though this was never stated officially. Tsinev probably moved to another leading KGB post in the late 1960s and was a deputy chairman of the USSR KGB by 1970.[12]

The presence of his allies in KGB leadership was a source of strength for Brezhnev; at the same time, the KGB was now able to influence decision making. The careers of Brezhnev's KGB friends, and also of Andropov himself, prospered. Andropov was promoted to full membership in the Politburo in April 1973—a move that clearly enhanced both his personal authority and that of the KGB as an institution—and in September 1976 he was elevated to the rank of Army general, unprecedented for a security chief since Beria days.[13] In addition, Tsvigun and Tsinev were awarded "Hero of Socialist Labor" titles in 1977 on the occasion of their sixtieth and seventieth birthdays, respectively. Such honors are rarely accorded to non-Politburo members, particularly those without ministerial rank. Even more remarkable was that they were both promoted to the rank of Army general, along with the chief of the Border Guards, V. A. Matrosov, in December 1978.[14]

The publicity campaign to promote the security police reached new heights in 1967. The fiftieth anniversary of the founding of the political police, celebrated on 20 December 1967, provided the impetus for a flood of literature on the Chekisty. Ceremonies commemorating the occasion, which took place throughout the Soviet Union, were given full coverage in the national and local press, while hundreds of articles on the state security organs appeared in newspapers and journals over several days.[15] In addition to leading party officials, representatives of security police from socialist countries also attended the fetes. As Frederick Barghoorn observed, of the 1967 ceremonies in honor of various institutions—the army, militia, courts, diplomatic services—"that accorded to the KGB certainly exceeded the others in duration, saliency, volume and the status of major organizing participants."[16]

The general tone of the speeches delivered by KGB officials was different from what it had been ten years before, on the fortieth anniversary of the state security organs. Whereas in December 1957 KGB Chairman Serov had spoken of the "serious damage" inflicted upon the people during the purges and the "spy mania" that resulted from the "cult of personality," Andropov's representation of these events was milder. In his speech, delivered at the Kremlin Palace of Congresses in the presence of the entire Politburo, he did not refer to Stalin at all and mentioned only that "political adventurists, at the reins of power in the

NKVD *attempted* to remove the security agencies from party oversight, to isolate them from the people, and displayed disregard of the law, which caused serious detriment to the interests of our state, Soviet citizens and the security agencies themselves."[17] He was careful to assure his audience that this institution was under full party control and scoffed at Western references to the KGB as a "secret police." Other KGB officials felt it necessary to point out that the "mistakes" under Stalin had not changed the "socialist nature" of the security organs or isolated them from the people, and some KGB republic chairmen did not even mention the illegalities committed by the security police.[18]

The appearance of literature glorifying the security police in the form of memoirs, biographies, histories, and adventure stories continued unabated from 1967 throughout the Brezhnev era. In 1972 the Soviets published a bibliography of over fifty pages devoted entirely to literature on Chekisty.[19] In May 1976 *Literaturnaia gazeta* reported a meeting of a special commission of the RSFSR Writers Union charged with promoting the police adventure story as a full-fledged genre, as part of plans for the centenary celebration of Dzerzhinskii's birth.[20] Although by 1977, according to one estimate, over two thousand books extolling the deeds of the security police had been published in the Soviet Union, the pace did not let up.[21] In early 1979 KGB First Deputy Chairman Tsvigun, speaking at a nationwide congress of creative arts federations in Moscow, appealed for greater artistic efforts on behalf of the KGB border guards and Chekisty, announcing that prizes had been created for the best works of literature and art on the subject.[22]

Among the more impressive examples of the new genre of Chekist literature was a large volume published by the Komsomol in 1972 appropriately entitled *Chekisty*.[23] The book, which included photographs of famous security policemen, including Rudolph Abel, was a collection of articles and stories devoted to the history of the security organs and its heroes. Intended to inspire feelings of patriotism and admiration among the younger generation, the book was filled with lofty quotations such as the following from an alleged conversation with a Chekist named Ivan Gaba: "'What do you think is important for Chekists?' I asked Gaba. He thought and then answered quietly: 'The most important thing—is to love people . . .' No this is not simply a phrase. This is the essence, the whole life of Ivan Vasilevich Gaba and his Chekist comrades."[24] As before, the Chekist was portrayed not simply as a dedicated protector of the nation's security but as a valiant soldier of the revolution, a moral guardian with lofty, almost religious ideals and qualities of perfection.

Particularly noteworthy for the KGB in terms of publicity was the year 1977. September brought the centenary of the birth of Vecheka chief Dzerzhinskii, which provided the opportunity for a round of self-congratulatory celebrations. Andropov himself marked the occasion with a fifty-five-minute speech (on 9 September) that was televised from the Kremlin, as well as being reprinted in all the major papers. Not surprisingly, Andropov stressed the continuity of the Vecheka with the present KGB, invoking the sacred image of Dzerzhinskii as the leader who continued to provide inspiration. He sought to convey the idea that the KGB was carrying on with the Vecheka tradition:

> Communist conviction and high professionalism, moral purity and loyalty to one's duty, constant vigilance and responsiveness, sensitivity, faith in people, general culture and a developed sense of civic responsibility—this is how Dzerzhinskii saw and the Soviet people today see the Soviet Chekist.[25]

Never mind that the first Chekists were a ruthless, uneducated, politically crude lot who bore little resemblance to this portrayal. The KGB, like the party, needed a mythology in order to legitimize its existence and to provide a focal point for patriotic sentiments.[26] Andropov also sought to impress on his audience that the enemies of socialism were persevering in their efforts to subvert the Soviet state, just as they had in the days of the Cheka. Hence Dzerzhinskii's revolutionary vigilance was just as important as it had been in the past. Andropov's brief address on the occasion of the sixtieth anniversary of the state security organs, delivered three months later, carried a similar message.[27] Significantly, Andropov did not mention past police excesses as he did in his anniversary address ten years earlier, and republic KGB chairmen failed to refer to the purges in their speeches.[28]

The campaign to glorify the state security organs clearly benefited not only the KGB as an institution but also Andropov personally. Andropov deserved much of the credit for raising the KGB's stature during the Brezhnev period. Indeed, his personal image—that of a dedicated, intelligent party man with reasonably moderate views—did much to enhance the image of the KGB. Nonetheless Brezhnev cannot have objected to these promotional efforts, and judging from his enthusiastic praise of the KGB and its officials, he seems to have actively backed them. After placing several of his protégés in the KGB leadership, he had a stake in enhancing the authority and prestige of this institution. But he apparently underestimated Andropov's ambitions and political prowess and failed to realize that Andropov was developing into a powerful political figure who could effectively challenge the political domination

[85]

of the Brezhnev "mafia." Unlikely as it may have seemed in 1967, Andropov proved more formidable than either Beria or Shelepin.

The Police and the Brezhnev Succession

The security police played an important role in Andropov's accession to the general secretaryship. The available evidence suggests that Andropov enlisted the KGB in a campaign against corruption in order to attack the Brezhnevites in the party and state bureaucracy, including the MVD. As was noted earlier, the KGB had been involved in investigations of economic crime since the early 1960s. Campaigns against such crime had been relaxed considerably after Brezhnev came to power, however, and it was not until the late 1970s that the problem of corruption again came to the forefront. Brezhnev, as part of his policy of gaining loyalty from party officials by ensuring job security ("stability of cadres"), had turned a blind eye to the phenomena of bribery and corruption that had become almost universal by the end of his tenure in office.[29]

The MVD, responsible along with the Procuracy and, in some cases, the KGB for uncovering such crime, was itself permeated with corrupt officials who frequently collaborated in illegal activities. In response to increasing complaints among the public over the ineffectiveness of regular law enforcement agencies, the party stressed the need for increased supervision over them and also made penalties for economic crimes more severe.[30] Criticisms of the MVD and the Procuracy for their failures to combat crime became particularly intense by the late 1970s and dismissals were stepped up.[31] There were scathing press attacks on the MVD and Procuracy in such republics as Kirgizia, Georgia, and Azerbaidzhan. Criminal investigators were accused of "formalism, bureaucratism, and red tape" in dragging out their investigations over long periods, with the result that many cases remained unsolved and innocent persons were often arrested wrongfully. Even more serious were the charges that employees of these law enforcement agencies engaged in corrupt activities themselves.[32]

It was perhaps not surprising, in view of the dismal record of the MVD and Procuracy in combating economic crime, that the KGB would step in. KGB officials began suggesting that their organization had important responsibilities in fighting corruption on the theory that such activity had implications for the security of the state. This idea was expressed by Georgian KGB Chairman Inauri in a remarkable speech in September 1980:

> The most decisive measures for eradicating crime and violations of public order and the strengthening of party, state and labor discipline are being adopted. The Committee of State Security and its local organs, fulfilling their basic functions, actively participate in this struggle. They have uncovered criminal activity of many smart dealers and intriguers, who embezzled the people's goods on a large scale. We believe that a successful struggle against crime, in addition to general protection of the community, also helps to ensure state security by narrowing the possibilities of our class enemies to act in favorable circumstances.[33]

A further sign of greater KGB interest in economic crime appeared in a three-part article in *Moskovskaia pravda* in November 1981. In a detailed account of how investigators from the Moscow KGB caught a group of diamond smugglers, the author seemed to be suggesting that a more intense crackdown on official corruption was long overdue and that the KGB might be enlisted in the struggle.[34]

The KGB, after all, was not tainted with the reputation of inefficiency and corruption that its legal counterparts had gained. In contrast with the regular law enforcement agencies, the KGB's status continued to rise. At the Twenty-Sixth Party Congress in 1981, four KGB officials were elected to full membership in the Central Committee—Andropov, Tsvigun, Tsinev, and Chebrikov. This represented a marked increase from the previous congress in 1976, when only Andropov was accorded full CC membership.[35] Brezhnev voiced high praise for KGB employees in his report to the Twenty-Sixth Congress, noting that "they resolutely suppress the activity of those who embark on anti-state, hostile activities, who infringe on the rights of Soviet people, on the interests of Soviet society. And this work of theirs deserves the deep gratitude of the party, of the whole people."[36] In response to these lofty words, the chief of the Leningrad KGB, D. P. Nosyrev, later noted: "This high estimation not only inspires Chekists, not only places greater obligations on the employees of the state security organs, but it gives birth to a new surge of creative force, a desire to work even more selflessly for the good of our socialist Motherland."[37]

Nosyrev himself was a consultant for a new film series on the security police that premiered on Soviet television in April 1982. The series, entitled "20 December," was a documentary about the heroic achievements of the early Chekists after the revolution. The intended parallels with the contemporary security police doubtless were not lost on viewers.[38] This series was one of many films, some fictional and some documentary, about the security police that had been produced in recent years. In at least one republic, Belorussia, special showings of these films were organized in cities and villages to commemorate the sixty-fifth anniversary of the security police in December 1982.[39]

The significance of the KGB's increased prominence and its heightened interest in economic crime was revealed in the dramatic events that unfolded in early 1982. The sequence began with the sudden death on 19 January 1982 of Brezhnev's most influential ally in the KGB, First Deputy Chairman Semen Tsvigun. Coincidentally Mikhail Suslov, one of the most powerful men in the party leadership, died a week later. Both these deaths were fortuitous for Andropov, who rose in political prominence markedly in the months that followed. According to rumors circulating in Moscow at the time, Tsvigun's death was precipitated by a KGB investigation, instigated by Andropov, of a bribery and corruption scandal involving close friends of Brezhnev's daughter, Galina. At the same time there were reports that Brezhnev's son, Iurii, first deputy minister of foreign trade, was being investigated for misuse of state funds. Tsvigun, himself a member of Brezhnev's family by marriage, reportedly tried to stop KGB efforts to discredit Brezhnev and ended up committing suicide.[40]

The death of Brezhnev's top man in the KGB not only solidified Andropov's grip on that organization but also placed several of those who had been protected by Tsvigun and Brezhnev in vulnerable positions. In addition to Galina Brezhnev's friends, who were arrested in February 1982, these persons included her husband, Iurii Churbanov, first deputy minister of internal affairs, and his boss, MVD chief Nikolai Shchelokov. Churbanov's spectacular political rise, after he married Brezhnev's daughter and joined the MVD in 1970, was no doubt a result of his familial connections. By 1975 he had become chief of the political administration of the MVD's Internal Troops and probably retained control over these highly important troops when he became a deputy MVD minister in 1977.[41] Shchelokov likewise had close ties with Brezhnev; they had been fellow students at the Dnepropetrovsk Metallurgical Institute and had worked together during the war and later in the party apparatus.[42]

The exposure of the scandal around Galina Brezhnev, together with the intensified criticism of the MVD, was a blow to this organization and a harbinger of further reprisals. The possibility of widespread arrests and demotions for corruption also must have created alarm among party apparatchiks all over the country. Interestingly, Eduard Shevardnadze, party chief in Georgia, which had been the subject of a particularly harsh crackdown on crime, had already revealed some anxiety in a speech to commemorate the sixtieth anniversary of the Georgian security police in December 1981.[43] Shevardnadze praised the KGB in his speech, referring in particular to the KGB's involvement in the anticorruption campaign. At the same time, however, he stressed that the state security organs were the "party's loyal assistants in implementing its general line," and issued a pointed reminder of what might happen if the KGB were to go too far: "We do not have a right to forget that there was a time when serious deviations from party principles were permitted in the activity of the state security authorities and instances of arbitrariness and illegality occurred. And we all know full well what the consequences were." Shevardnadze, who had served as MVD chief in Georgia from 1965 to 1972, did not have a reputation for being soft on corruption. It was he, for example, who had instigated the criminal investigation of former Georgian party chief Mzhavanadze in 1972. Nevertheless the fact that corruption in Georgia was still widespread and that he had a long association with the MVD and Shchelokov placed Shevardnadze in a precarious position.[44]

Andropov's move from the KGB into the Secretariat in May 1982 can hardly have assuaged the anxieties of the Brezhnevites about a threat to their own careers by a KGB-backed anticorruption campaign. From May onward Andropov was no longer a "dark horse" candidate to succeed Brezhnev but a prime contender for the job. The appointment of Vitalii Fedorchuk to take over as KGB chairman may have caused additional concern. For the first time since 1954 the Soviet leadership deviated from its policy of placing party *apparatchiks* in the post of KGB chairman and appointed a career Chekist instead.[45] Born in 1918 and a Ukrainian by nationality, Fedorchuk joined the ranks of the security police in 1939. He served in SMERSH during the war and continued to work in military counterintelligence, rising to chief of the KGB Third Directorate in the late 1960s. In 1970 Fedorchuk was made chairman of the KGB in the Ukraine, replacing V. F. Nikitchenko, who reportedly was considered too soft on dissidents. Fedorchuk soon gained a reputation as a ruthless and effective suppressor of dissent and a hard-liner on foreign policy.[46]

Fedorchuk's appointment was somewhat puzzling in view of his relatively low rank in the KGB leadership hierarchy. He did not appear to have close ties with Andropov, and he was junior in status to the two recently appointed first deputy chairmen, Tsinev and Chebrikov, who were both full members of the CC. The designation of both Tsinev and

[89]

Chebrikov to replace Tsvigun was also somewhat curious, particularly considering the fact that the timing of their promotions was unclear. On 23 February 1982 Tsinev alone was identified as first deputy USSR KGB chairman. Then, after a lapse of five weeks, it was revealed that Chebrikov also had been made a first deputy.[47] All this suggests that there was a conflict about who would fill the top KGB posts. Perhaps a compromise was reached by giving Tsinev and Chebrikov the same positions and elevating Fedorchuk to the chairmanship. Equally possible is that Fedorchuk's appointment was designed to prevent Andropov from retaining a strong hold on the KGB after he left that institution.[48]

It should be stressed that Andropov did not reach the general secretaryship in November 1982 without facing what appeared to be tough competition from Brezhnev's favored successor, CC secretary Konstantin Chernenko. Although Chernenko, who had been a full member of the Politburo only since 1978, did not have a substantial power base of his own, he probably had the support of most party officials loyal to Brezhnev. His close personal association with Brezhnev (which began when Chernenko worked under Brezhnev in Moldavia) was a key factor in his rise to political prominence. By the early 1980s Chernenko had managed to surpass his chief rival in the Secretariat, Andrei Kirilenko, and had assumed (in part at least) Kirilenko's portfolio of supervision over party cadres and Administrative Organs (which includes the police and the military). As Brezhnev's health deteriorated Chernenko also took over many of his functions, playing a prominent role in foreign and domestic affairs. Andropov's entry into the Secretariat changed the balance of power considerably, and throughout the summer and autumn of 1982 there were signs of intense rivalry between Andropov and Chernenko.[49]

The reasons for Andropov's victory are still a matter of dispute among Western experts. Having served in the KGB for fifteen years, he had not been able to cultivate a base of support within the party similar to the kind of patronage networks established by party leaders. Thus he had to rely on other sources of political support, in particular the KGB. Substantial personnel changes had occurred in the top echelons of the KGB from 1978 onward. Eleven of fourteen republic KGB chairmen were replaced, while the names of three new USSR KGB deputy chairmen appeared among the delegates to the Twenty-Sixth Party Congress in 1981.[50] It is not possible to determine the allegiances of all the new men, but it seems reasonable to assume that Andropov managed to build his own network of loyal officials in this organization, while Tsvigun's death no doubt strengthened Andropov's hold further. The

KGB, by virtue of its internal security and criminal investigation functions, had detailed information on corruption involving important party and state officials—a powerful weapon to use against the Brezhnev-Chernenko faction.

It is probably true that Andropov was favored as general secretary by some of his Politburo colleagues because of his intelligence, efficiency, and broad experience. Reportedly many officials, including Minister of Defense Ustinov and Minister of Foreign Affairs Gromyko, were tired of Brezhnev's do-nothing policies, which had caused economic stagnation and widespread corruption, and saw Chernenko as offering more of the same. In addition, as Jerry Hough has suggested, Andropov seems to have appealed for support to Kirilenko's former allies and protégés, most of whom had suffered politically in the wake of Chernenko's rise to prominence.[51] While these circumstances no doubt helped Andropov in overcoming opposition from Chernenko, it appears that Andropov's fifteen-year tenure as head of the KGB was an equally important factor in his successful bid for power. This hypothesis is supported strongly by the events that followed his accession.

The KGB after Brezhnev

One of the first promotions that Andropov made in the Kremlin leadership was that of Geidar Aliev, first secretary in Azerbaidzhan and a former KGB official. Aliev, who was elevated to the post of first deputy chairman of the Council of Ministers and made a full member of the Politburo in November 1982, had served for many years in the security police. According to one source it was Tsvigun, Aliev's boss in the Azerbaidzhan KGB from 1963 to 1967, who had recommended him to Brezhnev to head the party there. Once he had assumed this post he reportedly used the KGB to carry out a sweeping anticorruption campaign, dismissing many party and MVD officials and replacing them with his associates from the KGB.[52] Aliev gained a reputation as an outspoken and determined opponent of economic crime. In numerous interviews and speeches he urged that harsh reprisals be taken against officials engaged in such activity and decried the laxity of the regular law enforcement agencies.[53]

The promotion of an official with strong KGB connections and a record of speaking out against corruption became even more significant when Vitalii Fedorchuk was named to replace Brezhnev crony N. A.

[91]

Shchelokov as head of the MVD in December 1982 and Viktor Chebrikov was designated the new KGB chief. Given Fedorchuk's background, with over forty-five years in the security police, it was difficult to interpret his appointment to head the MVD as anything other than a move to increase KGB control over this apparatus. Although it was accompanied by a promotion to the rank of Army general, Fedorchuk's transfer was in fact a demotion in the political hierarchy. The MVD ranks lower than the KGB in terms of political authority and public image, and its leader has never enjoyed Politburo status. Whereas the KGB Chairman is responsible for intelligence collection, counterespionage, and domestic security, the MVD chief restricts his concerns to the more banal area of "ordinary" crime. In this case, however, Fedorchuk had the politically important job of launching an all-out campaign against economic crime and cleansing the MVD of corrupt and inefficient Brezhnevites. As Robert Sharlet noted, "the team of Andropov, Aliev, Fedorchuk and Chebrikov meant that the 'new puritans' were in command in Moscow, ready to wage war against crime, corruption and indiscipline."[54]

The campaign was set in motion when *Pravda* reported on 11 December 1982 that the problem of corruption had been discussed at the latest Politburo meeting and that the Procuracy and the MVD had been notified of the need to take immediate steps to maintain law and order.[55] A few days later the chief of the Moscow KGB, V. I. Alidin, made it clear in an article commemorating the sixty-fifth anniversary of the state security organs that the KGB would take an important role in the anticorruption campaign.[56] As criticisms of the MVD in the Soviet press became more frequent and emphatic, it seemed that the attack on the MVD was building steam. Writing in *Pravda* in early January 1983, the USSR Procurator General, A. M. Rekunkov, accused the regular police not only of being ineffective in fighting bribery, speculation, and theft but also of deliberately covering up these crimes.[57] By the summer of 1983 Fedorchuk made it clear that a widespread shake-up was occurring within the MVD when he announced in *Pravda* that this organization was being "purged of slackers and those who are ideologically and morally immature."[58]

In addition to Shchelokov, who was expelled from the Central Committee in June 1983, Iurii Churbanov appeared to be in trouble. He was not seen in public after Brezhnev's death, and there were persistent rumors that he had been exiled to Murmansk. Although he continued to be identified in his MVD position in 1983 and early 1984, he was not elected to the USSR Supreme Soviet in February 1984 as might have been expected, and by late 1984 he had been replaced as first deputy minister of internal affairs by former Moscow *Gorkom* secretary Vasilii Trushin.[59] At least two other leading officials in the USSR MVD left their posts in 1983, along with three republic ministers of internal affairs.[60] In several cases KGB officials were moved into the MVD as replacements. Thus, for example, Vasilii Lezhepekov, a deputy chairman of the USSR KGB since 1979, was named a deputy minister of internal affairs in July 1983.[61]

Chebrikov, the new KGB chairman, was no doubt involved in carrying out these purges of the MVD, at least insofar as he was delegating KGB personnel to that organization and providing information from KGB files on cases of corruption. Chebrikov was in many ways better suited to head the KGB than Fedorchuk had been. Although he had served in the KGB since 1967, his previous career experience was in the party apparatus and he did not have Fedorchuk's tough policeman's image. Chebrikov may have been Andropov's preferred candidate all along, but ambiguities concerning his status over the next year counter this impression.

Somewhat surprisingly, Chebrikov was not given the rank of Army general upon assuming his new post despite the fact that both Fedorchuk and Chebrikov's deputy, Tsinev, held this rank. Nor was Chebrikov promoted to candidate membership in the Politburo at the June 1983 CC Plenum, as might have been expected. On his sixtieth birthday in April 1983 Chebrikov was presented with an Order of Lenin rather than a Hero of Socialist Labor title.[62] While this title is not commonly given to those without Politburo status, recall that both Tsinev and Tsvigun received this honor on their birthdays in 1977. It is possible that Andropov was not on particularly good terms with Chebrikov because of the latter's connection with the Brezhnev Dnepropetrovsk "mafia." Perhaps Chebrikov's appointment to the KGB Chairmanship had been pressed upon Andropov as part of some sort of compromise surrounding his accession to the party leadership. It is equally possible that Andropov was simply anxious to dissociate himself from his KGB past and dispel the impression that his new role would lead to a rise in KGB influence.

Interestingly, the KGB's status and that of Chebrikov personally rose markedly after Andropov's illness forced him from public view in August 1983. In late October, not long after the KAL airliner incident, an article appeared in *Pravda* that discussed the scores of letters that had been pouring in from Soviet citizens to express their gratitude for the outstanding job the KGB was doing.[63] The article cited quotations from these letters with unusually effusive praise for Chekisty. Just a week later, on 4 November, Chebrikov was promoted to the rank of Army general and, at the CC Plenum the next month, was elevated to candidate membership in the Politburo.[64] Equally significant for the KGB were changes in the law on state crimes that were introduced in January 1984. The definition of several crimes was broadened and a new article on passing professional secrets was added, all of which gave the KGB more latitude in its investigation of political deviance. These changes were seen as symptomatic of the spirit of xenophobia that ensued after Brezhnev's death and led some to speculate on the possibility of a revival of Stalinist practices.[65]

Contrary to what might have been expected, Chernenko's assumption of the general secretaryship on 13 February 1984 did not result in a diminution of the KGB's status. The number of KGB officials elected to the USSR Supreme Soviet later that month rose to an unprecedented eighteen delegates. These delegates were no doubt decided upon well in advance (the nomination process begins several weeks before Supreme Soviet elections and is carefully orchestrated to ensure that only the selected delegates are named), but Andropov was so ill that he may not have had much influence over the selection process. The available evidence indicates that Chernenko was acting general secretary, or least a strong second in command, for some time before Andropov's death.[66] Thus he might have been partially responsible for the rise in the KGB's status following Andropov's incapacitation. It is also significant that in May 1984 *Literaturnaia gazeta* announced a contest sponsored by the KGB, the USSR Writers' Union, and the USSR Cinematographers' Union for books, movies, and television films about the state security agencies. The purpose of the contest, to run through July 1987 and commemorate the seventieth anniversary of the Vecheka on 20 December 1987, was to enlist new creative forces in an effort to raise the ideological and artistic level of works devoted to Chekisty.[67]

Given the fact that in the past Chernenko had supervisory responsibilities for the police, it is quite possible that he cultivated his own ties with KGB personnel, particularly among those who owed their loyalties to his mentor, Brezhnev. Chernenko's service in the NKVD Border guards in the 1930s gave him an additional link with the KGB.[68] Chernenko seemed to be on good terms with KGB Chairman Chebrikov. The latter, for example, made positive references to Chernenko in his Supreme Soviet election speech on 20 February 1984. Just two months later, on 19 April, Chernenko personally presented Chebrikov with a Marshal's Star, a badge that accompanies the rank of Army general, to which status Chebrikov had earlier been promoted.[69] Both Minister of Defense Ustinov and Mikhail Solomentsev, chairman of the Party

Control Committee, also received awards. The fact that Chernenko made the presentations at a special Kremlin ceremony, mentioning the importance of the roles of these men, suggested that they were deserving of special recognition.

Chernenko may have cultivated good relations with the KGB, but he did not seem interested in pursuing the anticorruption campaign with the same vigor as had his predecessor. The Soviet press still featured accounts of corruption cases, but they involved low-level officials, and criticisms of the MVD and the Procuracy were toned down. Not surprisingly, Chernenko had little incentive to purge the Brezhnev old guard, as this group constituted the core of his political support. Indeed his election to the general secretaryship was probably a result of the widespread fear among entrenched party bureaucrats that further purges would ensue under a younger, more dynamic leader like Gorbachev. Chernenko symbolized a partial return to the status quo and a respite from the uncertainty of Andropov's reign. Nonetheless, Chernenko's ill health made it clear that his tenure would not be a long one, and some Western experts even surmised that Gorbachev was designated Chernenko's successor at the time the latter was chosen.[70] Gorbachev was a strong second in command, overseeing ideology, culture, and foreign affairs, along with the economy and party cadres. As one of only two senior secretaries in the Politburo, aside from Chernenko, Gorbachev shared responsibilities with Grigorii Romanov, who had been promoted into the Secretariat in June 1983 and by early 1984 appeared to have secretarial oversight for Administrative Organs.[71]

Perhaps because of Gorbachev's growing influence the respite from the anticorruption drive was short-lived; by the summer of 1984 it had gathered new momentum. In June the major newspapers publicized instances of widespread corruption in Uzbekistan, revealing that several high-level officials, including *obkom* first secretaries, had been removed. The revelations followed a 23 June plenum of the Uzbek Central Committee, which was attended by Egor Ligachev, CC secretary and head of the Party-Organizational Work Department. This department, responsible for party appointments, was under the general oversight of Gorbachev. Details of corruption in Uzbekistan and various other regions continued to be publicized throughout the summer.[72]

It is possible that the stepped-up struggle against corruption was inspired not by Chernenko but by Gorbachev and Ligachev. Gorbachev may well have been strong enough to pursue this course without the support of Chernenko, particularly if he was able to enlist the cooperation of certain elements in the KGB, which had access to all the

[95]

information on these scandals. Significantly the authority of one key Brezhnevite in the KGB, First Deputy Chairman Tsinev, who might have been expected to block Gorbachev's efforts, was diluted in May 1984 when Nikolai Emokhonov was promoted to the same position.[73] Emokhonov had been brought into the USSR KGB in 1968 from a post as director of an aviation institute and by 1971 was a deputy chairman. He had no apparent connections with the Brezhnev group.[74] It became clear by the autumn of 1984 that neither Chernenko nor anyone else was strong enough to protect his fellow Brezhnevites from the vicissitudes of the anticorruption drive. On 9 November 1984 it was announced that former MVD chief Nikolai Shchelokov, who had close associations not only with Brezhnev but also with Chernenko and Tsinev, had been stripped of his military rank for abusing his official position.[75]

It is difficult to say where Romanov stood in relation to these developments. Although apparently he had supervisory responsibilities for the police and the military, he did not have the authority that Gorbachev enjoyed in the Secretariat. Romanov did seem to have close ties with members of the military establishment, but the abrupt dismissal of Nikolai Ogarkov in September 1984 (when Romanov was out of the country) indicated a possible decline in his position, a decline that was probably furthered by the death of Dmitrii Ustinov, another apparent ally, on 20 December 1984. Significantly, there were signs at about this time that Romanov was being edged out of his Administrative Organs portfolio by Ligachev.[76]

Gorbachev and the KGB

After gaining the post of general secretary in March 1985 Gorbachev moved with unprecedented speed to implement personnel changes in the party and government. His success in getting rid of so many potential political opponents in such a short time surprised Western Soviet experts, particularly because Gorbachev did not have a substantial power base, or patronage network, of his own when he took office. In retrospect it appears that Gorbachev relied on the same bases of support that Andropov used in his ascent to the top. First, he joined forces with former members of the Kirilenko faction who had been promoted by Andropov—men such as Nikolai Ryzhkov, Igor Ligachev, and Vitalii Vorotnikov. Even more significant for the purpose of our analysis here, Gorbachev appears to have appealed to the KGB for help in purging the

Brezhnev old guard. The promotions at the April 1985 CC Plenum offered evidence of the alliances forged by Gorbachev. KGB Chairman Chebrikov was promoted to full membership in the Politburo along with Ligachev and Ryzhkov. Chebrikov's status contrasted sharply with that of Minister of Defense Sokolov, who was promoted only to candidate Politburo membership.

On the basis of these alliances Gorbachev managed, in his first year alone, to remove potential opponent Grigorii Romanov, Brezhnev stalwarts Nikolai Tikhonov and Viktor Grishin, and three junior CC secretaries: Ivan Kapitonov, Boris Ponomarev, and Konstantin Rusakov.[77] Extensive changes occurred in the CC apparatus, with at least seven department heads removed or transferred, as well as in the republic and regional party hierarchies, where four of fourteen republic party chiefs and at least forty-six regional first secretaries were replaced. These personnel changes were a continuation of a purge begun by Andropov and stepped up by Gorbachev in preparation for the Twenty-Seventh Party Congress held in March 1986. The Central Committee elected at the congress revealed the extent of the changes: the turnover in membership since the last congress in 1981 was approximately 40 percent.

The main vehicle used by Gorbachev in carrying out these purges was the anticorruption campaign. By the late summer of 1985 hardly a day passed without a report in the national or republic press of cases of bribery, embezzlement, or other forms of economic crime. Increasingly these cases involved higher-level officials, including *obkom* secretaries and republic ministers.[78] The republic party congresses in early 1986 offered spectacular revelations about how widespread economic crime had become, particularly in Kirgizia, Azerbaidzhan, Moldavia, and Uzbekistan. The MVD and the Procuracy came under heavy fire, and it was reported that numerous officials from these agencies were dismissed from their posts for their failure to uncover—and in some cases for collusion in—criminal activities by party and state officials.[79]

As it turned out, even the MVD chief, Fedorchuk, fell victim to Gorbachev's axe. In early 1986 he transferred from his post as chief of the MVD to that of a military inspector and advisor to the Group of General Inspectors under the Ministry of Defense.[80] This was a clear demotion. Possibly Fedorchuk was at odds with Chebrikov and others dominating the KGB after Andropov came to power; hence having served in the difficult job of heading the MVD during an anticorruption drive, he was then dispensed with. Fedorchuk's replacement as chief of the MVD, Aleksandr Vlasov, was a former party *apparatchik* with no experience in law enforcement. Vlasov hailed from Siberia and may have had some connections with Ligachev or Ryzhkov, but he had also served as a party executive in Gorbachev's home base of the North Caucasus.[81]

While the regular law enforcement agencies were subjected to sharp attacks for their failure to combat crime, the KGB remained unscathed. Despite the fact that it is actually empowered by law to conduct investigations into certain types of economic crime, in particular misappropriation of state property, the KGB was not held responsible for having allowed white-collar crime to become so pervasive. At the party congress in Kirgizia, for example, the new party chief, A. M. Masaliev, assailed the widespread phenomenon of bribery, criticizing several party officials and the regular law enforcement agencies. He also noted that the local military commissariat needed "serious improvement." But he then went on to stress pointedly that "the responsibilities of the KGB are increasing under conditions of exacerbated tension."[82]

The KGB underwent some turnover in key posts, but these changes were not nearly as widespread as they were in the party apparatus and other state agencies. Two high-level KGB officials were dismissed before the Twenty-Seventh Congress: V. I. Alidin, KGB chief for Moscow City and *Oblast*, and USSR First Deputy KGB Chairman Tsinev. These dismissals were not surprising in view of the advanced age of both men; Alidin was seventy-five and Tsinev almost seventy-nine.[83] Furthermore Tsinev's authority in the KGB, as noted earlier, had been weakening. At the republic level two KGB chairmen were removed during Gorbachev's first year, but neither was criticized and one, Kazakh KGB Chairman Zakash Kamalidenov, remained in the party bureau and was moved back to his former post as a republic CC secretary.[84]

Numerous signs pointed to the fact that the Gorbachev leadership was cultivating good relations with the KGB by maintaining its high prestige and political status. Chebrikov himself was made a Hero of Socialist Labor and featured prominently in the Soviet press during Gorbachev's first year. In June 1985 *Kommunist* published an article by Chebrikov in which he gave a lengthy account of the successful struggle being waged by the KGB against Western intelligence agencies and defended his organization against "slanderous allegations" by "bourgeois propagandists" of violations of human rights.[85] On 30 September Chebrikov received considerable publicity when he traveled to Iaroslav to confer an Order of the October Revolution on the city. His speech delivered on this occasion was given full coverage in the newspapers and was broadcast on Moscow Television.[86] Only a few weeks later, on 6

November, Chebrikov was again in the limelight when he delivered the October Revolution anniversary speech in the Kremlin.[87]

Meanwhile Chebrikov's former boss in the KGB, Iurii Andropov, had been glorified in a seventy-five-minute documentary that appeared on Moscow Television on 15 June 1985. The documentary included a substantial segment on Andropov's career as KGB chief, featuring an interview with KGB First Deputy Chairman Emokhonov, along with shots of Andropov with his KGB colleagues. Thus not only Dzerzhinskii but also Andropov had developed into a cult figure for the public to revere and worship.[88]

The new party program, which was approved before the congress, contained in the section on defense references to the importance of the state security organs that were not included in the previous program, adopted in 1961.[89] Given the significance of the party program for ideological and propaganda purposes, these changes, which might not seem meaningful at first glance, appeared to reflect the view that the USSR's political security was equally as important as its military might. The high standing of the KGB was further conveyed by the elections to republic and CPSU party bodies in early 1986. Republic KGB chairmen were elected to full membership on party bureaus in nine of fourteen republics, while they achieved candidate membership in the other five republics. This was a marked increase in KGB representation on the key policymaking body at this level. At the CPSU Congress the number of KGB officials elected to the new CC rose to five—four full and one candidate member—continuing the trend begun under Brezhnev of increased KGB representation on party bodies.[90]

Significantly, the KGB chairman delivered a speech at the congress for the first time since 1961, when Shelepin addressed delegates to the Twenty-Second Party Congress. Chebrikov's speech was an unprecedented assertion of the powers and authority of the KGB.[91] Speaking in unusually harsh terms about those who might consider going against the political grain, he disclosed that several Soviet employees of state organizations had recently been arrested by the KGB for passing state secrets to the West and twice reminded the audience that people who violated state security would get full retribution for their crimes. No effort was made by Chebrikov to reassure his audience that the KGB would observe socialist legality, as might have been expected in such a speech. In addition, Chebrikov seemed to broaden the concept of the KGB's role by mentioning the necessity of "cleansing society of all negative manifestations."

Gorbachev's second year as general secretary saw a continuation of

[99]

extensive personnel changes. While some of these changes bore his own stamp, Western analysts noted the increasing influence of the Siberian "mafia," led by Igor Ligachev, second in command to Gorbachev in the Secretariat, and Soviet Prime Minister Nikolai Ryzhkov.[92] As before, corruption and bribery served as the primary justifications for removing many of these officials, and heavy criticism of the law enforcement agencies persisted.[93] The new leadership's greatest success in moving against potential opponents was achieved in December 1986 when Dinmukhamed Kunaev, an old Brezhnev ally, was ousted from his post as first secretary of the Kazakhstan Communist party amid press reports of corruption and nepotism.[94]

Presumably the Gorbachev regime was still relying on the KGB's services in its drive to purge the party and state apparatus of corrupt officials. Evidence of the KGB's continued high stature appeared in the summer of 1986, when the press gave extensive coverage to its successful exposure of an alleged foreign spy.[95] The arrest in September 1986 of American journalist Nicholas Daniloff, however, suggested that the KGB might have been acting too zealously from Gorbachev's point of view. There is no evidence that this was an autonomous KGB action, but the fact that it threatened Gorbachev's arms control initiatives raises the possibility that certain elements in the leadership were using the KGB against Gorbachev.[96]

The KGB, for its part, cannot have been happy about the reformist policies Gorbachev was promoting with increasing zeal. The campaign for openness in the press, the liberalization of cultural norms, and the discussion of substantive changes in the economic system no doubt caused considerable unease at KGB headquarters. To state the obvious, these policies do not lend themselves to strong societal controls by the political police.

Calls for reform of the judicial and legal systems, voiced with increasing frequency in the autumn of 1986, were another ominous sign for the KGB. More and more, legal experts were emphasizing the necessity to protect individual rights by introducing greater access to the criminal process for defense lawyers and full publicity for trials.[97] The Politburo itself, meeting on 2 October, urged a "restructuring" (*perestroika*) of the work of the procuracy, the police, the courts, and *other law enforcement agencies* to protect citizens' interests and stressed that illegal interference in investigations must be stopped. This call was followed by a Central Committee resolution, published in *Pravda* on 30 November, on the strengthening of socialist legality. Although the KGB was not specifically referred to, the strongly worded resolution, calling for a halt to arbitrary violations of citizens' rights in the course of arrests and investigations, seemed to be intended for the KGB along with other legal institutions.[98]

This became clear when the KGB was publicly called to account for such illegalities in early 1987. Press criticism of the legal organs had never gone so far as to include the KGB, but this taboo was breached with the so-called Berkhin affair. According to press accounts, a journalist named V. Berkhin was unlawfully arrested in July 1986 on trumped-up charges of "hooliganism" because he had attempted to expose corruption in the Ukrainian region of Voroshilovgrad. The case was first brought to light in a 29 November *Pravda* article, which laid the blame on the local Procuracy.[99] In early January 1987 *Pravda* published another piece on this case, this time mentioning that the arrest was part of a carefully planned action coordinated by a candidate member of the party *obkom* bureau, one A. Dichenko.[100] Four days later, on the front page of *Pravda*, Chebrikov made the startling revelation that Dichenko was in fact chief of the Voroshilovograd KGB.[101] After noting that Dichenko had been expelled from the KGB and that a number of other local KGB officials had also been disciplined, Chebrikov went on to state that the KGB was taking measures to ensure that its activities complied with legal norms.

Such an acknowledgment of KGB abuses was unprecedented. Even during the Khrushchev era, when the crimes of Stalin's security police were exposed, the KGB itself was never criticized. Indeed it had seemed an unwritten rule that the KGB's image of infallibility should never be tarnished. The fact that Chebrikov publicly admitted that his organization was at fault, several months after the case had been exposed, suggests that he may have been pressured to do so.

While it appears that the Gorbachev leadership was motivated by a genuine desire to rein in the KGB and curtail its arbitrary actions against Soviet citizens, it is possible that some purely political concerns were also involved in the Berkhin case. The fact that the Ukrainian KGB was the focus of the attack was a blow to Shcherbitskii, party first secretary there. An article on the scandal in the Ukrainian party paper, which appeared on the same day as Chebrikov's announcement, had failed to mention the KGB's involvement.[102] Thus Shcherbitskii may have been unaware that the KGB was to be implicated. It was not until 15 February that Shcherbitskii acknowledged publicly that the KGB bore primary responsibility for the persecution of Berkhin.[103] Subsequent purges of the Ukrainian party and KGB apparatus, including the dismissal of Ukrainian KGB Chairman Mukha in June 1987, suggested that the

Kremlin leadership was undermining Shcherbitskii's power base in the Ukraine, which evidently included the republic KGB. Given that Chebrikov himself hails from the Ukraine and worked under Shcherbitskii in Dnepropetrovsk, he may have been resisting these attempts.[104] Interestingly, Mukha's replacement, N. M. Golushko, had worked in Ligachev's home territory of Tomsk, which may mean that Ligachev rather than Gorbachev was responsible for his appointment.[105]

Whatever the facts are surrounding the Berkhin affair, it marked a turning point for KGB-party relations because the party leadership indicated that it would no longer guarantee the KGB immunity from public criticism when its officials violate legal norms. Furthermore local party leaders were given the message that they could not with impunity enlist the KGB to suppress exposure of malfeasance in their regions. The public acknowledgment that the KGB involved itself in such illegal activities and exerted its authority over other law enforcement agencies was enough to suggest that such interference would be prevented in the future.[106] Many analysts have discussed the parallels between Gorbachev and Khrushchev in their political strategies and goals. Like Khrushchev, Gorbachev has confronted established interests and tried to gain legitimacy by appealing to popular support, using the time-honored method of mass mobilization. In his efforts to circumscribe the powers of the KGB, however, Gorbachev went further than Khrushchev did. Gorbachev may attempt to close the loopholes that permit the KGB to violate legal norms. By making the KGB vulnerable to public criticism he revoked the KGB's unwritten charter to act with impunity on the party's behalf.

The seriousness of Gorbachev's efforts to curb KGB powers was manifested further when the Kremlin announced in mid-February 1987 that it was releasing some 140 Soviet citizens who had been convicted and imprisoned under Article 70 of the RSFSR Criminal Code.[107] Investigations for violations under Article 70 (anti-Soviet propaganda and agitation) fall under the responsibility of the KGB, whose officials have used this article as a key weapon in suppressing dissent. The release of political prisoners, while clearly part of a broader effort to influence world opinion, was a blow to the prestige of the KGB and to its effectiveness in the struggle against dissent. A subsequent amnesty for certain categories of prisoners, announced in July 1987, omitted from release those charged with state crimes. But for the first time it included prisoners convicted under the lesser charge of "disseminating fabrications discrediting the Soviet system" (Article 190-1) and "organizing group actions that violate public order" (Article 190-3) as well as religious offenses.[108] It is also significant that a review of the Criminal Code was said to be under way, raising the possibility that laws against political dissent would be made less severe and narrower in scope.[109]

As Elizabeth Teague noted, Gorbachev moved from economic to political reform in his second year largely because he realized that some relaxation of social and political controls was a necessary prelude to significant economic changes.[110] It may also be the case that having depended initially on KGB support to purge the Brezhnevites, Gorbachev decided by early 1987 that he was strong enough to embark on reforms that might antagonize this institution. What have been the KGB's reactions to Gorbachev's policies? *Glasnost'* thus far does not include open political discussions, so we can only conjecture about the KGB's views. But it seems fairly clear that Gorbachev's policies are not greeted with favor by most elements in the security police. A clear indication that the KGB (or segments thereof) opposes Gorbachev's reforms appeared in *Izvestiia* on 14 March 1987 when a reader wrote to complain about "telebridges," or satellite-linked discussions in which both Soviet and American audiences participate. (These events are a hallmark of *glasnost'*.) Apparently in an appeal for support the outraged reader, expressing indignation about these "dirty, anti-Soviet shows," sent a copy of his letter to the USSR KGB.[111]

Some KGB officials admitted mistakes on the part of their organization and talked about the need for restructuring. Speaking at the April 1987 plenum of the Kirgiz Central Committee, Kirgiz KGB Chairman V. A. Riabokon acknowledged KGB shortcomings and stressed that the KGB's paramount task was to replenish its apparatus with mature party officials.[112] In an April 1987 interview in the newspaper *Trud*, USSR Deputy KGB Chairman G. A. Ageev noted that Chekists "wholeheartedly approve of the party's revolutionary decisions on the acceleration of socioeconomic development and on the restructuring and renovation of all spheres of Soviet society." But he did not fail to caution about "subversive actions to discredit our party decisions and a desire to distort the revolutionary nature of restructuring."[113]

After maintaining a low public profile throughout the spring and summer of 1987, Chebrikov made a comeback on 11 September, when he delivered a forceful speech in honor of the 110th anniversary of the birth of Vecheka Chairman Feliks Dzerzhinskii.[114] Chebrikov noted that the KGB was restructuring its operations and he paid obeisance to the "positive changes in the USSR and in the Soviet state's large-scale foreign policy initiatives." But he also warned that the West was using Soviet democratization for subversive purposes and he stressed the danger that extremist elements would push the reforms too far. He ended by stating that "a clear awareness is needed that restructuring is occurring in our state and society under the leadership of the Communist Party, within the framework of socialism and in the interests of socialism. This revolutionary process will be reliably protected against any subversive intrigues."

This amounted to an assertion that the KGB would not allow the reformist trends in the Soviet Union to get out of hand. And indeed, the subsequent ouster in November 1987 of Moscow *Gorkom* Chief Boris Eltsin, an outspoken proponent of restructuring, suggested that the conservative forces in the Kremlin have placed limits on the extent to which political liberalization will occur in the Soviet Union. There are already signs that Gorbachev's reforms are arousing opposition from several other quarters, including elements within the party leadership who see these changes as a threat to the party's predominance and to their own privileged positions. Judging from his public statements, Ligachev is a leading force behind this conservative backlash. The long-term implications of this opposition and the significance of the reforms Gorbachev has tried to introduce will be considered in the conclusions to this book. Suffice to say here that Gorbachev's opponents might try to enlist the support of the KGB, whose vested interests seem to be threatened by Gorbachev's policies. Gorbachev has demonstrated that the powers of the political police can be challenged, but this may entail paying a heavy price.

Notes

1. On this point see George Breslauer, *Khrushchev and Brezhnev as Leaders: Building Authority in Soviet Politics* (London: Allen & Unwin, 1982); and Seweryn Bialer, *The Soviet Paradox: External Expansion, Internal Decline* (New York: Alfred A. Knopf, 1986), pp. 41–46.

2. Stephen Cohen, *Rethinking the Soviet Experience: Politics and History since 1917* (New York and Oxford: Oxford University Press, 1985), p. 119.

3. For a detailed study of Andropov's career see the author's article, "Andropov: Myths and Realities," *Survey* 28, no. 1 (Spring 1984):22–44. Also see Zhores Medvedev, *Andropov* (New York: W. W. Norton, 1983).

4. Andropov's biographies do not tell us what CC department he worked in, but they do state that he was first an inspector and then head of a subdepartment. The Party Organs Department is the one department known to have had these institutions at the time. See Knight, "Andropov," p. 30.

5. Jiri Valenta, "Soviet Decisionmaking and the Czechoslovak Crisis of 1968," *Studies in Comparative Communism* 8, nos. 1–2 (Spring–Summer 1975):155–156. It should also be pointed out that Andropov was not really a party apparatchik in the strictest sense,

as much of his career had been spent in foreign affairs. The remarks of Soviet defector and former diplomat Arkady Shevchenko are illuminating in this regard: "At first I was surprised that so many KGB officers had immediately accepted Andropov as one of them. He had no background, either in the agency or the military. I finally realized that his previous position in the Central Committee as supervisor of the Soviet bloc empire was closely linked with KGB functions. They knew their man." Arkady Shevchenko, *Breaking with Moscow* (New York: Ballantine, 1985), p. 315.

6. For information on Tsvigun see his obituary in *Pravda*, 21 January 1982, p. 4. Also see his biography in *Deputaty VS SSSR* for the years 1966–1979. N. S. Zakharov, a first deputy since 1963, was edged out shortly afterwards. (Zakharov was a professional Chekist who had been chief of the Guards Directorate of the KGB since 1957.) See *Deputaty VS SSSR. sed'moi sozyv* (Moscow: Izvestiia, 1966), p. 167.

7. See *XIV s'ezd KP Tadzhikistana. Stenograficheskii otchet* (Dushanbe, 1961), pp. 247–251. As KGB chairman in Azerbaidzhan, he continued to warn in the most ominous terms of the dangers posed by Western intelligence services. See, for example, S. Tsvigun, "Bditel'nost'—nashe oruzhie," *Bakiinskii rabochii*, 10 October 1965, pp. 2–3.

8. See S. K. Tsvigun, ed., *Lenin i VChK* (Moscow: Politizdat, 1975); idem, *Feliks Dzerzhinskii* (Moscow: Politizdat, 1977); and his two novels: *My vernemsia* (Moscow: Sovetskaia Rossiia, 1971), and *Tainyi front* (Moscow, 1973). Tsvigun wrote a sequel to *My vernemsia* entitled "Uragan," which was serialized in *Ogonek*, nos. 21–45 (1981). Semenov, who has written several fictionalized works on the KGB, is rumored to have been Tsvigun's son-in-law.

9. See, for example, four articles written by Tsvigun for the journal *Kommunist*: "Borotsia s ideologicheskimi diversiiami vragov sotsializma," no. 11 (July 1969): 102–112; "Ideologicheskaia diversiia—orudie imperialisticheskoi reaktsii," no. 5 (March 1972): 109–118; "Podryvnye aktsii—oruzhie imperializma," no. 4 (March 1980): 108–119; and "O proiskakh imperialisticheskikh razvedok," no. 14 (September 1981): 88–99.

10. See his biography in *Ezhegodnik BSE*, 1977, p. 625, and *Deputaty VS SSSR. odinnadtsatyi sozyv* (Moscow: Izvestiia, 1984), p. 470.

11. In 1981 Chebrikov wrote an article on the threat posed to young people by Western propaganda. It appeared in *Molodoi Kommunist*, no. 4 (April 1981): 28–34. This suggests that he was still involved in personnel matters, as this journal is intended for Komsomol members, who are an important source of KGB recruits.

12. Biographical information on Tsinev, appears in *Ezhegodnik BSE* 1977, p. 624 and *Deputaty VS SSSR*, 1984, p. 465. Meanwhile to make room for these new figures, others were transferred out. USSR Deputy KGB Chairman S. G. Bannikov, who had served in Moscow since 1959, was named a deputy chairman of the USSR Supreme Court in October 1967, while KGB Lt. Gen. N. F. Chistiakov, a key official in investigating espionage cases, was also made a member of the court. See *Izvestiia* 13 October 1967, p. 3. Bannikov served in the Supreme Court at least until 1976. On Chistiakov's career see note 43, chapter 2. Another deputy chairman, A. I. Perepelitsyn, died not long after Semichastnyi's removal. Perepelitsyn was a former KGB chairman in Belorussia (1954–1959) and had served in the USSR KGB since 1959, thus working under both Shelepin and Semichastnyi. See his obituary in *Krasnaia zvezda* [hereafter *KZ*], 16 August 1967, p. 4.

13. See *Pravda*, 11 September 1976, p. 1. MVD chief N. A. Shchelokov, another member of the Brezhnev "mafia," was promoted to this rank at the same time.

14. On the birthday awards see *Pravda*, 5 May 1977, p. 1, and 28 September 1977, p. 1. On the new military ranks see *Vedomosti VS SSSR*, no. 51, 1978, item 847.

15. For a list of over 170 items published in connection with the fiftieth anniversary of the KGB, see *Soviet Intelligence and Security Services, 1964–70. A Selected Bibliography of Soviet Publications Prepared by the Congressional Research Service of the Library of Congress* (Washington, D.C.: U.S. Government Printing Officer, 1972), pp. 225–238.

16. Frederick Barghoorn, "The Security Police," in *Interest Groups in Soviet Politics*, ed. H. Gordon Skilling and F. Griffiths (Princeton, N.J.: Princeton University Press, 1970),

p. 108. This seminal article was the first among writings of Western Sovietologists to deal specifically with the contemporary Soviet security police.

17. See *Izvestiia*, 21 December 1967, p. 1, emphasis added.

18. N. Zakharov, "Polveka sluzheniia rodine," *Vechernaia moskva*, 20 December 1967, p. 2; and G. Tsinev, "Boitsy nevidimogo fronta," *Sovetskaia rossiia*, 20 December 1967, p. 3. Also see a speech by G. Badamiants, chairman of the Armenian KGB: "Na strazhe zavoevanii oktiabr'skoi revoliutsii," *Kommunist*, 20 December 1967, p. 2.

19. N. S. Aksenova and M. V. Vasil'eva, *Soldaty Dzerzhinskogo soiuza beregut. Rekomendatel'nyi ukazatel' literatury o chekistakh* (Moscow: "Kniga," 1972).

20. *Literaturnaia gazeta*, 19 May 1976, p. 3.

21. *Soviet Analyst* 6, no. 19 (28 September 1977):5.

22. *Literaturnaia gazeta*, no. 3, 17 January 1979, p. 2.

23. L. K. Korneshov, ed., *Chekisty. Sbornik* (Moscow: Molodaia gvardiia, 1972).

24. Ibid., p. 365. A similar description of a typical Chekist appears in a 1981 book on the state security organs in Azerbaidzhan: "All good Chekists are infinitely kind people. A Chekist is not a punisher; he is more like a doctor. Sometimes he is compelled to use painful surgical intervention. But this is only when it is necessary and on the basis of an exact diagnosis." Z. M. Iusif-Zade, ed., *Chekisty Azerbaidzhana* (Baku: Azerneshr, 1981), p. 229.

25. See *Pravda*, 10 September 1977, p. 1.

26. For an interesting study of how the Soviets have used the cult of Lenin to provide legitimacy and evoke patriotism, see Nina Tumarkin, *Lenin Lives: The Lenin Cult in Soviet Russia* (Cambridge, Mass., and London: Harvard University Press, 1983). Also see Stephan Burant, "The Influence of Russian Traditions on the Political Style of the Soviet Elite," *Political Science Quarterly* 102, no. 2 (Summer 1982):273–293.

27. The speech was reprinted in Iu. V. Andropov, *Izbrannye rechi i stat'i* (Moscow: Politizdat, 1979), pp. 272–276.

28. See reports in the various republic newspapers for the dates 18–21 December 1977.

29. For an interesting and informative treatment of the problem of corruption in the USSR, see Konstantin M. Simis, *USSR: The Corrupt Society. The Secret World of Soviet Capitalism*, trans. Jacqueline Edwards and Mitchell Schneider (New York: Simon and Schuster, 1982). Also see Nick Lampert, "Law and Order in the USSR: The Case of Economic and Official Crime," *Soviet Studies* 34, no. 3 (July 1984):366–385.

30. In September 1979 the party issued a decree entitled "Improving the Maintenance of Law and Order and Intensifying the Campaign against Violations of the Law." See *RLRB*, RL 285/79, 24 September 1979, for a discussion of this decree. In September 1981 a new law was adopted that made penalties much harsher for such economic crimes as accepting money for providing goods and services and withholding goods from sale. According to Western reports, a new campaign against economic crime was launched with a secret letter from the CC CPSU, read at closed party meetings all over the country, on the urgency of the problem. See Elizabeth Teague, "Anti-Corruption Campaign Turns up Well-Connected Suspects," *RLRB*, RL 100/82, 1 March 1982.

31. Republic MVD chiefs were replaced in Georgia, Kazakhstan, Tadzhikistan, Uzbekistan, and Estonia in 1979 and in Kirgizia and the Ukraine in 1982. Significantly, the head of the MVD's Main Administration for Combating the Embezzlement of Socialist Property (BKhSS) also was removed in 1981. On Procuracy dismissals, see *RLRB*, RL 284/80, 7 August 1980.

32. See, for example, "Usilit' bor'bu s *raskhititeliami* narodnogo dobra," *Sovetskaia kirgiziia*, 8 December 1981, pp. 1–2; G. Gvetadze, "Iskoreniaia formalizma," *Zaria vostoka*, 7 April 1981, p. 2; and a speech delivered by G. A. Aliev at a plenary session of the Azerbaidzhan Communist party, reprinted in *Baskiinskii rabochii*, 24 October 1982, pp. 1–6.

33. A. Inauri, "Na strazhe zavoevanii oktiabria," *Zaria vostoka*, 25 September 1980, pp. 2–3.

34. O. Komarov, "Brilliantovaia lenta," pts. 1–3, *Moskovskaia pravda*, 20–22 November 1981.

35. Significantly, the MVD's representation on the CC, one full and one candidate member, was the same as it had been in 1976. The KGB's representation on republic party bureaus also rose—to seven full and seven candidate members—whereas the MVD had had no officials represented in these bodies since 1956. Elections to the Supreme Soviet revealed similar trends. See chapter 5 for further discussion of KGB representation in party and state bodies.

36. See *XXVI s'ezd KPSS. Stenograficheskii otchet* (Moscow: Politizdat, 1981), I:84.

37. L. A. Plotnikova, ed., *Chekisty* (Leningrad: Lenizdat, 1982), pp. 6–7.

38. See a glowing review of the program in *Pravda*, 11 June 1982, p. 3.

39. *Sovetskaia Belorussiia*, 21 December 1982, p. 3.

40. On the scandal involving Brezhnev's family see Teague, "Anti-Corruption Campaign"; and Medvedev, *Andropov*, pp. 93–98. For a fascinating fictionalized account of Tsvigun's death see Fridrikh Neznansky and Edward Topol, *Red Square* (New York: Quartet Books, 1983). Brezhnev's failure to sign Tsvigun's obituary (*Pravda*, 21 January 1982) gave rise to speculation that there had been a rift between the two, but this is doubtful. Brezhnev's signature could have been omitted without his consent.

41. Following the sudden death of First Deputy Minister of Internal Affairs Viktor Paputin in December 1979, Churbanov was promoted—over the heads of more senior deputies—to the vacancy. By the early 1980s Churbanov was the subject of considerable publicity, and his activities and speeches were reported extensively in the press. On Churbanov see *Ezhegodnik BSE*, 1977, p. 626; *Posev*, no. 5 (1980):8; and Herwig Kraus, "A Further Promotion for Brezhnev's Son-in-Law," *RLRB*, RL 102/80, 5 March 1980. For an example of his views on the problems of law and order see "Na strazhe poriadka," *Kommunist vooruzhennykh sil*, no. 20 (October 1980), pp. 32–39. For a discussion of the MVD Internal Troops see chapter 7.

42. After he became chief of the internal affairs apparatus in 1966, Shchelokov's political fortunes seemed to flourish. He was elected a full member of the Central Committee in April 1968; he achieved the rank of Army general in 1976; and his articles appeared regularly in the most authoritative party publications. For biographical information on Shchelokov see *Pozharnoe delo*, no. 1 (January 1967); *Deputaty VS SSSR*, 1979, p. 494; and a biographical sketch written by Konstantin Grushevoi that appeared in *Voenno-istoricheskii zhurnal*, no. 11 (1980):94–96. Interestingly Grushevoi, a prominent military leader who apparently knew Shchelokov well, died in February 1982, not long after Suslov and Tsvigun.

43. *Zaria vostoka*, 26 December 1981, pp. 1–2.

44. Shevardnadze's biography appears in *Deputaty VS VSSR*, 1984, p. 484. Also see *RLRB*, RL 332/72, 27 November 1972. On the exposure of the Mzhavanadze scandal see Simis, *USSR: The Corrupt Society*, pp. 53–64.

45. On Fedorchuk, see *Deputaty VS SSSR*, 1984, p. 446; S. Z. Ostriakov, *Voennye chekisty* (Moscow: Voenizdat, 1979) p. 130; and Peter Deriabin with T. H. Bagley, "Fedorchuk, The KGB and the Soviet Succession," *ORBIS* 26, no. 3 (Fall 1982):611–636.

46. See Roman Solchanyk, "Ukrainian KGB Chief Warns of Ideological Sabotage," *RLRB*, RL 422/81, 22 October 1981.

47. See *KZ*, 23 February 1982, p. 1 and 4 April 1982, p. 4. There is a precedent for having two first deputy KGB chairmen. Tsvigun and Zakharov both occupied this position briefly in 1967. Evidence of conflict surrounding Chebrikov's appointment emerged much later, when the second revised edition of the *Military Encyclopedic Dictionary*, published in 1986, revealed that Chebrikov had in fact been appointed a first deputy KGB chairman in January 1982 but did not reveal the month of Tsinev's promotion. See *Voennyi entsiklopedicheskii slovar'*, 2d ed. (Moscow: Voenizdat, 1986), p. 805. The first edition of this dictionary, published in 1983, had omitted Chebrikov's name entirely despite the fact that he was already KGB chairman.

48. It has been suggested that Fedorchuk's appointment was a blow to the military establishment, as he was a former head of the KGB's Third Directorate, responsible for monitoring the political reliability of the Soviet armed forces. See Myron Rush, "Succeeding Brezhnev," *POC* (January–February 1983):4n. This may indeed have been the case, but it is

doubtful that concern over the military was the primary factor in Fedorchuk's appointment. The intense in-fighting over the Brezhnev succession was at the time the overriding element in all these key KGB appointments.

49. For details see Knight, "Andropov," p. 42.

50. The three, apparently new deputy chairmen were S. N. Antonov, G. F. Grigorenko, and V. A. Kriuchkov. One of the dismissed republic KGB chairmen, V. T. Shevchenko, head of the Kazakhstan KGB, may have had connections with Brezhnev, as he served in the state security organs in Kazakhstan during Brezhnev's tenure there from 1954 to 1956. For other changes see appendix E.

51. See Jerry F. Hough, "Andropov's First Year," *POC* (November–December 1983): 49–64. Among the Kirilenko men who may have supported Andropov were Nikolai Ryzhkov, named CC secretary in November 1982; Nikolai Sliun'kov, named first secretary of Belorussia in January 1983; Vitalii Vorotnikov, who was made chairman of the RSFSR Council of Ministers in June 1983; and Igor Ligachev, who was named head of the Organizational-Party Work Department in April 1983. Hough claims that Chebrikov was also a Kirilenko protégé, as he worked under Kirilenko in Dnepropetrovsk, but this is by no means certain.

52. For biographical information on Aliev see *Deputaty VS SSSR*, 1979, p. 21, and Il'ia Zemtsov, *Partiia ili mafiia* (Paris: Reunis, 1976), pp. 70–90. Relations between Brezhnev and Aliev had always seemed close; the latter went out of his way to heap fulsome praise on the party chief, but Aliev may have been disappointed with Brezhnev's failure to promote him to a post in Moscow.

53. See interviews with Aliev in *Pravda*, 1 August 1979, p. 2; *Literaturnaia gazeta*, 18 November 1981, p. 4, and his speech cited in note 32.

54. Robert Sharlet, "Soviet Legal Policy under Andropov: Law and Discipline," in *Soviet Politics: Russia after Brezhnev*, ed. Joseph L. Nogee (New York: Praeger, 1985), pp. 85–106 (quotation, p. 94). Also see *Izvestiia*, 19 December 1982, p. 1. There is a precedent in the post-Stalin era for naming a state security official to head the regular police: V. S. Tikunov became minister of internal affairs in 1961 after serving for two years as a deputy KGB chairman. But Tikunov was basically a party *apparatchik* and not a career Chekist.

55. *Pravda*, 11 December 1982, p. 1.

56. Alidin stated, "Moscow Chekists will help the party and the people to solve economic problems successfully and to overcome negative phenomena—to stop the activity of plunderers of socialist property and eradicate bribery." See "Vsegda v stroiu," *Moskovskaia pravda*, 19 December 1982, p. 2.

57. A. Rekunov, "Bez sniskhozhdeniia," *Pravda*, 9 January 1983, p. 3.

58. V. Fedorchuk, "Na strazhe pravoporiadka," *Pravda*, 10 August 1983, p. 1. Somewhat later Fedorchuk announced that "a number of measures had been passed" for strengthening the ties of the internal affairs apparatus with state security organs. See *Agitator*, no. 19 (October 1983):29–32.

59. This change was revealed when Trushin was identified as first deputy chief of the MVD in *Moskovskaia pravda*, 29 December 1983. Churbanov was arrested on corruption and bribery charges in early 1987. See *Moscow News*, no. 8, 22 February 1987, p. 9.

60. The two USSR MVD officials were Boris Shumilin, a deputy MVD chief since 1968, and Valerii Luk'ianov, head of the Main Administration of State Motor Vehicle Inspection (GAI). See *Sobranie postanovlenii pravitel'stva SSSR*, no. 13 (1983); and *RLRB*, RL 344/83, 14 September 1983. The three republic MVD ministers who were dismissed were K. E. Ergashev, Uzbekistan (July 1983); E. G. Patalov, Armenia (November 1983); and G. N. Zhabitskii, Belorussia (December 1983). Patalov was replaced by the republic deputy procurator, A. S. Shaginin, who had previously served fourteen years in the security police. See *RLRB*, RL 421/83, 8 November 1983.

61. See *Izvestiia*, 16 July 1983, p. 1; and *RLRB*, RL 344/83.

62. *Pravda*, 27 April 1983, p. 2. Also see note 47, where it was noted that Chebrikov was not listed in the *Military Encylopedic Dictionary*. Both Tsinev and Fedorchuk were included.

63. *Pravda*, 27 October 1983, p. 4.

64. *Pravda*, 5 November 1983, p. 1, and 27 December 1983, p. 1. Another curious development involving Chebrikov was the fact that his travels to Eastern Europe were publicized in the press, which was unusual for a KGB chief. See chapter 9.

65. See chapter 6 for a discussion of these changes.

66. See, for example, Marc Zlotnik, "Chernenko Succeeds," *POC* (March–April 1984):17–31.

67. *Literaturnaia gazeta*, no. 20, 16 May 1984, p. 2.

68. See Chernenko's biography in *Deputaty VS SSSR*, 1984, p. 472. Interestingly, Border Guards Chief Matrosov was first identified as a USSR deputy KGB chairman in November 1984, when Chernenko was general secretary. See *KZ*, 16 November 1984, p. 3.

69. See *Pravda*, 21 February 1984, p. 3, and *KZ*, 20 April 1984, p. 1.

70. See, for example, Alexander Rahr, "The Party's Darling," *RLRB*, RL 102/85, 29 March 1985; and Archie Brown, "Gorbachev: New Man in the Kremlin," *POC* (May–June 1985):1–23 (esp. pp. 14–15).

71. Brown, "Gorbachev," and Terry McNeill, "Grigorii Vasil'evich Romanov, the Other Heir Presumptive?" *RLRB*, RL 24/85, 25 January 1985.

72. See *Pravda*, 26 June 1984, p. 2; *Partiinaia zhizn'*, no. 4, 1984, pp. 17–22; Ann Sheehy, "Major Anti-Corruption Drive in Uzbekistan," *RLRB*, RL 324/84, 30 August 1984; *Izvestiia*, 16 July 1984, p. 6; and *Pravda*, 26 July 1984, p. 2. An interview in *Literaturnaia gazeta* in August with MVD Chief Fedorchuk added to the impression that the positions of many party *apparatchiks* were threatened.

73. *Pravda*, 23 May 1984, p. 1.

74. His biography appeared in *Deputaty VS SSSR*, 1984, p. 145.

75. See *Izvestiia*, 9 November 1984, p. 4. A month later, faced with a trial for his misdeeds, he reportedly committed suicide. See *FBIS. Daily Report, Soviet Union* 3 (17 December 1984):R8.

76. See chapter 4 for further details on Romanov and the AO Department.

77. For an analysis of the changes in leadership over this period, see three articles by Elizabeth Teague, "Gorbachev Consolidates His Position," *RLRB*, RL 201/85, 20 June 1985; "The Twenty-Seventh Party Congress: Changes in the Politburo and Secretariat," *RLRB*, RL 111/86, 6 March 1986; and "Turnover in the Soviet Elite under Gorbachev: Implications for Soviet Politics," *RLRB* Supplement 1/86, 8 July 1986. Also see Thane Gustafson and Dawn Mann, "Gorbachev's First Year: Building Power and Authority," *POC* (May–June 1986), pp. 1–19.

78. See, for example, *Pravda*, 7 August 1985, p. 3; 20 October 1985, p. 2; and 29 October 1985, p. 2; *Izvestiia*, 14 August 1985, p. 6, and 10 September 1985, p. 6. Also see republic newspapers for this period and Elizabeth Teague, "Pockets of Opposition to Kremlin Policies," *RLRB*, RL 39/86, 22 January 1986.

79. See, for example, *Pravda*, 27 January 1986, p. 2; *Sovetskaia Kirgiziia*, 24 January 1986, pp. 1–5; *Bakiinskii rabochii*, 1 February 1986, pp. 1–5; *Pravda vostoka*, 31 January 1986, pp. 2–6; and Elizabeth Teague, "Attempts to Clean up Corruption in Soviet Law Enforcement Agencies," *RLRB*, RL 42/86, 23 January 1986. The extent of the purge in the MVD was revealed in May 1987, when it was announced that 100,000 employees had been dismissed in the past five years. See *Isvestiia*, 27 May 1987, p. 6.

80. See *Izvestiia*, 26 January 1986, p. 3; and *XXVII s'ezd KPSS. Stenograficheskii otchet* (Moscow: Politizdat, 1986), 3:547.

81. Vlasov's biography appears in *Deputaty VS SSSR*, 1984, p. 91. Also see Uri Ra'anan, "Before and after Chernobyl: Stresses in the Soviet Leadership," *ORBIS* 30, no. 2 (Summer 1986):249–258 (esp. p. 250).

82. *Sovetskaia kirgiziia*, 24 January 1986, p. 5.

83. Alidin had been in the KGB since at least the mid-1960s and had served as chief of the Moscow KGB since 1971. He was replaced by an official named N. E. Chelnokov. See *Moskovskaia pravda*, 27 May 1986, p. 1. Tsinev, like Fedorchuk, was made a member of the Group of General Inspectors of the Ministry of Defense. See *Voennyi entsik. slovar'*, 1986,

p. 803. It might be added that the list of delegates to the Twenty-Seventh Party Congress revealed that G. F. Grigorenko and S. N. Antonov, identified as USSR deputy KGB chairmen in 1981, were no longer in these posts. These men had long careers in the KGB and were well into their sixties. They may have left their posts shortly after Brezhnev died, as there was no mention of them in the press after 1981. Two new deputy chairmen (presumably their replacements) were identified among the delegates: V. A. Ponomarev (former chief of the KGB for Vladimir City and *Oblast*) and I. A. Markelov, whose former position is unknown. See the list of delegates printed in *XXVII s'ezd KPSS*, vol. 3. On Ponomarev see Vladimir Bukovskii, *Vladimirskaia tiurma* (New York, 1977), p. 66.

84. See *Kazakhstanskaia pravda*, 11 December 1985, p. 1. Kamalidenov, who was replaced by V. M. Miroshnik, may well fall victim to the extensive purges of the Kazakh party in the wake of Kunaev's dismissal. The other change was in Kirgizia, where N. P. Lomov was replaced by V. A. Riabokon. *Sovetskaia kirgiziia*, 28 December 1985, p. 1. In addition, K. P. Pulatov, First Deputy Chairman of the Tadzhik KGB, was appointed to head that republic's MVD in early 1986—a sign that the movement of KGB officials into MVD was a continuing trend despite the fact that the new USSR MVD chief was a party rather than a KGB man. See *Kommunist Tadzhikistana*, 21 January 1986, p. 1.

85. V. Chebrikov, "Sverias s Leninym, rukovodstvuias trebovaniem partii," *Kommunist*, no. 9 (June 1985):47–58.

86. See *Izvestiia*, 1 October 1985, p. 2.

87. *Pravda*, 7 November 1985, pp. 1–2.

88. *FBIS. Daily Report, Soviet Union* 3 (20 June 1985):R3. Signs of this cult had actually begun to appear earlier. In June 1984, for example, an article devoted to Andropov's seventieth birthday appeared in *Kommunist*. The article, which was biographical in form, did not fail to discuss Andropov's many accomplishments as head of the KGB. Interestingly, one of the authors, P. P. Laptev, had served as Andropov's personal assistant in the KGB and is currently first deputy chief of the CC General Department. The other, V. Sharapov, is currently one of Gorbachev's assistants. See P. Laptev and V. Sharapov, "Kommunist, goriachii patriot sotsialisticheskoi rodiny," *Kommunist*, no. 9 (June 1984):87–96. It might be added that a 1986 survey of literature on the Cheka indicated that several new publications appeared in 1985. See A. L. Litvin (Kazan'), "VChk v sovetskoi istoricheskoi bibliografii," *Voprosy istorii*, no. 5 (May 1986):96–102. Such continued glorification of Lenin's political police reflects favorably on the KGB.

89. The text of the new party program appeared in *Pravda*, 7 March 1986, pp. 3–8. In the section on defense the new program reads: "The CPSU regards the defense of the socialist homeland, the strengthening of the country's defense, *and the safeguarding of state security* as one of the most important functions of the Soviet state of the whole people" (emphasis added). In the earlier program "safeguarding of state security" had not been mentioned. The next paragraph contains a reference to the importance of "reinforcing the USSR's defensive might and *strengthening its security*"—with the last part omitted in the 1961 program.

90. The four full members from the KGB are Chebrikov, First Deputy Chairmen N. P. Emokhonov and F. D. Bobkov, and Deputy Chairman V. A. Kriuchkov. The candidate member from the KGB is G. A. Ageev, a deputy chairman. In addition, P. P. Laptev was elected to the Central Auditing Commission. The number of KGB delegates to the congress is close to what it was in 1981. See chapter 5 for more details.

91. *Pravda*, 1 March 1986, pp. 5–6.

92. On the Siberian "mafia" see Dawn Mann, "Is There a Siberian Mafia?" *RLRB*, RL 302/86, 29 July 1986.

93. For continued criticism of the law enforcement agencies for corruption—particularly in Moldavia, Latvia, and Uzbekistan—see, for example, *Sovetskaia moldavia*, 20 April 1986, p. 2; *Pravda*, 25 July 1986, p. 3; *Izvestiia*, 23 July 1986, p. 4, and 2 December 1986, p. 3.

94. On the political upheaval in Kazakhstan see *Pravda*, 17 December 1986, p. 2; *Izvestiia*, 24 January 1987, p. 3; *Pravda*, 11 February 1987, p. 2, and 9 March 1987, pp. 1, 3;

and Bess Brown, "Progress of Cleanup in Kazakhstan," *RLRB*, RL 79/87, 23 February 1987. It is important to note that Kunaev's replacement as party chief there, G. V. Kolbin, appears to be a member of the Siberian "mafia." See his biography in *Deputaty VS SSSR*, 1984, p. 200.

95. See *BBC Summary of World Broadcasts*, SU/8351/C1/1, 30 August 1986, for an account of a Soviet television program on the KGB's exposure of alleged spy Ilia Suslov.

96. It might be noted that Gorbachev was reported to be on vacation and away from Moscow at the time of the incident.

97. See, for example, *Literaturnaia gazeta*, 24 September 1986, p. 13, and 17 December 1986, p. 13; and *Izvestiia*, 4 October 1986.

98. *Pravda*, 3 October 1986, p. 1, and 30 November 1986, pp. 1–2.

99. Ibid., 29 November 1986, p. 6.

100. Ibid., 4 January 1987, p. 1.

101. Ibid., 8 January 1987, p. 1.

102. *Pravda ukrainy*, 8 January 1987, p. 1.

103. See *Pravda*, 15 February 1987, p. 2, for Shcherbitskii's comments. He had even failed to mention the KGB when he discussed the case at a journalists' congress on 14 February. See *Pravda ukrainy*, 15 February 1987, pp. 1–2.

104. Probably the most ominous personnel change for Shcherbitskii (and also perhaps for Chebrikov) was the dismissal of Dnepropetrovsk *Obkom* First Secretary V. G. Boiko, who had worked under both men in Dnepropetrovsk. See *Pravda*, 18 March 1987, p. 2.

105. See *Pravda ukrainy*, 26 May 1987, p. 1.

106. The Berkhin affair became even more scandalous when it was reported that Berkhin died in July 1987 as a result of his "illegal arrest." See *FBIS Daily Report, Soviet Union*, 22 October 1987, p. 52, citing a report in *Meditsinskaia gazeta*.

107. *Pravda*, 13 February 1987, p. 2.

108. For the text of the amnesty, see *Izvestiia*, 19 July 1987, p. 2

109. See chapter 6 for details. It might be added that Gorbachev's remarks about the state security organs made in his speech to the CC Plenum at the end of January 1987 can hardly have been reassuring to those at KGB headquarters. In contrast to the usual laudatory references to the security police made by party leaders, Gorbachev's words were unusually curt and restrained. See *Pravda*, 28 January 1987, p. 5.

110. Elizabeth Teague, "Gorbachev's First Two Years in Power," *RLRB*, RL 94/87, 9 March 1987.

111. "Uchit nenavisti?" *Izvestiia*, 14 March 1987, p. 7.

112. *Sovetskaia kirgiziia*, 14 April 1987, p. 7.

113. *Trud*, 19 April 1987, p. 4.

114. *Pravda*, 11 Sept. 1987, p. 3.

II
The Structure of the KGB

4

The KGB: Functions, Organization and Party Control

Given the highly sensitive nature of the KGB's role in the Soviet political system, it is not surprising that official sources are reticent about its functions and organization and even less forthcoming on how it is controlled by the party. However much the Kremlin leadership attempts to portray the KGB as a legitimate government institution that fits into the framework of the state bureaucracy, the KGB's very purpose precludes any straightforward official description of how it operates and what the parameters of its authority are. On the basis of what evidence we do have it appears that the KGB's official tasks are not clearly circumscribed but are fluid, depending on the political circumstances at any given time. This enables the regime to be flexible in using the political police as a means of both ensuring society's compliance with its rule and implementing foreign policy objectives. At the same time, because it is not monitored by the government or the party through the usual channels, the KGB has more operational autonomy than most other Soviet institutions. These points are illustrated in the following discussion of the KGB's role and organization as a government institution and the mechanisms for party control over the KGB.

Official Status and Role

The Committee of State Security (KGB) was established, on the basis of instructions from the CPSU Central Committee, by a decree (*ukaz*) of the Presidium of the USSR Supreme Soviet on 13 March 1954. No details on the KGB's purpose and functions were offered in the decree, which was ratified as a law by a full session of the USSR Supreme Soviet on 26 April 1956 and published in *Pravda* two days later.[1] The KGB was originally designated as a "state committee attached to (*pri*) the USSR Council of Ministers." Article 70 of the 1936 USSR Constitution was amended to include the KGB chairman as a member of the Council of Ministers (which was not an ex officio right of state committee chairmen). When the new USSR Constitution was adopted in 1977, Article 128 stated only that chairmen of state committees *of* the USSR were included in the Council of Ministers and did not mention the KGB. However, it was stipulated that heads of other agencies could be included, so presumably the KGB chairman retained this right.

On 5 July 1978 a new law on the USSR Council of Ministers changed the status of the KGB, along with that of several other state committees, to a "state committee *of* the USSR" (KGB USSR).[2] This meant that its chairman was henceforth a member of the USSR Council of Ministers by law. This could be an important distinction considering that the KGB is under the formal authority of the Council of Ministers. The USSR Council of Ministers is, according to the 1977 Constitution, the highest executive and administrative agency of the Soviet state. It "coordinates and directs" the work of the ministries and state committees and confirms their operational statutes and organizational structure. In exercising "systematic control," the Council of Ministers is empowered "to rescind acts of the USSR State Committees and to impose disciplinary punishments on its chairmen and deputy chairmen." It also has the right to designate the deputy chairmen of state committees, and to confirm the membership of their collegia, or highest decision-making bodies.[3] Although the powers of the Council of Ministers laid down by the Constitution apply to most ministries and state committees, they probably do not extend to certain key institutions, such as the KGB, the Ministry of Defense, and the Ministry of Foreign Affairs. By most accounts these latter bodies, dealing as they do with crucial matters of defense and security, are under the direct control of the party, and their subordination to the Council of Ministers is merely a formality.[4]

The situation is similar with the dual-chamber USSR Supreme

Soviet, which ostensibly has the ultimate authority over the Council of Ministers and its agencies, including the KGB. According to the Constitution, the Supreme Soviet forms the Council of Ministers and the latter is accountable to it. Any changes in the composition of the Council of Ministers, including the dismissal or appointment of ministers or chairmen of state committees, are supposed to be approved by the USSR Supreme Soviet. In addition, the USSR Supreme Soviet has the exclusive right to pass legislation concerning the obligations of ministries and state committees, which would include determining the scope and definition of crimes coming under the KGB's investigative purview.[5]

As most Western experts acknowledge, however, the powers of the Supreme Soviet are more ceremonial than real. It is a large, unwieldy body (composed of over 1500 delegates) and meets usually no more than twice a year for a few days to "rubber stamp" decisions that have already been reached by the party leadership. Between sessions the Presidium of the Supreme Soviet, consisting of some thirty-nine members, has the formal authority to exercise legislative and executive functions. It is assisted by several permanent, or standing, commissions composed of Supreme Soviet deputies who are to take part in the preparation of legislation, discuss policy issues, and supervise state agencies and organizations on behalf of the Supreme Soviet.[6]

The Legislative Proposals Commissions of each of the two chambers of the Supreme Soviet, which are charged with working out draft laws relating to the legal and judicial system and hearing reports by ministries and state agencies on questions of socialist legality, apparently have some formal oversight for the judicial and legal organs, including the KGB.[7] In theory the commissions have the right to request documents from ministerial agencies, as well as written responses to questions. The commissions also can request the personal appearance of the head of any agency before the commission and submit recommendations for actions to these agencies. However, the commissions have no authority to implement their requests and do not have the services of a permanent staff of experts. Additionally, in the case of the Legislative Proposals Commissions their authority over the KGB is diluted by the fact that members of the KGB actually serve on these commissions.[8]

As a USSR state committee with ministerial status, the KGB operates on the basis of a statute (*polozhenie*), which is confirmed by the USSR Council of Ministers and sets forth in legal terms the KGB's rights and duties. Unlike the majority of statutes governing ministerial agencies, which are published, this is not the case with the KGB and certain other agencies, including the Ministry of Defense.[9] Nevertheless Soviet text-

[117]

books on administrative law have offered some useful statements on the KGB's role and functions as perceived by the Soviet leadership.

During the first two decades of its existence the KGB's tasks were defined generally as encompassing four areas: the struggle against foreign spies and agents; the exposure and investigation of political crimes by Soviet citizens; the guarding of the USSR's state borders; and the protection of state secrets.[10] A 1979 Soviet legal textbook, edited by Iu. Kozlov and published by the prestigious Institute of State and Law of the USSR Academy of Sciences, gave a much broader interpretation of KGB functions, presumably because the concept of state security had expanded in scope by this time. A detailed and lengthy chapter written by Iu. T. Mil'ko on the administration of state security and the tasks of the KGB reflects a more open approach to this issue on the part of the regime as part of its ongoing effort to publicize and legitimize the KGB in the eyes of the Soviet public.[11] The discussion begins with the basic factors involved in ensuring the security of the Soviet state, which is presented as a "social and political" process, an aggregate of measures by numerous state agencies carried out in conjunction with military efforts. These measures include general "preventative" ones, such as "creating favorable external political and internal governmental conditions for overcoming the subversive actions of the enemy," and the more specific tasks of struggling against hostile actions. According to Mil'ko, the KGB takes an active part in both types of effort. Thus in addition to combating espionage and state crimes, the KGB "actively participates in working out and coordinating general preventative measures of ensuring state security, collaborating with ministries and agencies, their institutions, enterprises and organizations."[12] This implies a role in both domestic and foreign policymaking.

Mil'ko goes on to explain that the competence of the state security organs has changed over the years and depends on external and internal circumstances at any given time. "Under present circumstances," it is noted, "the external political security of the Soviet state acquires an especially important significance."[13] Recall that 1979 marked the beginning of a period of international tension and a deterioration of relations between the Soviet Union and the West. Thus it is not surprising that the problem of state security acquired special importance for the Soviet regime. The crucial point, however, is that by the end of the 1970s the role of the KGB appears to have expanded far beyond the functions ascribed to it·in the late 1950s and early 1960s.

It is instructive to cite in full the passage from Mil'ko describing specific KGB functions in 1979:

the timely exposure of aggressive plans and subversive acts being prepared by imperialists, which present a threat to the security of the USSR and other socialist countries; the prevention of espionage, terrorism, diversion and other subversive acts of intelligence and other special services of imperialist states and anti-Soviet organizations abroad; the protection of state secrets; the organization and guarding of USSR state borders and the prevention of their violations; the struggle against subversive political and ideological acts against the USSR by special services of the enemies, anti-Soviet centers abroad and other hostile elements; the timely exposure of circumstances giving rise to politically harmful manifestations and subversive activity by the enemy and taking measures to eliminate these circumstances; the active participation in prophylactic work of the organs of the Soviet state, directed towards liquidating crime in the country.[14]

Interestingly this passage makes an implicit reference to the foreign espionage, counterespionage and intelligence-gathering activities of the KGB by referring to the "timely exposure of aggressive plans and subversive acts" of the enemy and the prevention of espionage against the USSR. Moreover the passage indicates that in addition to foreign operations, guarding the border, and investigating crimes against the state, the KGB is also charged with a wide range of so-called prophylactic activities that are designed to eliminate circumstances giving rise to both political and ordinary crimes among Soviet citizens. In other words, the KGB is to ferret out potential threats to the state and ensure that unorthodox political and social attitudes do not develop among the population.

While changes in the Code of Criminal Procedure from 1961 onward have provided a legal basis for the expansion of the KGB's purview in investigating crimes—in particular its involvement in non-political economic crimes—these changes do not specify the prophylactic measures to suppress criminal and dissident attitudes or the involvement in policymaking that are suggested in the quotation. Such functions have thus accrued to the KGB on an ad hoc basis, presumably because the leadership has increasingly relied on this organization to ensure political and social stability. It might be added that statements in legal textbooks such as the foregoing have been confirmed by numerous other official sources and also by considerable practical evidence, discussed elsewhere, showing that the KGB has placed increasing emphasis on such methods as propaganda, reeducation, and "persuasion" to carry out its basic function of protecting state security.

[119]

Structure

The KGB is a union-republic state committee operating through corresponding state committees of the same name in the fourteen non-Russian republics. (All-union ministries and state committees, by contrast, do not have corresponding branches in the republics but execute their functions directly through the government of the USSR.) Below the republic level there exists in the *krais* and *oblasts* (regional territorial divisions) KGB administrations (*upravleniia*). There is no separate KGB for the RSFSR; *oblast* KGB administrations in the RSFSR are subordinated directly to the USSR KGB. At the lower levels in autonomous *okrugs*, or areas, the larger cities and *raions*, or districts, exist KGB *otdely* or *otdeleniia* (departments or sections). This was not always the case. Apparently as part of an overall program designed to reduce the manpower of the state security organs, *okrug*, *raion*, and most city departments were abolished when the KGB was created in 1954. Not until after 1970 were they reestablished.[15] The KGB also has a broad network of so-called special departments in all major state institutions, enterprises, and factories. They usually consist of one or more KGB officials whose purpose is to ensure that security regulations are observed and to monitor political sentiments among employees.[16] A separate network of special departments, discussed in chapter 8, exists within the armed forces. Finally, the KGB enlists the cooperation of large numbers of informers, who report regularly on the activities and opinions of their fellow citizens.

As a rule, union-republic ministries and agencies are less centralized than all-union ministerial agencies because some of their functions devolve to the branches. This is not the case with the KGB, which is highly centralized and controlled rigidly from the top. This characteristic was stressed by Mil'ko in 1979:

> As a whole the administration in the KGB operates on the same general principles as those of all union-republic state committees. However, this does not exclude a number of special characteristics, relating to a high degree of centralization. This is reflected above all in the fact that the basic planning-regulatory functions, the direction of the most important lines of struggle with subversive activity of the enemy, generalization of experience, control over the execution of measures to ensure state security, and selection and placement of leading cadres are concentrated in the USSR KGB. . . . This high degree of centralization in the sphere of state security, the strict uniformity of all chains of the administrative system, gives the USSR KGB the possibility of conducting its policies on an all-union level.[17]

Thus it would appear that the KGB at the center keeps tight control over the operations of its branches, leaving the latter little autonomous authority over policy or cadre selection. Moreover it seems that local government organs have little involvement in local KGB activities and personnel appointments. Indeed, as Mil'ko and others have pointed out, the high degree of centralization in the KGB is reflected in the fact that regional KGB branches are not subordinated to the local Soviets but only to the KGB hierarchy.[18] Thus they differ from branches of most union-republic ministerial agencies, such as the MVD, which are subject to dual subordination.

The KGB is directed by a chairman who is formally appointed by the USSR Supreme Soviet, one or two first deputy chairmen, and several (usually four to six) deputy chairmen, who are appointed in theory by the USSR Council of Ministers. The chairman of the KGB has a great deal of authority. He issues instructions and gives orders (formally in accordance with the laws and decrees of the government), which are obligatory for all elements of the KGB apparatus. He confirms statutes and regulations that apply to KGB bodies and "has the right to control the activity of all units of the committee, both at the center and in the localities."[19] Key decisions are made by the KGB Collegium, which is a collective leadership body composed of the chairman, deputy chairmen, chiefs of certain KGB departments, and one or two chairmen of republic KGB organizations.[20]

KGB officers have military ranks analogous to those of the Soviet army. Thus the current KGB Chairman, Chebrikov, and at least one of his two first deputies, Emokhonov, are Army generals, while deputy KGB chairmen are usually colonel generals. Republic KGB chairmen have ranks of lieutenant or colonel general, and their deputies and chiefs of regional KGB administrations are, as a rule, major generals. These ranks are higher than they were in the 1960s and early '70s. Semichastnyi, KGB chairman from 1958 to 1961, was only a colonel general, as was Andropov until 1976, when he became an Army general. Republic KGB chairmen usually ranked no higher than major general at this time.[21]

Official Soviet sources do not discuss the internal structure of the KGB beyond what has already been presented. Nevertheless some information on how the KGB is organized has been revealed by Soviet defectors and other sources that have been passed on to government, academic, and journalistic circles in the West. Although the information may be contradictory or outdated and as such cannot be accepted as fact, it is possible, by combining and cross-checking information from several sources, to come up with what is probably a fairly accurate picture of the basic organizational structure of the KGB. Indeed, this structure has been outlined in numerous Western publications, so it will be only briefly recapitulated here.[22]

The KGB is organized into six chief directorates and three to four directorates, as well as various other administrative and technical support departments. Open source Western estimates of KGB manpower have ranged from 490,000 in 1973 to 700,000 in 1986.[23] The First Chief Directorate is responsible for all foreign operations and intelligence-gathering activities. Estimates of its manpower in the late 1960s were in the range of 10,000 employees, but presumably it has grown significantly since then. The First CD is divided into both functional services—training and management of covert agents, intelligence analysis, collection of scientific and technological intelligence, "active measures" and so forth—and geographic departments for different areas of the world. This directorate reportedly recruits the best-qualified personnel of all the KGB directorates, those with a strong academic record and a higher education, knowledge of one or more foreign languages, and, not surprisingly, a flawless background in terms of political reliability. Those who work in this directorate apparently are considered the elite of the KGB, and their colleagues in the domestic services are viewed as less fortunate and slightly inferior.[24]

According to John Barron, KGB officers from the domestic side of operations do sometimes transfer to so-called Directorate K of the First Chief Directorate, which is responsible, among other things, for the supervision of Soviet citizens abroad.[25] In general, however, the personnel of the First CD, while working closely with the domestic apparatus in many situations, have careers that are separate from those serving inside the country, except at the very highest levels of the KGB.[26] This is not surprising in view of the fact that KGB officials within the Soviet Union are usually publicly identified as such, whereas those working abroad keep their identity secret. In addition, the training needs of foreign and domestic employees are quite different.

The first official who could be identified as heading the First CD was Colonel General Aleksandr Mikhailovich Sakharovskii. According to information from his obituary, which appeared in the Soviet press in 1983, and from a Western press report, Sakharovskii served in this post from about 1956 to the early 1970s.[27] He was a career Chekist who had joined the NKVD in 1939 at the age of thirty and rose in the ranks of the security organs. Sakharovskii was succeeded by a protégé of Andropov, Col. Gen. Vladimir Aleksandrovich Kriuchkov, who apparently retains this post today, serving simultaneously as a deputy chairman of the

KGB.[28] Kriuchkov was born in 1924 and, after a two-year stint in the Komsomol, began a career in the Procuracy in 1946. By 1956 he was in the diplomatic corps (ostensibly), serving as third secretary in the Soviet embassy in Budapest while Andropov was ambassador there. (Interestingly his official biography as a deputy to the Supreme Soviet, appearing in 1984, fails to mention his diplomatic service.) He followed Andropov to the Central Committee in 1959, working as head of a sector in the Department for Liaison with Ruling Socialist Countries. Judging from the articles he wrote while serving in this department, his main responsibility was Hungary.[29] When Andropov became KGB chairman in 1967 he brought along Kriuchkov, who started as head of the KGB Secretariat and rose rapidly in the hierarchy, becoming a deputy chairman by 1978.

The Second Chief Directorate is responsible for internal political control of Soviet citizens and foreigners residing within the Soviet Union, including both diplomats and tourists. In dealing with the latter, the Second Directorate works closely with the First Directorate. Barron claims that six of the twelve numbered departments in the Second Directorate are concerned with subverting foreign diplomats and denying them contact with Soviet citizens, while other departments exist specifically for dealing with tourists and foreign students.[30] In addition, there are departments for KGB investigations of political crimes, economic crimes, informant networks, and so on. Although there is no firm evidence of his position, Oleg Mikhailovich Gribanov was identified by several sources as head of the Second CD from approximately 1956 to the mid-1960s.[31] His successor has not been identified, but evidence suggests that from the mid-1970s to the mid-1980s Grigorii Fedorovich Grigorenko may have held this post.[32] Grigorenko, about whom there is little information, was not a delegate to the last party congress, so he is probably no longer in this post.

The Fifth Chief Directorate also deals with internal security. Created in the late 1960s to combat political dissent, it has taken up some of the tasks previously handled by the Second Chief Directorate. The Fifth CD has special operational departments for religious dissent, ethnic minorities, the intelligentsia and artistic community, and censorship of literature, as well as other issues. According to one source, Filipp Denisovich Bobkov, who became a deputy chairman of the USSR KGB in 1982, is chief of the Fifth CD. A long-time police professional, Bobkov joined the state security organs in 1945 at age twenty. In late 1985 Bobkov became a first deputy USSR KGB chairman, replacing Tsinev.[33]

The Seventh Directorate handles surveillance, providing personnel and technical equipment to follow and monitor the activities of both foreigners and suspect Soviet citizens. Much of this work is centered in the Moscow and Leningrad areas, where tourists, diplomats, foreign students, and members of the Soviet intelligentsia are concentrated. V. I. Alidin was reported by one source to be chief of the Seventh Directorate in 1967; he became chief of the KGB Administration for Moscow City and *Oblast* in 1971, and his successor was not identified.[34]

The Eighth Chief Directorate is responsible for the highly sensitive area of communications. This directorate provides technical systems, including cipher systems for other KGB departments and government agencies, and also monitors and deciphers foreign communications. According to Western reports, S. N. Lialin was chief of the Eighth Directorate before he became head of the KGB for Moscow City and *Oblast* in 1967. Lialin had a military-technical education and had entered the state security organs in 1951. Subsequently his KGB career was severely damaged by the defection of his nephew, Oleg Lialin, as a member of a Soviet trade delegation in September 1971.[35] This defection resulted in the expulsion of 105 Soviet officials from Britain. Evidence indicates that the head of the Eighth Directorate after 1968 was current First Deputy KGB Chief Nikolai Pavlovich Emokhonov. A former aviation ministry official with a higher degree from the Military Communications Academy, Emokhonov came to the KGB to head a directorate in 1968. Given his background, it seems likely that he was responsible for the Eighth Directorate, at least until he became a first deputy chairman in 1983.[36]

The KGB has at least three additional directorates, which will be discussed in subsequent chapters. The Third Chief Directorate, or Directorate of Special Departments, concerns itself with military counterintelligence and political surveillance of the Soviet armed forces. The Chief Directorate of Border Troops is responsible for guarding all Soviet land and sea borders, and the Ninth Directorate has the highly important function of guarding the Kremlin and key offices of the Communist party.

In addition to the various directorates and a special network of training and educational establishments, the USSR KGB has a personnel department, secretariat, technical support staff, finance department, archives department, administrative department, and party committee. Most of these bodies are duplicated within the different directorates. The party committees, which exist in every Soviet organization, have the function of political indoctrination of personnel. Heads of party committees arrange regular meetings to discuss party matters and serve as a liaison between the party and KGB at various levels, though it might be added that party membership is probably universal among KGB employees.[37]

Presumably at the republic level the KGB is organized in a similar way to that of the USSR KGB, though republic KGBs would not supervise border troops, which are administered separately. Nor would they include an element of the Third Directorate, which is organized primarily along service lines or by military district. In addition, functions such as communications and foreign espionage may be administered only in Moscow. It might be noted, however, that several republic KGBs exist in areas that border sensitive and highly strategic countries, such as Iran, Turkey, and Afghanistan. Thus the republic KGB organizations probably assist Moscow in carrying out sensitive intelligence missions across the border.

Party Control of the Security Police:
The CC Administrative Organs Department

Although the Soviet security police has always been a state rather than a party institution, the party has considered this agency to be its own vital arm and has sought to maintain the closest supervision and control over its activities. Thus when the Vecheka was established in December 1917, it was attached to the Council of People's Commissars (Sovnarkom), but the party leadership soon established its own mechanisms of authority over this body. Today the KGB is a USSR State Committee and hence nominally part of the Council of Ministers, but in reality it is the party, not the government, that exercises direction over this organization. As one Soviet source states, "the Communist party keeps its [KGB] activity under its unremitting control, offering a great deal of assistance in its practical work."[38]

Since the Soviet political police is a highly centralized institution that operates with a great deal of autonomy, party control over its activities has been concentrated in the top levels of the party apparatus. Aside from the Politburo, which probably issues general policy directives, another vehicle for such party control is thought to be the Administrative Organs Department of the CC Secretariat. Little has been written in the West about the Administrative Organs Department or its predecessor agencies. The organization and functions of the CPSU departments are never discussed explicitly in the Soviet press, and our information about how they operate is fragmentary.[39] This is particularly true

[125]

with the Administrative Organs Department, which is involved in the sensitive area of party supervision not only over the security police but over other legal organs and also defense institutions. Nevertheless it is possible on the basis of open sources to consider the history, functions, and role of the Administrative Organs Department in order to assess its importance as an organ of party control over the security police.

Forerunners of the AO Department

Initially the mechanisms for party control over the political police were vague, and before Lenin became incapacitated by illness in mid-1922 such control was exercised mainly on an ad hoc personal basis. According to George Leggett, Lenin himself personally watched over police activities in his dual capacity as party leader and chairman of the Sovnarkom.[40] Lenin's task was made easier by the fact that Vecheka chief Dzerzhinskii was always a loyal party servant who could be counted on to place the interests of the party above those of the institution he directed. As a member of the Central Committee, a candidate, later a full member, of the Orgburo and by 1924 a candidate member of the Politburo, Dzerzhinskii provided the link between the police and the party leadership.

When the party did attempt to create some formal mechanism for controlling the Vecheka, Stalin played a significant part. He served on a couple of short-lived three-man commissions formed by the Central Committee and the Defense Council to inquire into the Vecheka's activities. In early 1919, as a result of widespread criticism of the Vecheka, Lenin decided to subordinate it directly to the Politburo by having a Politburo representative sit on the Vecheka collegium with right of veto. Initially Nikolai Bukharin served as the representative, but Stalin succeeded him in 1920.[41]

Even more important for Stalin was his increasing domination over the party bodies responsible for selection of security police personnel. The party emphasized control over personnel as a key weapon for maintaining its authority over the police, and concerted efforts were made to staff the security police with trusted party members.[42] Initially it was the Orgburo, a preserve of Stalin's, that arranged for the posting of party officials to the Chekas. Gradually, however, the Secretariat, though in theory subordinate to the Orgburo, began to take precedence over the latter institution. After 1924 the main agency for all personnel appointments within both the party and government was the Organization and Assignment Department (*Orgraspred*) of the Secretariat. Leonard Schapiro, noting that Orgraspred became the key department of the Secretariat, wrote: "Its history is the story of Stalin's success in controlling the party."[43] According to the evidence Orgraspred also contributed to Stalin's success in dominating the police apparatus.

Most Western scholars have assumed that the main party body for control over the security police was the so-called Special, or Secret, Department of the CC Secretariat, which is known to have existed since about 1922.[44] Their assumptions were based on the fact that the Soviets themselves were reticent about the functions of this department, which indicated that its role was very sensitive. It also appears that this department was either closely tied with Stalin's personel secretariat or was in fact merged with it.[45]

According to emigré accounts, Stalin's secretariat and/or the Secret Department served as a link between Stalin and the security police, arranging highly secret assignments, such as the murder of Kirov and the assassination of Trotsky.[46] There is some confusion in these accounts, however, with an organization that existed within the police apparatus itself. Apparently both the OGPU and its successor, the NKVD, had a so-called Secret Political Department (*Sekretnyi-politicheskii otdel*), which carried out reprisals, including murder, against Stalin's opponents. In 1935 G. A. Molchanov, an NKVD official, was identified in the Soviet press as chief of this department.[47] Although this was distinct from the CC Secret or Special Department, their similar designations may have led to confusion about their functions. Adding to the confusion was the fact that the security police also had a Special Department (*Osobyi otdel*) for military counterintelligence.[48]

Considering that the CC Secret Department apparently had responsibility for handling classified documents and secret correspondence among the leadership, there is little doubt that it had close contact with the security police, particularly in implementing the purges of Stalin's opponents. But it seems that some police-related functions have been incorrectly attributed to this body, which basically served as a secretariat for the Politburo, the Orgburo, and the party Secretariat. According to the evidence cited by Schapiro, the CC Secret Department was not the forerunner of the Administrative Organs Department but of the General Department of the CPSU, which today serves as the chancery of the Central Committee.[49] The first predecessor agency of the Administrative Organs Department and hence the key organ of party control over the police was, as Schapiro hypothesized, more than likely Orgraspred.

[127]

When Orgraspred was created in 1924 it included sections for the various branches of both the party and state administration, including, presumably, one for the security police and legal and defense organs. After the CC Secretariat was reorganized in 1930 cadre responsibilities for party and state were split, and a separate Assignment Department was established to serve the personnel needs of the state machinery. Among the subsections of the Assignment Department was one for "Soviet Administration," which most probably concerned itself with what the Soviets today call "administrative organs"—the police, legal, judicial, and defense apparatuses.[50] When, in 1934, this subsection emerged as an independent CC department, the Political Administration Department, its task as described at the Seventeenth Party Congress was "to keep watch on party aspects of work in general Soviet organs, in the Red Army, its Political Directorate, in procuratorial organs and others."[51]

It is significant that a key figure in the system of party supervision over the security police was N. I. Ezhov, who was to become head of the NKVD in 1936. Ezhov was appointed chief of Orgraspred in 1930, and although it is not clear to which department he moved when Orgraspred was split later that year, he seems to have maintained a hand in supervising state security cadres. After becoming a CC secretary in early 1935, Ezhov is reported to have been responsible for overseeing administrative organs. Indeed, as Medvedev remarked, it was not surprising that Ezhov was appointed people's commissar of internal affairs, as he had been "checking NKVD activity for the CC."[52]

When, in 1939, the tasks of cadre selection were again concentrated in one body of the Secretariat, the CC Cadres Administration, Georgii Malenkov was placed in charge of it while at the same time becoming a CC secretary. Malenkov had served as Ezhov's assistant when Ezhov was CC secretary and had headed the CC Department of Leading Party Organs since 1935. Malenkov's main concern was with party cadres, but he also involved himself with state security affairs. In late 1938 he served, along with Beria, Molotov, and Vyshinskii, on a special CC subcommittee to investigate the activities of the NKVD; and Beria, chief of the NKVD from 1938 to 1946, was a close ally.[53] It is noteworthy that Beria relinquished his post as head of the NKVD in 1946, the same time that Malenkov was forced out of the Secretariat.

From 1946 to 1948, according to Khrushchev, A. A. Kuznetsov, a protégé of Andrei Zhdanov from Leningrad, assumed secretarial responsibilities for the political police.[54] Malenkov, who regained his position in the Secretariat in 1948, launched a plot with Beria against the

Leningrad group and managed to have Kuznetsov removed. Malenkov probably resumed the function of secretarial oversight for administrative organs, at least for two or three years. In 1948, as a result of yet another reorganization of the Secretariat, the Cadres Department was abolished and a separate Administrative Department was established.[55] By the early 1950s this was referred to as the Administrative Organs Department, a designation that has remained to this day.

The continual reorganizations and personnel changes within the CC apparatus that took place from 1948 until Stalin's death make it difficult to identify with certainty who was serving as chief of the AO Department. It appears, however, that several officials from the Main Political Administration (MPA) entered the department during this time. Among them were V. E. Makarov, who may have headed the AO Department in 1950–1951; V. V. Zolotukhin, who became a deputy department chief and apparently had close ties with Khrushchev; and N. I. Savinkin, who was to become AO Department chief in 1968.[56] The influx of MPA officials into the Administrative Organs Department may have been part of a general attack against Malenkov and Beria carried out by Stalin in 1951–1953 with the help of Khrushchev and others.[57] Indeed, the fact that these officials remained in their posts after the defeat of Beria and Malenkov indicates that their recruitment may have been a result of Khrushchev's influence.

Whatever role the Administrative Organs Department and its forerunners may have had in implementing party control over the security police during the Stalin era, the principal authority in this area was always Stalin himself. As Antonov-Ovseenko notes:

> It was a well-established custom in the Politburo for each member to oversee a certain area of governmental concern. But to say that Stalin "oversaw" the Organs [of state security] is to say nothing. He was constantly preoccupied with these agencies and never for one moment let the activities of the People's Commissar of Internal Affairs and the deputy commissars out of his sight.[58]

N. R. Mironov and the AO Department under Khrushchev

With Stalin's death, the defeat of Beria and the introduction of numerous measures to institute a regime of "socialist legality," the party agency responsible for overseeing the security police assumed a more important and more authoritative role. The existence of the AO Department was now mentioned openly in the Soviet press and its officials became more visible than they had been in the past. This was particularly the case after Khrushchev defeated the anti-party group in 1957 and launched his de-Stalinization campaign.

The official who did the most to raise the stature and influence of the AO Department and increase its effectiveness as an agency of party control over the police and legal organs was Nikolai Mironov. Mironov, who headed the department from 1959 to 1964, was an important figure whose career deserves attention.[59] Born in 1913 in Brezhnev's hometown of Dnepropetrovsk, Mironov worked in Komsomol and trade union organizations there before enrolling in 1937 in Dnepropetrovsk State University, where he managed to obtain a higher education by the outbreak of the war. According to the memoirs of Konstantin Grushevoi, Mironov was recruited by Brezhnev to serve as a military-political officer in June 1941.[60] He returned to Dnepropetrovsk after the war, serving as first secretary of the Oktiabrsk *Raion*, where he worked under Brezhnev, who was first secretary of the Dnepropetrovsk *Obkom* at the time. Mironov also was under the authority of Khrushchev, first secretary of the Ukraine. Mironov must have pleased his party bosses because he was promoted to first secretary of the Kirovograd *Obkom* only two years later. In 1951 he was brought to Moscow to serve in the military counterintelligence apparatus of the state security organs. He remained there, surviving the extensive purges of the police, until 1957, when he was appointed chief of the Leningrad KGB.

In 1959 as the de-Stalinization campaign gained momentum, Mironov replaced A. S. Zheltov, a former MPA chief, as head of the Administrative Organs Department.[61] At the same time, Shelepin protégé V. S. Tikunov, who had served in the AO Department since the early 1950s, rising to become a deputy chief, moved to the post of deputy chairman of the USSR KGB.[62] Mironov's arrival in the AO Department was followed by significant changes in both KGB and MVD personnel.[63] Unlike his predecessor, Mironov was a dynamic figure who soon emerged as a key spokesman for the campaign to institute a regime of socialist legality. During 1960–1964 he wrote no fewer than seven articles, which appeared in the most authoritative party and legal journals, as well as two books on the subject of strengthening legality and increasing party control over the police and legal organs. Mironov's writings, though far from revolutionary, were a radical departure from Stalinist concepts of law and reflected the spirit of innovation that characterized the Khrushchev era. Insofar as was possible within the framework of the Soviet political order, he advocated concrete steps to rid the legal system of its arbitrary nature and to make it an effective instrument of the party.

Mironov's approach was similar to that of Soviet legal theorists in the 1920s, in that he argued for lenient treatment of first offenders and those whose offenses were not of a serious nature. Mironov claimed that reeducation and persuasion, not imprisonment, were more effective in dealing with most crimes.[64] At the same time, he was a staunch advocate of severe punishment, including death, for more serious crimes. In his writings Mironov promoted Khrushchev's plans to have certain government functions transferred to "public organizations." He was a keen supporter of voluntary public-order squads, for example, to assist the militia in combating minor crimes.[65] Mironov was openly critical of the MVD, the Procuracy, and the courts for their failure to deter crime effectively and for corruption in their ranks, and he decried the widespread practice of interference by party officials in the judicial process to protect party members from prosecution.[66]

De-Stalinization was another major theme in Mironov's writings, which contain lengthy accounts of the crimes committed by Stalin and other leaders during the period of the "cult of personality." What is striking about his statements on the Stalin era is that they were considerably more explicit and strongly worded than most official accounts.[67] Yet while Mironov was outspoken on the past crimes of the state security organs, he took pains to stress that the party had taken strong measures to eliminate the "remnants of the cult of personality" in the state security organs and to ensure that socialist legality would not be violated.

In an effort to restore the damaged image of the security police and make its struggle against internal subversion more effective, Mironov argued for more "prophylactic" and "persuasive" measures, rather than physical compulsion. The KGB, he urged, should try to reform persons with subversive views by calling them in for educational talks and reporting their anti-Soviet views to their work collectives or Komsomol organizations so that group pressure could be applied. He urged KGB officials to make contact with the public by speaking at meetings and public gatherings.[68]

As chief of the Administrative Organs Department, Mironov had a substantial impact on party policy toward the state security apparatus and other legal organs from 1959 to 1964. Perhaps because he was a former KGB official, Mironov may have favored the security police over the regular police, but he also campaigned vigorously for an increase in party controls over the entire legal system, including the KGB, and he made the AO Department a key agency for implementing these controls. It is worth noting, for example, that the AO departments of several

[131]

republic central committees, which had been abolished in 1956–1957, were reestablished under Mironov's leadership.

Former GRU Colonel Oleg Penkovskiy, executed by the Soviets as a spy in 1963, offered an idea of just how powerful Mironov and his department were under Khrushchev:

> The Central Committee has a so-called Administrative Organs Department. Its chief is Nikolay Romanovich Mironov. He is a former high officer of the KGB. This section has nothing at all to do with administrative matters. It directs the work of the KGB, the Ministries of Internal Affairs of the Union Republics, the courts, the procurator's office, and us, the GRU. This Mironov is czar and God over us. Everything goes to him, and from him to Khrushchev and other members of the Presidium of the Central Committee CPSU. . . . Our General Serov stands at attention before him, indeed before any employee of his section.[69]

On 19 October 1964, just days after Khrushchev's ouster, Mironov died in a plane crash in Yugoslavia, along with First Deputy Minister of Defense and Chief of the General Staff Sergei Biriuzov and several other leading military officials.[70] There was considerable speculation in Moscow about the crash, and suggestions arose that it might not have been accidental. Mironov's policies and his loyalty to Khrushchev were said to have incurred the wrath of Shelepin and Semichastnyi, who therefore had strong motives for getting him out of the picture.[71] Adding to the speculation was the fact that Biriuzov had also been a source of controversy. As another loyal Khrushchevite, Biriuzov had supported Khrushchev in efforts to strengthen the role of the MPA and to reduce the size of the ground forces, thus causing disfavor among the Army high command.[72]

Whatever the facts are involving Mironov's death, it marked the beginning of an apparent decline in the influence of the AO Department. No successor was named to take his place until 1968, when N. I. Savinkin assumed the post of department chief. Apparently Savinkin had served as acting chief before this, but some controversy had delayed his formal assumption of the post. Many of the reforms advocated by Mironov (and Khrushchev) were reversed after Brezhnev came to power, particularly those involving the internal affairs apparatus.[73] Perhaps most significant of all the reversals was the fact that the de-Stalinization campaign was brought to a swift halt. A heavily edited version of a book written by Mironov in 1964 and re-published posthumously in 1969 demonstrated clearly that the new party leadership wished to revise many of the views he had expressed.[74] Unlike the first edition, there were no references in the new version to the crimes of the Stalin era; nor was there any mention of inefficiency and corruption within the MVD and Procuracy or of illegal party interference in the judicial process.

Savinkin, who has remained at the head of the AO Department to this day, has maintained a lower profile than Mironov. According to Michael Voslensky, he has not enjoyed the authority of his predecessor mainly because control over the KGB has been exerted at a higher level within the party.[75] Born in 1913, Savinkin did political work in the Soviet Army during the war and then attended the Lenin Military-Political Academy, graduating in 1950 and joining the staff of the AO Department in that year. Unlike Mironov, he has no legal training or background and has written little on the subject of the Soviet security and legal organs. He is said by some to have been a protégé of Brezhnev, but considering that he has survived in his post beyond the Brezhnev era, it is more likely that he is simply a loyal, uncontroversial party functionary.[76]

Organization and Functions of the AO Department

The Administrative Organs Department, as it has existed since the beginning of the Khrushchev era, has as its primary function that of party control over those organizations of the Soviet state classified as "administrative" or "administrative-political": the Ministry of Defense, Civil Aviation, DOSAAF, the MPA, GRU, Ministry of Internal Affairs, courts, Procuracy, and KGB.[77] The activities of leading AO personnel as well as their signatures on obituaries illustrate the department's oversight, at least in formal terms, for these administrative agencies. Thus for example, Savinkin and his deputies attend conferences, meetings, and ceremonies involving the military, the KGB, and other legal organs. According to emigré sources, the AO Department also supervises the drafting of legislation in order to ensure that the party's will is followed.[78]

The way in which party control is implemented over administrative agencies is not set forth explicitly in any published party rules or documents, but apparently the AO Department approves personnel appointments and exercises general oversight to ensure that these organizations are following party directives. A former deputy AO chief explained the functions of this department and its subordinate departments in overseeing the legal organs:

> One of the basic tasks of the administrative organs departments of party committees is constant control over the fulfillment of tasks assigned to

[133]

the militias, investigative agencies, the Procuracy, the courts and the corrective-labor institutions. This control must be efficient and specific. The employees of the departments must study and prepare suggestions for the further improvement of the activity of these organs, ensure the proper selection and training of cadres, resolutely suppress violations of the law by officials, strengthen the ties of the militia, courts and Procuracy with the public, improve the style of leadership of the lower branches of these organs by the republic and oblast apparatus.[79]

The KGB is included in the category of investigative organs and thus is under the formal purview of the AO Department. According to a former investigator from the Procuracy, Fridrikh Neznansky, the KGB's personnel appointments, along with all those in the legal system, are subject to approval by this department.[80] Nevertheless it is probable that the extent of supervision exercised by the AO Department varies considerably from organization to organization. The KGB is rarely mentioned specifically as being subject to such oversight, and it may well be that the party leadership gives the AO Department a freer hand with the MVD, Procuracy, and judiciary than with such highly centralized institutions as the KGB and the Ministry of Defense.

The Administrative Organs Department is directed by a chief, a first deputy chief, and two to three deputy chiefs. Below these officials are sector chiefs, who take charge of specific areas of the department's activities. Although no more than three sector chiefs could be identified for one period of time, there are probably more sectors for the different areas under the department's purview. Table 4.1 lists those officials who could be identified as serving in the AO Department from the early 1950s to the present, along with, wherever possible, their areas of oversight.

According to Peter Solomon, who based his information on interviews with Soviet criminologists, in the period from 1964 to 1968 the Legal Affairs Sector was small, including only five or six employees in all.[81] Solomon also notes that

> the duties of this sector were mainly supervisory and concerned with questions of cadres and policy execution. In the course of supervision, department instructors collected information about the legal system so that their superiors, the Department Chiefs, might keep informed about the legal realm. But neither the instructors themselves nor their departmental superiors played a large part in the initiation or advocacy of policy proposals.[82]

Although Solomon's reconstruction of the functions of this sector conforms with other information, it seems doubtful that a staff of only

TABLE 4.1
Administrative Organs Department of the CPSU Central Committee: 1955–1987

CHIEFS, DEPUTIES, AND SECTOR CHIEFS

A. S. Zheltov (1958–1959)
Chief

    V. V. Zolotukhin (1955–1960)
    Dep. Chief

N. R. Mironov (1959–1964)
Chief

    A. P. Uskov (?–1969)
    Sector Chief

    C. I. Grachev (1963–1968)
    Dep. Chief

N. I. Savinkin (1964–1968)
Acting chief, (1968–   )
Chief

    A. I. Ivanov (1967–?)
    Sector Chief

    N. P. Malshakov (1968–1971)
    First Dep. Chief

    V. I. Gladyshev (1974–1983)
    Dep. Chief

    V. I. Drugov (1975–Jan. 1986)
    First Dep. Chief

    V. A. Lepeshkin (Nov. 1977)
    Dep. Chief

    A. N. Soshnikov (1983–   )
    Dep. Chief (air defense, MPA, KGB
      border guards)

    V. A. Abolentsev (1985–   )
    Dep. Chief (Procuracy, judiciary)

    A. S. Pavlov (Feb. 1985–   )
    Chief, Legal Affairs Sector

A. A. Startsev (Sept. 1955–?)
Dep. Chief

V. S. Tikunov (early 1950s–1959)
Sector, Dep. Chief

N. I. Savinkin (1950–1964)
Dep., First Dep. Chief

K. I. Nikitin (June 1963–1966)
Chief, Legal Affairs Sector

V. I. Laputin (1963–1969)
Dep. Chief

A. Ia. Sukharev (1966–1970)
Chief, Legal Affairs Sector

S. A. Shishkov (1971–1978)
Chief, Legal Affairs Sector

A. E. Volkov (1972–?)
Sector Chief

I. P. Potapov (1973–   )
Sector Chief

A. I. Goliakov (Dec. 1974–   )
Sector Chief (DOSAAF)

V. V. Zamotin (1983–1986)
Sector Chief (civil aviation)

V. E. Sidorov (Mar. 1984–   )
Sector Chief (militia)

O. S. Beliakov (Jan. 1986–   )
Sector Chief (civil aviation; military)

I. A. Larin
First Dep. Chief (Aug. 1986–   )

NOTE: The information presented here was reconstructed by the author from identifications of these officials in the Soviet press. In most cases dates represent first or last time that an official was identified in the press, rather than the date of appointment or dismissal.

five or six would be sufficient to perform these tasks. While it is possible that the staff of the AO Department was cut after Mironov's death in conjunction with a decline in the department's authority, most of the sectors are probably larger than this. Considering that the chief, deputy chiefs, and sector heads spend much of their time attending official functions and meetings, they must have a fairly substantial staff to perform the daily business of the department.

Another source, a former Central Committee official with the pseudonym Pravdin, whose statements appear in a 1974 issue of *Survey*, claimed that the AO Department had six deputy chiefs.[83] He did not give figures on the number of sectors or the total AO staff but noted that each sector includes inspectors and instructors (junior employees responsible to the sector chiefs) and support staff. Assuming that the AO Department has more than three sectors (considering that sector chiefs for sensitive areas such as state security and defense might not be identified), it seems that a total staff of forty to fifty responsible workers plus technical support would be a reasonable approximation. This conforms with Pravdin's estimates on the size of other CC departments.

According to Soviet sources, administrative organs departments exist within republic central committees (where they are divided into sectors, as they are at the national level), as well as within the bureaus of *krai* and *oblast* party committees, and within some party bureaus of the larger cities.[84] Judging from reports in the Soviet press, republic AO officials perform much the same role as that of their counterparts in the central party apparatus. Chiefs and deputy chiefs of republic AO departments address seminars on socialist legality, militia gatherings, conferences of Procuracy officials, and plenums of republic supreme courts. The fact that AO officials not only appear but also speak at such gatherings indicates that they have a certain amount of authority over these organizations. We also have evidence from the press that AO Department heads do participate in selecting personnel for the regular law enforcement agencies, though apparently their authority is sometimes usurped by the party first secretary.[85] As far as the KGB and the military are concerned, the press reports only the attendance of AO chiefs at ceremonies to honor these institutions, so we have no way of knowing what role they play.

Further insights into the functions of the Administrative Organs departments, both at the national and republic level, are offered by looking at information on the background and career patterns of AO officials. Mironov has been the only CPSU AO chief with previous experience in the state security apparatus. Among the deputy and sector chiefs at this level, the only other identifiable career connection with the KGB is that of V. S. Tikunov, who moved from the AO department in 1959 to the post of deputy chairman of the USSR KGB and later, in 1961, became chief of MOOP. Most CPSU AO officials on whom there is career information have been former party apparatchiks who subsequently moved not into the KGB but into the MVD, Procuracy, or judiciary. Military connections are also uncommon, with the exceptions being the initial group from the MPA that entered the department in the 1950s and the recently appointed first deputy chief of the AO Department, Lt. Gen. I. A. Larin, who served previously in the Ministry of Defense.[86] The usual pattern has been a move from deputy chief or sector head to a post of deputy minister of one of these legal agencies, indicating, as Solomon pointed out, that AO officials are by no means superior in rank to the officials they supervise.[87] The most recent example of this pattern is V. I. Drugov, first deputy chief of the AO Department since 1975, who became a deputy chief of the MVD in early 1986.[88]

Somewhat more data are available on career backgrounds at the republic level. Of nineteen AO department chiefs serving in the period 1955–1987 on whom information exists, the majority came from party posts within the republic, while three had served in the legal or judicial apparatus and only one in the KGB. Of the twenty republic AO chiefs on whom subsequent career data are available, one half moved to the MVD or judicial organs and six assumed party posts, while only two AO chiefs transferred to the KGB (see table 4.2).

This information suggests that like their superiors in Moscow, republic party officials who supervise Administrative Organs have career ties mainly with the party itself and the ordinary legal and judicial organs, rather than with the security police or defense institutions. Other sources have confirmed this impression.[89] The fact that significantly more AO officials move to positions in the regular legal or judicial organs than into the KGB indicates that the former areas have been their primary concern during their tenure in administrative organs departments. It might be added that republic AO Department chiefs rarely are members of the republic party bureaus. If they exercised real authority over the security agencies, including personnel appointments, it might be expected that their status would be equal to that of heads of party cadres departments, who are often bureau members.

If, as it seems, republic AO chiefs have substantially less involvement with the KGB than with other administrative agencies, how is party control over the KGB exercised at this level? Given the KGB's key political task of suppressing internal dissent, it might be assumed that

[137]

TABLE 4.2
Republic AO Department Chiefs: Career Transitions, 1955–1987

FROM		TO	
Party Apparatus		*Party Apparatus*	
Sec. *obkom*	1	Chm., Rep. Party Control	3
1st Sec., *raikom*	3	Commission	
1st Sec., *gorkom*	2	1st Sec., *gorkom*	1
2nd Sec., *gorkom*	1	2nd Sec., *gorkom*	1
Rep. AO Dept.	2	CC Dept. Chief	1
Other CC Dept., Chief	3		
1st Sec. Rep. Komsomol	1		
Legal and Judicial Organs		*Legal and Judicial Organs*	
Dep. Rep. MVD	2	Rep. MVD Chief	6
Member, Rep. Sup. Court	1	1st Dep. MVD Chief	1
		Chm., Rep. Sup. Court	1
		Rep. Min. Justice	1
		Rep. Procurator	1
Other		*Other*	
Chm., Rep. State Commt.	2	Chm., Rep. State Commt.	
		for Labor Reserves	1
Rep. KGB	1	Chief, Rep. Main Archive Admin.	1
		Dep. Chm., Rep. KGB	1
		Chm., Rep. KGB	1
Total	19	Total	20

NOTE: Data for this table were compiled from reports in republic newspapers; selected *Deputaty verkhovnogo soveta* for certain republics; republic encyclopedias; Grey Hodnett and Val Ogareff, *Leaders of the Soviet Republics, 1955–72* (Canberra: Australian National University, 1973); and Val Ogareff, *Leaders of the Soviet Republics, 1971–80* (Canberra: Australian National University, 1981). The KGB career connections are as follows: D. Asankulov, chief of an *oblast* KGB Administration in Kirgizia, became head of the Kirgiz CC AO Department in 1966. Then in 1967 he was appointed chairman of the Kirgiz KGB. V. E. Poryvkin, chief of the AO Department of the Estonian CC from 1963 to 1971, became a deputy chairman of the Estonian KGB in 1971. It might be added that I. I. Cheban, a deputy chief of the AO Department in Moldavia, joined the Moldavian KGB in 1961, but as he was a deputy chief he was not included in the table. Also, A. D. Rudak, head of the Belorussian AO Department from 1954 to 1957, served as first secretary of the Minsk *Gorkom* in 1957–1960 and then became a deputy chairman of the Belorussian KGB.

much of the responsibility is in the hands of the highest republic party officials. As the final party authority in the republic, the first secretary no doubt has some involvement in KGB affairs, but the extent of his oversight for the KGB may be limited. It is doubtful, for example, that he would be in a position to appoint the republic KGB chairman or his deputies.[90] Judging from their activities as reported in the press, second secretaries, who have traditionally performed a watchdog role for the central party apparatus, have some responsibility for administrative organs. They attend all important functions concerning the internal affairs apparatus, the judiciary, and the Procuracy, as well as the KGB and the military. It is not uncommon for the second secretary to open meetings and address conferences of these institutions.[91]

It seems, however, that the role of the second secretary does not extend beyond the tasks of monitoring KGB activities for the party at the center and vetting personnel changes in conjunction with the republic AO department. As members of a highly centralized hierarchical organization, local KGB officials probably operate with considerable autonomy vis-à-vis the local party apparatus, responding mainly to directives from their KGB superiors, with the key controls maintained by the central party apparatus in Moscow. Yet even at the center AO Department officials appear to be more concerned with the ordinary legal and judicial organs than with the state security apparatus. All this implies, as suggested by Voslensky, that much of the supervision over the KGB is carried out directly by the CPSU Central Committee secretary responsible for overseeing the Administrative Organs Department.

The usual practice within the Central Committee Secretariat is to have a junior secretary, who is not a full member of the Politburo, overseeing a given department or several departments and reporting to a senior secretary, who is a full Politburo member and exercises authority over several areas of Central Committee activity. Unlike the situation at lower party levels, where there is a single second secretary (though not always identified as such), responsibilities within the CC CPSU Secretariat are not clear-cut and are often subject to rivalry among senior secretaries. This is particularly true with party cadres and administrative organs, which are the key areas for those aspiring to be heir apparent. As Michel Tatu suggested, the general secretary may encourage competition among the senior secretaries so that no individual threatens his authority.[92]

In any case, ambitious senior secretaries have always tried to include the Administrative Organs Department in their portfolios. Secretarial oversight for the AO Department can be inferred from activi-

TABLE 4.3
CPSU Secretaries Supervising Administrative Organs

L. I. Brezhnev*	Apr. 1963–Oct. 1964
A. N. Shelepin	Nov. 1964–1966
M. A. Suslov	1966–?
A. P. Kirilenko	mid-1970s–1981
D. F. Ustinov, junior secretary	1965–1976
Ia. P. Riabov, junior secretary	1976–1979
K. I. Chernenko*	1979–1984
I. V. Kapitonov, junior secretary	1979–1983, 1985
M. S. Gorbachev*	junior secretary, 1979–1980; senior secretary, 1981–1984
G. V. Romanov	Feb. 1984–June 1985
E. K. Ligachev*	junior secretary, Apr. 1984–Apr. 1985; senior secretary, Apr. 1985–Jan. 1986
L. N. Zaikov	junior secretary, Jan.–Mar. 1986; senior secretary, Mar. 1986–?
A. I. Lukianov, junior secretary	Jan. 1987–

SOURCES: Central Soviet press; Tatu, *Power in the Kremlin*, pp. 503–508; Jerry Hough, "Andropov's First Year," *Problems of Communism* (Nov.–Dec. 1984): 52–53, 57–59; and Alexander Rahr, "The Central Committee Secretariat," *Radio Liberty Research*, RL 439/84, 16 November 1984. According to Tatu, p. 349, Brezhnev may have shared his authority over party cadres and administrative organs with Nikolai Podgornyi from April 1963 to July 1964, when the former was divested of his post as head of state.

* Indicates simultaneous oversight for party cadres.

ties of the secretaries reported in the press, as well as by their signatures on obituaries of important police, judicial, or military officials. Table 4.3 lists the secretaries who appear to have held this responsibility from immediately prior to Khrushchev's ouster onward.

As table 4.3 shows, the most powerful senior secretaries have had administrative organs as part of their portfolio, in some cases combining this with oversight for party cadres. Indeed, with the exception of Andropov, those who reached the top party post supervised the Administrative Organs Department at some point before becoming general secretary. Andropov, who served in the Secretariat for only a six-month period prior to November 1982, was evidently involved mainly with foreign policy and ideology. But his fifteen years as head of the KGB gave him a solid base of support among AO cadres, and he no doubt retained his influence in this area after becoming a party secretary. During his tenure as party chief Andropov may well have assumed direct oversight for the Administrative Organs Department with Kapitonov, a junior secretary, acting as his deputy.

Significantly, both Chernenko and Gorbachev had some secretarial oversight for administrative organs prior to Brezhnev's death. There is strong evidence that Chernenko began to compete with Kirilenko in this area, as well as in that of party organs, in the late 1970s. And although the two men appeared to have vied for authority, Chernenko had emerged as victor by early 1982. Gorbachev's responsibilities for administrative organs were not as obvious, but his attendance at AO-related functions, his signature on obituaries, and the fact that he was chairman of the Legislative Proposals Commission of the Supreme Soviet (a body with theoretical oversight for administrative organs on behalf of the Supreme Soviet), indicates some involvement during the 1979–1984 period.[93]

By the time Chernenko became general secretary, Grigorii Romanov had taken on responsibilities for Administrative Organs, leaving party cadres to Gorbachev and his close associate, Igor Ligachev. Evidently no junior secretary was acting under Romanov in this area because Kapitonov's responsibilities had been shifted to light industry and consumer goods. Romanov monopolized the administrative organs portfolio from early 1984 until December of that year. He attended, often in the company of AO chief Savinkin, virtually all important functions relating to the police, military, and judicial organs, and signed obituaries of their top officials.

As part of an effort to eliminate opposition to his candidacy for general secretary, Gorbachev sought to deprive Romanov of secretarial authority for administrative organs. The first suggestion that Romanov was being challenged was Ligachev's attendance at a conference of AO department chiefs in December 1984.[94] Ligachev had in fact been head of the Legislative Proposals Commission of the Supreme Soviet since April 1984 but had not been attending AO-related functions. Then, on 4 March 1985, an important all-union conference of internal affairs officials took place in Moscow. The only CC secretary to attend was Ligachev.[95] Romanov's absence at this key conference was unusual, though he did continue to attend some AO functions of lesser importance. Ligachev's promotion to full Politburo membership in April 1985, which made him a senior secretary, along with N. I. Ryzhkov, posed an even greater challenge to Romanov because it meant that there were two senior secretaries overseeing administrative organs.

The competition was resolved by Romanov's unceremonious ouster from the party leadership on 1 July 1985. This meant that Ligachev, who was apparently serving as senior secretary responsible for ideology, party cadres, and administrative organs, had a very large portfolio indeed. Furthermore after Ryzhkov departed from the Secretariat

[141]

in connection with his appointment as Chairman of the Council of Ministers in November 1985, Ligachev was the only senior secretary, aside from Gorbachev himself. It was thus not surprising that Lev Zaikov, a member of the Secretariat since July 1985, would be promoted to full Politburo membership at the Twenty-Seventh Party Congress. Zaikov, who had been supervising the economy and defense industry, apparently added administrative organs to his portfolio in early 1986.[96] Although Zaikov had worked for several years under former Leningrad First Secretary Romanov, the fact that he had been chosen to succeed Romanov in this post in June 1983, when Gorbachev was supervising party appointments (Gorbachev personally attended the party meeting that elected him) suggested that Zaikov was looked upon favorably by the general secretary.

In January 1987 A. I. Lukianov was brought into the Secretariat to supervise administrative organs.[97] Lukianov, who had been chief of the CC General Department since 1985, has a background in legal affairs and reportedly attended Moscow University's Law Faculty when Gorbachev was there (in the early 1950s). But Lukianov was two years ahead of Gorbachev and there is little evidence that the two retained ties after this. Lukianov may have an association with the coterie of officials who worked with Andropov in the KGB. He served at one time for the Council of Ministers' Legal Commission, which may have involved him with the KGB, and his first deputy in the General Department was P. P. Laptev, a former KGB official and Andropov aide.[98] Lukianov is only a junior secretary, so Zaikov may have retained some authority for this area until he left the Secretariat to become Moscow Party Chief in November 1987. It is also possible that Ligachev will resume Senior Secretarial oversight for administrative organs, with Lukianov as his deputy. Another possibility is that Gorbachev will attempt to oversee Lukianov himself. After all, with his training as a jurist, it would not be surprising if Gorbachev were to evince a keen interest in legal affairs.

What changes, if any, can we expect in the role of the AO Department under the Gorbachev leadership? Is Gorbachev likely to follow in Khrushchev's footsteps and strengthen the authority of this department? As our discussion has shown, the role of the AO Department in supervising the security police is vague. Though formally classified as one of the institutions falling under the purview of the AO Department, the KGB is apparently not subject to the same controls to which the MVD and other legal institutions are subject. Presumably the party leadership is more reluctant to allocate to the AO Department decisions concerning KGB personnel and policy than decisions involving, for example, the militia or the Procuracy. Thus the main responsibility for the KGB rests at a higher level with certain CPSU secretaries.

Of course, the AO Department's function of monitoring on behalf of the party leadership—however circumscribed in the case of the KGB—still carries a certain amount of influence. In order to make decisions regarding KGB policy or to approve top KGB personnel appointments, for example, the party secretaries presumably rely on information and recommendations from the AO Department. Moreover, as the example of Mironov's tenure as its chief illustrated, the department's influence has at times been considerable. It is possible that as Gorbachev tightens his grip on the Kremlin leadership, he will delegate to the AO Department more direct authority over the KGB. If Gorbachev expects to make this department a more effective agency for police supervision, however, he will probably have to replace Savinkin, who is in his seventies, with a younger, more dynamic official.[99] Numerous personnel changes have already occurred in the AO apparatus both in Moscow and the republics since Gorbachev came to power, so perhaps it will not be long before Savinkin himself is replaced.[100] In the final analysis any significant shift in the extent of the AO Department's oversight of the KGB will depend not only on the qualifications of the official who succeeds Savinkin but also on how determined the party leadership is to curtail the KGB's operational autonomy by instituting tighter, more formalized party controls. As experience has demonstrated, Soviet leaders have been reluctant to do this because it might hamper the KGB's effectiveness in ensuring political support for the Kremlin.

Notes

1. See *Pravda*, 28 April 1954, p. 2.

2. This law was published in *Pravda* on 8 July 1978, pp. 1–2. It sets forth the full competence of the Council of Ministers, the procedure for carrying out its activities, and its relationship with other government institutions. For a detailed discussion of this law and the general organization of the Council of Ministers, see Ger P. Van den Berg, "The Council of Ministers of the Soviet Union," *Review of Socialist Law* 6, no. 3 (September 1980): 292–323.

3. Ibid. Also see Articles 127, 133, and 134 of the 1977 USSR Constitution and the entry on state committees in A. Ia. Sukharev, ed., *Iuridicheskii entsiklopedicheskii slovar'* (Moscow: Sovetskaia entsiklopediia, 1984), pp. 66–67.

4. As O. S. Ioffe, a former Soviet citizen and legal scholar, expressed it, "with regard to the relationship between individual ministries and the Council of Ministers, one may observe the ministries' direct subordination, if not to the full Council of Ministers, then to its Presidium (chairman and deputy-chairmen), or to the chairman of the Council of Ministers, or to that deputy chairman who acts as supervisor of the ministry concerned. Nevertheless, this type of subordination does not encompass certain ministries or state

committees: the Ministry of Defense, the Ministry of Foreign Affairs, and the KGB."
Olimpiad S. Ioffe, *Soviet Law and Soviet Reality* (Dordrecht, Boston, Lancaster: Martinus
Nijhoff, 1985), pp. 29–30.

5. See Articles 108 and 122 of the 1977 USSR Constitution and Iu. T. Mil'ko,
"Upravlenie v oblasti obespecheniia gosudarstvennoi bezopasnosti," in *Sovetskoe administrativnoe pravo: Upravlenie v oblasti administrativno-politicheskoi deiatel'nosti,* ed. Iu. M. Kozlov
et al. (Moscow: Iuridicheskaia Literatura, 1979), pp. 63–95 (quotation, p. 74).

6. See Article 125 of the USSR Constitution.

7. See Article 10 of the Statute on Standing Commissions, enacted on 23 October
1967 and translated in Harold J. Berman and John B. Quigley, Jr., *Basic Laws on the Structure
of the Soviet State* (Cambridge, Mass.: Harvard University Press, 1969), pp. 121–131. Also
see M. P. Evteev and L. V. Saratovskii, "O rabote kommissii zakonodatel'nykh predlozhe-
nii nad proektom osnov ugolovnogo sudoproizvodstva soiuza SSR i soiuznykh respublik,"
in *Voprosy sudoproizvodstva i sudoustroistva v novom zakonodatel'stve soiuza SSR,* ed. S. A.
Golunskii (Moscow: Gosizdat Iuridicheskoi Literatury, 1959), pp. 437–473. For a good
general discussion of the role of the standing commissions see Richard D. Little, "Soviet
Parliamentary Committees after Khrushchev: Obstacles and Opportunities," *Soviet Studies*
24, no. 1 (July 1972):41–60. Also see Robert W. Siegler, *The Standing Commissions of the
Supreme Soviet* (New York: Praeger, 1982).

8. From 1966 onward anywhere from two to five KGB delegates have served on the
two legislative proposals commissions.

9. See Dietrich A. Loeber, "Statutes of Agencies with Ministerial Status in the USSR:
List of Sources as of 1 July 1982," *Review of Socialist Law* 8, no. 4 (1982):359–367; and Iu. M.
Kozlov, *Sovetskoe administrativnoe pravo: Posobie dlia slushatelei* (Moscow: Znanie, 1984),
pp. 80–84.

10. See, for example, V. A. Vlasov and S. S. Studenikin, *Sovetskoe administrativnoe
pravo* (Moscow: Gosizdat Iuridicheskoi Literatury, 1959), p. 264; Iu. M. Kozlov, ed.,
Sovetskoe administrativnoe pravo: Osobennaia chast' (Moscow: Iuridicheskaia Literatura, 1964),
p. 252; and V. D. Sorokin, ed., *Sovetskoe administrativnoe pravo (osobennaia chast')* (Leningrad: Izd. Leningradskogo Universiteta, 1966), p. 245.

11. Mil'ko, "Upravlenie v oblasti obespecheniia gosudarstvennoi bezopasnosti."

12. Ibid., pp. 68, 77.

13. Ibid., p. 82.

14. Ibid., p. 83.

15. See Roy Medvedev, *Khrushchev,* trans. Brian Pearce (New York: Anchor Press,
1983), p. 70; and idem, *On Social Democracy* (New York: W. W. Norton, 1977), p. 160. Also
see an article by the former dissident Valentyn Moroz, "The KGB from My Own Personal
Experience," *Ukrayins'ke slovo,* 11, 18, and 25 December, 1983, Joint Publications Research
Service [hereafter JPRS] translation, Washington, D.C., USSR Report UPS-84-010-L, 7
March 1984, p. 34. The temporary abolition of lower-level KGB offices is confirmed by the
fact that the numerous textbooks on administrative law appearing before 1970 and sur-
veyed here do not mention the existence of KGB organizations below the regional (*oblast* or
krai) level. A 1970 textbook mentions KGB administrations in large cities. See A. E. Lunev,
ed., *Administrativnoe pravo* (Moscow: Iuridicheskaia Literatura, 1970), p. 506. In 1973
another source noted that the KGB had representatives (*upolnomochennye*) in large cities and
raions. See Iu. M. Kozlov, ed., *Sovetskoe administrativnoe pravo* (Moscow: Iuridicheskaia
Literatura, 1973), p. 531. Finally, Mil'ko, "Upravlenie," p. 86, writes of KGB departments
or sections at the *okrug,* city, and *raion* level. In some areas, such as Moscow, the
administrations for *oblast* and city are combined.

16. These special departments have been mentioned by numerous Soviet emigrés.
See, for example, Ioffe, *Soviet Law and Soviet Reality,* p. 161.

17. Mil'ko, "Upravlenie," pp. 86–87.

18. Ibid. Also see Sorokin, *Sovetskoe administrativnoe pravo,* p. 245.

19. Mil'ko, "Upravlenie," p. 87.

20. Ibid.

21. Shelepin's rank was not, to my knowledge, publicized. Serov was an Army general, a status no doubt attained during his long years of service in the state security organs. On military ranks for the KGB and those of the Soviet officer corps in general, see a decree of the USSR Supreme Soviet dated 26 April 1984, reprinted in *Vedomost VS SSSR*, no. 18, article 318, 1984 (pp. 432–435).

22. The following Western sources have been used for information on the general structure of the USSR KGB: "Soviet Intelligence Structure Outlined," *New York Times*, 10 November 1967, p. 14; Mischa Scorer, "The KGB," *The Listener*, 14 February 1974, pp. 204–207; John Barron, *KGB: The Secret Work of Soviet Secret Agents* (New York: Bantam Books, 1974), pp. 95–126; John Barron, *KGB Today: The Hidden Hand* (New York: Readers Digest Press, 1983), pp. 444–453; and "KGB: Das Schwert trifft auch Unschuldige," *Der Spiegel*, 2 July 1984, pp. 115–134. Most other Western publications on the KGB that have appeared recently rely on Barron for their information on organizational structure. Among the recent books on the KGB are Harry Rositzke, *The KGB: The Eyes of Russia* (Garden City, N.Y.: Doubleday, 1981); Brian Freemantle, *KGB* (New York: Holt, Rinehart & Winston, 1982); William R. Corson and Robert T. Crowley, *The New KGB: Engine of Soviet Power* (New York: William Morrow, 1985); and Jeffrey T. Richelson, *Sword and Shield: Soviet Intelligence and Security Apparatus* (Cambridge, Mass.: Ballinger, 1986).

23. For these estimates see Barron, *KGB Today*, p. 41; and Richard F. Staar, *USSR Foreign Policies after Détente*, rev. ed. (Stanford, Calif.: Hoover Institution Press, 1987), p. 107 (note 5). In Russian, *upravlenie* can mean either "administration" or "directorate." For lower-level KGB organs this is translated here as "administration," but for the USSR KGB it is translated here as "directorate."

24. See chapter 9 for more details on the First CD.

25. Barron, *KGB Today*, p. 446.

26. Of the approximately 150 domestic KGB officials on whom biographical information could be found, only a few had experience in the First Chief Directorate.

27. See *Krasnaia zvezda*, 15 November 1983, p. 4; and *The Washington Post* 15 November 1983.

28. For information on Kriuchkov see *Deputaty VS SSSR*, 1984, p. 219; List of Members of Diplomatic Corps, Budapest, May 1956, *Pravda*, 4 December 1958 and 12 November 1963; Barron, *KGB Today*, p. 81; and *Sovetskii entsiklopedicheskii slovar'* (Moscow: Sovetskaia entsiklopediia, 1986), p. 662.

29. See, for example, V. Kriuchkov, "Piatiletnii plan razvitiia Vengerskoi Narodnoi Respubliki (1961–1965)," *Planovoe khoziastvo*, no. 2 (1962):83–86; K. Ivanov and Vladimir A. Kriuchkov, *Vopleshchenie mechty k 20-letiiu osvobozhdeniia vengrii* (Moscow: Znanie, 1965).

30. Barron, *KGB: Secret Work*, p. 113.

31. See Iu. Krotkov, "KGB v deistvii," *Novyi zhurnal*, no. 109 (1972):194; Barron, *KGB: Secret Work*, pp. 85–87; and *CIA Directory of Soviet Officials* (Washington D.C., November 1973), p. 202. Gribanov did not attend the Party Congress in 1966, so he was probably out by this time.

32. Grigorenko, as a delegate to the Twenty-Fifth Party Congress in 1976, was identified as head of an unnamed Chief Directorate. In March 1981 as a delegate to the Twenty-Sixth Party Congress, he was identified as a deputy chairman of the USSR KGB. Because most other Chief Directorate heads have been identified, it is likely that Grigorenko held this post. See *XXV s'ezd KPSS. Stenograficheskii otchet* (Moscow: Politizdat, 1976), vol. 3, and *XXVI s'ezd KPSS. Stenograficheskii otchet* (Moscow: Politizdat, 1981), vol. 3.

33. See Peter Reddaway, *Soviet Policies on Dissent and Emigration: The Radical Change of Course since 1979*, Colloquium Paper Number 192, Kennan Institute for Advanced Russian Studies, Washington D.C., 28 August 1984, p. 16; *KZ*, 28 May 1983, p. 1, and 15 May 1986, p. 3; and *Sovetskii entsik. slovar'*, p. 148.

34. Alidin was removed from his post as head of the Moscow KGB in January 1986, probably in connection with his retirement.

35. Lialin's obituary appeared in *Moskovskaia pravda*, 24 February 1978. According to his obituary, Lialin continued to serve in the KGB until 1973 after leaving his post as chief of the

Moscow KGB in 1971, but his career was clearly damaged by the episode with his nephew.

36. *Deputaty VS SSSR* (Moscow, 1984), p. 145.

37. See appendix C for a chart describing the Central KGB apparatus.

38. V. M. Manokhin, ed., *Sovetskoe administrativnoe pravo* (Moscow: Iuridicheskaia Literatura, 1977), p. 449.

39. Among the best scholarly attempts to assess the role and functions of CC departments are two articles by Leonard Schapiro: "The General Department of the CC of the CPSU," *Survey* 21, no. 3 (Summer 1975):53–65, and "The International Department of the CPSU: Key to Soviet Policy," *International Journal* vol. 22 (Winter 1976–1977), pp. 41–55. Also see Robert W. Kitrinos, "International Department of the CPSU," *POC* 33 (September–October 1984):59–69.

40. George Leggett, *The Cheka: Lenin's Political Police* (Oxford: Clarendon Press, 1981), pp. 158–159, 166–169.

41. Ibid., pp. 132–133; 162–166; 396, note 38.

42. Ibid., pp. 160–161.

43. Leonard Schapiro, *The Communist Party of the Soviet Union* (New York: Vintage Books, 1971), p. 319.

44. See Merle Fainsod, *How Russia Is Ruled*, rev. ed. (Cambridge, Mass.: Harvard University Press, 1967), pp. 194, 200; Robert Conquest, *The Great Terror: Stalin's Purge of the Thirties*, rev. ed. (New York: Collier Books, 1973), p. 67; Simon Wolin and Robert Slusser, eds., *The Soviet Secret Police* (New York: Praeger, 1957), p. 16; and Schapiro, *CPSU*, pp. 452–453. Schapiro later revised his views in light of new information. See note 49.

45. Schapiro, "The General Department," pp. 53–54. For a very detailed treatment of Stalin's personal secretariat, see Neils Erik Rosenfeldt, *Knowledge and Power: The Role of Stalin's Secret Chancellery in the Soviet System of Government* (Copenhagen: Rosenkilde and Bagger, 1978). This book basically confirms most of Schapiro's assumptions but points out that Stalin's secretariat was also deeply involved with the police.

46. See N. Ruslanov, "Voskhozhdenie Malenkova," *Sotsialisticheskii vestnik*, nos. 7–8 (July–August 1953), pp. 128–129; and Boris Nicolaevsky's account, cited in Wolin and Slusser, *The Soviet Secret Police*, p. 385.

47. Alexander Orlov, *The Secret History of Stalin's Crimes* (New York: Random House, 1953), p. 59; Wolin and Slusser, *The Soviet Secret Police*, pp. 122–124, 378–379.

48. In Fainsod, *How Russia Is Ruled*, the CC Special Department and that of the security police are listed as one and the same in the index.

49. Schapiro, "The General Department," pp. 53–56.

50. Fainsod, *How Russia Is Ruled*, pp. 192–193.

51. Schapiro, "The General Department," p. 56.

52. Roy Medvedev, *Let History Judge: The Origins and Consequences of Stalinism* (New York: Alfred A. Knopf, 1971), p. 172. On Ezhov's background see ibid., pp. 171–172; and Abdurakhman Avtorkhanov, *Stalin and the Soviet Communist Party: A Study in the Technology of Power* (Munich: Institute for the Study of the USSR, 1959), p. 218. Avtorkhanov confirms that Ezhov was the secretary responsible for supervising the police and the legal organs.

53. On this CC subcommittee see Anton Antonov-Ovseyenko, *The Time of Stalin*, trans. George Saunders (New York: Harper & Row, 1981), p. 124; and Roy Medvedev, "New Pages from the Political Biography of Stalin," in *Stalinism. Essays in Historical Interpretation*, ed. Robert C. Tucker (New York: W. W. Norton, 1977), pp. 217–218.

54. N. S. Khrushchev, *The Crimes of the Stalin Era: Report to the 20th Party Congress of the CPSU*. Reprint from *New Leader*, 16 July 1956, p. 45.

55. See B. A. Abramov, *Organizatsionno-partiinaia rabota KPSS v gody chetvertoi piatiletki,"* *Voprosy istorii KPSS*, no. 3 (March 1979):55–65 (quotation, p. 64); and Fainsod, *How Russia Is Ruled*, p. 199.

56. For information on Savinkin see *Ezhegodnik BSE, 1976* (Moscow: Sovetskaia Entsiklopedia, 1977), p. 616; and *Deputaty VS SSSR*, 1984, p. 381. On Makarov, see his obituary in *KZ*, 3 September 1975, p. 3; and Werner Hahn, *Postwar Soviet Politics: The Fall of Zhdanov and the Defeat of Moderation, 1946–53* (Ithaca, N.Y., and London: Cornell

University Press, 1982), pp. 218–223; on Zolotukhin see *Voennyi vestnik*, no. 11 (1961):18. Zolotukhin was head of the Political Department of the Moscow Military District at the time Khrushchev was Moscow City party chief. For a discussion of the recruitment of MPA personnel into the CC Secretariat at this time see Timothy J. Colton, *Commissars, Commanders and Civilian Authority: The Structure of Soviet Military Politics* (Cambridge, Mass., and London: Harvard University Press, 1979), pp. 100–101.

57. For details see Hahn, *Postwar Soviet Politics*, pp. 140–143. Another former MPA official and close associate of Khrushchev was A. A. Epishev, who was appointed a deputy minister of state security in 1951 and later became head of the MPA.

58. Antonov-Ovseyenko, *The Time of Stalin*, p. 123.

59. Biographical information on Mironov was obtained from his obituary, *KZ*, 24 October 1964, p. 3, and *Deputaty VS SSSR*, 1962, p. 286.

60. Konstantin S. Grushevoi, *Togda v sorok pervom* (Moscow: Voenizdat, 1974), p. 65.

61. Zheltov had been in the AO Department only one year after serving as MPA chief from 1953 to 1958. (His biography appeared in *Deputaty VS SSSR*, 1962, p. 146.) His immediate predecessor could not be identified.

62. Tikunov's biography appeared in *Ezhegodnik BSE*, 1962, p. 614.

63. During 1959–1960, for example, seven new republic KGB chairmen were appointed.

64. See, for example, N. Mironov, "Persuasion and Compulsion in Combating Anti-Socialist Acts," *Soviet Review* no. 2 (1961) (a translation from *Kommunist*, no. 3, 1961).

65. N. Mironov, "Ukreplenie sotsialisticheskoi zakonnosti i pravoporiadka," *Partiinaia zhizn'*, no. 5 (1962):8–17 (esp. p. 10).

66. Ibid., pp. 13–15; and N. R. Mironov, *Progamma KPSS i voprosy dal'neishego ukrepleniia zakonnosti i pravoporiadka* (Moscow: Higher Party School, 1962), pp. 51–56. Mironov pointed out that the party statutes had no provision for exempting party members from prosecution by normal legal procedure. For a discussion of this type of party interference in the legal system see Robert Sharlet, "The Communist Party and the Administration of Justice in the USSR," in *Soviet Law after Stalin: Part III. Soviet Institutions and the Administration of Law*, ed. Donald Barry, F. J. M. Feldbrugge, George Ginsburgs, and Peter Maggs (The Hague: Sijthoff and Noordhoff, 1978), pp. 360–364.

67. Mironov, *Programma KPSS*, pp. 7–8. Also see N. R. Mironov, "Vosstanovlenie i razvitie leninskikh printsipov sotsialisticheskoi zakonnosti," *Voprosy istorii KPSS*, no. 2 (1964):17–29.

68. Mironov, "Vosstanovlenie i razvitie leninskikh printsipov," p. 20; Mironov, *Programma KPSS*, pp. 14–17.

69. Oleg Penkovskiy, *The Penkovskiy Papers*, trans. Peter Deriabin, intr. and comm. Frank Gibney (New York: Doubleday, 1965), p. 275.

70. This crash was a major disaster for the Soviets. Almost the entire issue of *Krasnaia zvezda*, 20 October 1964, was devoted to obituaries and condolences.

71. See, for example, Michael Voslensky, *Nomenklatura: Anatomy of the Soviet Ruling Class*, trans. Eric Mosbacher (London: The Bodley Head, 1984), p. 87.

72. On Biriuzov and the controversy involving Khrushchev and the military, see Roman Kolkowicz, *The Soviet Military and the Communist Party* (Princeton, NJ: Princeton University Press, 1967), pp. 264–279. I would also like to thank George Mellinger of the University of Minnesota for his insights into this question.

73. See Robert Sharlet, "Legal Policy under Khrushchev and Brezhnev: Continuity and Change," in *Soviet Law after Stalin: Part II. Social Engineering through Law*, ed. Donald D. Barry, George Ginsburgs, and Peter B. Maggs (The Hague: Sijthoff and Noordhoff, 1978), pp. 319–330; and Harold Berman, *Soviet Criminal Law and Procedure: The RSFSR Codes*, 2d ed. (Cambridge, Mass.: Harvard University Press, 1972), p. 76.

74. N. R. Mironov, *Ukreplenie zakonnosti i pravoporiadka v obshchenarodnom gosudarstve. Programnaia zadacha partii*, 1st ed. (Moscow: Iuridicheskaia Literatura, 1964); 2d ed. (Moscow: Iuridicheskaia Literatura, 1969).

75. Voslensky notes, "Nikolai Savinkin, the present head, was appointed only

when KGB activities were expanded and it was subjected to higher control. . . . The post of anonymous head of desk [AO Department chief] became rather unimportant after the appointment of Iurii Andropov to the post of head of the KGB and his election to the Politburo." *Nomenklatura*, pp. 87–88.

76. For sources on Savinkin see note 56.

77. On these "administrative-political" bodies see Manokhin, *Sovetskoe administrativnoe pravo*, pp. 13, 436–476.

78. Konstantin M. Simis, "The Making of the New Soviet Constitution: Conflict over Administrative Justice," in Robert Sharlet, ed., "Studies in Soviet Legal Policymaking and Implementation," a special issue of *Soviet Union* 6, no. 2 (1979):203–207. According to Simis, Savinkin and the AO Department were deeply involved in drawing up the 1977 Constitution and even vetoed a clause that established a process of judicial review over administrative decisions.

79. S. Grachev, "Partiinye organy i ukreplenie obshchestvennogo poriadka," *Partiinaia zhizn'*, no. 10 (1964):13.

80. Summary of report, "The Operation of the Penal System and the Mechanics of Coercion in the USSR," presented by Fridrikh Neznansky at the International Sakharov Hearings, third session, Summer 1979, p. 3.

81. Peter H. Solomon, *Soviet Criminologists and Criminal Policy: Specialists in Policy-Making* (New York and London: Columbia University Press, 1978), p. 204, note 14.

82. Ibid., p. 111.

83. A. Pravdin, "Inside the CPSU Central Committee," *Survey* 20 no. 4 (Autumn 1974):95–96.

84. See, for example, *Partiinoe stroitel'stvo. uchebnoe posobie*, 6th ed. (Moscow: Politizdat, 1981), pp. 179–194. In city party committees and in smaller regions these departments are usually combined with trade and financial organs departments. According to a study by Eugene Huskey, the AO Department for the Baltic Republic of Estonia has only four members on its professional staff—a chief, deputy chief, and two instructors. See Eugene Huskey, "Specialists in the Soviet Communist Party Apparatus: Legal Professionals as Party Functionaries" (forthcoming, *Soviet Studies*), p. 16. Thus probably because Estonia is such a small republic, the AO Department is not divided into separate sectors.

85. For example, the chief of the AO Department of the Turkmen CC, I. Bekiev, who was dismissed for covering up official corruption, was reported as "personally selecting personnel in a certain region." See *Pravda*, 24 October 1986, p. 3. On the other hand, the former first secretary of the Dnepropetrovsk *Obkom*, V. G. Boiko, was criticized for deciding on the appointments of the *oblast* procurator, the internal affairs chief, and the chief of the AO section. *Pravda*, 20 March 1987, p. 2.

86. Larin was first identified as AO first deputy chief in *KZ*, 8 August 1986, p. 1. He had been listed earlier among the delegates to the Twenty-Seventh Party Congress as an employee of the Ministry of Defense.

87. Solomon, *Soviet Criminologists*, pp. 203–204, note 8.

88. See *KZ*, 10 January 1986, p. 3. The other examples are as follows: K. I. Nikitin, chief of the Legal Affairs Sector from approximately 1963 to 1966, joined the AO Department in 1953 after working under Brezhnev in the Moldavian party apparatus. He became a deputy minister of MOOP in 1966. (See his obituary in *Pravda*, 7 August 1979, p. 3.) A. Ia. Sukharov, who took over as Legal Affairs Sector chief in 1966, became USSR deputy minister of justice in 1970, and his successor as head of this sector, S. A. Shishkov, became a deputy USSR procurator in 1978. V. I. Gladyshev, a deputy chief of the AO Department from 1974 to 1983, was appointed in 1983 to head the newly created network of political organs within the MVD. Finally, S. A. Emelianov, identified as an instructor in the AO Department, was made deputy procurator of the city of Moscow in 1983 and in 1984 was appointed chief procurator for the RSFSR. One official, A. P. Uskov, who worked in the AO Department from 1950 to 1969, then became a deputy minister of civil aviation.

89. Eugene Huskey, who studied biographical data on 232 leading Procuracy officials at the regional, republic, and all-union levels, found that temporary secondment to

AO departments was a common pattern in the Procuracy. Huskey, "Specialists in the Soviet CP Apparatus." Another recent personnel change at the *obkom* level might also be mentioned: G. P. Voshchinin, head of the Leningrad *Obkom* AO Department, was transferred to work in the USSR MVD. See *Leningradskaia pravda*, 29 March 1987, p. 3.

90. For a discussion of the republic first secretary's relations with the KGB regarding policy toward dissidents, see chapter 6.

91. Little has been written in the West about the functions of the second secretary, though it has been noted that this post may involve control over the KGB. See Peter Deriabin, *Watchdogs of Terror: Russian Bodyguards from the Tsars to the Commissars* (New Rochelle, N.Y.: Arlington House, 1972), pp. 344–347. On recruitment of second secretaries in the non-Russian republics see John H. Miller, "Cadres Policy in Nationality Areas," *Soviet Studies* 39, no. 1 (January 1977):3–36.

92. Michel Tatu, *Power in the Kremlin: From Khrushchev to Kosygin*, trans. Helen Katel (New York: Viking, 1970), pp. 350–351.

93. Among signs of Chernenko's oversight for administrative organs were his participation in Militia Day ceremonies, 10 November 1979; Aeroflot Day ceremonies, 6 February 1981; and Border Guards Day ceremonies, 27 May 1982. He also attended a conference of Army-party secretaries, 13 May 1982, and signed AO-related obituaries, including that of KGB First Deputy Chairman Tsvigun, *Pravda*, 21 January 1982. Gorbachev attended Aeroflot Day ceremonies on 9 February 1979, 8 February 1980, and 12 February 1982. He attended a civil aviation conference on 4 June 1982 and also signed Tsvigun's obituary.

94. See *Izvestia*, 21 December 1984, p. 2.

95. Ibid., 4 March 1985, p. 2.

96. His signature on the obituary of USSR Military Procurator A. G. Gornyi was the first sign of his new responsibilities. See ibid., 9 January 1986. In addition to Minister of Defense Sokolov and Chebrikov, the only Politburo members to sign this obituary were Zaikov and B. N. Eltsin, first secretary of the Moscow *Gorkom*. Zaikov and Eltsin were both candidate Politburo members at the time. The next month, on 21 February, Zaikov was the only CC secretary to attend Army-Navy Day celebrations. See *KZ*, 22 February 1986, p. 1.

97. In *KZ*, 22 February 1987, p. 1, it was reported that Lukianov attended Army-Navy Day ceremonies along with Savinkin. Lukianov was present at a meeting of the MVD collegium on 4 February 1987, as reported in *FBIS. Daily Report, Soviet Union*, 3 (5 February 1982):R6. On 10 April 1987 he attended Cosmonauts' Day ceremonies. See *Pravda*, 11 April 1987, p. 3. More recently, on 22 July 1987, Lukianov addressed a USSR MVD collegium session (*Pravda*, 23 July 1987, p. 3), and on 29 July 1987 he addressed a collegium of the USSR Procuracy (*Pravda*, 30 July 1987, p. 3).

98. See Alexander Rahr, *A Biographic Directory of 100 Leading Soviet Officials*, 3d ed. (Munich: Radio Liberty Research, March 1986), p. 123. Curiously, there is no information on Lukianov's career from 1961–69. Laptev's biography appears in *Deputaty VS SSSR*, 1984, p. 239; and in *Sovetskii entsiklopedicheskii Slovak*, 1986, p. 688.

99. It is interesting to note that in terms of official status, Savinkin actually ranks higher than did Mironov. Savinkin is a colonel general and a full CC member, whereas Mironov was only a major general and a member of the CC Auditing Commission. Nonetheless in terms of publications and public visibility, Savinkin has not been as prominent.

100. In addition to the departure of First Deputy Chief Drugov from the CPSU AO Department in Moscow, ten republic AO chiefs were replaced between March 1985 and July 1987, along with the AO chiefs for the Moscow *Gorkom* and Leningrad *Obkom*.

5
CPSU Cadres Policy and Career Patterns in the KGB

The previous chapter described the organizational structure of party control over the KGB and the vehicles through which such control is implemented, in particular the Administrative Organs Department. As was stressed, the determination of appointments and promotions is an important weapon for maintaining the authority of the party leadership over the security police, as it is with all elements of the Soviet bureaucracy. Judging from statements made by Khrushchev and other party leaders after Stalin's death, cadres policy was seen to be a key mechanism for implementing reforms in the state security organs. A central feature of this cadres policy, as claimed repeatedly in the official press, was the appointment of "trusted party apparatchiks" to KGB posts. This was apparently to ensure that the KGB did not follow the precedent of earlier state security organizations and turn against the party.

There was more, however, to the cadres question than this. After all, when Stalin brought in a long-time party apparatchik, Ezhov, to head the security police in 1936 and replaced numerous other top police officials with party men at the same time, this marked an intensification of police terror against the party itself. Furthermore it was openly acknowledged by the post-Stalin leadership that a large number of Stalinist security officials were allowed to remain in their posts after

1953. Ironically even N. R. Mironov, who from 1959 to 1964 headed the CC Administrative Organs Department, which oversees police appointments on behalf of the party, was a former state security official.

Clearly what the party leadership intended to achieve through its cadres policy was not rapid turnover within the police apparatus by the continual introduction of party officials. Party policy has, since 1954, rested on a broader strategy, designed not only to prevent the police from becoming too powerful or falling under the control of one leader but also to ensure that the overall security needs of the state are met by means of an efficient and well-functioning political police organization. This has meant, among other things, the recruitment and promotion of KGB officials who have the experience and qualifications necessary to carry out their functions as determined by the party. What, then, are the characteristics of these officials, and what are the common features of their careers? To what extent have factionalism and party politics entered into cadres policy toward the KGB, at the expense of nonpartisan considerations?

This chapter presents biographical information on leading members of the state security apparatus since Stalin's death and examines both the patterns of appointments and turnover in different posts and the changes in the party and government status of KGB officials from 1954 to the present—Central Committee membership, republic party bureau membership, attendance at party congresses, and representation on USSR and republic Supreme Soviets. Officials serving in the KGB Border Guards and in the foreign intelligence apparatus (with some exceptions) have been excluded from consideration here because both groups constitute separate bureaucracies that have little career interaction with the domestic KGB apparatus. Some career information on border guards is presented in chapter 7, but in the case of the KGB foreign intelligence cadres, biographical information is sparse.

The underlying assumption of this analysis of the KGB elite is that the patterns that emerge from looking at background characteristics and career patterns offer insights into general party policies toward the security apparatus and also tell us something about the KGB's functions within the Soviet system. By its very nature the KGB is an organization shrouded in secrecy. Unlike the party apparatus, the economic bureaucracy, or even the military, whose activities and programs are frequently discussed in the press, the KGB reveals precious little about its operations. In recent years KGB officials have enjoyed greater prominence, but policy issues and organizational questions are never discussed openly. Thus one of the few ways to learn about the KGB's role and its relationship with the party is to study biographical and career data on its officials. Somewhat surprisingly, a great deal of these data are available in the Soviet press. As a result of the regime's campaign to raise the public prestige of the KGB, its officials have "come out of the closet," frequently attending public functions and receiving awards and honors, all of which are reported in regional or national newspapers. The vast amount of commemorative literature on the state security organs, though usually focusing on the pre-1954 period, often includes information on more current KGB officials. In addition, obituaries of KGB officials are now published on a regular basis in both the national and republic press. Together with general sources of biographical data on Soviet officials, such as encylopedias and yearbooks, this information is sufficient to reach some tentative conclusions about the party's cadres policy as implemented within the KGB.

KGB Elite Composition: 1958–1962, 1980–1984

The first part of the following analysis involves a comparison of two groups of officials, fifty in each, occupying key posts in the KGB apparatus during two separate periods, 1958–1962 and 1980–1984.[1] These are not strictly homogeneous groups, in the sense that within each group the officials occupy positions of varying status: USSR KGB chairmen and deputy chairmen, leading officials in the USSR KGB apparatus, republic and *oblast* KGB chiefs, and some deputy republic KGB chiefs. Nevertheless both groups represent, for their respective periods, what could be termed the "KGB elite." As opposed to lower-ranking officials and rank-and-file officers, members of this elite play important roles in the implementation of KGB policy, and their appointments are probably approved at top party levels. They are thus part of what is called the *nomenklatura*. The eighteen-year gap between times of occupancy for the two groups reveals changes in elite recruitment that have occurred over time, particularly since the later period encompasses two years of post-Brezhnev rule. While many of those in the second group have remained in their posts under Gorbachev, sufficient career information on officials appointed after 1984 are not yet available, and so this period is not included in the analysis.

Before turning to the data, it is important to note that although the KGB chairman may make initial recommendations on appointments to leading positions within the KGB (such as deputy chairmen, chiefs of directorates, and republic KGB chairmen), these appointments are doubtless approved by the party leadership, probably the Politburo or Secretariat, rather than the Administrative Organs Department alone. In addition, the general secretary or another powerful party leader might impose a few of his own hand-picked nominees upon the KGB. Brezhnev, as we have seen, brought several of his allies into KGB posts directly below Andropov. There is no evidence as yet that Gorbachev has installed party supporters in leading KGB positions. Most of the recent appointments appear to have been made from within the KGB.[2] If Gorbachev consolidates his power further we might expect some future KGB appointments to reflect his influence. In summary, the process of appointments to the top level of the KGB elite is, like that of key party and state appointments, a complex one of power-brokering and consensus.

Tables 5.1 and 5.2, which are based on career data on these one hundred men, show that top KGB appointees were drawn from a variety of professional backgrounds, but the majority in both cases came from two groups: those whose main careers had been in the party or Komsomol and those whose careers had been spent in the state security organs. While the party did indeed coopt many apparatchiki into the KGB after the purge of Beria, a substantial number of "trusted Chekists" remained in their posts. Of the 1958–1962 group, 58 percent had joined the security police before 1950, though several of these men had career experience outside the police before joining. The same holds true for the KGB elite of the early 1980s. While cooptation into the KGB was still practiced, at least one-third of this group were officials who had spent their entire adult careers in the state security organs.[3] According to table 5.2, by 1982 their average time of service in the security police was twenty-seven years; over 40 percent had joined the police before 1950. Even those who had been brought into the KGB from the party or elsewhere during the Khrushchev era by the late 1970s had gained fairly long periods of service in the security police.

Aside from men like Shelepin, Semichastnyi, Ivashutin (currently head of the GRU), Andropov and a few others, who were coopted into the KGB and later moved out, the overwhelming majority of coopted officials remained in the KGB on a permanent basis. It is perhaps surprising that despite all the initial publicity about the introduction of party men into the ranks of the state security organs, the KGB became, soon after its establishment in 1954, a remarkably closed and stable bureaucracy. It seems that the party, which gives top priority to the security of the Soviet regime, considers that officials with substantial police experience will be the most effective in top KGB posts. (With the

[154]

TABLE 5.1
Leading KGB Cadres: Main Career Experience Outside State Security Organs

	1958–1962 GROUP		1980–1984 GROUP	
	NUMBER	PERCENTAGE**	NUMBER	PERCENTAGE
Party Apparatus	10	20.4	16	32.6
Komsomol	8	16.3	5	10.2
Soviet Army	6	12.2	4	8.2
MPA	2	4.1	1	2.0
Industry	2	4.1	4	8.2
Agriculture	2	4.1	—	—
MVD	1	2.0	2	4.1
Other	1	2.0	1	2.0
None*	17	34.7	16	32.6
Subtotal	49	100.0	49	100.0
Unknown	1		1	
Total	50		50	

* This indicates the first significant career experience was with state security organs.
** Because of rounding, sums may not equal 100 percent.
SOURCES: See appendix D and note 1 to this chapter.

appointment of Vitalii Fedorchuk to the KGB chairmanship in May 1982 the party even reversed its policy of placing a party official in this post and opted for police experience instead.) Whether or not Chebrikov was still considered a party apparatchik in December 1982, after fifteen years in the KGB, is a debatable point.[4] Members of these two groups thus gained a strong sense of identity with the KGB as an institution. Given the fact that a significant proportion of both groups joined the security police in the Stalin era (a third of the 1958–1962 group actually joined before or during the purges), it might also be expected that some of the Stalinist attitudes and values survived within the security police, even through to the post-Brezhnev period.

With regard to career background, it is interesting to note that the Komsomol appears to be the main source of recruitment to the KGB. Teaching and communications work were also evident in the experience of some KGB officials. Thus for example, K. F. Liadus, S. K. Tsvigun, V. G. Baluev, and Z. M. Iusif-Zade had all been teachers for a time, and V. V. Fedorchuk and A. P. Pork had worked as journalists. This is not surprising given the propagandistic nature of security police work as it

TABLE 5.2
Leading KGB Cadres: State Security Experience

DATE OF ENTRY	1958–1962 GROUP		1980–1984 GROUP	
	NUMBER	PERCENTAGE*	NUMBER	PERCENTAGE
Before 1936	8	16.7		
1936–1940	9	18.7	6	12.2
1941–1945	7	14.6	10	20.4
1946–1950	4	8.3	5	10.2
1951–1955	12	25.0	9	18.4
1956–1960	8	16.7	2	4.1
1961–1965	—	—	4	8.1
1966–1970	—	—	6	12.2
After 1970	—	—	7	14.3
Subtotal	48	100.0	49	100.0
Unknown	2		1	
Total	50		50	
		1960		1982
Average number of years' experience		15		27
Mean		14		30

* Because of rounding, sums may not equal 100 percent.
SOURCES: See appendix D and note 1 to this chapter.

has developed in the Soviet Union.[5] Such a background also might prove useful for those KGB officials who take up writing about the exploits of Chekisty. In general, however, experience in these areas was relatively brief as compared to time spent in the KGB.

Table 5.3, which gives ages of security police officials, adds to the picture of an employee who has made the KGB a lifetime career. We see that from 1960 to 1982 the average age rose by about twelve years, from 46.6 to 58.2. This, of course, correlates with the general pattern of aging within the party and state bureaucracies as a result of Brezhnev's policy of "stability of cadres." But the process of aging within the top level of the KGB apparatus appears to have been more marked than with most other bureaucracies. Jerry Hough, for example, compared the changes in age composition over similar periods for various party and state groups at the central and regional leadership levels.[6] In most cases the KGB elite

TABLE 5.3
Leading KGB Cadres: Age

	1960*		1982**	
	NUMBER	PERCENTAGE***	NUMBER	PERCENTAGE
Under 40	8	16.6		
40–45	13	27.1	1	2.1
46–50	10	20.8	3	6.4
51–55	11	22.9	8	17.0
56–60	4	8.3	16	34.0
61–65	2	4.2	9	19.1
Over 65	—	—	10	21.3
Total	48	100.0	47	100.0
Unknown	2		3	

Average age in 1960: 46.6 years
Average age in 1982: 58.2 years

* Age in 1960 of members of 1958–1962 group
** Age in 1982 of members of 1980–1984 group
*** Because of rounding, sums may not equal 100 percent.
SOURCES: See appendix D and note 1 to this chapter.

aged more rapidly than the officials Hough considered. This cannot be explained by a variance in the status of members of the two KGB groups: both groups contain roughly the same balance of USSR chairmen, deputy chairmen, and regional officials. Rather, there have been few departures from the KGB to other bureaucracies, and the members of the 1980–1984 group had simply been in their posts for long periods.

If we look at the dates of joining the Communist party (table 5.4), we see that the differences for the two groups are roughly comparable to the differences in age and length of state security service. Members of the Brezhnev and post-Brezhnev era elite had significantly longer periods of CP membership than the Khrushchev era group. The table shows that whereas over two-thirds of the 1958–1962 KGB elite were initiated into political life before the outbreak of the war, over three-quarters of the 1980–1984 group joined the party during or after World War II. This suggests that the two groups had rather different political orientations.

[157]

TABLE 5.4
Leading KGB Cadres: Date of Joining CPSU

	1958–1962 GROUP		1980–1984 GROUP	
	NUMBER	PERCENTAGE*	NUMBER	PERCENTAGE
Before 1920	2	4.7	—	—
1920–1925	2	4.7	—	—
1926–1930	5	11.6	—	—
1931–1935	7	16.3	3	7.0
1936–1940	14	32.6	5	11.6
1941–1945	10	23.2	15	34.9
1946–1950	3	7.0	10	23.2
1951–1955	—	—	7	16.3
After 1955	—	—	3	7.0
Total	43	100.0	43	100.0
Unknown	7		7	

Avg. length of CP membership in 1960: 23.3 years
Avg. length of CP membership in 1982: 34.6 years

* Because of rounding, sums may not equal 100 percent.
SOURCES: See appendix D and note 1 to this chapter.

TABLE 5.5
Leading KGB Cadres: Nationality

	1958–1962 GROUP		1980–1984 GROUP	
	NUMBER	PERCENTAGE*	NUMBER	PERCENTAGE
Russian	27	54.0	30	61.2
Ukrainian	6	12.0	6	12.2
Belorussian	3	6.0	1	2.0
Armenian	2	4.0	2	4.1
Georgian	1	2.0	1	2.0
Azerbaidzhan	2	4.0	2	4.1
Estonian	1	2.0	2	4.1
Latvian	1	2.0	1	2.0
Lithuanian	2	4.0	1	2.0
Kazakh	2	4.0	2	4.1
Kirgiz	1	2.0		
Tadzhik	1	2.0	1	2.0
Uzbek	2	4.0		
Total	50	100.0	49	100.0
Unknown			1	

* Because of rounding, sums may not equal 100 percent.
SOURCES: See appendix D and note 1 to this chapter.

TABLE 5.6
Leading KGB Cadres: Education

	1958–1962 GROUP		1980–1984 GROUP	
	NUMBER	PERCENTAGE*	NUMBER	PERCENTAGE
Complete higher	(30):	(78.9):	(34):	(89.5):
Technical	6	15.8	8	21.0
Military	4	10.5	5	13.2
Legal	2	5.3	6	15.8
Education	1	2.6	4	10.5
Economic			1	2.6
Higher Party School	7	18.4	5	13.2
Higher KGB School	0	0.0	2	5.3
Other/unspecified	10	26.3	3	7.9
Incomplete higher	1	2.6	1	2.6
Secondary	6	15.8	3	7.9
Primary	1	2.6	0	0
Total	38	100.0	38	100.0
Unknown	12		12	

* Because of rounding, sums may not equal 100 percent.
SOURCES: See appendix D and note 1 to this chapter.

Table 5.5 on nationality shows a predominance of Great Russian and Ukrainian backgrounds, with other ethnic groups minimally represented. This is to be expected, in view of the underrepresentation of ethnic minorities in the party and government as a whole.[7] Given that many of the positions in question involve the implementation of Russian control over national minorities, the number of non-Russians among KGB officials actually is fairly substantial.

While there was little change in the nationality composition of the KGB elite over the years, changes in educational background (table 5.6) were somewhat more noticeable, with the 1980–1984 elite slightly better educated on average. (Readers should be cautioned, however, that the large number of "unknowns" detracts from the representative quality of the information, particularly because gaps in educational data may indicate a lower rather than a higher level.) Since the early Khrushchev era the party has stressed the importance of having well-educated cadres in the security police, as it has in other organizations. The trend toward higher education in the KGB elite reflects the fact that this was becoming a key criterion for upward mobility.

A well-educated KGB officialdom is important for two reasons. First, KGB methods for dealing with internal dissent have changed significantly over the years. Violence has been largely replaced by more sophisticated psychological tactics. In combating what it sees as internal subversion, the KGB often deals with intellectuals, whose crimes lie in the realm of ideas. Thus they must be well educated to carry out their tasks effectively. Second, the regime has shown itself to be highly concerned with the KGB's public image. KGB officials are portrayed by the media not only as humane and benevolent but as well educated and cultured, very different from their predecessors. As a 1982 book on the state security organs pointedly noted:

> In 1921 only 1.3 percent of Cheka employees had higher education, while 19.1 percent had secondary education. Moreover, the simple statistics report this figure: 1.5 percent of Cheka employees in 1921 were completely illiterate. Today, the absolute majority of Chekists have higher education.[8]

It might be added that descriptions of KGB officials in the popular media correspond to the picture that emerges from the data here. The typical KGB employee is presented as one who spent most of his career in the security organs and who gained a higher education.[9]

The KGB in the National Republics, Moscow, and Leningrad

The information provided in the foregoing tables offers a general picture of the KGB elite; however, the rather selective nature of the sample and the disparities in the positions of those included do not allow for an examination of such questions as tenure and turnover. In the specific case of USSR KGB officials, such as deputy chairmen or directorate chiefs, it is not always possible to follow their careers in order to get a complete picture of the composition of the USSR KGB at any given time. The situation is different with the fourteen national republic KGB organizations and with those of Moscow and Leningrad (roughly comparable in importance to republic KGBs).[10] In this case it is possible to determine (with very few exceptions) the names as well as the dates of appointments and dismissals of KGB chiefs during the period 1955–1986. (Appendix E sets forth this information, including, wherever possible, information on first deputy KGB chiefs.) This permits us to analyze not

TABLE 5.7
Rates of Yearly Turnover and Average Tenure: 1955–1986

	KGB CHAIRMAN		FIRST SECRETARY		SECOND SECRETARY		MVD CHIEF	
	TURNOVER RATE (%)	AVERAGE TENURE (YRS)	TURNOVER RATE (%)	AVERAGE TENURE (YRS)	TURNOVER RATE (%)	AVERAGE TENURE (YRS)	TURNOVER RATE (%)	AVERAGE TENURE (YRS)
Armenia	9.4	8.0	9.4	8	18.7	4.6	15.6	5.3
Azerbaidzhan	18.7	4.6	9.4	8	18.7	4.6	15.6	5.3
Belorussia	9.4	8.0	12.5	6.4	25.0	3.5	18.7	4.6
Estonia	6.2	10.7	3.1	16.0	15.6	5.3	9.4	8.0
Georgia	0	32.0	6.2	10.7	15.6	5.3	18.7	4.6
Kazakhstan	18.7	4.6	18.8	4.6	31.2	2.9	15.6	5.3
Kirgizia	15.6	5.3	6.2	10.7	28.1	3.2	15.6	5.3
Latvia	9.4	8.0	9.4	8.0	21.9	4.0	9.4	8.0
Lithuania	6.2	10.7	3.1	16.0	12.5	6.4	6.2	10.7
Moldavia	15.6	5.3	6.2	10.7	18.7	4.6	6.2	10.7
Tadzhikistan	21.9	4.0	12.5	6.4	21.9	4.0	9.4	8.0
Turkmenistan	15.6	5.3	15.6	5.3	15.6	5.3	15.6	5.3
Ukraine	6.2	10.7	9.4	8.0	28.1	3.2	9.4	8.0
Uzbekistan	18.7	4.6	12.5	6.4	18.7	4.6	15.6	5.3
Moscow City	12.5	6.4	6.2	10.7	15.6	5.3	25.0	3.5
Moscow Oblast			6.2	10.7	9.4	8.0	9.4	3.4
Leningrad City	9.4	8.0	12.5	6.4	18.7	4.6	15.6	5.3
Leningrad Oblast			9.4	10.8	18.7	4.6		
Average for all areas:	12.1	8.5	9.4	8.9	19.6	4.7	13.6	6.5

NOTE: Turnover equals number of changes in a given job divided by 32 (years). Average tenure equals 32 (years) divided by the number of occupants.

SOURCES: Appendix E; CIA *Directory of Soviet Officials* for various years; Grey Hodnett and Val Ogareff, *Leaders of the Soviet Republics, 1955–72* (Canberra: Australian National University, 1973); Val Ogareff, *Leaders of the Soviet Republics, 1972–80* (Canberra: Australian National University, 1980); and various Soviet newspapers.

[161]

only recruitment and promotion policies at this level but also turnover and tenure.

Table 5.7 presents the turnover rate by republic (and for Moscow and Leningrad) for occupants of the posts of KGB chairman, party first secretary, second secretary, and MVD chief for the years 1955–1986. As this table shows, the post of KGB chairman is relatively stable, with an average yearly turnover of 12.1 percent, as compared with 19.6 percent for second secretaries and 13.6 percent for MVD chiefs. The post of first secretary has a somewhat lower rate of turnover: 9.4 percent. On average KGB chairmen hold their posts for 8.5 years; the average tenure for second secretaries is 4.7 years, for MVD chiefs, 6.5 years, and for first secretaries, 8.9 years. Grey Hodnett, who analyzed turnover and job tenure for all leading state and party posts in the fourteen non-Russian republics over the period 1955–1972, found that the KGB chairman was among those with longer tenures and lower turnover rates.[11] The data here accord with his findings and show that this trend has persisted to 1986. In fact, if we look only at the last fifteen years, 1972–1986, the turnover rate for the post of KGB chief was 10.0 percent, which is lower than the rate for the entire period. This indicates a trend toward even greater stability of tenure, despite the political upheavals in the wake of the Brezhnev, Andropov, and Chernenko successions.

What conclusions might we draw from this information? First, the post of KGB chairman in the republics (and chief of the Moscow and Leningrad KGB administrations) is generally one of considerable job security, with less likelihood of removal than for most other posts. The KGB chairman performs crucial functions of political control on behalf of the regime. As Hodnett points out in reference to first secretaries, the leadership may deem it necessary to place in this sensitive post persons with long experience (despite the risks of the development of parochialism). The loyalty of these KGB officials as reliable executors of central policy is ensured by giving them job security. It may also be the case that frequent removal of these officials is viewed as undesirable because it would create an image of instability in an organization that should, from the regime's point of view, be looked upon by the public as above reproach. The regime might offset this low turnover by a higher turnover in posts directly below the KGB chief: first deputies and deputies. The available information is not sufficient to document this, but as will be discussed later, KGB deputies not infrequently move into the post of KGB chairman within the same republic. This means that, at least in these cases, the center is not implementing "control through

[162]

rotation"—as it does, for example, with the post of second or organizational secretary in the republics.

As table 5.7 indicates, there is considerable regional variation in the turnover and tenure rates for all posts listed. The explanation no doubt lies partly in the realm of personalities and politics. The higher turnover rates for KGB chairmen in the Central Asian republics and Azerbaidzhan, however, may also be attributed to nationality problems and the rise of Islamic fundamentalism and political ferment in states bordering these republics. KGB chairmen in the Central Asian republics are usually nonnatives brought in from the outside to serve for limited periods. At the other end of the spectrum is Georgia, whose native Georgian KGB chairman, A. N. Inauri, has occupied his post for thirty-three years. He survived a major political upheaval in 1972 when the first secretary of Georgia, V. P. Mzhavanadze (reputedly a close friend) was ousted along with many other party officials because of large-scale corruption. Inauri has also seen six MVD chiefs come and go and lived through numerous other corruption scandals in the republic. Presumably Moscow has been willing to turn a blind eye to all this as long as Inauri remains loyal to the center and is able to suppress dissent effectively.

If we break down personnel changes by year for the different republics, we see that changes in the post of KGB and MVD chiefs usually occurred independent of each other and without concurrent changes in the post of first secretary. There was some correlation, in that eleven of sixty-two changes in occupancy of the KGB chief took place in the same year as a change in the first secretary's post. But in general it seems that decisions to replace a KGB or an MVD chief are made at the center and that these changes have less relation to republic party politics than might be supposed. As the example of Inauri shows, the police may well remain unscathed when leading members of the republic party leadership lose their posts.

KGB personnel changes are probably related to developments within the Moscow leadership. In 1959–1960, ten republic KGB chiefs were replaced along with seven first secretaries and eight MVD chiefs. This marked a period of consolidation of Khrushchev's power after the defeat of the anti-party group. It was also a time when the party was moving its cadres into KGB ranks and the newly appointed KGB chief, Aleksandr Shelepin, was filling some KGB posts with his allies. Shelepin's replacement by Semichastnyi in 1961 did not lead to substantial personnel changes in the KGB because Semichastnyi was closely associated with Shelepin, who retained authority over the police after he moved into the Secretariat.

[163]

The period from 1967 to 1970 witnessed considerable change in republic KGB personnel, not only because Andropov was named to head the USSR KGB in 1967 but also because Brezhnev had defeated his adversary, Shelepin, and was probably bringing some men of his own choosing into KGB posts. Among them would be Geidar Aliev, who was closely allied with Brezhnev's relative Tsvigun, replacing him as chairman of the Azerbaidzhan KGB in 1967; Aleksei Beschastnov, a long-time security official who knew Brezhnev during the war and was appointed chairman of the Uzbek KGB in 1969; and Vasilii Shevchenko, who had worked in the state security organs of Kazakhstan when Brezhnev was first secretary there and was named to head the Tadzhikistan KGB in 1970.[12] It might also be noted that Vitalii Fedorchuk was made chairman of the Ukrainian KGB in 1970, reportedly because the incumbent Nikitchenko (a Khrushchev ally) was too soft on dissent in the Ukraine.[13]

The next series of personnel changes began in 1982 and were no doubt closely related to the prolonged succession crisis in the Kremlin. In the four-year period from 1982 to 1986, seven republic KGB chiefs were replaced, along with the chief of the Moscow KGB. Although it is possible to relate some of the dismissals to the general purge of Brezhnevites (such as Vasilii Shevchenko's removal in 1982 from the post of KGB chairman in Kazakhstan, where he had been since 1975), not enough is known about all the new appointees to speculate on their connections with the Moscow leadership.[14]

Closely related to job security and mobility are the questions of age, recruitment, and promotion of KGB officials directly below the national level and what patterns emerge (table 5.8). Altogether there were seventy-eight occupants of the post of KGB chief for the fourteen republics, Moscow, and Leningrad during the 1954–1986 period. The average age of these officials when they were appointed was 49.3 years. If we subdivide this period, the average age for those appointed from 1954 to 1969 was 46.3 years, while from 1970 to 1986 it was 53.6 years. This correlates with the data on tenure and turnover and also with age statistics available for other republic officials. According to one study, for example, the average age of republic first and second secretaries rose from 46 to 54 in the period 1955 to 1975.[15]

During the 1954–1969 period, thirty-four of the forty-one KGB chiefs on whom information is available were recruited from within the state security apparatus. Ten had been first deputy or deputy chairmen within their respective republics; three had been KGB chairmen of other republics and twenty-one came from elsewhere within the state security apparatus. Of the twenty-four from the 1970–1986 group on whom

TABLE 5.8

Republic KGB Chairmen, Chiefs of Moscow and Leningrad KGB
Administrations, 1954–1986

otal Occupants: 78	Age on Appointment	
	AVERAGE	MEDIAN
otal group for which data available: 58 persons	49.3 years	49.5 years
ppt. 1954–1969: 34 persons	46.3 years	46.0 years
ppt. 1970–1986: 24 persons	53.6 years	54.0 years

Transitions: Previous and Subsequent Posts

From

PPT.	STATE SECURITY APPARATUS				OUTSIDE			
	CENTRAL KGB	REP. OR REGION KGB	UNSPECI- FIED	MVD	PARTY	STATE	ARMY	UNKNOWN
54–1969 (49 persons)	6	17	11	2	3	1	1	8
70–1986 (29 persons)	7	11	5	0	1	0	0	5

To

	STATE SECURITY APPARATUS			OUTSIDE				
	CENTRAL KGB	REP. OR REGION KGB	UNSPECI- FIED	PARTY	STATE	RETIRED	STILL IN JOB	UNKNOWN
54–1969 (49 persons)	9	6	3	3	2	6	2	18
70–1986 (29 persons)	2	2	2	2	1	2	14	4

SOURCE: See note 1 this chapter.

information is available, twenty-three came from within the state security apparatus. Two had been KGB chairmen of other republics, and six
had been deputy or first deputy chairmen within that republic. The small
proportion of both groups that was recruited from the party, state, or
military indicates that cooptation from the outside is even rarer at this
level than in the USSR KGB apparatus.[16]

The picture of the KGB as a "closed profession" emerges even more
clearly from looking at what happened to KGB chiefs when they left their
posts. It might be assumed that those in the category "unknown"
either retired or moved into low-visibility KGB jobs at the center.
Together with those on whom we have information, by far the largest

proportion of KGB chiefs either moved back into the central apparatus or retired. Only a few moved to party or state positions. (In two cases KGB republic chairmen became first secretaries of the same republic. Geidar Aliev became first secretary of Azerbaidzhan in 1969 and, more recently, Boris Pugo became first secretary of Latvia in April 1984, but this is unusual.) For many KGB officials the post of republic chairman or chief of the Moscow or Leningrad KGB Administrations has represented the pinnacle of their careers. The likelihood of achieving a higher position (such as chief of a main administration or a deputy chairman of the USSR KGB) is not great. This occurred in only six out of seventy-eight cases.[17]

The sparsity of data on first deputy and deputy KGB chiefs for the republics, Moscow, and Leningrad precludes making numerical estimates on the turnover rate and average tenure for this group. Appointments and dismissals from these posts are rarely announced in the press. Nor is it possible to determine how many deputy chairmen are serving in the various republics. As a rough estimate there is probably one first deputy KGB chairman and two or three deputies at any given time, though it is often the case that first deputies are not identified as such and are simply referred to as deputy chairmen when their names appear in the press.

Limited information on age, recruitment, and transfer patterns for forty-five such officials serving in the period from 1954 to 1986 indicates that it is taking an increasingly longer time to reach the post of deputy or first deputy.[18] Individuals appointed during 1970–1986 were almost fifty years old on average when they were appointed to their posts, whereas those appointed during 1954–1969 were only forty-one years old on average. Almost three-fourths of those KGB deputies on whom we have information were appointed from within the state security apparatus. Those recruited from the party had been serving in the party apparatus of their respective republics. Data on transfer and promotions show that although it is not uncommon for a deputy or first deputy to achieve the post of republic KGB chairman, this is hardly a position to which he can automatically aspire. He might be sent instead to the central KGB in Moscow or to another republic. As was the case with ten members of this group, he might also be moved to other areas of the Soviet legal system—the Ministry of Justice, Procuracy, or MVD. Such transfers from the KGB are not uncommon, but it is rare for the reverse to happen. Another common alternative may be that of remaining in one's post until retirement. Length of tenure for KGB deputy chairmen seems to vary widely. There are examples of KGB deputies serving for fifteen to twenty

TABLE 5.9
Native Occupancy of Republic KGB Posts: June 1954 to June 1986

	CHAIRMEN		
REPUBLIC	NATIVE	NON-NATIVE	DEPUTY CHAIRMEN
Armenia	91%/3*	9%/1*	Predominantly native; 1st dep, mixed
Azerbaidzhan	26%/2	74%/5	Predominantly native; 1st dep, usually nonnative
Belorussia	0	100%/4	Predominantly native; 1st dep, usually native
Estonia	78%/2	22%/1	Predominantly native; 1st dep, usually native
Georgia	100%/1	0	Predominantly native; 1st dep, usually nonnative
Kazakhstan	22%/2	78%/5	Mixed; 1st dep, usually native
Kirgizia	34%/1	66%/5	Mixed
Latvia	44%/3	56%/1	Predominantly nonnative; 1st dep, usually native
Lithuania	100%/3	0	Mixed; 1st dep, usually nonnative
Moldavia	0	100%/6	Predomonantly native; 1st dep, usually native
Tadzhikistan	0	100%/8	Mixed; 1st dep, usually native
Turkmenistan	0	100%/6	Mixed; 1st dep, usually native
Ukraine	100%/3	0	Predominantly native; 1st dep, usually native
Uzbekistan	0	100%/7	Mixed; 1st dep, mixed
Total	42.5%/20	57.5%/49	

SOURCE: See note 1 to this chapter.
* Percentage figures equal total length of tenure of occupants divided by 32 (years), for each category. Numbers equal total occupants for each category.
NOTE: Occupants of posts of deputies and first deputy were often not identifiable.

years. Others serve for only two or three years before being transferred or promoted. Among those who were promoted to the post of republic KGB chairman, their tenure as deputies or first deputies ranged from two to eight years.

Career patterns of both republic KGB chairmen and deputies may depend upon the specific situation in the individual republics, and thus may be closely related to nationality policies. Table 5.9 sets forth information on native occupancy (or occupancy of the indigenous nationality) of the post of KGB chairman in the fourteen national republics from June 1954 to June 1986. It also includes rough estimates, based on limited data, on the extent of native occupancy for the posts of KGB deputies and first deputies. Perhaps the most interesting aspect of the table is that despite the importance of the position of republic KGB chairman for political control, which includes preserving Russian dominance over

[167]

national minorities, a surprisingly large number of KGB republic chairmen have been members of the republic's indigenous ethnic elite. In the Ukraine, Lithuania, and Georgia the post has always been occupied by a native; in Armenia a native occupied this post for all but three years and in Estonia for all but eight years. Moscow has adhered to a rigid policy of having nonindigenous cadres as KGB chairmen in only five of the fourteen republics: Belorussia, Moldavia, Tadzhikistan, Turkmenistan, and Uzbekistan.[19]

The variance among the different republics in native occupancy of the post of KGB chairman is difficult to explain. Hodnett, in his study of recruitment policy in the national republics, found similar republic variations with other job categories. While identifying some factors that account for these differences, Hodnett concluded that ethnic occupancy patterns are very complex and have little relation to such factors as the proportion of the indigenous nationality in the population of each republic.[20] Moscow's avoidance of a strict policy of appointing nonnatives to the top republic KGB post suggests that several considerations are involved when these appointments are made. First, there are geographical and religious factors. Republics such as Tadzhikistan, Turkmenistan, Uzbekistan, and Azerbaidzhan, which all border Muslim countries, may be seen to need tighter Russian control than other republics. Another consideration may be that of availability of qualified native cadres. In some of the less developed republics there may not be a large pool of such cadres from which to choose for the post of republic KGB chairman. This might be the case with Moldavia and Kazakhstan, for example, which both have low rates of native occupancy for many leading republic posts. Belorussia's situation is somewhat more difficult to explain. Native occupancy for other positions, including those of first and second secretary, is high, and like the Ukrainians and Armenians, Belorussians frequently serve as officials outside their republic. Curiously, two Belorussians have been KGB chairmen in other republics, but none in their own.[21]

As table 5.9 indicates, nonnative occupancy of the post of KGB chairman sometimes is offset by having a predominant number of natives in the posts below chairman. But this is not always the case, as the examples of Turkmenistan and Uzbekistan show. Conversely, the limited data show that in cases in which a native is KGB chairman, the first deputy is often a nonnative and hence probably serves as a watchdog for Moscow, not unlike the second secretary. This has occurred in Armenia, Azerbaidzhan, Georgia, and Lithuania but not in the Ukraine, where the majority of all KGB officials have been Ukrainians.

Although there appears to be a policy regarding either native or nonnative occupancy in at least nine republics, the situation has been fluid in the five remaining republics: Azerbaidzhan, Estonia, Kazakhstan, Kirgizia, and Latvia. As of 1986 all but Kirgizia and Kazakhstan had indigenous ethnic cadres occupying the post of KGB chairman. This could be a sign that Moscow has decided to encourage more native occupancy for this job. If so, the impetus for this change might well relate to the expanding role and changing public image of the KGB. While the main function of the republic KGB chairman remains that of political control, his role has increasingly broadened in scope. In contrast to earlier periods, when KGB officials maintained a low profile, the republic KGB chairman has become a more visible public figure engaging in a wide range of activities that include giving speeches and taking an active part in the republic party leadership. Thus his role is subtly shifting from behind-the-scenes control to one that involves propaganda and public relations. This might partly explain a greater effort to place native cadres in the post of KGB chairman, though this policy will be implemented only to the extent that it does not endanger the KGB's primary objective in the republics: ensuring Russian dominance.

Political Participation: Recruitment to Party and State Leadership Bodies

Election of KGB officials to party and state governing bodies, including those at the republic level, is probably carried out according to the dictates of the central party authorities. The extent to which the KGB and other Soviet institutions have been represented in these bodies is thus a reflection of a conscious and deliberate policy by the party leadership to confer political status on various groups. This applies also to the supreme soviets at the national and republic levels, which play only a small role in the policy process but whose delegates nevertheless represent members of the Soviet elite. In the case of party organizations (in particular, the Politburo, CPSU Central Committee, and republic party bureaus) membership carries not only status but also a role in decision making.

Considering first the USSR and republic supreme soviets, table 5.10 indicates a trend, with some exceptions, toward increased proportions of KGB delegates. The 1975 decline in KGB representation on republic supreme soviets relates partly to the fact that more republic KGB chair-

[169]

TABLE 5.10
KGB Representation on Supreme Soviets

		NATIONAL REPUBLIC SUPREME SOVIETS*					
	1955	1963	1967	1971	1975	1980	1985
Total KGB delegates	15	15	13	13	10	17	17

			RSFSR SUPREME SOVIET					
	1955	1959	1963	1967	1971	1975	1980	1985
Total KGB delegates	N/A	3	6	5	6	7	8	8
Percentage of total delegates		.4	.7	.5	.7	.8	.8	.8

			USSR SUPREME SOVIET**				
	1958	1962	1966	1970	1974	1979	1984
Total KGB delegates	6	8	12	10	13	15	18
Percentage of total delegates	.4	.5	.8	.7	.9	1.0	1.2

SOURCES: Selected issues of *Izvestiia* (for lists of delegates to RSFSR Supreme Soviet); republic party newspapers (for national republic Supreme Soviet); and *Deputaty VS SSSR* for various years (for delegates to USSR Supreme Soviet).

NOTE: Border Guards excluded from total KGB delegates for republic, RSFSR, and USSR supreme soviets.

* 1959 republic supreme soviets were excluded because delegates' occupations were usually not designated.

** 1954 USSR Supreme Soviet was excluded because the KGB had not yet been established, but there was a total of 17 delegates from the MVD, which incorporated the regular and the security police. This was a proportional representation of 1.3%.

men were being elected to the USSR Supreme Soviet and that they are not usually elected delegates to both. By 1980 the number of deputy chairmen and *oblast* KGB chiefs elected to republic supreme soviets had increased to offset this trend. The number of KGB delegates to the RSFSR Supreme Soviet has risen steadily since the Khrushchev era—from three in 1959 to eight in 1980 and 1985. These delegates usually include chiefs of a few *oblast* or *krai* KGB administrations, chiefs of the Moscow and Leningrad KGB Administrations, and certain USSR KGB officials.

The proportion of KGB delegates elected to the USSR Supreme Soviet has tripled since 1958. In the last election (February 1984) all KGB republic chairmen were elected for the first time. State security representation on the USSR Supreme Soviet has not been this high since 1950, when twenty-five MGB officials were elected. Interestingly, it is now higher than it was after the 1946 Supreme Soviet elections, when fourteen state security officials were elected (one percent of the total delegates). Despite the rather minor role that the Supreme Soviet plays in policymaking, these trends are important as they reflect the political status of the KGB.

It might also be noted that KGB delegates are well represented in the Standing Commissions of the Supreme Soviet. In 1966, when numerous new standing commissions were formed, KGB membership was restricted to the two Legislative Proposals Commissions (a total of five KGB delegates served on these commissions). But they soon extended their committee membership to other areas—including the prestigious Foreign Affairs Commission, to which Chebrikov was elected in 1979. In 1984 KGB delegates were elected to serve on the following USSR Supreme Soviet commissions:[22]

Soviet of Nationalities

Legislative Proposals
Industry (two members)
Construction and Construction
Materials Industry (two
members)
Transport and Communications
Trade and Public Services
Science and Technology
Health and Social Welfare
Planning and Budget
Youth Affairs
Mandate

Soviet of Unions

Legislative Proposals
Environmental and Natural
Resources
Energy
Mandate

While the Standing Commissions have little real authority, the KGB's participation signifies their increasingly broad role in the country's public life.

Increases in KGB representation on party organizations is even more noticeable. Table 5.11 shows that the number of KGB officials among delegates to CPSU congresses has risen considerably, though it still represents a small proportion of total delegates. A more significant indicator of political participation is KGB membership on the CPSU Central Committee. By 1986 four KGB officials were full members of the

[171]

TABLE 5.11
KGB Representation on Leading Party Bodies

		DELEGATES TO CPSU PARTY CONGRESSES				
	1956	1961	1966	1976	1981	1986
Number	7	16	24	26	37	36
Percentage of total delegates	.5	.3	.5	.5	.7	.7

		CPSU CENTRAL COMMITTEE MEMBERSHIP					
	1956	1961	1966	1971	1976	1981	1986
Full	1	0	1	1	1	4	4
Candidate	1	1	0	2	3	0	1

	REPUBLIC CENTRAL COMMITTEE MEMBERSHIP* (REPRESENTATION OF KGB DEPUTY CHAIRMEN)				
	1966	1971	1976	1981	1986
Full	0	0	0	1	2
Candidate	4	3	5	5	2
Auditing Commission	1	0	0	2	2
None	4	6	4	3	6
Unknown	5	5	5	3	2

SOURCES: Stenografic reports for the various CPSU party congresses and selected issues of republic newspapers.
 * KGB chairmen are always full members of republic central committees.

Central Committee— KGB Chairman Chebrikov, First Deputy Chairmen Emokhonov and Bobkov, and Deputy Chairman Kruichkov, while Deputy Chairman Ageev, was elected to candidate membership. Of course this representation is small in comparison with organizations such as the military, which had twenty-three officers elected to the Central Committee at the last congress. But the KGB is a much smaller organization and, given the sensitive nature of its functions, might be expected to maintain a less visible presence on the Central Committee.[23] What is significant is the marked increase in KGB representation since 1961.

At the republic level KGB chairmen are always full members of the republic central committee. The membership of deputy chairmen, however, has varied. Unfortunately, because it is not always possible to identify deputy chairmen, definite conclusions cannot be reached about their status in all cases. Nevertheless table 5.11 offers some tentative data that indicate a slight trend toward higher central committee status among this group from the early 1970s onward. It would be useful to determine the party status of all *oblast* KGB chiefs, but again problems of identification preclude such an analysis. In his study of twenty-five *obkoms*, Joel Moses concluded that in 1970 the regional KGB chief was a full member of the *obkom* bureau in all cases.[24] More recent information in the Soviet press has indicated either full or candidate bureau membership for *oblast* KGB chiefs.[25]

Table 5.12 offers information on membership of republic KGB chairmen and chiefs of the Moscow and Leningrad KGB administrations in their respective party bureaus, which are the top leadership bodies at the republic and regional levels. It appears from looking at the table that once Khrushchev had consolidated his power, there was a marked drop in the bureau membership of KGB chiefs. This was partly related to his general policy of reducing bureau size, but it was also a result of his aim of curtailing police powers. What is perhaps surprising is that the trend continued after Brezhnev became general secretary. In 1968–1970 only two KGB chiefs had bureau status. This might be explained by the fact that Brezhnev and his supporters were in the process of replacing KGB officials associated with Shelepin and Semichastnyi at this time. The new KGB appointees were then gradually given bureau status.

As table 5.12 shows, variations occurred among the different republics, but the general trend has been one of increased KGB representation on republic bureaus. This process correlated with Brezhnev's policy of courting nonparty institutions as a means of broadening his base of support and bringing representatives of these institutions into the party leadership. Brezhnev's successors have continued this trend, with KGB representation on party bureaus reaching an unprecedented nine full and seven candidates in early 1986, at the time of the republic and regional party congresses. As a result of this policy KGB officials are now formally included in party decision making at this level.

Observations

As this analysis suggests, the process of appointment and promotion in the KGB below the topmost level appears to be highly centralized, with little connection to republic or regional politics. KGB appointments may be divorced from local party politics, but there is strong evidence that party leaders in Moscow have at times influenced KGB personnel decisions. KGB officials can be assured of relatively secure jobs without the likelihood of abrupt dismissal. Yet they pay for this security by having

TABLE 5.12
CP Bureau Membership of KGB Chiefs of Republics; Moscow, Leningrad (16): 1955–1986

Republic	55	56	57	58	59	60	61	62	63	64	65	66	67	68	69	70	71	72	73	74	75	76	77	78	79	80	81	82	83	84	85	86
Armenia																											C	C	F	C	C	C
Azerbaidzhan		F															C	C	C	C	C	F	F	F	F	F	F	F	F	F	F	F
Belorussia																	C	C	C	C	C	C	C	F	F	F	F	F	F	F	F	F
Estonia																	F	F	F	F	F	F	F	F	F	F	C	F	F	F	F	F
Georgia	F	F	F	F	F	F	F	F	F	C	C	C	C	C	C	C	F	F	F	F	F	F	F	F	F	F	C	C	F	F	F	C
Kazakhstan	F	F	F	F	F	F	F	F	F	F	F	F	F				F	F	F	F	F	C	C	F	C	C	C	F	F	F	F	C
Kirgizia	F	C	C	C	C	C	C	C	C	C	C	C	C				C	C	C	C	C	C	C	C	C	C	C	C	C	C	C	C
Latvia								C															C	C	C	C	C	C	C	C	C	C
Lithuania	F			F	F	F	F	C	C	C	C	C					C	C		C	C	C	C	C	C	C	C	C	C	C	C	C
Moldavia		F	F	F	F	F	F	F	F	C	C	C					C	C	C		C	C	C	C	C		C	C	C	C	C	C
Tadzhikistan				F	F	F	F	F	F	F	F	F	F				F	F	F	F	F	F	F	F	F	F	F	F	F	F	F	F
Turkmenistan	F	F		C	F	C	C															C	C	C			F	F	C	F	F	C
Ukraine																			C	C	C	C	C	C	C	C	C	C	C	C	C	C
Uzbekistan	C	C	F	F	F	F	F	F	C								F	F	F	F	F	C	C	C	F	F	C	C	F	C	C	F
Total	5F 1C	6F 2C	5F 1C	6F 2C	7F 1C	4F 2C	4F 1C	5F 2C	3F 3C	2F 3C	1F 3C	1F 3C	1F 1C	1F 1C	1F 1C	1F 1C	3F 4C	3F 4C	3F 5C	3F 5C	2F 5C	5F 7C	5F 7C	5F 6C	5F 4C	5F 4C	7F 7C	7F 5C	7F 6C	7F 6C	6F 5C	9F 5C
Moscow City & Oblast											F	F	F	F	F	F	F	F	C	C	F	F	F	F	F	F	F	F	F	F	F	F
Leningrad City & Oblast											F	F	F	F	F	F	F	F	F	F	F	F	F	F	F	F	F	F	F	F	F	F
GRAND TOTAL	5F 1C	6F 2C	6F 2C	7F 2C	7F 2C	4F 2C	4F 1C	5F 2C	3F 3C	4F 3C	3F 3C	3F 3C	3F 1C	1F 1C	1F 1C	1F 1C	4F 4C	4F 4C	4F 5C	4F 6C	4F 5C	7F 7C	7F 7C	7F 6C	7F 4C	7F 4C	9F 7C	9F 5C	9F 6C	9F 6C	8F 5C	11F 5C

SOURCES: Selected issues of republic party newspapers; *Leningradskaia pravda* and *Moskovskaia pravda*.

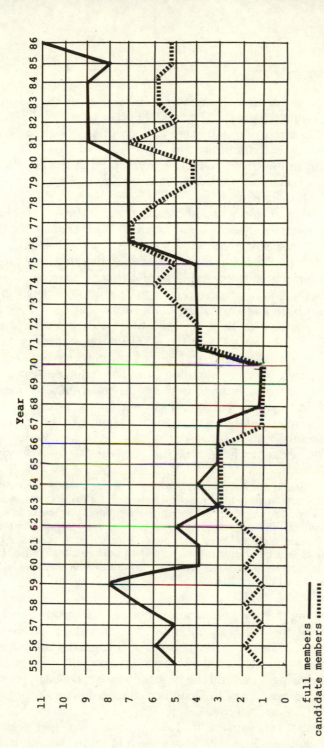

FIGURE 5.1 *Trends in CP Bureau Membership of KGB Chiefs of Republics and Moscow and Leningrad, 1955–1986.*

few opportunities for upward mobility. In most cases the position of chairman or deputy chairman of a republic KGB is the final point in a KGB official's career. Although there are exceptions, such as Tsvigun and Fedorchuk, the chances for a republic KGB official to achieve a prominent post in the USSR KGB are not great. High-level posts in the USSR KGB have often been filled by party apparatchiks or from within the USSR KGB hierarchy itself.

Judging from recruitment and career patterns, the KGB represents a highly professional bureaucratic group with distinct characteristics that set it off from other Soviet elites. As indicated by the backgrounds of members of the KGB elite, the party has placed a high premium on experience and expertise at the expense of *partiinost* (party spirit). After the initial introduction of party and other cadres into the newly created KGB, there has been a relatively small influx of outsiders, except at the very highest levels. The KGB has become a closed bureaucracy of specialists similar to the military. As a result state security officials display a homogeneity in their backgrounds and career experiences that no doubt gives them a common outlook and has created a strong esprit de corps. Judging from numerous memoirs and reminiscences, this sense of solidarity has been particularly strong among the older group of KGB officials, who joined the security agencies before or during the war. Thus, for example, one KGB official of this generation writes about entering the "Chekist family" during the war years:

> Having settled in and become accustomed to things, we learned vigilance and conspiracy, acquired the practical habits of the Chekist profession. . . . Thank you for your friendship, mutual help and purposefulness, as a result of which all these years, day by day, in deciding operative tasks, knowledge has perfected itself and moved into action to prevail over lesser forces and the indestructable Chekist traditions, established by Dzerzhinskii, have been strengthened. Now all this has become an inseparable part of our characters.[26]

Even among the new generation a common background and sense of being part of the "Chekist tradition" has continued to breed this communal spirit. Thus the KGB chairman of Georgia, Inauri, noted that "new generations of state security workers have come to replace the first Chekists. Work experience and the best traditions have been passed on . . . and the KGB machinery in Georgia's cities and *raions* constitutes a single, united Chekist collective."[27]

The fact that members of the KGB enjoy a privileged position in Soviet society and, until recently, have been immune from public criticism probably reinforces their feeling of eliteness. They have been consistently described in the media as possessing superior qualities in terms of both character and ability. According to an article on the Leningrad KGB, Chekists must have

> not only an intense and thorough knowledge of their profession, but also the necessary qualities for this, the most important of which are a party caste, political maturity, ideological conviction, acute vigilance. Now more than ever before, first and foremost, must be the ability to evaluate from the class position all the variations, complexities and contradictions of contemporary phenomena of international life. . . . Persistence, erudition, steadfastness, conviction, tremendous capability for work, stability, and a deep knowledge of life—these are the more typical qualities of Chekists accepted for service in the Leningrad Oblast KGB.[28]

Presumably the KGB has been able to recruit such highly educated, highly qualified cadres not only because of the professional prestige but also because of the perquisites and high salaries that it offers.[29]

There is little indication as yet that Gorbachev will make a sharp departure from what appears to be a well-established cadres policy toward the KGB. To be sure, he has challenged the KGB's immunity from public criticism by allowing (or perhaps even encouraging) the press to discuss KGB violations of legality. And an interview with USSR Deputy KGB Chief G. A. Ageev, who appears to be responsible for KGB personnel, suggested that the KGB's public image was being lowered a few notches. Ageev noted that "the demands made on the nature of the Soviet Chekist are certainly a very long way from any characteristics of a superman. Any Soviet person raised on the principles of the socialist way of life, patriotism and love for the motherland can become a Chekist."[30]

Gorbachev may be diminishing the KGB's elite status by allowing its image of perfection and infallibility to be questioned, but he probably will not revoke the privileges and perquisites enjoyed by KGB personnel or damage its spirit of professionalism. There have been some changes among leading KGB personnel under Gorbachev, but he has not been replacing entrenched KGB bureaucrats with party apparatchiks. Perhaps Gorbachev does not yet have the power to carry through with such changes. More likely he simply does not consider it politically wise to attack the KGB's vested interests in this way. The party and the KGB reached a *modus vivendi* during the Brezhnev era that has served both institutions well. It is difficult to see why Gorbachev would want to destroy this relationship, unless he is attempting to change the system radically.

What are the implications of the high degree of institutional cohesion within the KGB and the relatively small amount of interaction with other bureaucracies? Does this situation create the basis for conflict with other institutions, as the KGB collectively defends its functional interests and perhaps attempts to influence the outcome of political struggles? We can probably assume that, like the military, the KGB does indeed have strong institutional interests to protect. But the party has done its best to ensure that the needs of the KGB are well met and that its privileged position is secure. Thus the likelihood of any attempt at collective action on the part of the KGB has been small. The trend toward increased representation of KGB officials on party leadership bodies at all levels suggests, however, that KGB officials are no longer mere executors of party tasks but are becoming integrated into the decision-making process and thus have gained more influence over Kremlin policy.

Notes

1. See appendix D for a list of these officials and career data on them. The information was drawn from a broad number of sources and compiled by the author over several years. The main sources are republic and national newspapers; *Deputaty verkhovnogo soveta SSSR* for the years 1958–1984; selected *Deputaty verkhovnogo soveta* for certain republics; various republic encyclopedias, the yearbooks (*ezhegodniki*) of the *Bol'shaia sovetskaia entsiklopediia*; and Soviet histories of the state security apparatus for various regions. Among the English-language sources are *Soviet Intelligence and Security Services*, vols. I (1964–1970) and II (1971–1972), prepared by the Congressional Research Service of the Library of Congress (Washington, D.C.: U.S. Government Printing Office, 1972 and 1975); CIA *Directory of Soviet Officials* for various years; Grey Hodnett and Val Ogareff, *Leaders of the Soviet Republics, 1955–72* (Canberra: Australian National University, 1973); and Val Ogareff, *Leaders of the Soviet Republics, 1972–1980* (Canberra: Australian National University, 1981). I was also allowed to use the biographical file on KGB officials of Mr. Peter Kruzhin of Radio Liberty, Munich, Germany, and the files of Professor Robert Slusser of Michigan State University.

2. Two new USSR KGB deputy chairmen were identified at the Twenty-Seventh Party Congress in March 1986: V. A. Ponomarev and I. A. Markelov. Ponomarev is a career KGB official, and because Markelov's previous career is unknown, he too probably comes from the security apparatus. See chapter 3, note 83. The other seven deputy chairmen were appointed before Gorbachev came to power. (F. D. Bobkov, who has been in the security police since 1945, was elevated from deputy to first deputy chairman in late 1985.) See appendix C. On republic-level changes see note 14.

3. Frederic Fleron defines cooptation into the party apparatus as having seven years' or more experience in a nonparty career before being given a party appointment. See Frederic Fleron, "Representation of Career Types in the Soviet Political Leadership," in *Political Leadership in Eastern Europe and the Soviet Union*, ed. R. Barry Farrell (Chicago: Aldine, 1970), pp. 123–124. I use the term more loosely, though in most cases it implies that an individual had already pursued a nonstate security career before he was brought into the KGB.

4. As was noted in chapter 3, even Andropov was not a party apparatchik in the strict sense of the term.

5. A study by Ellen Mickiewicz has drawn attention to the connection between communications officials and security police. See "The Functions of Communications Officials in the USSR: A Biographical Study," *Slavic Review* 43, no. 4 (Winter 1984):641–656. Mickiewicz identified yet another official, Abdulakhat Abdullaev, chairman of the Uzbek State Committee for Cinematography, who began his career in the KGB.

6. Jerry F. Hough, *Soviet Leadership in Transition* (Washington, D.C.: Brookings Institution, 1980), pp. 69–71.

7. This has not always been the case with the security police, however. During the time when Beria had control over the political police (roughly 1938–1953) a significant number of leading police cadres were from his Caucasian *khvost*.

8. L. A. Plotnikova, ed., *Chekisty* (Leningrad: Lenizdat, 1982), p. 501.

9. See, for example, the sketches of KGB employees that appear in Z. M. Iusif-Zade, ed., *Chekisty Azerbaidzhana: Dokumenty, ocherki, rasskazy* (Baku: Azerneshr, 1981), pp. 227–271; and in *Rytsari dolga: vospominaniia chekistov* (Donetsk: Donbas, 1982).

10. The Moscow and Leningrad KGB administrations cover both city and *oblast*. Their heads, who are called not chairmen but chiefs (*nachal'niki*), are roughly of the same stature as republic KGB chairmen (both usually hold the rank of Major General). Moscow and Leningrad were included to give representation to the RSFSR, which does not have a separate KGB organization, and thus not restrict our analysis to non-Russian areas.

11. Grey Hodnett, *Leadership in the Soviet National Republics: A Quantitative Study of Recruitment Policy* (Oakville, Ontario: Mosaic Press, 1978), pp. 61–73.

12. On Aliev see Il'ia Zemtsov, *Partiia ili Mafiia* (Paris: Reunis, 1976), pp. 73–94; Shevchenko's biography appears in *Deputaty VS SSSR* 1979, p. 487; Beschastnov's biography appears in *Deputaty VS SSSR*, 1974 p. 543. He also wrote an article about his wartime experiences in which he discussed his acquaintance with Brezhnev and spoke very highly of him. See *Chekisty Rasskazyvaiut*, book 5 (Moscow: Sovetskaia Rossiia, 1983), pp. 168–169. Andropov, having worked mainly in the field of foreign affairs, presumably had few protégés in either the party or KGB at the republic level when he was appointed head of the KGB in 1967. However he brought in some of his Central Committee associates, such as V. A. Kriuchkov and P. P. Laptev, to serve in the USSR KGB.

13. See Yaroslav Bilinksy, "Shcherbytskyi, Ukraine and Kremlin Politics," *POC*, 32 (July-August 1982), pp. 9–10; Borys Lewytzkyj, *Politics and Society in Soviet Ukraine, 1953–1980* (Edmonton, Alberta: Canadian Institute of Ukrainian Studies, 1984), pp. 117, 136.

14. It might be added that two republic KGB chairmen (Mukha in the Ukraine and Petkiavichius in Lithuania) have been replaced thus far in 1987, along with the Leningrad KGB chief D. P. Nosyrev, thus making a total of six changes at this level since Gorbachev came to power. See appendix E for details. With the exception of the new Ukrainian KGB chief, Golushko, we have no biographical data on the new officials. Thus it might be assumed that they are KGB rather than party men. Golushko, who has been in the KGB since 1963, may have worked with Ligachev. See chapter 3, note 105.

15. See John H. Miller, "Cadres Policy in Nationality Areas," *Soviet Studies* 29, no. 1 (January 1977):20.

16. Of the four recruited from the party apparatus, one, D. Asankulov, had been in the state security organs since 1946 but was made head of the Administrative Organs Department of the Kirgiz Central Committee one year prior to his appointment as chairman of the Kirgiz KGB. See *Deputaty VS SSSR*, 1974, p. 35.

17. The most notable case is that of Fedorchuk, who served as chairman of the Ukrainian KGB from 1970 to 1982. Others include A. I. Perepelitsyn, S. G. Bannikov, S. N. Lialin, S. S. Belchenko, and L. I. Korobov. The first two became USSR deputy KGB chairmen and the others became heads of KGB directorates.

18. Sources for the information are cited in note 1.

19. This counters the commonly held assumption among Western scholars that the head of the republic KGB is invariably a Russian. See, for example, Seweryn Bialer, *Stalin's*

Successors: Leadership, Stability, and Change in the Soviet Union (New York: Cambridge University Press, 1980), p. 214.

20. Hodnett, *Leadership in the Soviet Republics*, pp. 88–112. Also see Miller, "Cadres Policy in Nationality Areas."

21. These were E. B. Nordman, chairman of the Uzbek KGB from 1974 to 1978, and D. Asankulov, chairman of the Kirgiz KGB from 1967 to 1978. For Nordman's biography see *Uzbek Sovet entsiklopediiasi* (Tashkent, 1976), 8:62–63. On Asankulov see nŏte 16.

22. See *Deputaty VS SSSR, 1984.* Chebrikov was the only delegate from the KGB not to serve on a standing commission in 1984. Presumably he was not reelected to the Foreign Affairs Commission because his duties as KGB chairman precluded his membership. For a detailed study of Supreme Soviet Standing Commissions, see Robert W. Siegler, *The Standing Commissions of the USSR Supreme Soviet* (New York: Praeger, 1982).

23. The KGB's estimated manpower of 500,000 to 700,000 employees is small in comparison to the estimated five million members of the Soviet Armed Forces. See *The Military Balance 1986–1987* (London: International Institute for Strategic Studies, 1986), p. 36. In addition to these five KGB officials, P. P. Laptev, a former KGB official and Andropov aide, was elected to the Central Auditing Commission.

24. See Joel C. Moses, *Regional Party Leadership and Policy-Making in the USSR* (New York: Praeger, 1974), pp. 160–161. Phillip Stewart, in his book, *Political Power in the Soviet Union: A Study of Decision-Making in Stalingrad* (Indianapolis and New York: Bobbs-Merrill, 1968), found that the head of the KGB was included as a full member of the Stalingrad *Obkom* bureau from March 1954 to at least January 1961 (p. 98). According to Frederick Barghoorn, who examined seven *oblast* newspapers in 1966–1967, the KGB chief was either a full or candidate member of the *obkom* bureau in the seven *obkoms* involved. See Frederick Barghoorn, "The Security Police," in *Interest Groups in Soviet Politics*, ed. H. Gordon Skilling and Franklyn Griffiths (Princeton, N.J.: Princeton University Press, 1971), pp. 112–113.

25. See the obituary of Karagandinsk Oblast KGB Chief L. A. Chechurin, who was a full member of the *obkom* bureau, in *Kazakhstanskaia pravda*, 16 July 1986, p. 3. Also see *Pravda*, 4 January 1987, p. 3, and 8 January 1987, p. 1, where A. Dichenko, the disgraced chief of the Voroshilov Oblast KGB, is identified as a candidate member of the *obkom* bureau. This case is discussed in chapter 3.

26. N. Nelidov, "Pokoncheno bespovorotno," in *Ne zhaleia zhizni*, ed. A. Tleuliev (Alma Ata: Izdatelstvo Kazakhstan, 1977), pp. 239–240.

27. *Zaria vostoka*, 25 December 1981, p. 2.

28. Plotnikova, *Chekisty*, pp. 501–502.

29. According to former KGB employee Aleksei Myagkov, "as well as power over 'simple mortals,' freedom in personal behavior, and the opportunity to get drunk at official expense, KGB agents have other material privileges. An officer receives three or four times the daily pay of a skilled worker, he also has a splendid flat, the right to buy goods in special shops at reduced prices and much else beside." Aleksei Myagkov, *Inside the KGB* (Survey: Foreign Affairs Publishers, 1976), p. 91. Also see Gordon B. Smith, "Socialist Legality and Legal Policy in the Soviet Union," in *Public Policy and Administration in the Soviet Union* (New York: Praeger, 1980), p. 118; and Arkady Shevchenko, *Breaking with Moscow* (New York: Ballantine, 1985), p. 322. According to Shevchenko, "only the KGB pays its people well enough for them to afford the best in western clothing."

30. See *Trud*, 19 April 1987, p. 4.

III
The Functions of the KGB

6

The KGB and Internal Security

The KGB's interactions with society and the ways in which it performs its domestic role are strongly influenced by political events in the Kremlin. It is not uncommon, for example, to see shifts in Soviet policy toward dissent, as executed by the KGB, accompany changes in the Soviet leadership. The continuous tension between the party's desire to reform and its need to retain tight political control, which we have seen throughout the Soviet period, is strongly reflected in how the KGB goes about its task of ordering regime-societal relations. Thus while distinct changes in the KGB's domestic operations have occurred since Stalin died, we can also observe certain constants that are associated with the nature of the system itself. It is particularly important to bear this in mind when considering the reforms that have been advocated by the Gorbachev leadership. The campaign against dissent has been curtailed, and there has been a relaxation in societal controls, but these changes must be seen within the larger context of Soviet history, which has witnessed repeated cycles of relaxation and repression.

The Soviet Union is a single-party state where the CPSU enjoys a monopoly over political power. Throughout the Soviet system—from the center of decision making in Moscow to the factories, enterprises, and small villages—the party extends its all-pervasive controls. By means of the party's vast propaganda apparatus Soviet citizens are constantly reminded of its presence as a guiding force in their lives. Although the CPSU has successfully employed the traditional methods of political indoctrination, education, and propaganda to gain support from the Soviet public, the regime has never been able to rely solely on these noncoercive means even at the best of times. Because the leadership is not elected by Soviet citizens or accountable to them in any formal way, it lacks the legitimacy that democratically elected leaders enjoy and stands in isolation from the people. No matter how popular a given party leader may be or how successful the regime is in implementing its goals, there is always the danger that small pockets of discontent, having few outlets of free expression, could threaten the political stability of the regime. Thus the party leadership has continued to require an effective political police to buttress its rule. Younger more progressive leaders such as Gorbachev may endeavor to make the Soviet system more open by reducing police constraints on the population, but it is difficult to imagine any Soviet leader who is committed to the CPSU's monopoly of power questioning the necessity for the KGB.

As this study has stressed, the KGB's internal security functions, which are exercised primarily through its Second and Fifth Chief Directorates, extend far beyond uncovering and investigating state crimes. Soviet legal textbooks, statements by KGB officials, and testimonies of political dissidents attest to the wide range of tasks that the KGB has increasingly taken on as part of its domestic security role. These tasks can be divided roughly into three categories. First is the KGB's coercive punitive role—the arrest and investigation of Soviet citizens (and in some cases foreigners) for certain political and economic crimes, the fabrication of cases against dissidents on nonpolitical charges, and the forcible commitment of individuals in psychiatric hospitals. This role also encompasses various extrajudicial methods of repression, such as the use of covert violence, threats, and harassment.

The second function is a "prophylactic" one that is designed to prevent political crimes and suppress deviant political attitudes. The KGB exercises this function in a variety of ways. If, for example, the KGB learns that a Soviet citizen is having contact with foreigners or is speaking in a negative fashion about the Soviet regime, this citizen is called in for a "chat" and efforts are made to set him or her straight. The KGB also devotes effort to education and indoctrination of the Soviet public on the dangers of Western influences and the necessity of being "vigilant," and it participates in the extensive system of censorship. Finally, the third internal security task of the KGB is that of providing the Soviet leadership with information about dissent and the political attitudes and opinions of the Soviet public as a whole.

These three domestic security functions are exercised on behalf of the party leadership, which sets the general guidelines that the KGB is to follow. The regime has numerous policy options at its disposal in protecting itself against internal dissent. The policies that it chooses to adopt at any given time are influenced by a variety of factors: the international situation, economic concerns, and internal Kremlin politics. A question of primary interest here is the input that the KGB itself has into this policymaking. As a purveyor of information to the party leadership on the extent and nature of dissident activities, the KGB presumably influences Kremlin decision making in this realm. It is also important to consider the degree of autonomy enjoyed by the KGB in carrying out Kremlin directives. In other words, where is the line drawn between policymaking and policy implementation? To what extent is the KGB allowed to choose its own strategies and methods in protecting the regime from threats to its political stability? The following examination of the KGB's internal security role should shed light on these issues.

Punitive and Coercive Measures: Post-1965 Changes in the Legal Codes

In carrying out its task of ensuring state security, the KGB is empowered by law to uncover and investigate certain political crimes set forth in the RSFSR and other republic criminal codes. Changes in the republic codes of criminal procedure from 1961 to the present have extended the purview of the KGB's investigatory apparatus, while revisions in the criminal codes have broadened definitions of political crimes, making it easier to prosecute Soviet citizens on criminal charges. Although there have been waves of repression and relaxation during this period, in general the trend of tightening the legal codes—and hence increasing the punitive powers of the KGB—has been reflected in the treatment of political dissent. Because legal changes through 1965 have been examined in earlier chapters, only revisions in the legal codes since that time will be considered here.

In September 1966 two articles were added to the RSFSR Criminal Code which did not formally affect the KGB's authority but which nevertheless have proved significant in the struggle waged by the KGB against dissent. These are Articles 190-1 ("circulating false statements which defame the Soviet state") and 190-3 ("organization or active participation in group activities which violate public order.")[1] Although these crimes were placed under the investigative purview of the Procuracy rather than the KGB, the articles were designed specifically for the purpose of making it easier to prosecute political dissenters. Article 190-1 is similar to article 70 ("anti-Soviet agitation and propaganda"), but it carries a milder sentence and anti-Soviet intent does not have to be proved as a motivating factor in the crime, as it does in Article 70. It was interpreted in the West as a response to the difficulties that arose during the Sinyavskiy-Daniel trial of February 1966, when the defendants claimed that they had no anti-Soviet intentions. Article 190-3 was said to have been introduced because of group demonstrations that took place in the wake of the trial.[2] As experience has shown, the fact that the KGB has no formal authority to investigate cases under Articles 190-1 and 190-3 has not prevented it from orchestrating prosecutions behind the scenes.

Other far-reaching changes in the laws on state crimes that directly affect the authority of the KGB were introduced by a decree of 11 January 1984.[3] The definition of treason (Article 64 of the RSFSR Criminal Code) was made broader to encompass acts that affect not only the external security of the USSR but also its internal political stability. Though perhaps not having an immediate effect on the number of prosecutions for treason, the change reflected a greater stress on state security by the Soviet regime since the early 1980s. Article 70 (anti-Soviet agitation and propaganda) now includes the preparation, dissemination, or possession not only of anti-Soviet literature but also of "other forms of works containing such material." Such works, according to Soviet sources, might include records, drawings, tapes, photographs, and videos that Soviet authorities see as a distinct political threat.[4] Indeed, Soviet legal experts have subsequently made it clear that persons organizing viewings of videos that contain anti-Soviet propaganda can, if the intention of undermining Soviet authority is evident, be prosecuted under Article 70.[5]

Another important change in Article 70 was the amendment to paragraph 2, in which a more severe sentence (up to ten rather than seven years) is prescribed for "actions carried out with the use of funds or other material means obtained from foreign organizations or from persons acting in the interests of these organizations." This seemingly could apply to any Soviet citizen who has received support from abroad, including, for example, writers who receive foreign royalties, those who get support from the Solzhenitsyn Fund (The Russian Social Fund to Aid Political Prisoners and Their Families), or "refusniks" who receive aid from Western Jewish organizations. Thus the amendment was intended to discourage dissidents or potential dissidents from turning to sources abroad for financial help.

Finally, a new article was added to the list of state crimes, Article 76-1, "the transmission of information constituting an official secret to foreign organizations." Because no definition was offered of what constitutes an official secret, it might be assumed that virtually all information passed to foreigners could be construed as such. Thus any Soviet citizen who has contact with foreigners is vulnerable to prosecution under this article, particularly in view of the fact that most Soviets are government employees and therefore have access to "official secrets." This article might also be used to justify the denial of exit visas to applicants on the grounds that they have access to official secrets. According to the decree of 11 January 1984, the organs of state security have responsibility for investigating cases based on Article 76-1. This confers on the KGB virtually blanket authority to investigate any contacts between Soviet citizens and foreigners. Furthermore, on the grounds of protecting official or work-related secrets, the KGB can justify greater involvement in the day-to-day activities of state agencies and organizations.

In general the amendments to the law on state crimes placed significantly more power in the hands of the KGB. Taken in conjunction with such measures as the law of 25 May 1984, which made Soviet citizens liable for fines for allowing foreigners to stay with them without permission from the authorities,[6] the changes appeared to be part of a trend toward a more closed and xenophobic society. Gorbachev is attempting to reverse that trend. According to Soviet officials, the legal codes are currently being examined with a view to making substantial changes.[7] We will not know the precise impact on KGB operations for some time, but the changes could curtail the KGB's legal prerogatives. For example, in addition to calls for the protection of individual rights during investigations and trials, some experts have advocated explicit legal definitions of what constitutes secret or official information.[8] This would limit the KGB's authority to arrest individuals on vague charges of violating secrets.

But the existing legal codes remain in force and the legal changes that have been introduced have not significantly broadened political freedoms. Thus, for example, a law on the right of citizens to appeal to courts against illegal actions by Soviet officials was passed in July 1987. But Article 3 of the new law stipulates that appeals will not be permitted in connection with official actions regarding measures of state security.[9] For the time being, Gorbachev's attempts to relax political controls are being carried out on an ad hoc basis by means of pardons, amnesties, and fewer arrests.

[187]

Arrests and Prosecutions

As noted earlier, the intensity of KGB campaigns against political crime has varied considerably over the years. The Khrushchev period was marked not only by efforts to de-Stalinize and introduce a system of legality that curbed arbitrary police powers but also by a relatively liberal policy toward the arts and a more tolerant attitude toward political nonconformity. In general, as Robert Sharlet put it:

> Khrushchev, who made selective criticism of Stalinism the hallmark of his regime, basically construed "socialist legality" in a pro-individual, anti-arbitrariness direction, symbolizing his public commitment to the restoration and reinforcement of normative means at the expense of the Stalinist prerogatives.

Brezhnev, by contrast, tended to use the term "socialist legality" "to signal his pro-state, anti-deviance orientation in the administration of criminal justice."[10] As part of a general campaign for law and order the Brezhnev leadership enlisted the forces of a rehabilitated KGB to carry out a vigorous specialized campaign against political dissent. Though conducted under the guise of adherence to legality, this campaign actually involved continual flagrant violations of the law.

This systematic campaign against dissent is generally seen to have begun in 1965 with the arrests of Andrei Sinyavsky and Yulii Daniel, whose case was investigated by the KGB under Article 70 of the RSFSR Criminal Code. The trial gave rise to a wave of protests from Soviet intellectuals and set in motion a cycle of repression and dissent that continued with varying intensity throughout the Brezhnev era. While the main strategy of the dissidents was to defend their actions as complying with Soviet legal codes, the regime itself chose to respond by flouting legal codes and elevating *partiinost'* (party spirit) over *zakonnost'* (legality), mainly through the KGB.[11]

Peter Reddaway, who compiled detailed statistics on the annual rates of political arrests from the Khrushchev period to mid-1984, discerned some interesting trends in the regime's strategy over these years.[12] There was a sharp rise in arrests beginning in 1966 and continuing, with some fluctuation, through 1973. During this period the average rate of arrests was 185 per annum. The expansion of contacts between dissidents and the West and the increasing coverage of human rights abuses in the *Chronicle of Current Events* and other *samizdat* publications gave the regime an especially strong impetus to crack down on dissent in 1972. As Reddaway noted, the development of détente with the West was an additional factor.[13] The regime wanted to stress that relaxation of international tensions did not imply relaxation at home but the opposite.

Reddaway chronicled a sharp reversal in the regime's harsh policy toward dissent beginning in the autumn of 1973. Apparently foreign policy considerations, in particular the USSR's international image and the Kremlin's desire for a European security conference, gained precedence over domestic concerns. Despite a distinct rise in the level of dissent during these years, including the formation of independent groups to monitor Soviet compliance with the Helsinki accords, the Soviet regime seems to have decided that harsher policies toward dissent would jeopardize the benefits it sought from détente: SALT II, most-favored nation status with the U.S., and American trade credits. According to Reddaway, the rate of political arrests for the period 1975–1978 dropped to an average of eighty-seven per annum, less than half of what it had been.[14] Although it would be an exaggeration to say that in combating dissent, the KGB's hands were tied during this period, its actions were clearly constrained by the leadership's change in policy.

By late 1979 it became clear that Brezhnev's policy of détente was not bearing fruit, and the Kremlin may have felt that it had little to lose by initiating an antidissident campaign that was unprecedented in its severity. To be sure, the decision to invade Afghanistan lowered the political stakes of such a campaign even further, considering that the Soviet Union was now the butt of worldwide condemnation for its aggression. According to Reddaway, from the autumn of 1979 onward the rate of politically motivated arrests more than doubled, sentences were made longer, and emigration was drastically reduced.[15]

This trend continued after Brezhnev's death. According to Amnesty International more than 200 persons were arrested for exercising the right to freedom of expression or religion in 1983. Though Amnesty's arrest figures for 1984 and 1985 were somewhat lower (132 and 135, respectively), this may have reflected a lack of information coming from the Soviet Union, and most experts put the numbers much higher.[16] It should also be noted that these figures do not include either the political dissidents arrested on ordinary criminal charges or those confined in psychiatric hospitals.

It appears that political arrests continued with roughly the same frequency until the late summer or autumn of 1986. At this time Gorbachev began to push for political reform, which included a relaxation of the campaign against dissidents. This lent credibility to his efforts to "democratize" Soviet society and served to portray the Gorbachev

[189]

regime in a favorable light at a time when the USSR was engaged in sensitive arms control negotiations. In November 1986 *USSR News Brief*, a bimonthly newsletter from West Germany on the Soviet human rights movement, noted that several political prisoners had been prematurely released, others had had sentences revoked, and the number of political arrests had decreased.[17] The trend of fewer arrests continued into 1987, accompanied by the release of well over a hundred political prisoners. It should be stressed, however, that the KGB by no means ceased its arrests altogether.

What role has the KGB played in implementing the policies described earlier, particularly during times when the Kremlin has taken a tougher line on dissent? In principle the KGB has the right to make arrests and conduct investigations only for crimes specifically under its authority. While Reddaway classified annual arrests according to the type of dissident groups involved—religious, would-be emigrés, those with sociopolitical or nationalist concerns—there are no comprehensive statistics on the criminal charges made against dissidents over these years. After the addition of Article 190-1 to the RSFSR Criminal Code in 1966 it became just as common to prosecute dissidents under this article, which in theory is the responsibility of the Procuracy, as it was to make arrests under Article 70. And of course dissidents have frequently been arrested on a variety of ordinary criminal charges such as hooliganism (Article 206), parasitism (Article 209), and so on, while religious believers are most often charged under Article 142 (violation of laws on separation of church and state) or Article 227 (organization of religious groups that encroach on individual rights). In general, Articles 142, 190-1, 190-3, and 70 appear to be the most commonly applied to political prisoners. Of these only Article 70 is under the investigatory purview of the KGB.[18]

As a rough estimate it might be said that the KGB has had the formal legal authority to investigate a maximum of about one-third of all political cases. Although the majority of political arrests have been made for crimes falling under the purview of the Procuracy or the MVD, the KGB itself often enlists the MVD (or Procuracy) to instigate the proceedings. The practice of criminalizing political cases, which became increasingly common after Andropov assumed the KGB chairmanship in 1967, has the advantage of avoiding the publicity of political trials, which can reflect unfavorably on the USSR's image abroad. It also serves to discredit dissidents in the eyes of the public. An interesting statement about this practice has been attributed to former USSR KGB Chairman V. V. Fedorchuk, who served as head of the KGB in the Ukraine from 1970 to 1982: "In the course of 1980 we did a great job: we rendered harmless forty Ukrainian nationalists. In order to avoid needless international frictions, the majority of them were sentenced for ordinary criminal offenses."[19]

The general impression that emerges from *samizdat* and emigré accounts is that the KGB orchestrates most cases brought against religious or political dissenters regardless of the specific charges.[20] A good example is the case of Vladimir Brodskii, a founding member of the unofficial peace group "Trust" (*Doverie*). In August 1985 Brodskii was tried and sentenced by a Moscow court to three years in an ordinary regime camp on charges of "malicious hooliganism" (Article 206, part 2 of the RSFSR Criminal Code), which is under the investigative purview of both the Procuracy and the MVD. The *samizdat* documents, which give a detailed account of the case, show that the KGB was taking an active behind-the-scenes role well before Brodskii's arrest, harassing him at his workplace, and making threatening telephone calls.[21] *The Chronicle of Current Events* and *USSR News Brief* are replete with examples of KGB officers attending house searches of dissidents who later were charged for ordinary criminal offenses, as well as examples of persons arrested by the militia and taken to militia headquarters, only to be interrogated by KGB agents. The fact that KGB officers frequently threaten dissidents with arrest on ordinary criminal charges confirms that the KGB does in fact order the Procuracy or MVD to make such arrests.[22]

KGB Relations with the MVD and Procuracy

Although the MVD, which supervises the regular police, and Procuracy are compelled to carry through with such arrests on KGB instructions, there is some evidence of discontent about this situation, particularly on the part of the MVD. The former Soviet dissident Vladimir Bukovsky even recalls cases in which the MVD would not cooperate after the KGB had turned over political dissenters to their custody: "Sometimes the police punished us, but more often they simply let us go. Their interdepartmental hatred for these self-appointed police officers from the KGB never abated."[23] According to the former Ukrainian dissident Valentyn Moroz:

> There is also an irreconcilable conflict between the KGB and the militia (criminal police). The driving force here is ordinary envy. The militia does a lot of work, dirty and dangerous work (in view of the mass

alcoholism, hooliganism and thievery in the Soviet Union) but militia pay
and privileges are far less than what the KGB receives.[24]

There is less evidence of such antagonism between the Procuracy
and the KGB or of unwillingness on the part of Procuracy employees to
cooperate with the KGB in battling dissent. The Procuracy takes an
active role in cases instituted against political or religious dissenters.
Aside from the KGB, the Procuracy is probably the most prestigious and
authoritative of the institutions involved in the adminstration of justice.
At least 90 percent of procurators are party members and most have a
higher legal education.[25] Students graduating from legal faculties
reportedly choose the Procuracy over other areas of the regular legal
apparatus because of its higher status and better working conditions.[26]

Although Procuracy officials are in no way immune from public
criticism or dismissal from their jobs (as the ongoing anticorruption
campaign has demonstrated), in general they represent a stable, reasonably comfortable bureaucracy. In exchange for the status accorded to
them by the party, Procuracy officials seem to obey the dictum that
political concerns take precedence over legality. They may resent the
KGB's superior status, but procuratorial employees probably share with
the KGB similar views regarding dissent. (It might be added that there
are occasional examples of cross-postings of KGB and Procuracy officials,
though this is not common.)[27]

Of course the Procuracy plays a very different role in the criminal
process from that of the MVD. It is responsible not only for investigating
crimes but also for supervising investigations, whether carried out by the
MVD, the KGB, or investigators from the Procuracy itself. Among the
Procuracy's multifarious supervisory functions is that of ensuring that
crimes are investigated according to the legal requirements. A new law
on the Procuracy, enacted by the USSR Supreme Soviet in November
1979, replaced the 1955 Statute on Procuratorial Supervision and set
forth the supervisory rights of the Procuracy more comprehensively.[28]
While several Soviet legal experts have subsequently claimed that the
new law greatly strengthened the authority of the Procuracy vis-à-vis the
other investigatory organs, there is little evidence to support this claim
as it relates to the KGB.[29] Given the evidence of continued flagrant
violations of the laws on criminal procedure by KGB investigators, often
with the seeming cooperation of the Procuracy, it might be assumed that
the Procuracy turns a blind eye to questions of legality in political cases.
Although the Procuracy has a special department for supervising
investigations by the KGB, according to Gordon Smith, "an evaluation of

the efficacy of [this department] is impossible, as no published cases exist of a procurator protesting the illegal actions of a KGB official."[30]

KGB Methods and Strategy

What about the cases the KGB is legally empowered to investigate? In general the KGB prefers to avoid publicity and operate behind the scenes, but these cases are sometimes exploited by the KGB for propaganda purposes.[31] The first highly publicized trial was that of Sinyavskiy and Daniel, followed by the trial of Galanskov and Ginzburg in 1968 and Bukovsky in 1971. The most sensational trial and the most devastating for the human rights movement was that of Petr Iakir and Viktor Krasin, who were charged in August 1973 with anti-Soviet agitation and propaganda (Article 70). Iakir and Krasin, who had been involved with the production and dissemination of the *Chronicle of Current Events*, not only admitted their guilt but gave evidence on more than two hundred others connected with the *Chronicle*. As one Western source noted, "the trial amounted to a public demonstration of the KGB's success in suppressing the *Chronicle*. More, it reflected handsomely on KGB Chief Iurii Andropov's ability to crush internal dissent."[32] By all accounts the KGB's success was the product of painstaking efforts (150 volumes of evidence were assembled for the trial) and a carefully planned strategy.[33]

One of the most interesting aspects of the case was the fact that Andropov, who apparently was following developments closely, actually visited Krasin in his cell to persuade him to participate in a news conference following the trial. According to Krasin, Andropov was extremely friendly and understanding, presenting himself as someone wanting to be helpful. He promised to change Krasin's camp sentence to one of exile if Krasin cooperated, which he did. Andropov's visit demonstrated how important it was to the KGB and to Andropov personally to exploit the case for propaganda purposes. As Krasin noted sardonically, "[Andropov] needed my voluntary agreement. And of course, he needed this press conference and because of this he came to Lefortovo Prison himself."[34] Although terror and violence were not used, this trial was not without similarities to the show trials of the 1930s.

Increasingly KGB show trials in the Brezhnev era stressed the foreign connection, thus portraying KGB investigators as uncovering sinister Western plots. Sinyavskiy and Daniel, aside from reported contacts with Western publishing houses, were basically shown as acting on their own.[35] In 1973 with the trial of Krasin and Iakir, the charges of foreign involvement became more pronounced, though there was no attempt to prove direct links with foreign governments. In this respect the trials of Iurii Orlov and Anatolii Shcharanskii in 1978 marked a turning point. Orlov, the founder of the Moscow Helsinki Monitoring Group, charged under Article 70, was accused of having "contacts with representatives of foreign states." He was alleged to have fabricated reports about human rights abuses in the Soviet Union and distributed them to foreign embassies. Accusations against Jewish activist and Helsinki monitor Shcharanskii were considerably more serious. He was formally charged with treason (Article 64) for alleged dealings with the CIA and sentenced to thirteen years' imprisonment.[36]

What is perhaps most striking about dissident impressions of the KGB is how sophisticated its methods have become in comparison with those of the Stalinist political police. Part of this has to do with the fact that KGB investigators, unlike their predecessors, are well educated, intelligent, and well trained. In general they are familiar with the literature circulated in *samizdat*, as well as with the goals and methods of the dissenting political and religious groups in the Soviet Union. They have been taught the most effective psychological techniques for interrogations and the importance of appearing to observe, insofar as possible, the formalities of Soviet law. The stress on psychological techniques is evidenced in the legal literature—the textbooks and handbooks designated for investigators that have appeared in print since Stalin's death. These publications have emphasized the use of psychological devices in order to gain cooperation from those being interrogated.[37]

A growing awareness of the image projected by investigators is also evidenced in the legal literature. Thus for example, a recent article in one of the law journals discusses the importance of the prestige of investigators as a professional group for the effective execution of their tasks. A favorable image, writes the author, is crucial for enlisting the help of the population in the investigation of crimes as well as for successful interaction between the investigator and the individual being questioned. According to the author, social psychologists stress the significance of the investigator's outward appearance (dress and other signs) as well as educational level, title, rank, and other factors in making a favorable impression.[38]

The accounts of political dissidents have offered testimony to this sophisticated approach on the part of KGB investigators, particularly among the younger generation of Chekists. Valentyn Moroz, for example, wrote of the "new methods and new people" that have come to the KGB:

The old KGB officer was a sadist, who killed people or had them killed. The young officer is a time-server who joined the KGB because they pay more. . . . Young KGB officers achieve more through cunning than through brutality. A beating in prison is not such an effective instrument as one may think. It closes up a person and mobilizes his powers of resistance. Today's KGB officer knows this. Therefore as a rule he employs the following tactics: there is brutality all around. The guards are brutal; the surroundings are brutal. Only the investigative officer is a normal human being. He is polite. He might even bring the prisoner some butter or items from home. And there develops an involuntary attachment to him. These psychological details, insignificant at first glance, are highly dangerous. More than one prisoner has relaxed and weakened, without himself noting this, before a "civilized" KGB officer, although he most likely would not fear Stalin himself.[39]

This "civilized" approach has apparently been employed by KGB agents since the mid-1960s and was perfected during Andropov's tenure as KGB chief. (Andropov's interview with Viktor Krasin epitomizes the success of this method.)

Aleksandr Petrov-Agatov, a Soviet writer who served in the camps from 1947 to 1967, was rearrested in 1968 for writing anti-Soviet poetry. He later described the change in his treatment from years past:

As was true twenty-two years ago, they ordered me to strip naked, but without the shouts and threats. Every now and then could be heard: "be so kind," "please," "excuse me." I could have imagined that I was at a barber shop and they were on the point of asking "Are we disturbing you?"[40]

The author, Vladimir Voinovich, questioned by the KGB in 1975, noted: "I knew the usual police method, crude flattery, which changes into crude pressure and the other method, widely used even in the days of the third section: we are just like you. We are also people. We too see our weaknesses."[41]

Typically when a KGB officer "invites" someone for an interview, it is a "friendly chat." The officer tries to convey the impression that he is merely an ordinary person who bears no malice and is simply trying to learn a few facts about the interviewee. Thus for example, a Kalinin KGB investigator summoned the wife of a dissident for a two-and-a-half-hour talk so that he could "get to know her better." He was very amiable and told her all about himself. At the end of the interview he gave the woman his telephone number, telling her to ring whenever she wished and adding, "the organs are always ready to help you."[42] This encounter was by no means atypical. Many of those who have been questioned by the

[195]

KGB mention how friendly and agreeable the investigator appears to be.[43] As the late Andrei Amalrik observed:

> Help is their favorite word. Like the tsarist secret police, the KGB is ever eager to dry the tears of widows and orphans. Even people who have served time claim that KGB agents often say they "helped" them, so as to restrain them from committing even more dangerous deeds, or to protect them against the wrath of the people.[44]

In general, then, the techniques employed by the KGB today are very different from those used in Stalin's time. The regime's emphasis on legality and the introduction of the new legal codes has greatly influenced the changes. Such Stalinist practices as nighttime arrests and interrogations and physical torture in the form of sleep deprivation, starvation, continuous interrogation, and forcing prisoners to stand for hours on end are no longer permitted.[45] In Stalin's day it was common for an interrogator to address the prisoner using the familiar "ty" instead of the more polite "vy" for "you" and consciously to degrade him. Today's investigator not only observes the legal formalities but shows more respect and a more businesslike approach.

As was true in the Stalin era, the goal of the KGB interrogator is to obtain a confession or recantation from the political prisoner. Not only does this validate the charges made by the KGB and demoralize the political opposition, it also can be used for broader propaganda purposes. As was demonstrated in the case of Krasin and Iakir, the KGB often meets with success usually by offering a reduction in the sentence in return for recantation. Another example is that of the Lithuanian priest Dmitri Dudko, who was successfully persuaded to disavow his views and condemn his past activities in a 1980 Lithuanian press article. Faced with ten years in a labor camp followed by five years in exile, Dudko succumbed to KGB pressures.[46] It is perhaps significant that even recently, with the release of numerous political prisoners, police officials have made efforts to obtain recantations or requests for pardons.[47]

Although the general trend points to psychological rather than physical measures by the KGB, it should be noted that some instances of physical brutality against prisoners under investigation were reported in the 1970s. In fact, Petro Grigorenko and his wife asserted in 1977 that the KGB had on more than one occasion displayed to political prisoners a copy of a decree sanctioning physical coercion of prisoners under certain circumstances.[48] As a rule, however, KGB agents do not employ straightforward violence against dissidents. Rather, they have been known to use "covert violence," which is one form of extra-judicial repression discussed below.

Psychiatric Confinement

The forcible confinement of dissidents in psychiatric hospitals, where harmful drugs are often administered, is an alternative means to that of arrest.[49] Individuals are committed to psychiatric hospitals in the USSR by means of three different procedures. The first, civil commitment, is applied to persons who are not charged with criminal offenses but are deemed to pose an "evident danger" to themselves or to others. Such persons may be confined to a psychiatric hospital for an indefinite period without their consent or that of their families. If the person resists or if the family opposes confinement, the MVD is authorized to intervene. A second means, the criminal procedure of psychiatric confinement, is applied to those who are accused of a criminal offense and are sent for a psychiatric examination by the investigator in the case, who is from the Procuracy, the MVD, or the KGB. If the accused is deemed unaccountable for the offense as a result of mental illness or temporary derangement, he or she may be committed indefinitely to either a special psychiatric hospital (for those whose crimes are especially dangerous) or an ordinary psychiatric hospital.[50]

Third is a procedure whereby those already imprisoned for a criminal offense are transferred from their place of confinement to a psychiatric hospital. This is usually applied to particularly troublesome political prisoners who refuse to change their ways in the camps. Ordinary psychiatric hospitals are under the authority of the Ministry of Health; special psychiatric hospitals are under the MVD. According to Amnesty International, these hospitals are run like prisons and all leading medical personnel have MVD ranks.[51]

The brutal practices employed against political prisoners in psychiatric hospitals, in particular the indiscriminate use of harmful drugs, has been well documented, as have the frequent violations of procedural and legal norms by officials dealing with those said to be mentally ill. In the period from 1962 to 1977 at least 210 persons were confined to Soviet psychiatric hospitals for political rather than medical reasons.[52] The indignation and protest aroused in the West over Soviet psychiatric abuse, which reached a crescendo in the early 1970s, caused Soviet authorities to curtail this practice somewhat in late 1973. But from about 1977 to 1985 an average of twenty commitments per annum was reported.[53]

In the absence of definite figures for 1986 and 1987 it can only be said that the Gorbachev regime continues to commit political dissidents, and there is no evidence thus far of pardons for these victims.[54] Soviet authorities use psychiatric confinement as an alternative to other methods for several reasons. First, it avoids the unfavorable publicity that often arises with criminal trials. Second, by labeling dissenters madmen, authorities hope to discredit their actions and deprive them of potential support. Finally, this method offers the opportunity to persuade dissidents to recant their views. The KGB's role in applying these psychiatric methods is formally quite limited: KGB investigators may recommend a psychiatric examination only for persons accused in cases under their purview. In practice, however, the KGB's involvement is much greater. Because the KGB is usually running MVD and Procuracy cases against dissenters from behind the scenes, it probably makes recommendations for psychiatric evaluations in these instances as well.

KGB officers have in the past made their powers clear to political activists. A former chief of the Moscow KGB, Mikhail Svetlichnyy, remarked to Petro Grigorenko and his friends in 1966, "If you go out on the street, even without disturbing traffic, with banners reading 'Long Live the Central Committee' we shall still put you in lunatic asylums."[55] Vladimir Bukovsky notes that KGB investigators openly threaten people who refuse to give testimony or do not disavow their views by asking "Do you want to go to the loony bin?"[56]

Samizdat and emigré accounts offer clear testimony to the KGB's involvement at all stages of the process of psychiatric confinement for political reasons. In their "Manual on Psychiatry for Dissidents," Bukovsky and Semyon Gluzman write:

> Your convictions, openly expressed public stance, actions or acquaintances have made you an object of close attention of a KGB operative squad. Because of certain objective circumstances it is undesirable to institute criminal proceedings against you. In this case, the KGB (often not directly, but through the police or procuracy, the specifically Soviet institution of informers and collaborators, etc., etc.) will tell medical establishments that they believe you are suffering from mental illness and will indicate the reason for their interest in you.[57]

Although psychiatric hospitals are not under its authority, the KGB maintains an active presence in these institutions. Grigorenko, who was held in the infamous Serbsky Institute in Moscow, claimed that the department head, Professor Lunts, came to work in the uniform of a KGB official, as did certain other doctors.[58] As Bloch and Reddaway note, it is not important whether or not Grigorenko's observations were accurate because Lunts, for example, "works closely and apparently smoothly with the KGB, which regularly refers dissidents to his section."[59]

The abuse of psychiatry has recently been addressed in several Soviet press articles. An article in the professional journal of the Procuracy discussed the problem of unwarranted psychiatric examinations of those under arrest:

> A study of materials on criminal cases shows that forensic psychiatric examinations are designated in many cases without sufficient ground, which delays the judicial proceedings, violates the rights of the participants in the criminal process and lowers the effectiveness of the legal procedures.[60]

Though the abuse discussed in the Soviet press involves mainly corruption and inefficiency on the part of psychiatrists rather than persecution of dissent, these criticisms could have political implications.

Extrajudicial Repression

Covert violence emanating from the KGB cannot be termed widespread, but there is evidence that it has been practiced on a limited basis against lesser-known political dissenters. Such violence has taken various forms. Political prisoners are sometimes placed in a so-called pressure cell (*press-kamera*) for the purpose of obtaining a confession. These cells contain specially selected criminal prisoners who are instructed by the prison administration to beat up their cellmates.[61] The KGB is also believed to be responsible for numerous beatings of dissidents who are not in prison by thugs or hooligans, along with various other types of violence. It is difficult to prove the KGB's direct involvement, but several prominent political activists, including Sakharov, have claimed that the KGB hires professional criminals to inflict violence on dissidents.[62] The KGB has attempted poisoning dissidents on at least two occasions, involving the Georgian dissident Zviad Gamsakhurdia and the writer Vladimir Voinovich.[63] Equally disturbing are several unsolved and highly suspicious murders of religious and cultural activists in the Ukraine, Latvia, and elsewhere during the late 1970s and early 1980s. According to one source, at least twelve priests were murdered in Latvia in 1981–1982.[64] Such murders not only eliminate certain troublesome dissidents; they also intimidate others.

Among the other extrajudicial methods used by the KGB to suppress dissent are those that could be characterized as harassment: dismissal from employment, surveillance by KGB agents, illegal searches, and "chats" conducted by the KGB with those suspected of deviant political behavior. In these cases procedural requirements are not adhered to and the KGB acts in an arbitrary manner. The purpose of such harassment is to wear down or frighten individuals so that they cease their dissident activities without the KGB having to arrest them. *Samizdat* literature is replete with reports of KGB harassment from the mid-1960s to the present, and prominent dissidents such as Grigorenko and Sakharov have described these methods in detail.

The extrajudicial persecution of Sakharov and his family was relentless, involving continual surveillance, illegal interrogations, searches, threats, and blackmail. In May 1981 Sakharov wrote to Brezhnev complaining about KGB persecution of his daughter-in-law, Elizaveta Alekseeva, following her attempts to emigrate from the USSR:

> The interrogations [by the KGB] were accompanied by threats of arrest and of physical reprisals, by shouting and by insults and intimidation forbidden by law. The refusal which Alekseeva received and the subsequent interrogations, represent the culmination of many years of actions undertaken with regard to her by the authorities.[65]

Summoning dissidents, their relatives, or would-be emigrés for a "chat" is a tactic that has been used by the KGB with increasing frequency. The *Chronicle of Current Events* even devoted a special section to this type of intimidation.[66] "Chats" are distinguished from formal interrogations in that persons called in are not under investigation but have simply "aroused the KGB's interest." They occur without a summons or deposition and are therefore completely illegal. Often they can be described as "fishing expeditions," in which the investigator asks the individual about friends and acquaintances, reading habits, and other activities. Sometimes the purpose of a "chat" is to make threats, as in the following case reported in the *Chronicle*:

> On 19 August [1980], KGB officials came to see Vladimir Shepelev at work and invited him for a "chat." During the "chat," which lasted about two hours, two KGB officials told V. Shepelev that since 1978 he had been engaged in activity of an anti-social, anti-Soviet nature, which was harmful to the interests of national security. They showed Shepelev a file which contained letters and statements signed by him at various times (mostly "Right to Emigration Group" documents). V. Shepelev was told that if he continued with this activity, criminal proceedings would be

instituted against him and documents in his "case" would be added to a criminal case file.[67]

Shepelev was given a formal "warning," which he refused to sign. According to several *samizdat* sources, an unpublished decree was ratified by the USSR Supreme Soviet in December 1972 on the procedure for issuing a warning as a "prophylactic measure." Such a warning is given to persons whose activities are seen to be "anti-social" or verging on criminal violation. The individual is told that he or she will be prosecuted if such activities continue and asked to sign the warning, which is then placed in his or her file. If criminal proceedings are opened at a later time, this becomes part of the formal evidence.[68] Warnings have been issued to dissidents by the KGB on a regular basis since the early 1980s.[69] The fact that this procedure was never made public indicates that this is yet another extralegal method at the KGB's disposal.

Preventive Measures: Censorship

Illegal interrogations, "chats," and warnings also fall into the category of KGB methods that can be termed "prophylactic" or preventive, as their purpose is often not simply to gain information but also to intimidate dissidents into giving up their activities and thereby to avoid the necessity of arresting them. As Reddaway pointed out, the KGB has tried as a general rule to avoid arrests whenever possible because arrests create undesirable publicity and make dissidents into martyrs. According to Reddaway, arrests are even viewed by some KGB officials as a sign of failure.[70] The KGB is acutely conscious of its own image and would prefer to be seen as a moral guardian and a benevolent institution that sets people straight rather than as a repressive police force. A certain number of arrests serve as a reminder of the powers of the KGB and a deterrent to dissidents, but large-scale arrests, particularly when they involve well-known figures, have negative consequences both internally and internationally. Increasingly the emphasis has been placed on prevention of political crimes rather than prosecution.

One important aspect of the KGB's preventive work has been censorship of literature and other media, which it exercises at both an informal and a formal level. Informally the KGB acts as a censor when its employees harass writers and artists, arrange for their expulsion from professional organizations or from their jobs, and threaten them with

[201]

prosecution for their unorthodox views. Such forms of intimidation have forced many Soviet writers and artists to exercise self-censorship by producing only what they think will be officially approved. In other cases harassment forces them to emigrate.[71] The KGB is known to maintain strong surveillance over the USSR Union of Writers, as well as over the Journalists' and Artists' Unions, where KGB representatives occupy top administrative posts. In fact one source claimed that a secretary of the Writers' Union, Viktor Il'in, was a former KGB general.[72] KGB officials are said to work with authors on the basis of informal oral consultation. According to Valery Golovskoy, a Soviet emigré and author of a study on censorship, "no works of literature or art containing any trace of a problem concerning these organizations [KGB and MVD] can get through the censorship process without long and painstaking consultation."[73] KGB representatives also attend theater productions to ensure that they conform with official norms, and newspaper editors send letters from readers to the KGB when they appear to contain anti-Soviet sentiments.[74]

The KGB plays an important role in the system of formal censorship, which was first established in the early 1920s. The chief censorship agency in the USSR is the Main Administration for Safeguarding State Secrets in the Press, which is still referred to by its original name, Glavlit. Officially Glavlit is under the authority of the USSR Council of Ministers, but in practice it is supervised by both the CC Propaganda Department and the KGB. Glavlit has overall responsibility for the entire system of censorship, maintaining subordinate divisions down to the regional level and employing over 70,000 censors.[75] Its basic task is to screen all material appearing in the Soviet media to ensure that nothing appears that reveals military or state secrets or violates the regulations imposed on the media.

In view of the fact that the KGB is charged with protecting such secrets, it stands to reason that it would take an active part in the work of Glavlit. While the CC Propaganda Department provides the general ideological and political guidelines for Glavlit, the KGB reportedly defines classified information and deals with certain administrative and personnel matters, such as security clearances for employees. At least one of Glavlit's deputy chiefs is said to be a KGB official.[76] The KGB assists in Glavlit's compilation of its yearly index (*Perechen'*), a thick volume that is updated throughout the year listing all military, technical, statistical, and other subjects that may not be publicized without special permission from the Central Committee. The censor is responsible for making sure that no material listed in the index appears in the media.

The KGB also has its own "special departments" in research institutes to check manuscripts prepared by the staff to ensure that they do not contain classified information.[77] It might be added that KGB border guards carry out the function of checking printed matter, art works, films, and cassette recordings to prevent forbidden materials from crossing the borders. Apparently Glavlit draws up the instructions on what materials are to be kept out.[78]

In a sense the KGB's function with respect to Glavlit is more of a technical one, as the CC Propaganda Department and media editors have the main responsibility for the political content and the overall tone of media coverage. Nonetheless the KGB maintains an active presence in Soviet press agencies such as Novosti and Tass, which provide international news coverage. Not only do KGB agents posing as journalists engage in intelligence gathering; the KGB reportedly issues content guidelines for materials designated for foreign consumption.[79] In sum the KGB's role in censorship is both a deterrent and a punitive one. The KGB both helps to determine the extent of censorship by setting limits for the media and punishes those who disobey the censorship laws.

It is difficult at this point to determine the effect of *glasnost'* on the system of censorship and the KGB's specific role. In March 1987 it was revealed that Pavel K. Romanov, head of Glavlit since 1966, had been replaced by V. A. Boldyrev. There was also some suggestion that Glavlit's powers have been reduced.[80] But free expression clearly does not extend to criticism of the Soviet political system. Although the Gorbachev regime has relaxed restrictions on literature and communications, it will doubtless continue to rely on a strong system of censorship—enforced, in part at least, by the KGB.

Political Indoctrination

One important component of KGB preventive activities is political indoctrination and propaganda. Although this function has generally been assumed to belong to the party and the various mass media agencies, the KGB also takes an active role. At local and regional levels KGB officials regularly visit factories, schools, collective farms, and Komsomol organizations to deliver talks on political vigilance. This is not a new phenomenon. Such speaking engagements have been part of KGB duties since the early 1960s. Nonetheless as increasing emphasis has been placed on *preventing* manifestations of political discontent, KGB officials at all levels have been contributing more to the political indoctrination process.

According to an official with the Kalinin *Oblast* KGB Administration, for example, evening meetings are organized at educational institutions or workers' collectives during which KGB officials answer questions from the audience.

> Appearing before factory workers, collective farm employees, students and teachers, Chekists use concrete examples to reveal the subversive activities of imperialist spies, and show the true essence of the slanderous distortions of bourgeois propaganda. The interest in such evenings has become so great that the administration created a large group of lecturers from retired Chekists.[81]

A typical example of the subject matter was the keynote speech at a June 1985 conference for those in higher education, which was delivered by the chief of the Ashkhabad *Oblast* KGB. He spoke on "plenum decrees and questions of the further improvement of the ideological-political education of student youth under conditions in which imperialism is strengthening its ideological sabotage."[82]

KGB officials at higher levels perform similar functions of political indoctrination. In September 1983 I. F. Perbeinosov, deputy chairman of the Kazakh KGB, spoke at a republic seminar-conference on political indoctrination held in Alma Ata.[83] Later, in December 1985, the Armenian party newspaper *Kommunist* reported extensively on a regional seminar-conference held in Erevan and devoted to the problem of propaganda and ideological work in labor collectives.[84] According to the report, ideological workers from the party committees of seven union republics and nine autonomous republics and *oblasts* in the RSFSR attended along with journalists, scientists, and "other comrades who are directly involved in propaganda work and ideological activities." In addition to L. M. Zamiatin, chief of the now defunct CPSU CC International Information Department, another official came from Moscow—R. E. Rybin, identified as a "department head" in the USSR KGB. Rybin gave a report on ideological sabotage by class enemies and education to promote political vigilance. It is possible that the KGB department referred to here is one responsible specifically for propaganda and ideology, particularly as a Soviet emigré source has claimed that such a department exists in the KGB and that it plants articles in the domestic press.[85] This department is probably within the Second Chief Directorate, which is responsible for internal security. It might be added that First Deputy KGB Chairman Bobkov was reported in April 1987 to have addressed a meeting of regional party secretaries on improving ideological work,[86] so he could be responsible for overseeing this effort.

Articles and speeches by KGB officials reflect the growing stress on the KGB's ideological and propaganda roles. Z. M. Iusif-Zade, Azerbaidzhan KGB chairman, wrote a lengthy piece in a party journal in late 1983 on the importance of political indoctrination as part of the campaign against Western subversion and described the contribution made by Chekists to this task.[87] Writing in *Kommunist* in June 1985, KGB Chairman Chebrikov noted that "KGB members actively participate in work conducted by party organs to raise the political vigilance of Soviet people, systematically deliver lectures at enterprises and institutions, hold talks in collectives and make extensive use of the potential of the press, radio serial, and television for this purpose."[88] According to USSR Deputy KGB Chairman G. E. Ageev, the KGB also directs its propaganda at young children.[89]

The Communist party has always devoted a great deal of effort to political indoctrination of its citizens by various means: public lectures, political study, and the use of the mass media. Yet as Stephen White points out, Soviet authorities have manifested increasing concern about the effectiveness of this elaborate system of political socialization.[90] The party began a campaign in the late 1970s to improve ideological work, but according to White, numerous problems remain. Among them is the flow of information from abroad in the form of radio broadcasts, literature, videofilms, and other products of Western culture. Personal contacts with foreigners as a result of trade, scientific and cultural exchanges, and the international telephone and postal services have added to the problem. As White states, "greater interaction between the USSR and the outside world is certainly among the factors that have most seriously complicated the work of ideological officials at all levels."[91]

In view of the party's difficulties in overcoming the obstacles to successful political indoctrination, it is not surprising that the KGB has been enlisted to help in these efforts. Indeed from the point of view of internal security, the flow of "subversive" ideas from the West represents a tremendous threat and is clearly one of the KGB's chief concerns. Computers have added to the problem, mainly because they threaten the regime's monopoly over communications. As one Western study noted, "with the advent of increasingly powerful personal computers . . . the situation changes. Such computers, once in use, become miniature information systems. With word processing software and a printer hookup they can serve as printing presses."[92]

What is the content of the KGB's propaganda? The principal message of speeches and articles by KGB representatives is that the USSR is threatened by large-scale efforts of Western intelligence agencies

[205]

to penetrate the Soviet Union by sending spies through channels of cultural, scientific, and tourist exchange and by provocations against Soviet citizens at home and abroad. In addition, Soviet citizens are said to be barraged by hostile propaganda from the West as part of an effort to undermine the Soviet system. Thus the threat is seen as twofold: espionage efforts by Western intelligence agencies and what is called "ideological sabotage."

One KGB official who spoke about ideological sabotage frequently and in alarmist terms was the former USSR First Deputy KGB Chairman Tsvigun, who devoted numerous articles to the problem from the early 1970s onward. (Tsvigun may well have had overall responsibility for dealing with dissent.) He portrayed the USSR as besieged by ideological enemies, which included Western intelligence agencies, emigré organizations, Zionists, and other groups. He argued that these enemies spared no efforts at penetrating the Soviet Union with their subversive messages. According to a 1981 article by Tsvigun, this ideological sabotage, aimed at the "erosion of communist ideology," was intensifying and was characterized by new, more sophisticated methods. Tsvigun's message was emphatic: to meet the threat, "the state security organs' responsibility for protecting Soviet society against the intrigues of imperialist states' intelligence services and other special services increases still further."[93] In other words the KGB's services were more necessary than ever before.

Andropov, as KGB chairman, also voiced repeated concern about ideological sabotage, though in less alarmist tones. In September 1977 he spoke about "attempts to discredit Soviet reality and carry out in the ideological sphere other essentially subversive acts, which have fittingly come to be called ideological sabotage."[94] In 1979 he elaborated on the problem of ideological sabotage, stressing that it was not part of the conventional ideological struggle that objectively ensues from the existence of two opposing systems:

> Ideological sabotage is above all a form of imperialism's subversive activity against socialism. Its goal is to weaken and destabilize the socialist system. It is conducted by special means and often represents direct interference in the internal affairs of socialist countries, which contradicts the generally recognized rules of international law and socialist laws.[95]

This was a sign that the propagation of Western or politically harmful ideas would be interpreted as a direct threat to the Soviet Union's internal interests and a violation of Soviet law.

Who were the victims of the ideological saboteurs? Although Andropov did not make frequent references to dissidents in his public statements, nevertheless he made it clear that these hostile influences prey upon unorthodox political sentiments. Andropov stressed that although no danger is posed to the Soviet system by isolated antisocial acts,

> if they are taken together, considering their connection with the content and goals of the ideological sabotage of imperialism, such actions are not harmless. After all, our enemies are counting, by way of the gradual erosion of the belief in communist ideals on leading individual "confused" persons increasingly far along an alien and dangerous path. ... Through the erosion of the consciousness of individual persons they are striving to shake the political institutions of socialism and our entire social system. We can not ignore such actions.[96]

KGB officials in the Transcaucasian and Central Asian republics have been particularly concerned about "subversive ideological activity" to arouse religious and nationalist feelings. Azerbaidzhan KGB Chairman Iusif-Zade, for example, noted in late 1980 that "in connection with the situation in Iran and Afghanistan, the intelligence services of the United States are trying to make use of Islam, especially in areas with a large Moslem population, as a means of influencing the political situation."[97] In a speech delivered in December 1984 V. Golovin, chairman of the Uzbek KGB, stated that "imperialist political bosses are stepping up ideological sabotage and intensifying attempts to inspire nationalist attitudes and anti-Sovietism, to instill a foreign ideology and morality in the consciousness of the Soviet people."[98]

While KGB officials want to alert Soviet citizens to the dangers of ideological sabotage, as well as to stress the importance of a strong and effective state security agency, they try to balance the picture in order not to convey the idea that "so-called dissent" is a serious problem. Thus for example, former KGB Deputy Chairman Tsinev observed,

> In an effort to deceive the world public, ideological saboteurs try to pass off a pitifully small group of renegades, called "dissidents" in the West, as some sort of opposition to the socialist system. However, it has long been demonstrated that these spiritual Vlasovites represent no one except themselves, receive no sympathy in Soviet society and are angrily condemned by our people.[99]

In addition to minimizing the problem of dissent, KGB officials have gone to great lengths to portray dissidents in a negative light as weak, politically immature, money grubbing, morally degenerate, and,

[207]

as Andropov once claimed, sometimes mentally unstable.[100] One recent book on the state security organs described several members of the Helsinki Watch group as lazy outcasts who wanted to live off others: "physical labor was beneath him"; "he understood freedom to mean freedom from responsibility to society."[101]

Chebrikov's June 1985 article in *Kommunist* was significant because it synthesized and refined KGB statements about internal security.[102] Written shortly after Gorbachev came to power and the subsequent promotion of Chebrikov himself into the Politburo as a full member, this article could be considered an authoritative statement of KGB views on dissent. Although Chebrikov's tone was more moderate than that of officials such as Tsvigun, he devoted considerable space to the threat posed by ideological sabotage. Like Andropov, he stressed how such sabotage differs from the ideological struggle that arises over class differences and is "not an obstacle to normal political relations between states with different social systems." Ideological sabotage, by contrast, interferes in the USSR's internal affairs. Its scale, according to Chebrikov, is increasing and its methods have become more refined and insidious.

What was notable about Chebrikov's article was the stress placed on links between dissidents and foreign intelligence agencies. Chebrikov referred to "actions by individual elements hostile to our system who have embarked on this path under external influences and by renegades who do not represent any class or strata of Soviet society and act in the interests of foreign intelligence and anti-Soviet centers."[103] Later he pointed out how ideological sabotage, by inciting individuals to violate the law, was actually criminal activity, implying rather ominously that those foreigners who disseminate hostile propaganda and incite Soviet citizens to antistate activity are themselves criminally liable.[104]

Chebrikov's speech was in tune with the general Soviet media at the time, which increasingly emphasized the "foreign connection" in reporting on internal dissent. In February 1985 an hour-long documentary entitled "Conspiracy against the Land of the Soviets" appeared on Soviet television. The program centered on efforts by the CIA and other Western intelligence agencies to recruit Soviet citizens for espionage and subversion. Presented from a historical perspective, the film featured interviews with Soviet citizens allegedly recruited as spies and apprehended by the KGB. It asserted that agencies such as Amnesty International and the Solzhenitsyn Fund were actually controlled by the CIA and gave examples of Jewish activists such as Shcharanskii and Iosif Begun, who were supposedly CIA recruits. The central message of the program was summed up by the presenter in these words:

> All dissidence—no matter what noble phrases it may cover itself with—ends up as the same thing, subservience to the C.I.A. and therefore alliance with Nazis, Zionists, former members of the Polizei, and other human rabble. All this subservience in turn ends up in one and the same thing—war against one's own people. The war may be psychological or it may be the real thing, because the distance between anti-Soviet slander and actual shooting is not all that great.[105]

In August 1986 Soviet television featured a program about a former scientific editor at the Novosti press agency, Ilia Suslov, who was found guilty of selling defense secrets to West Germany. As the presenter stressed, Suslov's crime was discovered thanks to the "tremendous amount of work by the USSR KGB." Again the program, which featured a confession by Suslov, was intended to convey the message that Western intelligence agents are pursuing active efforts to subvert vulnerable Soviet citizens.[106]

The strong language of these broadcasts, along with Chebrikov's statements, reflect the hardened stance toward dissent that was evident in the 1984 changes in the Criminal Code. The concept of what constitutes a crime against the state was not only broadened but was also tied closely to the threat from the West.

Information Gathering and Policy Input

This brings us to the question of how the KGB influences Kremlin policy toward internal dissent. Has the tone of KGB propaganda changed since Gorbachev embarked on his program of political reform? Significantly KGB Chairman Chebrikov made no major speeches in the eighteen months following the Twenty-Seventh Party Congress. No other leading KGB officials spoke out until April 1987, when an interview with USSR Deputy KGB Chairman Ageev was printed in *Trud* (discussed earlier).[107] Ageev's tone was somewhat less menacing than that of Chebrikov and other officials during 1985–1986. He stated that ideological sabotage was "still an integral part of the policy of leading imperialist countries"; and as noted earlier, he claimed that the USSR's enemies were attempting to distort the significance of Soviet attempts at reform. But he did acknowledge that *glasnost'* and restructuring "deprives our enemies abroad of their threadbare 'arguments' and causes a certain confusion over the choice of means for further ideological actions." Chebrikov, however, reasserted his views on the threat of dissent in strong terms on 11 September 1987, making it clear that democratization offered new opportunities for Western subversion: "All strata of our country's population are targets of the imperialist special services . . . our opponents are trying to push representatives of the artistic intelligentsia into positions of carping, demagogy, nihilism . . ."[108]

The KGB, as the primary institution responsible for identifying and dealing with dissidents, has been the main source of the regime's information on the dissent movement and on the political mood within the country. Interestingly, Chebrikov himself made a reference to the KGB's information-gathering function when he noted that the KGB was conducting a careful study of the causes of "antisocial actions" in Soviet society and was working in conjunction with "other state organs and ideological institutions in the country."[109] This suggests that in addition to providing regular reports on dissent, the KGB has some kind of program of sociological research to evaluate manifestations of political discontent within the country. Computers have no doubt improved KGB methods of processing information and conducting research. We have no concrete evidence on the extent to which KGB employees use computers, but as one Western study noted, "it is not hard to imagine applications that would. be within their interests and capabilities."[110] These would include the development of large centralized data bases as well as surveillance systems and the use of personal computers by individual KGB officers.

This information-gathering function by its very nature gives the KGB influence over policy, particularly in light of the fact that Soviet leaders themselves have no direct contact with dissidents and nonconformists and thus rely on the KGB to inform them about motives, foreign connections, and estimates on numbers and support for various groups. Clearly the situation has changed somewhat under Gorbachev, but in the past the KGB's input made itself felt. According to Walter Parchomenko, author of a 1986 study on images of dissent presented in the Soviet media,

it is the local officials (especially the KGB) who shape and articulate official images and who are held responsible for identifying and dealing with dissidents and nonconformists. Whether or not key Soviet leaders accurately perceive dissidents and nonconformists or see only shadowy and exaggerated figures depends heavily not only on their interest in this

[210]

low-urgency subject, but, more importantly, on the reporting of local officials. These are the individuals who collect and interpret information about issues related to dissent and nonconformity and decide which information to suppress and which to transmit to central officials. From this point of view, local officials are political actors who exert an important influence on the direction of the dissent conflict.[111]

Both Parchomenko and Reddaway traced the themes put forth in general media propaganda on dissent (*Pravda*, *Izvestiia*, *New Times*, Moscow Radio, etc.) in the pre-Gorbachev period, and it appears that these themes coincided with those expressed specifically by KGB officials.[112] This is not surprising in view of the fact that, as Parchomenko suggested, KGB information was largely responsible for shaping these themes and images. Parchomenko hypothesized that the leadership accepted the official images of dissent as true despite their stereotypic and exaggerated quality and was guided by them in making policy. As a result, Parchomenko concluded, Soviet officials overreacted to dissident behavior with irrationally severe policies, thereby turning loyal critics into enemies. Why were the official images of dissent exaggerated and falsified? According to Parchomenko, the KGB has a vested bureaucratic interest in overestimating the danger posed by dissidents and foreigners because it reinforces the importance of a strong security police.[113]

Reddaway took issue with Parchomenko on the question of leadership acceptance of official images, claiming that Soviet leaders realized inwardly that the propaganda overstated foreign involvement and went too far in attributing evil and base motives to dissidents. Thus he concluded, "dissent policy is in fact guided more by rational (if possibly mistaken) calculation than by false stereotypic images of propagandists."[114] Reddaway also took the view that the KGB had no significant input into dissent policy: "What KGB input there is into policy comes from the highest level, where the leadership is almost wholly made up of drafted-in party officials like Andropov and Chebrikov."[115]

How do we explain these differences in interpretation, particularly in light of the apparent shift in Kremlin policy toward dissent that occurred in late 1986? The answer relates both to the political influence enjoyed by the KGB at a given time and to overriding domestic and foreign policy considerations. As was noted earlier, the KGB's stature in the Kremlin appeared to be high from the late 1960s to mid-1986. Although the leadership at times initiated more lenient approaches toward dissent, these appear to have been based on tactical considerations rather than on any fundamental reassessment of the threat from dissidents as a result of an ebb in KGB influence. Furthermore it is

[211]

possible that unpublicized information emanating from KGB officials, which is filtered up through the top levels of the KGB and transmitted to the leadership, did not exaggerate the political threat and gave a more reasoned assessment, which did indeed have an impact on leadership decision making.

Judging from the evidence, a discrepancy arose after Gorbachev came to power between KGB views of dissent and those of the more reform-minded elements in the leadership. One particularly striking sign of this appeared in a March 1987 article in *Moscow News*. The author, Len Karpinskii, assailed "those who were prepared to label any Soviet citizen's openly expressed criticism of the realities in social life as a 'hostile act'" and "a certain group of influential persons who had a vested interest in describing any criticism as 'dissent.'"[116] Karpinskii, who obviously was referring to the KGB, also stressed how the West takes advantage of Soviet persecution of dissenters by using it as evidence of evil Soviet intentions. Thus he indicated, the campaign against political nonconformists has played into the hands of Soviet opponents. Of course this may not have reflected the view of all of Gorbachev's colleagues, but the implication was that the Kremlin was reassessing its policies toward dissent and that the KGB's version of events would no longer be accepted without question.

What about implementation of Kremlin policy? Much of the evidence indicates that the KGB, until recently at least, has been given considerable latitude in carrying out the general directives of the party leadership. In other words, broad policy guidelines are decided upon by the Politburo, but the KGB makes the day-to-day decisions on specific courses of action. It is not certain that the KGB regularly consults the party before making individual arrests unless these involve well-known dissidents whose cause has attracted Western attention. With some exceptions local party officials are rarely if ever mentioned in *samizdat* literature as actors in the campaign against dissent.[117] Given the rigidly hierarchical, centralized organization of the KGB, it might be assumed that permission for arrests is secured from higher-ranking KGB officials rather than from local party authorities.[118]

This is not to say that republic party leaders, for example, have no involvement in the struggle against dissent. In the Ukraine the fate of the party leadership has been closely tied to this problem. Yet the impression conveyed by unofficial reports from the Ukraine is that the KGB has not always been a "loyal instrument" of the party in carrying out its policies. This was particularly the case after Fedorchuk became Ukrainian KGB chief in 1970 and began pursuing policies that were more severe than those advocated by party leader Petr Shelest. According to the *Ukrainian Herald*,

> the KGB completely slipped out from under the control of the CPU leadership. The number of KGB men and undercover agents increased sharply. The head of the Republic's KGB, Fedorchuk, sent off reports to Moscow, [charging] that the leadership of the CPU was not helping the KGB in carrying out its work effectively.[119]

Within two years Shelest was ousted and replaced by Vladimir Shcherbitskii, who, like Fedorchuk, advocated a harder line against dissent.

In reading dissidents' accounts of their struggles with the authorities one is struck by the general assumption that the KGB rather than the party is responsible for everything: "The KGB won't let me emigrate"; "The KGB decided to clamp down"; and so on. Interestingly, a report from the *Chronicle* suggested that the KGB actually blocks channels of information to the Politburo: "The KGB's dangerous freedom of action has increased considerably in recent years. . . . Personal communications of the chief of another state to the leaders of the USSR is [sic] perhaps the only kind of information that automatically gets through the barriers of aides and cannot be blocked by the KGB."[120] In his "Letter to Foreign Colleagues," Sakharov makes a similar suggestion:

> I have twice addressed requests for intervention to L. Brezhnev, Chairman of the Presidium of the USSR Supreme Soviet. In July 1980 I sent him a telegram, and in May 1981 a letter. I presume that neither of my missives reached Brezhnev, nor even his office, and that they were blocked by the KGB.[121]

Most dissidents seem to hold the view that the KGB is extremely powerful and enjoys considerable autonomy in implementing regime policy. The ethnic German refusnik and psychiatrist German Vulfert makes a typical observation:

> It is possible with confidence and without exaggeration to consider the KGB the pillar and bulwark of Soviet society and of the entire Soviet system. It is the KGB alone that determines the stability and inviolability of this anti-human structure. . . . The USSR is a country where the punitive organs of the KGB rule with impunity.[122]

This impression is exaggerated, even as it applied to the height of KGB influence under Brezhnev. But the fact that it represents the perception of many victims of KGB repression is itself significant. As Vladimir Solovyov observed:

[213]

> I confess that I don't know which there is more of in the USSR, KGB-phobia or real activity by the KGB. But is that question really important? Is it important by which means we are terrorized—by reality or by our imaginations? In the final analysis, our imagination, too, is a product of reality.[123]

Although the party leadership clearly determines the general policy toward dissent, it has an interest in promoting the idea that the KGB is responsible because the KGB can then be blamed for the injustices suffered by Soviet citizens. Furthermore the image of the KGB's omnipotence has no doubt helped to prevent anti-Soviet behavior. A recent Western study based on interviews with 2667 former soviet citizens concluded that, although those who had actually been persecuted by the KGB were not as a rule deterred from subsequent nonconformity, the widespread perception of the KGB as a highly competent and effective punitive organization did act as a general deterrent.[124] As Seweryn Bialer observed of the Soviet system, "without doubt, the key to stability has been the high visibility of the coercive apparatus and policies."[125]

Can we expect that Gorbachev's seemingly new approach to the problem of dissent will severely limit the scope of the KGB's domestic activities, as well as the influence it has enjoyed as a purveyor of information to the Kremlin? The policy of openness may indeed undercut the KGB's monopoly of information on political currents within the country, thereby depriving it of an important means of influencing Kremlin policy. In addition, the KGB's coercive operations against dissidents have been curtailed.

But this may be only a temporary phenomenon rather than a long-term trend. Strikes in the Ukraine and Belorussia, as well as the December 1986 riots in Kazakhstan, indicated the potential danger of social and economic unrest within the Soviet Union, particularly as expectations rise in anticipation of the much-discussed reforms.[126] More recently, in August 1987, large public demonstrations in the Baltic republics have raised the possibility that *glasnost'* will gain a momentum of its own and give rise to expressions of more fundamental grievances with the system itself. If this were to occur, the Gorbachev leadership would be compelled to revert to greater reliance on the coercive operations of the KGB. Meanwhile the KGB, which has evolved into a sophisticated and efficient organization of political control, may well accommodate itself to the changed environment under Gorbachev and develop new techniques to deal with the problem of ensuring political stability.

Notes

1. *Vedomosti VS RSFSR*, no. 38, item 1038, 1966.

2. See Leopold Labedz and Max Hayward, eds., *On Trial: The Case of Sinyavskiy (Tertz) and Daniel (Arzhak)* (London: Collins and Harvill, 1967).

3. See *Vedomosti VS SSSR*, no. 3, item 58, 1984. For a discussion of these changes see Julia Wishnevsky, "New Additions to the Law on Crimes against the State," *RLRB*, RL 78/84, 16 February 1984; and Zigmas A. Butkus, "Major Crimes against the Soviet State," Library of Congress, 1985. Also see a Soviet interpretation of the changes: S. D'iakov and P. Samoilenko, "Izmeneniia i dopolneniia zakona ot 25 Dekabria 1958 goda 'ob ugolovnoi otvetstvennosti za gosudarstvennye prestupleniia," *Sotsialisticheskaia zakonnost'* [hereafter *SZ*], no. 11 (1984):34–37; and appendix B.

4. D'iakov and Samoilenko, "Izmeneniia," p. 35; *Kommentarii k ugolovno-protsessual 'nomu kodeksu RSFSR* (Moscow, 1984), pp. 157–158. Also see Chebrikov's speech to the Twenty-Seventh Party Congress, quoted in *Pravda*, 1 March 1985, pp. 5–6, where he voiced concern over the use of "video technology" for "harmful, amoral propaganda." On the spread of video networks see Taras Kuzio, "Illegal Video Networks in USSR," *Soviet Analyst* 16, no. 7 (8 April 1987).

5. See an interview with Professor Iurii Liatunov in *Zhurnalist*, no. 12 (December 1986):58–59. Liatunov also pointed out that a new article, 228-1, which makes it a crime to create or show films that propagate the cult of violence and cruelty, was incorporated into the RSFSR Criminal Code in August 1986. This is a lesser offense than that covered by Article 70 and does not require anti-Soviet intent. Also see an interview with Deputy USSR Procurator General S. Shishkov in *Pravda*, 28 February 1987, p. 6.

6. See *Vedomosti VS SSSR*, no. 22, item 380, 1984; and, for a discussion of the law, Julia Wishnevsky, "The Decree on Administrative Liability for Violation of the Rules on Contacts with Foreigners," *RLRB*, RL 287/84, 25 July 1984.

7. See an interview with MVD chief Vlasov in *Komsomolskaia pravda*, 11 January 1987, pp. 1–2; *Vesti iz SSSR* (*USSR News Brief*), no. 3 (15 February 1987):8, which cites an announcement by Foreign Ministry spokesman G. Gerasimov; and no. 4 (28 February 1987):8, citing V. Kudriavtsev, director of the Institute of State and Law.

8. According to one such expert, "it would seem appropriate to develop and anchor in legislation a system of criteria for defining which information is of a secret nature or for official use only. A lack of clarity on this point could lead to all a situation in which information concerning the shortcomings and failures of specific organizations and officials would fall wrongly into this category." See. V. A. Kriazhkov, "Glasnost' raboty sovetov: sotsiologiia i pravo," *Sovetskoe gosudarstvo i pravo*, no. 12 (December 1986):35–42, quotation, p. 41.

9. For the text of this law, see *Izvestiia*, 2 July 1987, p. 1.

10. Robert Sharlet, "Legal Policy under Khrushchev and Brezhnev: Continuity and Change," in *Soviet Law after Stalin: Part II. Social and Engineering through Law*, ed. Donald Barry, George Ginsburgs, and Peter B. Maggs (The Hague: Sijthoff and Noordhof, 1978), pp. 319–330 (quotation, p. 322).

11. See Robert Sharlet, "Dissent and Repression in the Soviet Union," *Current History* 73, no. 430 (October 1977):112–117, 130: and Peter Reddaway, "Policy towards Dissent since Khrushchev," in *Authority, Power and Policy in the USSR: Essays Dedicated to Leonard Schapiro*, 2d ed., ed. T. H. Rigby, Archie Brown, and Peter Reddaway (New York: St. Martin's Press, 1980), pp. 158–192.

12. See Peter Reddaway, *Soviet Policies on Dissent and Emigration: The Radical Change of Course since 1979* (Colloquium Paper No. 192, Kennan Institute for Advanced Russian Studies, Washington, D.C. 28 August 1984).

13. Reddaway, "Policy towards Dissent since Khrushchev," pp. 172–174.

14. See ibid., pp. 174–179; Reddaway, *Soviet Policies on Dissent and Emigration*, pp. 6–10.

15. See Reddaway, *Soviet Policies on Dissent and Emigration*, pp. 11–26; and Peter Reddaway, "Dissent in the Soviet Union," *POC* 32, No. 6 (November-December 1983): 1–15 (esp. pp. 9–10).

16. *Amnesty International Report*, 1984, 1985, 1986 (London: Amnesty International Publications, 1984–1986).

17. *Vesti iz SSSR*, no. 21 (15 November 1986):1.

18. *Prisoners of Conscience in the USSR: Their Treatment and Conditions. An Amnesty International Report* (London: Quartermane House, 1975); 2d ed. (London: Amnesty International Publications, 1980); *Amnesty International Reports* for the years 1978–1985; and *Vesti iz SSSR*.

19. Quoted in Yaroslav Bilinsky, "Shcherbytskyi, Ukraine and Kremlin Politics," *POC* 32, no. 4 (July-August 1983):10.

20. There are countless examples of such cases reported in *A Chronicle of Current Events* [hereafter *CCE*], the *samizdat* journal that has appeared in Moscow since 1968 and is published in English by Amnesty International Publications and in Russian by Khronika Press, New York. Also see *Vesti iz SSSR*; Dina Kaminskaya, *Final Judgement: My Life as a Soviet Defense Attorney*, trans. Michael Glenny (New York: Simon & Schuster, 1982), pp. 173–176, 184, 210; and an excellent and comprehensive study by Ludmilla Alexeyeva, *Soviet Dissent: Contemporary Movements for National, Religious, and Human Rights* (Middletown, Conn.: Wesleyan University Press, 1985).

21. *Arkhiv samizdata*, Radio Liberty, Munich, Germany no. 2/86, 17 January 1986, AS no. 5587.

22. It might be added that the Soviet press actually acknowledged such illegal KGB interference when it exposed the Berkhin affair, discussed in chapter 3. According to press accounts, the local KGB chief coordinated the entire campaign of persecution against the journalist Berkhin, ordering the local procurator to arrest him.

23. Vladimir Bukovsky, *To Build a Castle: My Life as a Dissenter*, trans. Michael Scammell (New York: Viking, 1978), p. 150.

24. Valentyn Moroz, "The KGB from My Own Personal Experience," *Ukrayins'ke slovo*, 11–25 December 1983, JPRS translation, USSR Report, UPS–84–010–L, 7 March 1984, pp. 33–41, (quotation, p. 37).

25. See William Butler, *Soviet Law* (London: Butterworths, 1983), p. 161.

26. Gordon B. Smith, ed., *Public Policy and Administration in the Soviet Union* (New York: Praeger, 1980), p. 116.

27. See chapter 5 and a study of procuratorial career patterns by Eugene Huskey, "Specialists in the Soviet Communist Party Apparatus: Legal Professionals as Party Functionaries" (forthcoming, *Soviet Studies*, 1988).

28. This law was reprinted in *Pravda*, 2 December 1979, pp. 2–3.

29. See, for example, B. A. Galkin, "Zakon 'O Prokuratore SSSR' i dal'neishee sovershenstvovanie prokurorskogo nadzora," *Vestnik Mosksovskogo Universiteta. Seriia 11. pravo*, no. 3 (1980):3–18; G. I. Skaredov, "Prokurorskii nadzor i protsessual'naia samostoiatel'nost'sledovatelia," ibid., no. 6 (1980):11–17.

30. Gordon Smith, *The Soviet Procuracy and Supervision of Administration* (Leyden: Sijthoff & Noordhoff, 1978), p. 20. As of 1979 the chief of the department for supervising KGB investigations in the USSR Procuracy was Mikhail Rogov, a Procuracy employee since 1952. See *SZ*, no. 7 (July 1979):73.

31. It should be noted that the KGB's role does not end when the investigation is over. All defense lawyers in political trials must be granted special access by the KGB before they can plead in court; and the KGB maintains guard over the courtroom to make sure that only KGB-approved audiences are permitted to attend these supposedly public trials. See Dina Kaminskaia, *Final Judgement*, pp. 31–32. For an interesting study of the defense counsel and the debate over expanding his role in the pretrial process, see Eugene Huskey, "The Politics of the Soviet Criminal Process: Expanding the Right to Counsel in pre-Trial Proceedings," *American Journal of Comparative Law* 35, No. 1 (Winter 1986):93–112.

32. Mark Hopkins, *Russia's Underground Press: The Chronicle of Current Events* (New York: Praeger, 1983) p. 67.

33. Ibid., p. 67.

34. Viktor Krasin, *Sud* (New York: Chalidze Publications, 1983), p. 76.

35. See Labedz and Hayward, *On Trial.*

36. For an analysis of the Orlov case, see Walter Parchomenko, *Soviet Images of Dissidents and Nonconformists* (New York: Praeger, 1986), pp. 106–169; for a Soviet report on the Shcharanskii case, see *Pravda*, 21 May 1978, p. 6. Shcharanskii was released in late 1985 and sent to the West in exchange for the return of a Soviet spy.

37. See, for example, A. R. Ratinov, *Sudebnaia psikhologiia dlia sledovatelei* (Moscow: Izdatel'stvo Vyshei Shkoly Moop SSSR, 1967); A. V. Dulov, *Osnovy psikhologicheskogo analiza na predvaritel 'nom sledstvii* (Moscow Iuricheskaia Literatura 1973); and A. N. Vasil'ev, *Sledstvennaia taktika* (Moscow: Iuridecheskaia Literatura, 1976).

38. I. E. Bykhovskii, 'Sledovatel' i ego deiatel'nost 's positsii sotsialnoi psikhologii,' *Pravovedenie*, no. 1 (January 1985):83–86.

39. Moroz, ''The KGB from My Personal Experience,'' p. 37–38.

40. Aleksandr Petrov-Agatov, ''Arestanskie vstrechi: nevydumannaia povest','' *GRANI* (Frankfurt), no. 82 (December 1971):99–119 (quotation, pp. 102–103).

41. Vladimir Voinovich, ''Proisshestvie v Metropole,'' *Kontinent*, no. 5 (1975):51–97 (quotation, p. 51). Voinovich goes on to recount how the KGB tried to poison him.

42. *CCE*, (London) nos. 59–61 (1982):153.

43. See, for example, ibid., no. 58 (1981):26–27.

44. Andrei Amalrik, *Notes of a Revolutionary*, trans. Guy Daniels (New York: Alfred A. Knopf, 1982), p. 316.

45. For an interesting study of methods used by the Soviet and Chinese political police prior to the 1950s, see a declassified CIA report, *Communist Control Techniques: An Analysis of the Methods Used by Communist State Police in the Arrest, Interrogation and Indoctrination of Persons Regarded as ''Enemies of the State''* no. 055375 (2 April 1956; declassified 14 January 1977).

46. See *Russkaia mysl'*, 18 October 1985, p. 7. Also see a reference to his arrest and recantation in L. A. Plotnikova, ed., *Chekisty* (Leningrad: Lenizdat, 1982), p. 464.

47. According to most accounts, however, requests for pardons have not been an absolute requirement for release. See *Vesti iz SSSR*, nos. 5–6 (31 March 1987):1–2; and *Soviet Nationality Survey* 4, no. 4 (April 1987):1–5.

48. See Julia Wishnevsky, ''Is There an Official Decree in the USSR on the Use of Physical Coercion?'' *RLRB*, RL 269/77, 18 November 1977.

49. Several excellent, well-documented studies of the abuse of psychiatry in the USSR have been published in the West. Among the sources used here are Sidney Bloch and Peter Reddaway, *Russia's Political Hospitals*, 2d. exp. ed. (London: Futura, 1978); *The Political Abuse of Psychiatry in the Soviet Union* (London: Working Group on the Internment of Dissenters in Mental Hospitals, 1977); *Political Abuse of Psychiatry in the USSR: An Amnesty International Briefing* (London: Amnesty International, March 1983); *Soviet Political Psychiatry: The Story of the Opposition.* (London: International Association on the Political Use of Psychiatry, Spring 1983); and Alexander Podrabinek, *Punitive Medicine* (Ann Arbor, Mich.: Karoma Publishers, 1979). In addition, there are numerous firsthand accounts by victims of Soviet psychiatric abuse, including Bukovsky, *To Build a Castle*; Victor Nekipelov, trans. and ed. Marco Carynnyk and Marta Horban *Institute of Fools: Notes from the Serbsky*, (New York: Farrar, Straus, Giroux, 1980); and Petro Grigorenko, *Memoirs*, trans. Thomas P. Whitney (London, New York: W. W. Norton, 1982).

50. A decree of the USSR Supreme Soviet dated 13 June 1985 broadened the legal scope for psychiatric confinement of persons charged for socially dangerous crimes. According to revisions made in Article 11 of the Fundamental Principles of Criminal Legislation, the court may recommend compulsory medical treatment not only for persons under investigation or trial who are mentally ill (the original law) but also (according to the revision) for those whose temporary mental confusion prevents a determination of their

mental state at the time the crime was committed. See *Vedomosti VS SSSR*, no. 25, item 444, 1985.

51. Amnesty International, *Prisoners of Conscience in the USSR*, pp. 190–191.

52. Bloch and Reddaway, *Russia's Political Hospitals*, p. 279.

53. Working Group on the Internment of Dissenters, *Political Abuse of Psychiatry in the USSR*, p. 1; and *Amnesty International Reports*, 1984, 1985, 1986.

54. See issues of *Vesti iz SSSR* for this period and an interview with human rights advocate and former Soviet psychiatrist Anatoly Koryagin in *The Washington Post*, 19 May 1987, p. A19.

55. Bloch and Reddaway, *Russia's Political Hospitals*, p. 108.

56. Bukovsky, *To Build a Castle*, p. 358.

57. Vladimir Bukovsky and Semyon Gluzman, "A Manual on Psychiatry for Dissidents," *Survey* 21, nos. 1-2 (94-95) (Winter-Spring 1975):181.

58. Grigorenko, *Memoirs*, p. 385. For more recent evidence see the account by a former Jewish refusnik, Grigorii Steshenko, in *Arkhiv samizdata*, no. 40, 19 December 1986, AS no. 5838. According to Steshenko, the chief doctors at psychiatric institutions work closely with KGB officials and take orders from them.

59. Bloch and Reddaway, *Russia's Political Hospitals*, p. 226.

60. I. Bobrova et al., "Osnovaniia naznacheniia sudebnopsikhiatricheskoi ekspertizy po ugolovnym delam," *SZ*, no. 2 (1986):46–48. Also see Peter Reddaway, "Does Moscow's Purge of Corrupt Psychiatrists Threaten the Psychiatric Gulag?" *RLRB*, RL 295/87, 23 July 1987.

61. See Julia Wishnevsky, "The Use of Torture in Soviet Penal Institutions: The Pressure Cell," *RLRB*, RL 329/83, 6 September 1983.

62. See an interview with Sakharov in the *Christian Science Monitor*, 10 August 1976; Reddaway, "Policy towards Dissent since Khrushchev," p. 183; *Russkaia mysl'*, 22 November 1985, p. 2; and *Vesti iz SSSR*, nos. 13-14 (31 July 1983):7, no. 21 (15 November 1986):6. In some cases more direct KGB involvement in assaults on dissidents has been documented. See *Vesti iz SSSR*, no. 21 (15 November 1981):7, no. 21 (15 November 1984):5, and nos. 23-24 (31 December 1985):7.

63. See Julia Wishevsky, "New Tactics in Treatment of Dissidents," *RLRB*, RL 45/77, 23 February 1977; Voinovich, "Proisshestive v Metropole."

64. *Die Welt*, 22 July 1982, p. 1. Also see *Soviet Analyst* 4, no. 2 (16 January 1985):4; Alexseyeva, *Soviet Dissent*, p. 82; and Pyotr Grigorenko, "Etot Demokrat Andropov," *Novoe Russkoe Slovo*, 30 July 1982, p. 3. Grigorenko notes that after Fedorchuk became KGB chairman in the Ukraine a series of puzzling murders of dissidents occurred.

65. *CCE* (London), no. 63 (1983):128–29. Also see Grigorenko, *Memoirs*, p. 385.

66. See, for example, *CCE* (London), no. 63 (1983):58–59, and no. 64 (1984):26–32.

67. Ibid. no. 63 (1983):58–59. For more recent examples see *Vesti iz SSSR*, no. 20 (31 October 1986), and no. 21 (15 November 1986).

68. *CCE* (New York), nos. 28–31 (31 December 1972–17 May 1974):99–100, no. 32 (17 July 1974):57–59.

69. *USSR News Brief* reported at least twenty such warnings from1981 through 1985, and this probably represents only a small portion of the actual number.

70. Reddaway, "Policy towards Dissent since Khrushchev," pp. 160–161.

71. See, for example, Anatoly Kuznetsov, "Russian Writers and the Secret Police," in *Man, State and Society in the Soviet Union*, ed. Joseph. Nogee (New York: Praeger, 1972), pp. 485–494; Kuznetsov's discussion of self-censorship in Martin Dewhirst and Robert Farrell, eds., *The Soviet Censorship* (Metuchen, N.J.: Scarecrow Press, 1973); an interview with Georgii Vladimirov in *Posev*, no. 8 (August 1983):31–38 (JPRS translation L/11780, 7 December 1983, pp. 32–42); and Vladimir Voinovich, "The Writer in Soviet Society," *Posev*, no. 9 (September 1983):31–38 (JPRS translation 11765, 30 November 1983, pp. 47–58).

72. Voinovich, "The Writers in Soviet Society," p. 51.

73. Valery Golovskoy, *Is There Censorship in the Soviet Union? Methodological Problems of Studying Soviet Censorship* (Washington D.C.: Kennan Institute Occasional Papers No. 201, 1985), p. 21.

74. Lilita Dzirkals, Thane Gustafson, and A. Ross Johnson, *The Media and Intra-Elite Communication in the USSR* (Santa Monica, Calf.: Rand Corporation September 1982), p. 35. This interesting and informative study is based primarily on interviews with Soviet emigrés formerly involved in the Soviet media.

75. For information on Glavlit and the system of censorship see Golovskoy, "Is There Censorship?"; Dewhirst and Farrell, *The Soviet Censorship*; Dzirkals et al., *The Media and Intra-Elite Communication*; Julia Wishnevsky, "The Sixtieth Anniversary of Glavlit," *RLRB*, RL 213/82, 26 May 1982; and Julia Wishnevsky, "Information on the Operations of Glavlit Section no. 2," *RLRB* RL 494/76, 8 December 1976.

76. Dzirkals et al., *The Media and Intra-Elite Communication*, p. 38; Golovskoy, *Is There Censorship?* p. 9.

77. Dzirkals et al., *The Media and Intra-Elite Communication*, p. 35.

78. *RLRB*, RL 494/76, pp. 5–6.

79. Dzirkals et al., *The Media and Intra-Elite Communication*, p. 34.

80. See *Sovetskaia kultura*, 21 March 1987, for the announcement of Romanov's retirement. On the reduction of Glavlit's powers see a statement attributed to *Ogonek* editor Vitalii Korotich in *La Stampa*, 13 March 1987.

81. V. I. Bukhalov et al., eds., *Poklialis' my v vernosti otchizne . . . Dokumental'nye ocherki vospominaniia i stat'i o kalininskikh chekistakh* (Moscow: Moskovskii Rabochii, 1983), p. 244.

82. Reported in the Turkmen paper, *Mugallymlar Gazeti*, 7 June 1985, p. 2 (JPRS translation, UPS–85–078, 5 November 1985, p. 144).

83. *Kazakhstanskaia pravda*, 24 September 1983, p. 2.

84. *Kommunist* (Erevan), 3 December 1985, pp. 1–2, 4 December 1985, p. 2.

85. Dzirkals et al., *The Media and Intra-Elite Communication*, p. 34.

86. *Pravda* 3 April 1987, p. 2.

87. *Kommunist Azerbaidzhana*, no. 12 (December 1983), pp. 11–17.

88. V. Chebrikov, "Sverias s Leninym, rukovodstvuias trebovaniem partii," *Kommunist*, no. 9 (June 1985):47–58. (quotation, pp. 51–52).

89. See *Trud*, 19 April 1987, p. 4. Ageev added that KGB employees took an active part in constructing a *Molodaia gvardia* (Young Guard) children's home outside Moscow.

90. See Stephen White, "Propagating Communist Values in the USSR," *POC* (November-December 1985):1–17.

91. Ibid., p. 17.

92. Walter R. Roberts and Harold E. Engle, "The Global Information Revolution and the Communist World," *The Washington Quarterly* 9, no. 2 (Spring 1986):141–156 (quotation, p. 150).

93. S. K. Tsvigun, "O proiskakh imperialisticheskikh razvedok," *Kommunist*, no. 14 (September 1981):88–99 (quotation, p. 89). Also see S. Tsvigun, "Podryvnye aktsii—oruzhie imperializma," *Kommunist*, no. 4 (March 1980):108–119.

94. Report delivered by Andropov on 9 September 1977 at a meeting commemorating Dzerzhinskii's birth, reprinted in Iu. V. Andropov, *Izbrannye rechi i stat 'i* (Moscow: Politizdat, 1983), pp. 135–149 (quotation, p. 145).

95. Speech delivered at a KGB meeting in February 1979, reprinted in ibid., pp. 161–168 (quotation, p. 162).

96. Ibid., p. 165–166.

97. *Bakiinskii rabochii*, 19 December 1980, p. 3.

98. *Pravda vostoka*, 20 December 1984, p. 3. Maj. Gen. N. Ovezov, first deputy chairman of the Turkmen KGB, accused the West of "using radio propaganda to revive and provoke religious and national factions." *Soviet Turkmenistany*, 19 December 1982, p. 3 (JPRS translation). *USSR Report: Political and Sociological Affairs*, no. 1413 (December 1983), p. 27.

99. G. Tsinev, "Na strazhe bezopasnosti rodiny oktiabria," *Agitator*, no. 23 (1977):

35–38 (quotation, p. 38).

100. Andropov, *Izbrannye rechi i stat 'i*, p. 147.

101. Plotnikova, *Chekisty*, pp. 459–460.

102. Chebrikov, "Sverias s Leninym."

103. Ibid., p. 49

104. Ibid., pp. 54–55.

105. *BBC. Summary of World Broadcasts* (SU/7884/C/1–11, 25 February 1985).

106. Ibid. (SU/8351/C1/1, 30 August 1986).

107. *Trud*, 19 April 1987, p. 4

108. *Pravda*, 11 September 1987, p. 3.

109. Chebrikov, "Sverias s Leninym," p. 57.

110. S. E. Goodman and W. K. McHenry, "Computing in the USSR: Recent Progress and Policies," *Soviet Economy* 2, no. 4 (1986):327–354 (quotation, pp. 339–340). There have been no discussions in the press of the use of computers by the KGB specifically, but there have been general articles on the importance of cybernetics for use by various law enforcement organs. See, for example, G. A. Tumanov and A. P. Gerasimov, "Metodologicheskie vozmozhnosti kibernetiki v gosudarstvennopravovoi sfere," *Sovetskoe gosudarstvo i pravo*, no. 9 (1982):29–37.

111. Parchomenko, *Soviet Images of Dissent*, pp. 65–66.

112. Ibid.; and see Peter Reddaway, "Images of Dissent in Soviet Propaganda" (unpublished paper, June 1985).

113. Parchomenko, *Soviet Images of Dissent*, p. 183.

114. Reddaway, "Images of Dissent," p. 46.

115. Reddaway, "Soviet Policies on Dissent and Emigration," p. 29.

116. Len Karpinskii, "It's Ridiculous to Waver before an Open Door," *Moscow News* no. 9, 1 March 1987, pp. 11–12.

117. Exceptions would be a report in *CCE* (London), no. 63, p. 67, where the KGB is said to have agreed together with an official of the regional party committee, upon the arrest of dissident Pavel Kampov, and a *samizdat* account by a former prisoner in a Dnepropetrovsk psychiatric hospital, Grigorii Steshenko, who claimed that party authorities followed his case closely and had the final say about his fate. See note 59.

118. This high degree of centralization in the KGB is illustrated by the personal involvement of high-ranking KGB officials in cases of dissent. Andropov, as was mentioned earlier, met with political prisoner Viktor Krasin in his cell; A. Inauri, chairman of the Georgian KGB, had a private discussion in October 1974 with D. Koridze, an investigator with the Procuracy who was suspected of collaborating with dissidents; in 1969 Ukrainian KGB Chief Nikitchenko met with Vasilii Chornovil following the latter's release from prison. See *CCE* (New York), no. 34 (31 December 1974):56; Borys Lewytzkyj, *Politics and Society in Soviet Ukraine, 1953–1980* (Edmonton, Alberta: Canadian Institute of Ukrainian Studies, 1984), p. 136.

119. Lewytzkyj, *Politics and Society in Soviet Ukraine*, p. 117.

120. *CCE* (London), no. 63 (1982):152.

121. Ibid., p. 131.

122. Radio Free Europe/Radio Liberty, *Materialy samizdata*, no. 5/86, 3 February 1986, AS no. 5594.

123. Vladimir Solovyev, "Knowing the KGB," *Partisan Review* 99, no. 2 (1982): 167–183 (quotation, p. 170).

124. Donna Bahry and Brian D. Silver, *The Intimidation Factor in Soviet Politics: The Symbolic Uses of Terror* (Working Paper No. 31, Soviet Interview Project. University of Illinois at Urbana-Champaign, February 1987).

125. Seweryn Bialer, *The Soviet Paradox: External Expansion, Internal Decline* (New York: Alfred A. Knopf, 1986), p. 20.

126. Elizabeth Teague, "Gorbachev's First Two Years in Power," *RLRB*, RL 94/87, 9 March 1987. Kirgiz KGB chairman V. A. Riabokon voiced particular concern about nationalist unrest, noting in reference to the Kazakhstan riots that "we have drawn for ourselves the proper conclusions from the lessons of events in Alma-Ata." *Sovetskaia Kirgiziia*, 14 April 1987, p. 5.

7

KGB Security and Border Troops

In addition to punitive powers and seemingly unlimited access to politically sensitive information, the KGB's authority is buttressed by the presence of troops under its direct control. According to official Soviet sources, the KGB has two types of troops at its disposal: troops of state security and border troops.[1] The border troops, which constitute the largest component of KGB forces, are organized under a separate unnumbered chief directorate. Having an ostensibly straightforward and legitimate function of protecting the USSR's borders, these troops receive considerable publicity, and information on their history, leading personnel, and basic organization is not difficult to find.

This is not the case with the troops of state security, which are shrouded in secrecy. Although Soviet sources have not specified the functions of these special troops, it is generally thought that one of their main tasks is to guard the top leadership in the Kremlin as well as key government and party buildings and officials at the republic and regional levels. Such troops are presumably under the Ninth, or Guards, Directorate of the KGB. Other types of KGB security troops may perform communications, counterterrorist, and counterinsurgency functions.

KGB troops are small in number by comparison with regular armed forces, but the fact that they provide the KGB with a coercive potential makes them politically significant. In addition, at times the border troops have performed important military functions. Thus these troops deserve close attention, particularly because information on them presented in

Western sources has often been contradictory. The complex history of the border and state security troops, which have undergone numerous reorganizations and transmutations since 1917, is one source of the confusion. In the case of the security troops, additional confusion is caused by the existence of other special troops under the MVD, in particular the internal troops, which perform similar functions. This chapter will attempt to clarify some of the issues raised in Western writings by describing the history, organization, and functions of the two types of KGB troops.

Troops of State Security: History

Not surprisingly, the Vecheka found itself in need of its own armed forces fairly early in its existence. By late March 1918 a Vecheka combat detachment had been formed: the provincial chekas had already established their individual contingents. In June of that year these forces were united into a single Corps of Vecheka Troops, numbering some thirty-five battalions whose purpose was to suppress insurrection and counter-revolution. After his appointment as People's Commissar for Internal Affairs in early 1919, Dzerzhinskii combined the command of all troops fighting counterrevolution, and Vecheka troops were absorbed into the Internal Security Troops (*Voiska Vnutrennei Okhrany Respubliki*, or VOKhR), which were nominally under the control of the NKVD but actually fell under Vecheka authority.[2]

In September 1920 a new system of Internal Service Troops (*Voiska Vnutrennei Sluzhby*, or VNUS), was created. This body absorbed VOKhR and all other special troops responsible for guard duties and internal security and was subordinated to both the NKVD and the Red Army. VNUS was short-lived, however; in January 1921 it was dissolved and its troops transferred from the NKVD to military command, except for railway and waterway militias, and the forces serving the Vecheka, which were established as separate troops under the sole authority of the Vecheka.[3]

Among the Vecheka troops were units of special purpose, which were combined in April 1921 into a Detachment of Special Purpose (*Otriad Osobogo Naznacheniia*, or OSNAZ) numbering some 1097 men under the Vecheka collegium. Incorporated into OSNAZ was the Sverdlovsk Detachment, which had originally been established under the Central Executive Committee for the purpose of guarding government and party buildings and ensuring order at public gatherings. The head of Lenin's personal Kremlin guard, I. Ia. Belenkii, a Chekist, enlisted soldiers from OSNAZ to do service in the Kremlin.[4] These soldiers may have been precursors of today's KGB guard troops.

At the same time, a separate corps of elite troops—units of special purpose (*Chasti Osobogo Naznacheniia*, or CHON)—had been recruited from party and Komsomol members to guard important political, economic, and military installations, as well as to suppress counter-revolutionary uprisings. These were under the authority of the Central Committee. When they were dissolved in 1924 or 1925, their functions apparently devolved to OSNAZ.[5] In June 1924, OSNAZ was made a special division with three rifle regiments and was renamed the Dzerzhinskii Division two years later. It formed part of the internal troops, which were then under the OGPU and, in addition to guard functions, helped to suppress local uprisings and banditry in different areas of the country.[6]

The internal troops remained directly under the state security organs until July 1934, when the NKVD was established. At this time the Main Administration of Border and Internal Troops (GUPVO) was created, which was separate from the newly established Main Administration of State Security (GUGB). Henceforth throughout the numerous reorganizations that took place among the internal affairs and state security apparatuses, the internal troops remained separate from the state security organs until 1950, though presumably they were at the latter's disposal. In 1950 for reasons that remain unclear, they were transferred from the MVD to the MGB, which retained control over them until Beria formed the united MVD in March 1953. After a separate MVD and KGB were set up in 1954, the internal troops were placed under the authority of the former.[7]

It seems that at some point in the mid-1920s, the state security organs developed special troops units distinct from the internal troops, which were then passed on to the Main Administration of State Security when it was established under the NKVD in 1934. These units, rather than the internal troops, have had the exclusive task of special guard for the party and state elite. According to Peter Deriabin, who served in the Guards Directorate after World War II, a so-called Operative Department was formed for this purpose within the OGPU in 1926, after Dzerzhinskii died, and was later placed under the authority of the GUGB.[8] This department, the forerunner of today's Ninth Directorate of the KGB, was itself reorganized numerous times and subjected to several name changes, but it has remained under the security organs.

[223]

The chief of the Operative Department from 1926 to 1937 was a Hungarian Jew named Karl V. Pauker, a former barber and a valet at the Budapest opera. After Pauker's arrest in mid-1937 a succession of others served in this post until 1940, when, according to Robert Conquest, the Operative Department was split into two sections, one for general guard duties and the other for so-called Defense of Leadership.[9] Deriabin claims that the Operative Department had been renamed the First Department (of the GUGB) as far back as 1934 and that later, when the state security organs were separated from the NKVD in April 1943, the First Department became the Sixth Directorate of the NKGB.[10] According to Deriabin, in 1946 the Sixth Directorate was divided into two guard administrations: one for Stalin and one for other key officials. Both administrations were placed under the MGB along with the post of Kremlin Kommendant, occupied since 1939 by N. K. Spiridonov, a border troops veteran.[11] Conquest reports that the post of Kremlin Kommendant had in fact been removed from the authority of the Soviet army in 1935, when Divisional Commander R. A. Peterson was dismissed from this position. After Peterson's departure NKVD troop officers apparently occupied this position.[12]

By February 1947 the two guard administrations and the Kremlin Kommendatura had been organized into a single Main Guards Directorate (Glavnoe Upravlenie Okhrany), which may have been placed under the direct authority of Stalin and his loyal assistant Poskrebyshev, though apparently it was still nominally under the MGB.[13] A U.S. intelligence report for this period, now declassified, confirms Deriabin's account of the organization of the guards administration.[14] It also indicates, along with Deriabin, that internal troops and regular Army troops were stationed in the Kremlin with the state security troops. During the early 1950s these troops were a focal point of the Kremlin power struggles. When Beria made his attempt to seize power from his colleagues after Stalin died, he brought in new men to head both the Guards Directorate (Sergei Kuzmichev) and the Kremlin Kommendatura (Andrei Vedenin). Apparently he intended to use MVD troops in Moscow to back his planned coup. (Both security and internal troops were then under the MVD.) After Beria was defeated by his opponents, who relied on the support of the regular military forces and the help of MVD officials Kruglov and Serov, the MVD apparatus was dismantled and the Guards Directorate became the Ninth Directorate of the KGB.[15]

The Ninth Directorate

Kuzmichev was dismissed as head of the Guards Directorate immediately after Beria's arrest. According to Deriabin, he was replaced by Aleksandr M. Lenev, an ally of Khrushchev from the Moscow *Gorkom* (City Party Committee).[16] By 1954 Vladimir Ustinov, another Khrushchev associate from the same committee, had become head of the Guards Directorate.[17] Clearly Khrushchev considered it important to have a trusted supporter in this post.

When Ustinov became first secretary of the Moscow *Gorkom* in 1957, he was succeeded in the Ninth Directorate by N. S. Zakharov, a career Chekist who had been Ustinov's deputy since 1954. Zakharov personally served as Khrushchev's bodyguard during his visit to the United States in 1959. An indication of the importance of the Ninth Directorate is that both Ustinov and Zakharov had the rank of deputy chairman of the USSR KGB. By 1963, in fact, Zakharov had become first deputy chairman, apparently while still occupying his post as chief of the Ninth Directorate.[18] Zakharov's survival in his post after Khrushchev's fall (until late 1967 or early 1968) would indicate that his ties with the state security organs were greater than those he had with Khrushchev personally. Zakharov's successor could not be identified. Deriabin claims that it was Tsvigun, but we have no evidence to confirm this.

It is interesting that the Kremlin Kommendant, A. Ia. Vedenin, survived the Beria purge and remained in his post until his retirement in 1967. Vedenin, a former political officer in the Red Army, seems to have been a neutral figure in the power struggles of these years, although the post of Kremlin Kommendant apparently continued to be under the authority of the state security organs (probably the Ninth Directorate) rather than the regular military after 1954. When Vedenin's obituary was published in June 1984 he was described as a "retired USSR KGB staff member."[19] Vedenin's successor, Lt. Gen. S. S. Shornikov, has not been identified publicly as a KGB officer, but he served in the military counterintelligence branch of the state security organs for fifteen years prior to 1967, so it seems likely that he was under the KGB.[20]. After almost twenty years in his post, Shornikov retired sometime in 1986 and was replaced by Maj. Gen. G. D. Bashkin.[21]

The Ninth Directorate, whose troops are distinguished by their blue shoulder tabs, has carried on the functions of its predecessors: guarding party and state leaders, along with the Kremlin and other important official buildings probably down to the regional, or *oblast*, level. It has also been suggested that KGB guards are responsible for handling and storage of special and nuclear munitions, although other sources claim that the KGB no longer has this responsibility.[22] There are no reliable estimates on the troop strength of the Guards Directorate. Deriabin assessed its total strength in 1952 as 17,000, but he may have included internal troop units, such as the Dzerzhinskii Division, in his calculations, as these troops were under the MGB at the time.[23] Another source cited a figure of 15,000 KGB guards troops in 1967.[24] The 1986 estimate from the London-based International Institute for Strategic Studies gives a figure of 40,000 special KGB troops, which is said to include the Kremlin guard, special guards, and signal troops.[25]

The Army and the security forces were on opposing sides in the struggle between Beria and his opponents, but it is not clear that KGB guard troops are intended, along with the MVD internal troops, as a counterforce to the regular military. Although the strength of MVD troops has been estimated at between 250,000 and 340,000 men, reportedly only one operational division, the Dzerzhinskii Division, is located in Moscow.[26] Furthermore as one source has pointed out, the overwhelming majority of internal troop units are not equipped with artillery and tanks but are only infantry units.[27] It is not known what type of equipment the state security forces possess, but it is doubtful that they could successfully oppose the military in an armed confrontation.

Some have suggested that the internal troops are actually at the disposal of the KGB.[28] Their units are garrisoned with KGB troops in the Kremlin and are apparently intended to serve as support troops to the KGB in the event of a popular uprising that would threaten the leadership. Given their political reliability and special training, KGB and MVD troops would be more effective than regular army troops in such a crisis. Nevertheless they remain under separate commands. The fact that the internal troops were formally transferred from the state security organs to the internal affairs ministry after Beria's fall suggests that the Kremlin leadership considers it prudent to keep these troops under a separate command from the KGB lest the latter attempt to interfere by force in a Kremlin power struggle. In any case, the strength of the troops of the Ninth Directorate lies more in the importance of their highly sensitive political functions than in their numbers.

Other State Security Troops

More than one source has claimed that in addition to guard troops, the KGB has several units of signal troops. These troops are reportedly responsible for installation, maintenance, and operation of secret communications facilities for the leading party and government bodies, including the Ministry of Defense. Their function is seen as an extension of the tasks performed by state security signal, or special communications, troops in World War II, which reportedly numbered approximately 15,000 men.[29] Although official Soviet sources do not make explicit reference to KGB signal troops, evidence indicates that such signal troops do exist. At a ceremony to celebrate the fiftieth anniversary of the MOD Signal Troops in 1969, among those listed in the press as having attended was P. N. Voronin, lt. gen. of Signal Troops, and a representative from the KGB.[30] KGB signal troops are probably under the command of the Eighth (Communications) Directorate.

There is also another body of special KGB troops, perhaps successors to the earlier operational troops, which are intended for counterterrorist and counterinsurgency operations. Such troops are reportedly employed, along with MVD internal troops, to suppress public protests and disperse demonstrations, such as that of the Crimean Tatars in July 1987.[31] KGB troops in Moscow are also alleged to perform certain types of sabotage and diversionary missions. Some sources have reported the presence of special KGB troop units in Hungary in 1956, in Czechoslovakia in 1968, and, more recently, in Afghanistan, where several KGB officers have been killed. Aleksei Myagkov, a former officer in the KGB's Third Directorate, noted that KGB sabotage troops are trained to operate on enemy territory as advance units before the outbreak of a war.[32] These operational units are probably separate from the guards and communications troops, but their subordination, precise functions, and numbers remain unknown.

KGB Border Troops: History

The early history of the border, or frontier, troops was marked by numerous reorganizations. Initially the Vecheka did not have primary responsibility for guarding the borders. On 28 May 1918, celebrated today as the official anniversary of the border troops, Lenin signed a Sovnarkom decree that formally established a frontier guard under the Main Administration of Border Protection. This administration was functionally subordinate first to the People's Commissariat of Finance, then to the Commissariat of Trade and Industry and, a few weeks later, to the People's Commissariat of Foreign Trade, but its troops were under the command of the Red Army.[33]

As Leggett notes, Chekas established along the frontier exercised a supporting role, and the Cheka's Special Departments in the Red Army served as watchdogs in the front zones.[34] Not until November 1920 was responsibility for border protection vested in the Vecheka directly under its Special Department, headed at the time by V. R. Menzhinskii. Shortly thereafter the frontier troops were formally transferred to Vecheka control. By the summer of 1921 Vecheka border troops reportedly numbered 95,000. Except for the period from October 1921 to September 1922, when border troops were transferred temporarily to the Red Army, responsibility for frontier protection remained in the hands of the security police (GPU/OGPU) until 1934.[35]

In early 1924 following the establishment of the OGPU, the structure of the border troops was reorganized. Border troops, which had been reduced in number to 30,000 in 1922, and border administration were united into a single agency, the Department of Border Protection. The approximately eight border districts were subdivided into detachments (*otriady*), commandant posts (*komendatury*), and border outposts (*zastavy*)—a structure that has been preserved, with some changes, to this day. Then toward the end of 1926 a Main Administration of Border Protection and OGPU troops was established, uniting the Department of Border Protection and the Administration of OGPU troops, which included the special troops. As international tensions and the threat of war grew, the Soviet regime decided to strengthen border protection further and in the early 1930s increased the numbers of border troops by 50 percent. In addition, four new institutions were set up to train commanding officers of the border troops.[36]

Border troops engaged in a variety of operations during the 1920s and early 1930s, which have been described in detail by Soviet historians. They waged a continuous struggle against armed insurgents and partisans in border regions, particularly the Basmachi bands from Afghanistan and Iran. They also captured people who were described as "spies, saboteurs and terrorists" attempting to cross the Soviet borders and foiled thousands of attempts to smuggle contraband. The scope of their operations is conveyed by the fact that in the period between 1922 and 1925 alone border guards in the western district reportedly captured a total of 11,641 border violators, including 2604 smugglers and over 600 "spies and terrorists." Border troops also participated, along with the regular Soviet armed forces, in defending the Soviet border in the Far East against attacks by the Japanese.[37]

When the NKVD was established in July 1934, it included the Main Administration of Border and Internal Troops (GUPVO), which was separate from the Main Administration of State Security. In December 1934 the Worker-Peasant Militia was incorporated into this administration but was again made a separate administration within the next year or so. Border and internal troops remained under one administration until March 1939 when, with the situation along Soviet borders tense and uncertain, at least four separate NKVD administrations, or directorates, were established according to the different services—border, internal, convoy, and railway troops.[38] When a separate NKVD and NKGB were established (first from February to June 1941 and again in April 1943) these troop administrations were placed under the NKVD.

The Border Troops in World War II

By the eve of the war the total stength of the NKVD border troops had reached between 157,000 and 158,000 men, almost two-thirds (100,000) of whom were positioned along the western border.[39] When Germany attacked the Soviet Union on 22 June 1941 these troops sustained the initial blow, containing the enemy advance for several hours and in some places for several days. Spread very thinly, they were equipped with only hand weapons and grenades and had no reserves, so they suffered heavy losses.

From the outset of the war border troops served as a reserve force for regular military units. Within the first days the NKVD formed fifteen infantry divisions totaling 15,000 troops from the various border districts. These divisions became part of the 29th, 30th, 31st, and 24th armies, which served, along with the 28th and 32nd armies, as a reserve front. These armies took a direct part in the battles of Smolensk and Moscow. Other divisions comprising both border and internal troops fought actively on the Southwest Front—in the Crimea, at Stalingrad, and in the North Caucasus. At the end of 1942 NKVD border and internal troops formed the 17th Army, which took part in a fierce battle with the enemy at Kursk in July 1943. During the course of the entire war 113,700 border troops participated directly in combat.[40] Border guards who found themselves behind enemy lines participated in the partisan movement aimed at sabotaging the enemy in occupied territory.[41]

One of the main tasks of the border and internal troops in the period of the German advance was that of securing the rear of the Red

Army. On 25 June 1941 the Sovnarkom passed a resolution charging the NKVD with this task. The leadership of the rear security troops was exercised by the Main Administration of Border Troops until April 1942, where a separate Administration of Troops for Securing the Rear was formed. In May 1943 this became a main administration, or directorate. The rear security troops were under the dual subordination of the General Staff, which directed all their maneuvers at the front, and the NKVD, which had overall control over the transmission of these troop units from one front to another.[42] The rear security troops were charged with a variety of tasks: uncovering and arresting enemy agents who managed to reach the rear of the front, liquidating small enemy groups and armed detachments, protecting communications in the rear, guarding Army receiving stations for prisoners of war, and apprehending deserters. In 1942 alone rear security troops are said to have caught more the 1500 spies and diversionists and liquidated more than 135 groups of bandits and 3000 enemy "sympathizers and accomplices."[43]

When the Red Army moved westward, "liberating" German-occupied territory, rear security troops were charged with clearing away enemy remnants, ensuring order in the front zones, and carrying out intelligence tasks. During 1945 border troops guarding the rear of the advancing Soviet army in East Germany, Hungary, Czechoslovakia, and Poland helped to restore order, fight pockets of local resistance, and unmask war criminals.[44]

For the special purpose of securing newly established Soviet borders, thirty-seven detachments composed of border and regular Soviet troops were moved into the border districts from Karelia down to the Black Sea in 1943. Their main tasks, in addition to rebuilding border fortifications, consisted of fighting "bourgeois-nationalist" groups that resisted Soviet rule, particularly in the Ukraine, Belorussia, and Baltic areas. In some cases efforts to rout local nationalist groups lasted several years. According to one Soviet source, border troops in the Baltic District, together with the regular state security police, continued to fight these groups until 1950.[45]

In the Far East campaign border troops mounted the initial surprise attack against the Japanese on 9 August 1945. It was thought that these troops, with their knowledge of the territory along the enemy cordon and the approaches to enemy strongholds, would be best suited for the advance attack. With this goal troops of the Transbaikal, Khaborovsk, and Maritime Border Districts had been placed under the operational command of corresponding front commanders, and a carefully planned attack had been prepared. The attack involved 320 border detachments, each numbering between thirty and seventy-five men, though in some cases the numbers were greater. Land border forces were supported by naval border guards. Moving at night in small groups, they crossed marshes and forded rivers to reach Japanese garrisons unseen and launched surprise coordinated assaults on Japanese strongholds all along the Soviet border, a total of over 2700 kilometers in length. Their success in overrunning Japanese fortifications enabled regular Soviet military forces to exploit the surprise by launching their offensive without air or artillery preparation.[46]

Most Western experts have assumed that the future combat role of the Soviet border troops would be similar to their role in World War II: that of absorbing the initial enemy blow and then securing the rear of the regular army, as well as the numerous other policing and paramilitary missions discussed earlier.[47] Technological developments in weapons and communications actually have made it unlikely that Soviet border forces would face an unexpected large-scale enemy attack that would leave them vulnerable and without the immediate support of the Red Army. It is possible, however, that border troops would be used to launch a surprise conventional attack on neighboring territory, as they did against the Japanese.

Soviet sources are vague about the postwar organization of the border troops. The troops continued under the authority of the internal affairs apparatus (renamed MVD in 1946) until 1950, when the MGB, or Ministry of State Security, acquired both the border and internal troops. (The militia had been placed under the MGB some time before this.) All these troops came under the united MVD created by Beria in March 1953, and after the KGB was established the next year, they were placed under the internal affairs apparatus. Not until 1957 were the border troops transferred back to the state security organs.[48]

Because the border guard, throughout much of its pre-1957 history, was not under the authority of the state security organs, border guard officials had careers that were distinct from those of regular state security officers and were often closely associated with the internal troops. The career of S. I. Donskov, who served after the war as chief of the Internal Troops and later became a deputy chief of the USSR KGB Border Troops, is a typical example of cross-posting of these officials.[49] This is not surprising in view of the fact that border and internal troops were united in one administration from 1934 to 1939 and were later combined in the Main Administration for Securing the Rear of the Red Army during the war. Although careers of internal and border troops officials have tended to follow separate tracks since the border troops were moved to the KGB

[231]

in 1957, it might be expected that border and internal troops would again work closely in the event of a future war, and that plans for a coordinated or combined administration have been worked out.

The Chief Directorate of Border Troops of the USSR KGB: Organization and Personnel

The Border Troops Directorate is headed by a chief, currently Army general V. A. Matrosov, who is assisted by one or more first deputy chiefs, several deputy chiefs, and a chief of staff. Within the directorate there is also the Political Administration, which has functions similar to that of the MPA (Main Political Administration) of the Soviet Army and Navy: political indoctrination and surveillance on behalf of the party. In addition, Western sources claim that there is an intelligence administration within the Border Troops Directorate. This cannot be confirmed, but it is likely given the fact that such an administration was identified during the war years. According to declassified U.S. intelligence documents, this administration had branches in all border districts. Each branch in turn contained two sections; the first was designated for domestic intelligence and border counterintelligence (observation of the loyalty of the Soviet border population and detection of espionage by foreign agents) and the other section concerned itself with foreign intelligence collection and counterespionage in adjacent foreign territory.[50] Presumably the intelligence administration operates along similar lines today.

The Border Troops Directorate is divided into approximately nine border districts that cover the 67,000 kilometers of the USSR state border.[51] Border district boundaries are distinct from civil or military district boundaries. The total force strength of the KGB border troops has not been revealed by Soviet sources. As was indicated earlier, border troops numbered approximately 158,000 on the eve of World War II. Given the increase in the Soviet population, the annexation of new territory, and the vast manpower resources allocated to the regular military since the war, the most recent estimate by the London-based International Institute for Strategic Studies of 230,000 border troops is by no means exaggerated and could even be too low.[52]

Table 7.1 presents an organizational chart showing the main structure and leading personnel of the KGB Border Troops Directorate since 1957. In most cases the dates represent first and last identifications in the posts and thus are only approximate. Occupants of key posts could not always be identified over the period covered, which accounts for lapses.

TABLE 7.1
Chief Directorate of Border Troops of USSR KGB: 1957–1987[a]

Chief:	Col. Gen. P. I. Zyrianov (1957–1972)[b]
	Army General V. A. Matrosov (1972–)
First Deputy Chiefs:	Lt. Gen. V. F. Lobanov (1973–1977)
	Maj. Gen. V. K. Gurianov (1978–)
	Lt. Gen. I. P. Vertelko (Nov. 1985–)
Deputy Chiefs:	G. A. Petrov (1961)
	Ia. T. Reznichenko (1969)
	Lt. Gen. F. A. Kuzmichev (May 1971–)
	Maj. Gen. G. I. Vlasenko (May 1971–)
	Vice Adm. N. N. Dolmatov (1974–)
	Lt. Gen. S. A. Bannykh (1961–1967)
	Lt. Gen. P. I. Ionov (1969–)
	E. D. Solov'ev (Jan. 1973)
	Maj. Gen. I. P. Vertelko (May 1973–)
	Rear Adm. N. N. Kozorezov (1978–)
	Lt. Gen. I. P. Polezhaev (May 1980–)
	B. I. Korovin (1983; Jan. 1986–)
	V. S. Donskov (1986–)
	V. I. Shishlov (April 1987–)
	A. S. Shindaev (April 1987–)
Chiefs of Staff:	Lt. Gen. S. A. Bannykh (1961–1963)
	K. F. Sekretarev (1963–1967)
	Lt. Gen. V. A. Matrosov (1967–1972)
	Lt. Gen. V. F. Lobanov (1973–1977)
	Maj. Gen. Iu. A. Neshumov (1977)
	Lt. Gen. I. Ia. Kalinichenko (May 1986–)
Intelligence Administration Chiefs:	?
POLITICAL ADMINISTRATION	
Chiefs:	Lt. Gen. N. A. Romanov (May 1958)
	Lt. Gen. G. I. Zabolotnyy (1959–1968)
	V. Ia. Lezhepekov (1969–1974)
	Maj. Gen. V. T. Shchur (1974–1975)
	Maj. Gen. V. V. Gaponenko (Jan. 1976–1978)
	A. M. Latyshev (1979–1981)
	Maj. Gen. V. S. Ivanov (May 1982–1986)
	Maj. Gen. N. V. Britvin (May 1987–)
BORDER DISTRICT COMMANDERS	
Baltic BD	Lt. Gen. N. A. Romanov (1959–)
	I. Ia. Kalinichenko (May 1977; May 1981)
	Lt. Gen. G. F. Moiseenko (1981–?)
Central Asian BD	Maj. Gen. V. Kh. Lapin (1958–1962)
	Lt. Gen. F. A. Kuz'michev (May 1962; 1971)
	Iu. A. Neshumov (Jan. 1976)
	Maj. Gen. I. G. Karpov (1977–1980)
	G. A. Zgerskii (1981–1982)
	V. F. Zaporozhchenko (May 1983)
	Maj. Gen. V. I. Shliakhtin (Dec. 1984; May 1985)

[233]

TABLE 7.1 (cont).

Eastern BD	Lt. Gen. M. K. Merkulov (May 1966–1976)
	Lt. Gen. V. S. Donskov (1976–1986)
	Maj. Gen. I. K. Petrovas (1986–)
Far Eastern BD	Maj. Gen. L. Ia. Sen'kov (Mar. 1966–Apr. 1970)
	Lt. Gen. V. M. Krylovskii (Jan. 1976; Mar. 1981)
	K. E. Kortelainen (1981–Jun. 1982)
Northwest BD	P. I. Ionov (Mar. 1966)
	Lt. Gen. K. F. Sekretarev (May 1969; 1971)
	Lt. Gen. A. G. Viktorov (May 1976–)
Pacific BD	P. S. Ivanov (1961; Mar. 1966)
	Maj. Gen. V. F. Lobanov (Mar. 1969)
	Maj. Gen. V. Konstantinov (Dec. 1975; Mar. 1976)
	Lt. Gen. V. K. Gaponenko (Dec. 1980–)
Transcaucasus BD	P. V. Piskunov (1954–1963)
	V. A. Matrosov (1963–1967)
	Maj. Gen. N. D. Peskov (May 1967–May 1969)
	L. Ia. Sen'kov (Mar. 1971)
	A. G. Viktorov (1975–1976)
	Maj. Gen. N. I. Makarov (1977–1981)
	V. E. Sentiurin (Sept. 1981–July 1983)
	Lt. Gen. G. A. Zgerskii (Nov. 1985–)
Western BD	Maj. Gen. B. A. Ivanov (May 1963; Mar. 1966)
	Lt. Gen. N. V. Lavrinenko (1972–1981)
	Lt. Gen. I. Ia. Kalinichenko (Jun. 1981–1986)
	Lt. Gen. V. I. Stus (1986–)
Transbaikal BD[c]	Maj. Gen. N. V. Lavrinenko (Oct. 1969; 1970)

[a]. Information for this table comes from a cumulation of references to border guards officials in the Soviet press, particularly *KZ* and republic newspapers. The CIA *Directory of Soviet Officials* for various years and several editions of *Deputaty VS* for the USSR and certain republics have also been used.

[b]. Zyrianov was actually chief of the border guards since 1952, but they were not under KGB control until 1957.

[c]. Unlike the other BDs, the Transbaikal BD is rarely mentioned in the Soviet press so it may no longer exist. The only recent reference to this district was in a Soviet book that mentioned '*zabaikal'tsy*,' or troops of the Transbaikal, among the various border troops. See *Dal'nevostochnyi pogranichnyi*, p. 281.

As the table indicates, the turnover of border district commanders has been quite heavy in certain districts, such as the Central Asian and Transcaucasus BDs, while in other districts the commanders remained in their posts for up to ten years. It is not uncommon for commanders to be transferred from one district to another. Presumably this trains them for general border troop administration in Moscow by giving them experience in more than one area.

The somewhat limited biographical information available on leading officers indicates that most have spent their entire careers in the border troops, rising in the ranks to their command posts. Col. Gen. P. I. Zyrianov, chief of the USSR Border Troops from 1952 to 1972, joined these forces in 1927 at the age of twenty. By 1943 he was commander of what was then the Maritime (*Primorskii*) BD and nine years later reached the top post in the border troops.[53] Similarly, Army General V. A. Matrosov, chief of the border troops since 1972, joined these forces in 1938 at the age of twenty-one. In 1955 Matrosov graduated from the Military Juridical Academy of the Soviet Army and in 1959 completed higher academic courses at the General Staff Academy. He became commander of the Transcaucasus BD in 1963, serving there until his appointment as chief of staff of the USSR Border Troops in 1967.[54]

Information on post-1957 occupants of key positions in the border troops below that of chief reveals a similar pattern. All six BD commanders for whom career data are available were career border troops officers, as were the only two deputy BD commanders about whom there is information.[55] The same appears to be the case with those serving in the Political Administration of the Border Troops, whose officers as a rule have spent most of their careers in this work.[56]

Although it appears that border troops officers have little career interaction or overlap with the regular, non-militarized KGB hierarchy, there are two interesting exceptions. Karl Efremovich Kortelainen, an Estonian born in 1930 and educated at the General Staff Academy, joined the border troops in the early 1950s, rising to become commander of the Far Eastern BD in 1981. In June 1982 he was appointed chairman of the Estonian KGB.[57] Another unusual career is that of Lt. Gen. V. Ia. Lezhepekov, who was identified in the press as chief of the Political Administration of the USSR Border Troops from 1969 through about 1974. By 1976 Lezhepekov was identified as a deputy chairman of the USSR KGB and thus part of the regular KGB hierarchy. Interestingly, he moved to the MVD in July 1983, becoming a deputy minister.[58]

Despite these exceptions, moves from the border troops to other areas of the KGB are rare, and the Border Guards Directorate functions as a distinct and separate hierarchy. This is confirmed by data on regular KGB officials, discussed in chapter 5. It is thus not surprising that personnel changes in the border troops appear to have little relation to changes in the KGB leadership or to Kremlin power struggles. Both Zyrianov and Matrosov survived upheavals in the state security organs and the party leadership without being replaced.

If border guard officials seem to be immune from the vagaries of Kremlin politics, they also have relatively weak representation on political bodies in comparison with other KGB officials and members of the military hierarchy. No USSR Border Troop chief has ever gained membership in the Central Committee, even as a candidate, or been elected to the USSR Supreme Soviet. Matrosov was elected to the latter body when he was commander of the Transcaucasus BD in 1966, but he has not been a delegate since then. The USSR Border Troop chief is elected regularly to the RSFSR Supreme Soviet, however.

Commanders of certain border districts—Baltic, Central Asian, Eastern, and Transcaucasian—have regularly been elected to central committees in republics coinciding geographically with these districts: Latvia, Turkmenistan, Kazakhstan, Georgia, and the Ukraine, respectively. At the Twenty-Third Party Congress of the Turkmen CP in January 1986, the Commander of the Central Asian BD, V. I. Shliakhtin, was elected a member of the Turkmen CC party bureau. Presumably this unusual development reflects the importance of this border district, both militarily and politically, to the Soviet regime. Border guard officials are sometimes elected to republic supreme soviets, which have little direct political influence but do confer prestige on the organizations represented. In contrast with border guard officials, KGB republic chairmen and commanders of military districts are not only elected to the USSR Supreme Soviet and republic central committees but also are frequently included as full or candidate members of republic party bureaus.

Despite their low political profile, border troops officers enjoy a great deal of prestige and public exposure. Matrosov was promoted to the rank of Army general in December 1978 and in 1984 was made a USSR deputy KGB chairman.[59] He appears frequently in public and has had numerous interviews, speeches, and articles published, as have his subordinates. Border Troops Day, established in 1958 to commemorate the founding of the Soviet frontier guard, is celebrated every year on 28 May with much fanfare. Leading border troop, KGB, military, and party officials gather in Moscow and in various other republic capitals to mark the occasion, which usually receives prominent press coverage. Anniversary celebrations for the founding of individual border districts are also widely publicized. The sixtieth anniversary of the Transcaucasus BD, for example, was commemorated on 23 July 1982 by a large gathering in Tbilisi attended by the party first secretaries of Georgia, Azerbaidzhan, and Armenia, who gave lengthy speeches in honor of the border guard.[60]

Books and articles glorifying the border guards are published in the Soviet press at a steady rate. These publications discuss the heroism of

[236]

border troops in World War II, as well as their current activities in protecting the USSR's "sacred borders."[61] The KGB has made a concerted effort to enlist the talents of Soviet writers and artists in depicting the achievements of the border guard. In November 1978 a conference of representatives of creative unions was held in Moscow for the purpose of encouraging such artistic endeavors.[62] In February 1985, Soviet television broadcast a four-part documentary series, "Steps on the Frontier," on the work of the border guard.[63]

The constant barrage of propaganda glorifying the border troops serves several purposes. First and most obvious, it is intended to evoke feelings of patriotism among the Soviet people. The border troops are the first line of defense for the Soviet Union, and they symbolize both the integrity and inviolability of Soviet borders, which the public is supposed to hold sacred. Second, the propaganda is designed to encourage qualified young men motivated by patriotism to join the border troops and also to enlist the population in supporting these troops. Much importance is attached to the support of the Komsomol, volunteer people's militia, and local population in border areas. The latter are encouraged, for example, to report on any strangers seen near the border. Another purpose of the propaganda is to demonstrate to the Soviet public that the borders are continually under threat by spies, subversives, and possible military aggression, thereby justifying the need for acute "vigilance" on the part of the regime. Finally, the glorification of the border troops—in particular the frequent mention by name of individual border guards who have acted heroically—does much to raise the morale of these troops. Given the loneliness and physical hardship as well as political sensitivity of their work, this is an important aspect of the propaganda.

Legal Jurisdiction and Function of Border Troops

The border troops are by law under the jurisdiction of the USSR KGB. The Chief Directorate of Border Troops of the USSR KGB operates independently of the other KGB directorates and does not have components in the regular KGB apparatus that exist at the republic level and below. Rather, it has a separate hierarchy organized according to border districts. Border troops, while under the operational authority of the KGB, are conscripted as part of the biannual call-up of the Ministry of Defense, and their induction and discharge are regulated by the 1967

[237]

USSR Law on Universal Military Service, which covers all armed forces of the USSR.[64]

The legal status, duties, and rights of the border troops are set forth in the Law on the USSR State Border, confirmed by the USSR Supreme Soviet on 24 November 1982.[65] This law, which took effect on 1 March 1983, replaced an earlier statute (*polozhenie*) on the USSR State Border of 5 August 1960.[66] The new law is more detailed and comprehensive than the earlier statute, taking into account the technological changes that have affected border protection and strengthening regulations governing the border regime. Article 28 defines the basic duties of border troops. Among them are repulsing armed incursions into USSR territory; preventing illegal crossings of the border or the transport across the border of weapons, explosives, contraband, or subversive literature; monitoring the observance of established procedures at border crossing points; monitoring the observance by Soviet and foreign ships of navigation procedures in Russia's territorial waters; and assisting state agencies in the preservation of natural resources and the protection of the environment from pollution. Not surprisingly, the law does not mention the intelligence functions of the border guards.

These duties are similar to those outlined in the 1960 statute except that they are broader and set forth in considerably more detail. The new law, for example, states specifically the types of subversive materials border guards are to prevent being conveyed across the border: "printed or duplicated materials, manuscripts, documents, video or sound recordings, films or other printed or pictorial matter containing information that could be detrimental to the state's political or economic interests, security, public order or the population's health or morals." In contrast to the 1960 statute, which mentions simply "forbidden objects or materials" that are to be kept out, the 1983 law implies that border guards are to exercise a censorship function, acting as guardians of the people's morals by determining what material is detrimental to Soviet society and what is not.[67]

Article 29 of the 1983 Law on USSR Borders enumerates the legal prerogatives of the border troops, which are more extensive than those set forth in the 1960 statute. The border guards have the right, among other things, to examine documents and possessions of persons crossing the borders and to confiscate articles; to conduct inquiries in cases of violations of the USSR state border; and to take such actions as arrest, search, and interrogation of individuals. In accordance with a decree (*ukaz*) passed in February 1972 and incorporated into the 1983 law, border guards can carry out the administrative detention for up to three days of persons who violate border procedures, providing the Procurator has been informed within the first twenty-four hours, or up to ten days with the Procurator's sanction, if the violator has no documents verifying his or her identity.[68] Border troops thus have the right to impose so-called administrative sanctions against border violators, as well as to conduct inquiries into cases of border violations, but they are not empowered to carry out criminal investigations.

Border troops, responsible for protecting land and sea borders, and air defense forces, responsible for Soviet airspace, are empowered under Article 36 to use weapons and combat equipment in repulsing armed attacks, incursions, or provocations on the USSR border and in preventing hijacking of Soviet aircraft when no passengers are on board or against any type of border violation on land, sea or air — "in cases where violators use force or cannot be detained by any other means." If necessary, weapons and combat equipment of the regular armed forces are to be used.

In contrast to the earlier law, the 1983 law places greater emphasis on the active participation of the public in protecting the borders. Article 38 notes that people's volunteer militia detachments (*druzhiny*) are to be established for this purpose in border district communities and at border crossing points. In addition, state agencies, public organizations, and officials are to educate citizens on the "political and economic significance of protecting the USSR State Border" and instill in them "a spirit of high vigilance" (Article 39). Discussions of the new border law in the Soviet press indicate that such public support for the border guards is considered to be an especially important aspect of border protection policy.[69]

In general the 1983 border law reflects a more aggressive policy of border protection as compared with the earlier statute. The final article (Article 40) states firmly that persons guilty of violating or attempting to violate the USSR state border or border policy "bear criminal, administrative or other liabilities." Such an article was not a feature of the 1960 statute. Furthermore the new legislation, in addition to tightening the entire border regime, gives border guards wider latitude in carrying out their functions.

Training, Deployment, and Equipment

As Soviet sources repeatedly stress, the border guard is not only a soldier, but a defender of Soviet ideology. His mission is not merely military but also political, entailing difficult and sensitive tasks. Thus in addition to enduring the physical hardships of border duty, the border guard must be prepared to shoot Soviet citizens who attempt to escape across the border and also to detect contraband and morally harmful literature that comes to the borders. Vigilance and dedication to the communist cause are important prerequisites for border guards, who may be faced with temptations in their work. Soviet sources claim that border guards are frequently offered bribes by persons attempting to violate border procedures.[70] Thus the biannual recruitment of troops for the border guard stresses political reliability along with physical preparedness. Among the officer corps, 85 percent were members of the Communist party by the late 1960s whereas 45 percent were reported to have higher education. Among regular enlisted men in 1969, 56 percent had at least a middle education and 85 percent were members of Komsomol.[71]

Enlisted men are trained with their operational units, whereas officers are trained in special KGB Border Guard schools. The Dzerzhinskii KGB Higher Border Command School was established in Alma Ata in 1960 from what was formerly the Alma Ata Border School, and in Moscow a regular border school was transformed into a higher border school in 1965. For military-political officers the Voroshilov Higher Border Military-Political Academy, located outside Leningrad, has existed since the 1930s. In 1972 a higher border military-political school was created in Golytsin, near Moscow. More recently higher border command faculties were set up at the Frunze Military Academy and the Lenin Military-Political Academy.[72] The period of instruction at the higher border command schools is four years. Officer candidates, who are screened carefully by their local KGB offices before admittance, take general higher education courses along with specialized military and political ones.[73]

To ensure a high level of *partiinost* and discipline among the border troops, much attention is devoted to political training and indoctrination. For this purpose a network of political organs similar to but independent of the MPA exists within the KGB Border Troops. At the top of the hierarchy is the Political Administration of the USSR KGB Border Troops in Moscow. Unlike the MPA, it is not part of the Central Committee apparatus. Below this administration political departments exist within all the border districts, detachments, and educational institutions, while a network of full-time party political officers works among all border troop units. These officers conduct political study groups, give propaganda lectures, and work to increase the level of combat effectiveness among the troops.[74]

In 1963 a system of military councils was established in the border districts. These are collegial decision-making bodies, like those in the armed forces, that exist at border district headquarters and include the commanding military-political officer. They were reportedly created to increase the decision-making role of the political officer. In 1969 the high-level Military Council of the Border Troops, which includes the chief of the Political Administration, was set up in Moscow.[75] Political officers play an important role in publicizing the activities of border troops by making speeches and writing books and articles on their mission and achievements. In short, they serve as public relations men for the border troops. A monthly journal, *Pogranichnik* (The Border Guard) has been published by the Border Troops Political Administration since 1938.[76]

It has been suggested by Western sources that the KGB's Special Departments (*Osobye otdely*), which exist throughout the regular military apparatus for the purpose of political surveillance of troops and officers, are also deployed in the border troops.[77] (Apparently this was the case during World War II, but at that time the border troops were not under the state security organs.[78]) Given the fact that today the border troops form an organization that is separate from the regular KGB hierarchy, it stands to reason that the KGB leadership would consider it necessary to use such a system of political surveillance, but its existence has not been mentioned in the Soviet press.

The nine border districts are subdivided into detachments (*otriady*) covering specific sections of the border, border command posts (*pogranichnye komendatury*), passport control points (*kontrol'no-propusknye punkty*), and border outposts (*zastavy*).[79] Soviet sources do not reveal the number or size of detachments or other border units, but judging from unclassified Western estimates, border detachments probably include between three and five *komendatury*, and their strength ranges from 1200 to 2000 men. It is believed that five or six border outposts, the basic level of organization, are grouped into one *komendatura*.[80] Detachments also include maneuver groups, which are mobile units, probably available for emergencies, such as a border provocation and small air units for reconnaissance and supplies. Border districts with water areas and sea coasts also include maritime or coast guard units.[81]

The border area is divided into a border zone, which encompasses the territory of the district and settlements adjacent to the state border, and the border strip, an area of approximately two kilometers in depth running directly along the border. Entry into a border zone is forbidden except by permanent residents or those who have obtained authorization from the Ministry of Internal Affairs, which regulates entry into the zone. Entry into the border strip is forbidden without special permission from the border troops.[82]

The border clashes that occurred between the Soviets and the Chinese in March 1969 along the Ussuri River, including the Battle of Damanskii Island, in which over thirty border guards were killed, had a great impact on Soviet border policy. This border engagement, as well as other skirmishes with the Chinese that occurred in the early 1970s, provided the impetus for greater stress on border security and combat readiness. According to one authoritative Soviet source, in the period between the Twenty-Third and Twenty-Fourth Party congresses (1966–1971) the CPSU and the Soviet government made a series of decisions that improved border security: because of a "complicated situation on certain portions of the USSR state border, and also an activization of enemy intelligence activity" new border districts and detachments were created. In addition, the border guards' arms and equipment were substantially improved and updated.[83] It is not clear what new border districts were in fact created but, as was noted earlier, nine border districts have been identified since the early 1970s.

With regard to equipment, high-speed ships and launches, modern helicopters, and airplanes capable of protecting the border under all climatic and geographic conditions, independently or in conjunction with land and sea units, have been supplied to the border troops in recent years. Ground border troop units have been equipped with advanced radar stations, searchlight installations, signaling and electronic-optical equipment, cross-country vehicles, and up-to-date weaponry.[84] Although Soviet sources stress that border guards should be able not only to render border violators harmless but also to fight in the event of an armed invasion, the equipment and weapons at their immediate disposal are probably intended mainly for the former task. The 1983 Law on the State Border indicates that the weapons and combat equipment of the border guards would be reinforced by that belonging to the Soviet Army or Navy in the event of a serious border conflict. In fact one Western source notes that tanks used in the border clashes with the Chinese actually belonged to the Soviet Army.[85]

In this age of satellites and sophisticated reconnaissance technology it is unlikely that the border guards will face a surprise armed invasion, and their tasks of detecting secret agents who attempt to slip across the border have also been made easier. But they do play an important role in keeping Soviet citizens from fleeing abroad, as well as in preventing the flow of "subversive" materials into the Soviet Union.

In the event of a future conventional war the border guards would again fulfill the politically sensitive tasks of guarding the rear of the Army and hunting down enemy agents, but it is possible that they would also engage in direct offensive operations, as they did in World War II.

The Soviets place greater emphasis on the sanctity of their borders than do most Western states, and clearly the ability to protect their borders, including airspace, which is the responsibility of the air defense forces, has a significance that extends beyond any physical threat or economic concern. (This concern was brought to light clearly with the violation of Soviet airspace by the young West German, Mathias Rust, in May 1987, which resulted in a purge of the Soviet military.[86]) In a sense Soviet border troops embody one of the most essential prerequisites of the modern police state: the ability to maintain tight control over the flow of people and communications both into and out of the country. This control is essential if the CPSU is to retain its monopoly of power. Thus the border guards can count on the Kremlin leadership to continue to promote their public image and to provide them with the best possible training, equipment, and weapons.

Notes

1. Iu. M. Kozlov, (ed.), *Sovetskoe administrativnoe pravo* (Moscow: Iuridichestkaia Literatura, 1973), p. 531.

2. Lt. Gen. V. Kotkov and Col. V. Zhuravlev, "Iz istorii vnutrennikh voisk," *Voenno-istoricheskii zhurnal*, no. 11 (1972):90–95; V. I. Chugunov, "Voiska vnutrennei okhrany respubliki," *Sovetskaia voennaia entsiklopedüa* [hereafter *SVE*] vol. 2 (Moscow: Voenizdat, 1976):316; George Leggett, *The Cheka: Lenin's Political Police* (Oxford: Clarendon Press, 1981) pp. 32–35, 74–77, 93–94.

3. Leggett, *The Cheka*, p. 225.

4. I. G. Belikov et al., eds., *Imeni Dzerzhinskogo: Boevoi put' ordena Lenina krasnoznamenoi divizii im. F. E. Dzerzhinskogo* (Moscow: Voenizdat, 1976), pp. 30–33; N. Zubov, *Oni okhraniali Lenina* (Moscow: Molodaia gvardiia, 1984), p. 105.

5. Col. P. Dmitriyev, "Special Purpose Unit," *Soviet Military Review*, no. 2 (1980): 44–45; Leggett, *The Cheka*, pp. 226–227.

6. Belikov, *Imeni Dzerzhinskogo*, pp. 30–33.

7. On the history and current operations of the internal troops see ibid., I. K. Iakovlev, "Vnutrennie voiska," *SVE* 2 (1976):164–165; Mikhail Lavrik, ed., *Prikazano zastupit'!* (Moscow: Molodaia Gvardiia, 1974); Iu. Churbanov, "Ideinye boitsy," *KZ*, 3 August 1973, p. 2. There is also a good Western study of the internal troops: William Fuller, Jr., "The Internal Troops of the MVD SSSR" (College Station Papers, No. 6) (College Station, Texas, 1983).

8. Peter Deriabin, *Watchdogs of Terror: Russian Bodyguards from the Tsars to the Commissars* (New Rochelle, N.Y.: Arlington House, 1972), pp. 285–286.

9. Robert Conquest, *Inside Stalin's Secret Police: NKVD Politics 1936–39* (Stanford, Calif.: Hoover Institution Press, 1985), pp. 17–18, 46–48, 102.

10. Deriabin, *Watchdogs*, pp. 285–286.

11. Ibid., pp. 302–307. Also see Spiridonov's obituary in *KZ*, 19 March 1976, p. 4.

12. Conquest, *Inside Stalin's Secret Police*, p. 84.

13. Deriabin, *Watchdogs*, pp. 307–310, 356.

14. See *Survey of Soviet Intelligence and Counterintelligence* (Intelligence Division GSUSA, Department of the Army, 9 January 1948, declassified NND 770011), pp. 38, 54, 60.

15. Deriabin, *Watchdogs*, pp. 318–336.

16. Ibid., pp. 335–338.

17. For biographical information on Ustinov see *Ezhegodnik BSE* 1958, p. 644; and Ibid.

18. Zakharov's biography appears in *Deputaty VS SSSR. sed'moi sozyv* (Moscow, 1966), p. 167. Deriabin claims that Zakharov was later sent to a remote area of the Crimea. (See Deriabin, *Watchdogs*, pp. 252, 339).

19. See *KZ*, 16 June 1984, p. 3. Vedenin wrote memoirs—see *Gody i liudi* (Moscow: Politizdat, 1964)—but they reveal little about his post as Kremlin Kommendant.

20. On Shornikov's service in KGB military counterintelligence, or Special Departments, see S. E. Ostriakov, *Voennye chekisty* (Moscow: Voenizdat, 1979), p. 273. Supporting the hypothesis that the Kremlin kommendant is under the authority of the KGB is the fact that the death in 1974 of the kommendant of the city of Moscow, A. N. Shekalov, was announced by both the Moscow party apparatus and the Moscow KGB administration. See *Moskovskaia pravda*, 12 June 1974, p. 4.

21. Bashkin was identified in *Moskovskaia pravda*, 6 November 1986, p. 4.

22. See James T. Reitz, "The Soviet Security Troops—The Kremlin's Other Armies," in *Soviet Armed Forces Review Annual*, ed. David R. Jones, Gulf Breeze, Fla.: Academic International Press, 1982), vol. 6, p. 302; and chapter 8.

23. Deriabin, *Watchdogs*, pp. 318–319.

24. Mischa Scorer, "The KGB," *The Listener*, 14 February 1974, p. 204.

25. *The Military Balance 1986–87* (London: International Institute for Strategic Studies, 1986), p. 46.

26. Fuller, *Internal Troops*, pp. 1, 24. The higher estimate is that of the International Institute for Strategic Studies, *Military Balance*.

27. Fuller, *Internal Troops*, p. 24.

28. See John J. Dziak, "Soviet Intelligence and Security Services in the Eighties: The Paramilitary Dimension," *ORBIS* (Winter 1981):771–786 (quotation, p. 775).

29. See Reitz, "Soviet Security Troops," p. 301; these troops are also mentioned in International Institute for Strategic Studies, *Military Balance*, 1986–87, p. 46. Former KGB Chairman Semichastnyi referred to such signal troops operating in World War II under the authority of the state security organs. See Vladimir Semichastnyi, "Chekisty v velikoi otechestvennoi voine," *Pravda*, 7 May 1965, p. 4. At the same time, a declassified U.S. intelligence report notes that a special directorate of signal troops was formed under the NKVD in 1943. The troops of this directorate, though not under the formal authority of the state security organs, may have been at the latter's disposal. The same report goes on to mention the existence in the postwar period of signal troops under the MVD. Among their functions was that of maintaining and operating long-distance telephone lines for high-level government and party communications. It is possible that these MVD signal troops were transferred to the state security organs at some later date. See *Survey of Soviet Intelligence*, pp. 32, 59, 153.

30. See *KZ*, 31 October 1969, p. 1.

31. See reports on clashes between KGB troops and the Crimean Tatars in *FBIS. Daily Report, Soviet Union*, National Affairs, 27 July 1987, p. 11.

32. See Dziak, "Soviet Intelligence and Security Service," pp. 782, 785; Iurii Krotkov, "KGB v deistvii," *Novyi zhurnal*, book 109 (1972), p. 194. Krotkov claims that the former chief of the KGB's Second Directorate, Oleg Gribanov, led a group of KGB units employed for punitive operations in Hungary in 1956. In addition, numerous obituaries of KGB officers killed tragically in the line of duty have appeared in *KZ* since the Afghanistan invasion in late 1979; Aleksei Myagkov, "The Soviet Union's Special Forces," *Soviet Analyst* 9, no. 1 (8 January 1980):3–4.

33. See A. I. Chugunov, *Bor'ba na granitse, 1917–1928* (Moscow: Izdatel'stvo Mysl', 1980), pp. 18–21; and V. S. Ivanov et al., *Chasovye sovetskikh granits: kratkii ocherk istorii pogranichnykh voisk SSSR* (Moscow: Politizdat, 1983), pp. 31–33.

34. Leggett, *The Cheka* pp. 90–92, 227.

35. Ibid., pp. 228–229; Chugunov, *Bor'ba*, pp. 35–43. According to Ivanov, *Chasovye sovetskikh granits*, pp. 60–61, newly created departments for border protection under the GPU took over responsibilities from the Special Departments in July 1923 in Soviet Russia. The Special Departments may have continued to supervise border protection in other republics, however.

36. Ivanov, *Chasovye*, pp. 59–67; *V. I. Lenin i okhrana gosudarstvennoi granitsy SSSR. Sbornik dokumentov i statei* (Moscow, 1970), pp. 151–152; and Chugunov, *Bor'ba*, pp. 42–43.

37. Ivanov, *Chasovye*, pp. 70–96; V. A. Matrosov and V. K. Gaponenko, "Pogranichnye voiska," *SVE* 4 (1977):365–367; V. I. Stus et al., eds., *Dal'nevostochnyi pogranichnyi. ocherk istorii voisk krasnoznamennogo dal'nevostochnogo pogranichnogo okruga* (Khaborovsk: Khaborovskoe Knizhnoe Idatel'stvo, 1983), pp. 69–115; and L. D. Gerson, *The Secret Police in Lenin's Russia* (Philadelphia: Temple University Press, 1976), p. 230, citing P. I. Zyrianov et al., eds., *Pogranichnye voiska SSSR 1918–1928. Sbornik dokumentov i materialov* (Moscow: Nauka, 1973), pp. 525–528.

38. I. I. Evtikhiev and V. A. Vlasov, *Administrativnoe pravo SSSR: Uchebnik dlia iuridicheskikh institutov i fakul'tetov* (Moscow: Iuridicheskoe Izdatel'stvo, 1946), pp. 190–191; Simon Wolin and Robert Slusser, eds., *The Soviet Secret Police* (New York: Praeger, 1957), p. 47; Iakovlev, "Vnutrennie voiska," p. 165. One Soviet source claims that six directorates were formed in 1939. See G. P. Sechkin, "Pogranichnye voiska nakunune velikoi otechestvennoi voiny (Sentiabr 1939-iun' 1941 g.)" *Istoriia SSSR*, no. 3 (May-June 1982):36–50 (esp. p. 43).

39. Ivanov, *Chasovye*, p. 152; Sechkin, "Pogranichnye voiska," p. 43.

40. Ivanov, *Chasovye*, pp. 151–160; A. I. Chugunov, ed., *Pogranichnye voiska SSSR v velikoi otechestvennoi voine, 1941. Sbornik dokumentov i materialov* (Moscow: Akademiia Nauk, 1976), pp. 6–11.

41. Ivanov, *Chasovye*, pp. 166–172.

42. Ibid., pp. 178–179; A. I. Chugunov, ed., *Pogranichnye voiska SSSR v velikoi otechestvennoi voine, 1942–45* (Moscow Akademiia Nauk SSSR, 1976), p. 10.

43. Ivanov, *Chasovye*, pp. 179–181. Also see Maj. Gen. V. F. Nekrasov, "Vklad vnutrennikh voisk v delo pobedy Sovetskogo naroda v velikoi otechestvennoi voine," *Voenno-istoricheskii zhurnal*, no. 9 (September 1985):29–33.

44. *Pogranichnye voiska, 1942–45*, pp. 33–41; *Pogranichnye voiska SSSR, 1945–50. Sbornik dokumentov i materialov* (Moscow: Nauka, 1975), pp. 8–17.

45. Ivanov, *Chasovye*, pp. 191–195; *Krasnoznamennyi pribaltiiskii pogranichnyi* (Riga: Avotsi, 1983), p. 188.

46. *Pogranichnye 1942–45*, pp. 844–845; *Dal'nevostochnyi pogranichnyi*, pp. 166–190; and V. Platonov and A. Bulatov, "Pogranichnye voiska perekhodiat v nastuplenie," *Voenno-istoricheskii zhurnal*, no. 8 (August 1965):11–16.

47. See, for example, Reitz, "Soviet Security Troops," p. 300.

48. Ivanov, *Chasovye*, p. 199.

49. See his obituary in *KZ*, 30 December 1972, p. 4. Other examples are Lt. Gen. P. M. Bogdanov, chief of staff of the MVD Internal Troops, 1956–1959, who had served as chief of the border troops in Belorussia from 1939 to 1941 (see his obituary in *KZ*, 1 April 1973, p. 4); Maj. Gen. A. P. Kozlov, a border troops officer who later served in command positions in the internal troops after the war (*Voenno-istoricheskii zhurnal*, no. 6 (June 1981): 54–55; and Lt. Gen. A. G. Sidorov, a border troops officer during the early years of the war and later (until 1982 or 1983) deputy chief of the MVD Internal Troops. See *KZ*, 26 November 1975; and A. G. Gorev, *Sluzhu vo vnutrennikh voiskakh* (Moscow: Voenizdat, 1983), p. 5.

50. See Reitz, "Soviet Security Troops," p. 281; and *Survey of Soviet Intelligence*, pp. 61–62.

51. Matrosov and Gaponenko, "Pogranichnye voiska," p. 366. Although Soviet sources do not refer specifically to the current number of border districts, altogether nine BDs have been identified in the press since the early 1970s. During World War II German intelligence services identified seventeen Soviet BDs. See *Espionage-Sabotage-Conspiracy: German and Russian Operations 1940 to 1945*. Washington D.C.: (Office of Naval Intelligence, US Department of the Navy, April 1947, D 498–1: declassified 1972), p. 35. These districts were apparently consolidated and their numbers reduced considerably after the war. Then sometime in the late 1960s one or two new BDs were created. See Ivanov, *Chasovye*, pp. 230–231.

52. *The Military Balance*, 1986–87, p. 30. For a discussion of the various estimates on KGB troop strengths see Reitz, 'Soviet Security Troops,' pp. 287–288.

53. See his biography in *SVE* 6 (1979): p. 368; and *Literaturnaia gazeta*, no. 22 (29 May 1968): 1–2.

54. On Matrosov, see *Deputaty VS SSSR. Sedmoi sozyv* (Moscow, 1966), p. 288; *KZ*, 28 May 1971, p. 2; and *Voennyi entsiklopedicheskii slovar'*, 2d ed. (Moscow: Voenizdat, 1986), p. 43.

55. These six BD commanders are S. A. Bannykh, who commanded several BDs before 1961 and then became chief of staff of the USSR Border Troops (*KZ*, 2 April 1979, p. 4); P. V. Piskunov, former chief of the Transcaucasus BD (*Deputaty VS SSSR*, 1958 p. 315); F. A. Kuz'michev, a former commander of the Central Asian BD (*Deputaty VS SSSR, 1966*); M. K. Merkulov, a former commander of the Eastern BD (S. A. Konovalov, comp., *Nezrimyi front*, Alma Ata: Izdatel'stvo 'Kazakhstan,' 1967, pp. 298–299); K. E. Kortelainen, a former commander of the Far Eastern BD (see note 57); and K. F. Sekretarev, chief of the Northwest BD from 1969 to the mid-1970s (see *Deputaty VS Latviiskoi SSR. vos'moi sozyv*, Riga, 1972, p. 129). The two deputy commanders are A. M. Leont'ev (see his obituary in *KZ*, 3 November 1960, p. 4); and A. Gafarov (see *Kommunist Tadzhikistana*, 16 March 1967; 28 May 1982).

56. Examples are V. P. Nagibin, chief of the Political Department of the Northwest BD in 1976 (*Verkhovnyi sovet Estonskoi SSR. deviatyi sozyv*, Tallin, 1976, p. 103); E. D. Solov'ev, by 1976 chief of the Political Department of the Western BD (see his obituary in *KZ*, 13 November 1979, p. 4); and V. S. Vinogradov, since 1979 chief of the Political Department of the Baltic BD (*Verkhovnyi sovet Estonskoi SSR. desiatyi sozyv*, Tallin, 1980, p. 280). V. V. Gaponenko, former chief of the Political Directorate of the USSR Border Guards, moved out of political work and subsequently became a BD commander, as did N. A. Romanov, another former Political Directorate chief, who became head of the Baltic BD.

57. On Kortelainen see *Deputaty VS SSSR*, 1984, p. 210; and *Dal'nevostochnyi pogranichnyi*, p. 276.

58. For Lezhepekov's various appointments see *Pravda*, 29 May 1969; *KZ*, 14 March 1971, p. 4, and 16 November 1979; and *Izvestiia*, 16 July 1983, p. 1.

59. See *KZ*, 28 December 1978, p. 1, and 16 November 1984, p. 3, where Matrosov was first identified as a USSR deputy chairman.

60. See *Zaria vostoka*, 24 July 1982, pp. 1–2.

61. These publications are too numerous to list here. Examples are listed in notes 33, 37, 44, and 45 and a few more recent ones: A. I. Chugunov, *Na strazhe sovetskikh rubezhei 1929–1938* (Moscow: Voenizdat, 1981); M. I. Il'in, ed., *Granitsa. Povesti i rasskazy* (Moscow: Voenizdat, 1983); P. S. Shchedrov et al., eds., *Dozornye granitsy* (Minsk: Belarus, 1983); N. A. Arzumanov, ed., *Zastava imenii* (Moscow: Sovetskaia Rossiia, 1984); and Pavel Ermakov, *Goriachie peski: Dokumental'naia povest' i ocherk* (Moscow: Izdatel 'stvo DOSAAF, 1984).

62. See *KZ*, 14 November 1978, p. 3. Also see an article by Tsvigun, "Khudozhnik i granitsa," *Literaturnaia Gazeta*, no. 3, 17 January 1979, p. 2.

63. See *BBC Summary of World Broadcasts*. (SU 7901/C1, 16 March 1985). Parts of this documentary were rebroadcast in May 1985 in honor of Border Guards Day. See *ibid*. (SU 7967/C5, 3 June 1985).

64. See *Izvestiia*, 13 October 1967, pp. 3–4, for the text of this law.

65. The law was published in *Izvestiia* on 26 November 1982, pp. 1–3. For a discussion of its legal implications see two articles in *Sovetskoe gosudarstvo i pravo*; no. 9 (September 1983): V. I. Troitskii and L. A. Steshenko, "Novoe v sovetskom zakonodatel'stve o gosudarstvennoi granitse SSSR," pp. 34–40; and B. M. Klimenko, "Mezhdunarodnoe pravo i zakon o gosudarstvennoi granitse SSSR," pp. 41–47.

66. See *Vedomosti VS SSSR*, no. 34 (1018) (30 August 1960):747–756.

67. The border guards are reportedly guided by instructions from Glavlit on what materials are to be kept out. See chapter 6, note 84. Religious literature occupies a prominent place in forbidden printed matter. A 1983 article in a Soviet paper described how Soviet border guards uncovered a truckload of bibles being smuggled across the border. See *Sel'skaia gazeta*, 5 October 1983, p. 3.

68. For the original decree see *Vedomosti VS SSSR*, no. 6 (1972), Article 52. According to USSR Deputy KGB Chairman G. E. Ageev, over 200 violators of the USSR border were detained at border checkpoints in 1986. See an interview with him in *Trud*, 19 April 1987, p. 4.

69. See an interview with Maj. Gen. Iu. G. Nitsyn, Deputy Chief of Staff, USSR Border Troops, in *Argumenty i Fakty*, no. 27 (5 July 1983):6–7.

70. See, for example, an interview with Maj. Gen. V. S. Ivanov in *Trud*, 28 May 1983, p. 2. According to Ivanov, at the time chief of the Political Directorate of the USSR Border Troops, "this year alone thousands of attempts by foreigners to make unoffical contacts with border guards have already been recorded. They attempt to give our people bribes in the form of souvenirs, knickknacks, alcoholic drinks, money and also 'works' that make you want to wash your hands right after looking at them."

71. Ivanov, *Chasovye*, p. 230. Unfortunately, more recent statistics on educational levels were not available.

72. Ibid. Also see F. Popenko, "Vysshee pogranichnoe," *Voennoe znamia* no. 3 (March 1984):14–15.

73. See *KZ*, 27 June 1981, p. 3; and Popenko, "Vysshee pogsanichoe."

74. See P. Ivanchishin, "Okhrana granitsy sovetskogo otechestva" *Politicheskoe samoobrazovanie*, no. 4 (April 1978):48–54.

75. Ibid.; Ivanov, *Chasovye*, p. 230.

76. Ivanov, *Chasovye*, p. 239. *SVE* 4, p. 363.

77. Reitz, "Soviet Security Troops," p. 292; John Barron, *The KGB: The Secret Work of Soviet Secret Agents* (New York: Bantam Books 1974), pp. 19–20.

78. See chapter 8.

79. Matrosov and Gaponenko, "Pogranichnye voiska," p. 368.

80. See Mark L. Urban, "The Soviet Border Troops," *Ground Defense International*, no. 75 (1981):15–17; and Reitz, "The Soviet Security Troops," p. 285.

81. Matrosov and Gaponenko, "Pogranichnye voiska," p. 368.

82. See both the 1960 statute and the 1982 Law on the USSR State Border.

83. Ivanov, *Chasovye*, pp. 230–231.

84. Ibid.; *Pravda*, 28 June 1976, and *Sovetskaia Moldavia*, 28 May 1983, p. 2. For a further discussion of military equipment of the border troops see Urban, "The Soviet Border Troops," p. 17.

85. See Article 36 of the 1982 Law on the Border, and Urban, "The Soviet Border Troops."

86. It is most ironic that this incident occurred on 28 May, Soviet Border Guards Day. Although the border guards do not bear direct responsibility for Soviet airspace, their failure to detect the low-flying plane was doubtless an embarrassment.

8

The KGB's Special Departments in the Soviet Armed Forces*

As the previous chapter pointed out, the regime relies on KGB troops rather than on its regular armed forces to perform such highly sensitive tasks as guarding the leadership and quelling domestic disturbances. Probably these special troops are recruited very selectively and are deemed more politically dependable than regular troops. It was also noted, however, that the party leadership does not consider KGB forces, which are relatively small in number, to be a deterrent to possible challenges to its rule by the military. Indeed the party has other, more effective methods of ensuring the military's loyalty.

Until recently most scholars attributed the continued acceptance of civilian authority by the Soviet military to a system of party controls, known since 1958 as the Main Political Administration (MPA) of the Soviet Army and Navy. The MPA, which operates as a department of the CPSU Central Committee, is a large and complex network of political organs embedded within the armed forces at all levels.[1] In the late 1970s, however, some scholars challenged this assumption by demonstrating that the MPA is not all that effective as an instrument of control. Timothy Colton, for example, concluded that "the fact that the Soviet military has

*Portions of this chapter appeared in an article in ORBIS 28, no. 2 (Summer 1984): 257–280.

not exercised its potential for disruptive political action cannot be explained in terms of party mechanisms for penetration and control of the military command."[2] Colton, claiming that conflict between the party and the armed forces has been exaggerated in the West, attributed the latter's political quiescence to its basic conservatism and indifference toward most aspects of politics that do not affect it directly. In his view the military is loyal to the party because its interests have been well served by the party's politics.

Another study, by Amos Perlmutter and William LeoGrande, claims that the military is subordinate to party authority by virtue of the party's ideological dominance.[3] The armed forces have been politicized to the extent that even in cases of severe factional conflict they participate "not as the military per se, but as part of the Party, the Party-in-uniform." Thus the military functions as a dual elite whose coercive potential will be used only to support one faction or another within the party, never against the party.

These studies have done much to enhance our understanding of civil-military relations, but they do not provide a complete picture. Given the military's enormous potential for organized forceful opposition, can it really be taken for granted that the party leadership relies either on the political integration of the armed forces or on the supremacy of ideology as the principal guarantee against a threat to its predominance? In addition to the party and the military, it is important to consider a third variable in civil-military relations: the security police.[4]

Western analysts often lump the KGB and military together when considering the various interest groups that exist separately from the party apparatus. Yet despite the fact that both these institutions represent coercive forces, they perform very different tasks. The role of the Soviet armed forces is to defend the Soviet Union from foreign invasions and to project Soviet strength abroad. The KGB's role is above all a political one, involving not only foreign intelligence and counter-intelligence but also the crucial domestic function of ensuring internal stability. Thus while the military protects the country as a whole from outside incursions, the KGB acts on behalf of the leadership to protect it from both foreign enemies and its own people.

Ever since the early days of the regime an important internal security function of the political police has been that of ensuring the political reliability of the armed forces. This has been carried out through a network of so-called Special Departments (*Osobye otdely*). Barrington Moore, in his 1954 study *Terror and Progress USSR*, observed that whereas there is a tendency for the *zampolit* or party political officer "to be absorbed into the military forces to an extent sufficient to blind this eye of the party," the political police representative is much less likely to be deflected from his task.[5] "On the whole," Moore concluded, "it would seem that police controls might increase in importance within the military forces at the expense of strictly party ones."[6] Much of the evidence has confirmed Moore's assumption. Although, as Colton demonstrated, the interests of the MPA and armed forces appear to have converged, the KGB's network of political controls over the military has become stronger.

Officially designated as a military counterintelligence organization, nonetheless the KGB's Directorate of Special Departments, or Third Chief Directorate, performs tasks that extend far beyond counterintelligence and encompasses extensive political surveillance of the military and other military security duties. The Soviets themselves have begun to publish books and articles on the past and present activities of the Special Departments that strongly suggest that this apparatus plays a much more important role in the armed forces than Western experts have realized. Through examination of these writings and other materials this chapter sets forth the history, functions, and purpose of the KGB Special Departments and assesses their contribution to the role of the political police as well as their broader significance for civilian-military relations in the Soviet Union.

Evolution of the Special Departments

The history of the Special Departments in the Soviet armed forces dates from 16 July 1918, when a resolution of the Council of People's Commissars created under the Vecheka a Cheka on the Eastern front.[7] Shortly thereafter Cheka organs were established at other fronts. Although these organs conducted counterintelligence operations against enemy agents, their main task was to fight counterrevolution, treason, and criminal activity within the Red Army itself. Such close political supervision and extensive control were seen as essential during a period when the Red Army depended heavily on former tsarist officers, many of whom were politically unreliable. Although the Red Army eventually became more dependable, the political surveillance functions of the Special Departments were to remain paramount.

From the outset the difficulty of reconciling the authority and prerogatives of the military, the party, and the police presented the regime with problems. Apparently there was considerable conflict over jurisdiction between the Army Chekas and the organs of *Voenkontrol* (Military Control) of the *Revvoensovet* (Revolutionary War Council), which were also responsible for counterintelligence and counter-espionage. In an attempt to resolve the issue, the two organizations were merged, and by 1 January 1919 a single organization for military counter-intelligence—the Special Department (*Osobyi otdel*, or OO) of the Vecheka—was established. It was headed initially by a top Vecheka official, M. S. Kedrov. In August 1919 the chief óf the Vecheka, Feliks Dzerzhinskii, assumed direct control over the OO, retaining this job until July 1920, when V. R. Menzhinskii took it over. Subordinate Special Departments were established in all provincial Chekas, military fronts, and armies, while OO commissars were assigned to divisions, regiments, and other units. They were empowered to make arrests, conduct searches, carry out investigations of counterrevolutionary crimes, and, in areas under martial law, carry out executions. The OOs were important enough to be allocated one-third of the total Vecheka budget in 1920.[8]

A problem of jurisdiction remained however, because the OOs were actually under the dual authority of the central Special Department and the Revvoensovet, both of which could issue orders to them. The situation had been complicated by the July 1918 creation of a hierarchy of political commissars under the Revvoensovet to supervise the political loyalty of military personnel. These commissars shared command with military officers and, like OO officials, could arrest members of the military for counterrevolutionary activity. Conflicts over authority and overlapping functions soon arose between political commissars and OO personnel. The problem was brought to Lenin's attention in January 1919 when a dispute occurred between the head of the Political Department and the head of the OO at the Caspian-Caucasian front. Lenin was forced to intervene.[9]

The problem of the OO's subordination generated considerable discussion at the Eighth Party Congress held in March 1919. At this time it was decided to place the OOs of the fronts and armies directly under the Political Department (later named the Political Administration) of the Revvoensovet while leaving "general leadership and control" to the Vecheka Special Department at the center. This change was introduced because the party wanted to keep a closer watch on the political loyalty of the Army. It was also part of a general move against the so-called Army opposition, who wanted more independence for the Red Army command from the party's political commissars.[10]

[252]

During the civil war years "army Chekists" from the Special Departments were occupied with routing out treasonous elements from the Red Army, particularly among former tsarist officers. From 1919 to 1921 they uncovered several major conspiracies against the Soviet regime. They also performed a variety of tasks, including the arrest of deserters, the security of arms and ammunition depots, and general surveillance over Red Army facilities. In November 1920 the OOs took over responsibility for guarding the borders; special sections for border security were set up in the main border regions, with border units and posts subordinate to them. Their function was to protect the borders from foreign intelligence agents, White Guard emissaries, and smugglers. The OOs shared responsibility for border protection with the Red Army command from October 1921 to September 1922, when this task was again placed under the sole authority of the OOs. This situation apparently lasted until July 1923, when, in Soviet Russia at least, OO control was replaced by the new GPU Department for Border Protection.[11]

After the civil war ended and the ranks of the Red Army were reduced, the OOs concentrated on fighting kulaks and various nationalist bands. They also conducted several operations abroad designed to ensnare members of Russian emigré groups and to transmit disinformation to Western intelligence services. By the mid-1920s, when the threat of subversion from abroad had subsided, the OOs devoted increasing effort to internal control of the armed forces. Their purpose was to protect Army and Navy personnel from "bourgeois influences" and to expose the "slightest manifestation of political corruption" or "unhealthy attitudes" among military units. Their functions thus became increasingly politicized, and like the rest of the OGPU, they were drawn into the various power struggles within the party. (The OOs are reported to have played an active part in the defeat of the "Trotskyite-Zinovievite Opposition" in 1926–1927, for example.)[12]

As the police apparatus in general became more powerful, the OOs gained more authority. In 1931 they were made completely independent of the Revvoensovet and responsible only to the Special Department at the center. The creation in 1933 of the Main Military Procuracy, which prosecuted members of the armed forces and was closely linked with the security police, gave the latter an additional repressive weapon. And as John Erikson points out, political commissars were increasingly seen as ineffective in controlling the Army, particularly at the higher levels, where the commander and the commissar were often the same person. The integration of the Army into the party, with substantial numbers of Soviet military personnel becoming party members, began to change the

[253]

problem of control of the armed forces considerably: "Under such conditions," noted Erikson, "it was inevitable that the weight of effective surveillance should be shifted on to the secret police and its organs."[13]

These changes strengthened the role of the OOs as political watchdogs against the military command and paved the way for their participation in the massive purges of the armed forces during 1937–1938. Both the political and the command staff fell victim to the purges, in which the OOs played a key role by compiling dossiers on the officers. One OO representative told a high-ranking Soviet officer during the purges, "In every person I see an enemy of the people, and not a single one will escape, slip through, or deceive me."[14] Alleging foreign espionage plots, the OOs helped to implement a purge of 20 to 30 percent of the officer corps.[15] There can be little doubt that this experience had a profound impact on the attitude of the military toward the political police and serves as a reminder, even today, of the latter's potential powers if not closely controlled by the party.

The OOs soon suffered a blow in return when in late 1938 a purge of the NKVD was initiated and most of the higher OO apparatus was liquidated. To replace the purged element, new personnel were brought in from the party and the Army. Among the new men were several who later rose in the KGB hierarchy during the Brezhnev era including Vitalii Fedorchuk, briefly chairman of the KGB and subsequently, from December 1982 to February 1986, Minister of Internal Affairs.[16]

The Special Departments in World War II

World War II brought about significant changes in the organization and functions of the Special Departments (see table 8.1). In February 1941, shortly before the German attack, military counterintelligence was transferred from the state security organs to the People's Commissariat of Defense, although a Third Directorate was retained in the state security organs to ensure the political security of the internal and border troops.[17] At the same time, the state security organs themselves were separated from NKVD, and the NKGB (People's Commissariat of State Security) was formed. OO officers were subordinated both to higher OO officials and to military commanders. This dual subordination apparently led to considerable friction between the military command and the military counterintelligence apparatus, particularly after the German attack. According to one Soviet source, "there were cases where individual

TABLE 8.1
Organizational History of the Special Departments
(Soviet Military Counterintelligence)

July 1918	Extraordinary Commission (Cheka) established to fight counterrevolution on the Eastern front, followed by the creation of Chekas on other fronts.
January 1919	Special Department (Osobyi otdel, or OO) of Vecheka created.
February 1922	Special Department (OO) of Vecheka becomes OO of GPU (State Political Administration).
November 1923	OO of GPU becomes OO of OGPU (Unified State Political Administration).
July 1934	OO of OGPU becomes OO of newly created Main Administration of State Security (GUGB) of the People's Commissariat of Internal Affairs (NKVD).
February 1941	OO of NKVD transferred to Third Office of People's Commissariat of Defense and Third Office of Navy Commissariat.
July 1941	Military counterintelligence transferred back to NKVD as OO of NKVD.
April 1943	OO of NKVD becomes Main Administration of Counterintelligence (GUKR) of People's Commissariat of Defense, or SMERSH, with a separate SMERSH organization within the Navy.
May 1946	SMERSH disbanded. Military counterintelligence reorganized into Special Department (OO) and subordinated to newly created Ministry of State Security (MGB) as the Main Administration of Counterintelligence (GUKR).
March 1953	OO of MGB becomes OO of newly established MVD (Ministry of Internal Affairs), which unites functions of former MGB and MVD.
March 1954	United MVD disbanded. Separate MVD and KGB (Committee of State Security) created. Third Directorate, or Directorate of Special Departments (OOs), established within KGB. Subsequently designated a Chief Directorate.

SOURCES: Compiled by the author from sources in note 7 to this chapter.

commanders tried to use army Chekists for various service tasks, which had little relation to their basic functions."[18] Thus in July 1941, when the NKGB was reintegrated into the NKVD, military counterintelligence was again placed completely under NKVD control.

The beginning of World War II found Soviet military counterintelligence deficient in several respects. The purges of the Special Departments shortly before the war meant that many of its officers and staff were new and inexperienced. Furthermore before the German attack little attention had been paid to training cadres or planning for wartime counterintelligence. Thus the OOs had no alternative but to organize and train for military counterintelligence when they were "already face to face with the enemy."[19] According to recently declassified U.S. intelligence documents from the period, the ineffectiveness of Soviet military counterintelligence permitted the Germans to gain considerable information about the disposition and strength of the Red Army at the beginning of the war and subsequently to penetrate some of the highest levels of the Soviet wartime command.[20] One Soviet history of the OOs even acknowledges: "There were misfortunes, mistakes, defeats. And so that they are not repeated, they should not be forgotten."[21]

April 1943 brought yet another reorganization. The Special Departments of the NKVD were abolished and military counterintelligence was transferred back to the People's Commissariat of Defense. The new organization, known as the Main Counterintelligence Administration (GUKR or SMERSH), was headed by the former Special Department chief, the notorious V. S. Abakumov.[22] Some Soviet histories, glossing over the deficiencies of Soviet military counterintelligence prior to 1943, attribute the change to various factors, such as the need to "unify the defense leadership in the final stages of the war."[23] But other Soviet sources point out that the reorganization was part of an effort to improve Soviet military counterintelligence.[24] SMERSH did prove to be more effective than its predecessor. Counterintelligence behind German lines became much more vigorous, and many German spy networks were broken up. Nevertheless throughout the war Soviet military counterintelligence continued to be hampered by several weaknesses, which were enumerated in a U.S. intelligence document:

> First, constant emphasis on repression and coercion breeds resentment and disaffection even in normally loyal persons. Secondly, the very comprehensiveness of espionage regulations and security measures disperses the efforts of the counterintelligence agencies and forces them to depend primarily upon routine and stereotyped methods. Consequently, while inexpert agents are easily detected, skilled foreign agents with authentic credentials can operate with considerable impunity. Thirdly, the tight segregation of information and the frequent use of internal or special codes afford special opportunities for penetration and the use of clandestine communications. Lastly, overstress on counterintelligence has led to relative neglect of criminal detection, in relation to both the effort and the moral outlook of the operating agencies.[25]

The functions of counterespionage and counterintelligence resided mainly with SMERSH organs at the higher levels while lower SMERSH organs were concerned with monitoring the political loyalty of the troops and ferreting out possible traitors. They were assisted in their tasks by military procurators. The severity and ruthlessness that SMERSH operatives used in dealing with even the slightest malfeasance have been well documented.[26] Often this took the form of periodic sweeping campaigns of repression aimed at intimidating soldiers through exemplary punishment. According to one account,

> most of the accusations made by Smersh were of a standard variety. Thus, while during peacetime the NKVD was always busy combatting "wrecking" which was said to be occurring everywhere, during wartime a similarly all-inclusive accusation was that of "cowardice." Commanders and soldiers defeated by the enemy or forced to leave their equipment behind were tried for "cowardice."[27]

Trial and punishment were carried swiftly, without regard to the procedural norms. As one Soviet source acknowledges,

> The combat situation made it necessary to introduce changes in the organization of the work of the organs of inquiry, preliminary investigation and the Procuracy. . . . Here in combat areas the investigation and judicial process had to be accomplished more quickly than in peacetime with the shortest possible delay. Experience showed that military procurators and investigators successfully completed the investigations of criminal cases swiftly and objectively. At the front about 70 percent of criminal cases were investigated in a period of up to five days or even several hours.[28]

SMERSH personnel saturated the Red Army at all levels. U.S. intelligence documents estimated that 3 to 4 percent of the Soviet armed forces in World War II were engaged in intelligence or counterintelligence, while roughly 12 percent of all military personnel were agents or informers of military counterintelligence.[29] Counterintelligence sections existed at all levels of organization down to divisions. According to one source, the administration of counterintelligence for an army averaged about 100–110 men, exclusive of guards and representatives among the troops. Departments for counterintelligence of corps and divisions were smaller. A division counterintelligence department consisted of about seven to eleven persons. Below the division level there were no counterintelligence departments or sections, but representatives were placed within the staff of regiments, battalions, and companies. In the various subordinate units SMERSH also used regular soldiers as agents or residents, who in turn recruited informers.[30]

As might be expected, regular military officers were resentful of the Chekists in their midst and cooperated with efforts to ensnare "cowards" only when forced to do so. The relationship between SMERSH officers and the political commissars, or *zampolits*, as they were called after 1942, was also characterized by antagonism. Memoir literature offers several examples of *zampolits* siding with military commanders to protect troops from persecution by SMERSH personnel at the front.[31] It should be pointed out, however, that military counterintelligence organs had been staffed with large numbers of political officers at the beginning of the war, which may have mitigated to a certain extent the tension between the two groups. In addition, both *zampolits* and SMERSH personnel were responsible for ensuring the loyalty of the troops, and both were held accountable for defections and desertions. Because they shared a common task they had to meet frequently to exchange information and discuss the political morale of the troops.

In addition to counterintelligence, counterespionage, and political security of the troops, SMERSH performed other key tasks. Special SMERSH operational groups carried out missions that involved kidnapping German officers, liquidating enemy agents, cutting communication lines, and other sabotage efforts.[32] SMERSH maintained surveillance over the civilian population in operational zones not covered by the territorial NKVD agencies. After the Red Army took the offensive in 1943, SMERSH organs advanced with the troops and helped to ensure the security of the army front line as well as rear services and communications. Along with local security police SMERSH hunted down, arrested, and often shot on the spot anyone suspected of having collaborated with the Germans. They also suppressed any form of nationalist opposition in territory "liberated" by the Red Army. As Ostriakov put it, SMERSH "helped the people of liberated countries in establishing and strengthening a free domestic form of government."[33]

After the German surrender another function of SMERSH was to screen former Soviet prisoners of war before they were repatriated to the Soviet Union. This task was reportedly carried out ruthlessly and inhumanly, with large numbers of deaths. Ostriakov acknowledges that "there was a tendency to regard Soviet POW's with distrust. Even military counterintelligence made such mistakes."[34] The variety of functions performed by SMERSH in World War II and immediately afterward suggests that in any present-day conflict the role of the Special Departments would be similarly broad and extend beyond the immediate tasks of military counterintelligence. In fact the Special Departments probably played an active role when the Soviets moved into Czechoslovakia in 1968 and into Afghanistan in 1979.[35]

The KGB's Special Departments: Organization and Personnel

SMERSH was disbanded in 1946, and military counterintelligence was returned to the hands of the state security apparatus as the Main Administration of Counterintelligence (GUKR) of the Ministry of State Security (MGB). The military counterintelligence staff was reduced significantly, and many former SMERSH personnel were transferred to other MGB departments. When at the instigation of Beria the MGB was amalgamated into the MVD (Ministry of Internal Affairs) in 1953, military counterintelligence became part of this organization, which was headed by Beria himself. These changes were short-lived because of Beria's swift demise, in which Marshal Zhukov and other military leaders played an important part. According to the Soviet defector Vladimir Petrov, the Special Departments had contributed to Zhukov's temporary fall from favor after World War II. If so, this gave Zhukov strong incentive to participate in moves against the police.[36] In 1954, when the KGB was established, military counterintelligence was renamed the Directorate of Special Departments, or the Third Directorate of the KGB. Sometime in the early 1980s it became a chief directorate.[37]

As part of an effort to bring the security police back under party control, several former Beria associates in military counterintelligence were purged and replaced with cadres from the military-political organs. D. S. Leonov, who became chief of the Special Departments in 1954, was typical of the new OO leadership. At the age of fifty-four Leonov had over thirty years of political work in the Soviet Army behind him. In 1959 he was replaced by Brezhnev's ally G. K. Tsinev, who had also been an Army political officer and had joined the Special Departments shortly after Stalin died.[38] It is important to note, however, that personnel changes affected mainly the top level of military counterintelligence; most of the lesser officials survived the 1953 shake-up.

Little information is available on how the Third Chief Directorate is organized. During World War II SMERSH was organized along functional lines, with separate departments for surveillance, investigation, counterespionage, censorship, security, information, personnel, and so on.[39] An independent military counterintelligence organization existed

[259]

within the Soviet Navy. Some Western sources claim that the Third Directorate, which is now responsible for all of the armed forces, including the Navy, is organized at the top level according to service branches. John Barron listed twelve major departments within the Third CD, which are said to oversee the Ministry of Defense and General Staff, the Main Intelligence Administration (GRU), conventional ground forces, naval forces, air forces, border troops, militia and internal troops, missile forces, nuclear forces, civil aviation, and the Moscow military district.[40]

If such service departments do exist, they are obviously not equal in terms of size and stature. For example, the Ground Forces Department would have much greater responsibility than departments in charge of border troops or civil aviation. In addition, the OOs of other military districts and some force groups, such as the Group of Soviet Forces Germany (GSFG), may have the status of main departments or, in the case of the GSFG, a subdirectorate.[41] Most functional divisions, such as surveillance and security, are probably duplicated and subordinated to these main departments or subdirectorates, but some, such as counterespionage and personnel, may serve as independent departments of the Third Directorate with branches at various levels. This would mean that the Third Directorate is organized somewhat like the MPA, with both service and functional divisions.

No figures are available on the manpower of the Third Directorate, but reports from Soviet defectors permit broad estimates of the Third Directorate's personnel strength. Today the OO network in the armed forces is undoubtedly much smaller than it was during the war, but KGB Special Departments still exist in all military institutions and installations, all military districts, groups of forces, armies, corps, divisions, and brigades. Regiments and independent battalions probably do not have Special Departments as such, but rather two or three operational case officers from the Third CD.[42] One former OO officer, Aleksei Myagkov, who served in the Group of Soviet Forces in Germany from 1969 to 1974, offered some figures on the Special Department there. Based on his figures, there appears to have been about one OO officer (excluding agents and informers) for every 600 men—about .17 percent. If this ratio is applied broadly to the total manpower of Soviet armed forces today, we arrive at a figure of about 8500 Special Department personnel.[43]

The OO network among Soviet forces stationed abroad may be denser than among forces within the Soviet Union, and ground forces in general may also have a higher ratio of OO personnel in their midst than, for example, the Soviet Navy. Nevertheless even if the figure of 8500 is an overestimate, it does not take into account the OO departments or staff officers who exist in all the defense-related industries, missile installations, Aeroflot and among the MVD internal troops, border guards, and other troops. If we add these, plus the staff of the Third Directorate at KGB headquarters in Moscow, an estimate of about 12,000 for the total manpower is probably not an exaggeration, particularly in light of Timothy Colton's estimate of the total MPA strength in the late 1970s at about 40,000.[44]

According to most sources, political reliability is the main criterion for recruitment into the KGB, including its Special Departments, although educational background is also stressed. OO personnel departments select OO officers, drawing mainly from the military and the MPA. These selections may be vetted by the Administrative Organs Departments of the Central Committee, but we have no firm evidence of this. The Third Directorate sends its officer personnel to special training schools, one of which is known to be in Novosibirsk. Although specializing in military counterintelligence, the new recruits receive courses on all aspects of KGB operations, which allows them to move to other areas of the KGB without much additional training.[45]

OO officials, or "military Chekisty," represent a specialized group within the KGB, and their career patterns and backgrounds are fairly homogeneous. Profiles of eighteen KGB officials who have served in the Third Directorate at some time since 1954 offer a picture of the OO career type at the upper echelons.[46] With the exception of Geidar Aliev, all are Slavs by nationality. Higher education appears to be the norm among these officials. Most started their working careers by joining the Special Departments during the war or before, though at least three served in the MPA before joining the Special Departments. About half of these officials subsequently moved out of the Third Directorate into other work in the KGB or elsewhere. Judging from their subsequent careers, their service with the Special Departments placed them in a good position for upward mobility. In particular Mironov, Aliev, Fedorchuk, Ivashutin, and Tsinev all rose to positions of considerable prominence in the KGB, the party, or government. It is significant that from May to December 1982 both the chairman (Fedorchuk) and one of the first deputy chairmen (Tsinev) of the KGB were former military Chekists. Interestingly, however, officials with a background in the Special Departments have not fared well under Gorbachev. During 1986–1987 Fedorchuk, Tsinev, Aliev, and D. P. Nosyrev, head of the Leningrad KGB, all lost their posts. This suggests that a network of Army Chekists has existed within the KGB and that some political faction within the party or KGB leadership decided to move against it. This hypothesis is supported by the fact that Brezhnev, who worked as a political officer during World War II, had close ties with OO officers, and the Brezhnevites have been under attack by the Gorbachev leadership.

It is not possible to determine exactly who has headed the Third Chief Directorate since Tsinev occupied that position. Fedorchuk may have been chief from about 1967 to 1970, when he became chairman of the KGB in the Ukraine, and according to some sources I. A. Fadeikin was chief in the early 1970s. At present the evidence suggests that Lt. Gen. N. A. Dushin is the current head of the Third CD. Ostriakov refers to him as occupying a key position in the Special Departments, and he was identified as the head of an unnamed chief directorate when he attended the Twenty-Seventh Party Congress in 1986.[47]

Functions of the Special Departments

According to official Soviet sources, the main function of the KGB's Special Departments is military counterintelligence. Yet the Soviets conceive of counterintelligence in much broader terms than we in the West do, and the functions of the Special Departments extend far beyond the struggle against espionage and the penetration of the armed forces by foreign agents into the armed forces. The Special Departments, for example, are responsible for all security clearances of military personnel and for ensuring that security regulations and procedures are strictly observed in all branches of the armed forces.[48] Thus they have control over (or at least immediate access to) military personnel files and all information relating to the political reliability of members of the armed forces.

The Special Departments are charged with protecting all state and military secrets, including those involving nuclear weapons, which places them in a position of considerable strategic importance. Ostriakov has pointed out, "the reliable defense of Soviet forces from all types of espionage took on special significance when the basic defensive strength of the country came to consist of the most contemporary weapons systems, especially ballistic-nuclear weapons."[49] According to Western sources, the KGB actually had custody and transport responsibilities for nuclear charges, which were separated from missiles and aircraft until the late 1960s.[50] At that time the KGB apparently relinquished its physical control over nuclear warheads, but as Stephen Meyer noted, "the KGB may not be totally removed from the nuclear control processes."[51] Not only does it maintain a strategic communications network that is independent of the military communications system, but its responsibilities for protecting nuclear secrets presumably give the KGB access to nuclear weapons installations as well as to military plans regarding the use of nuclear weapons. Thus the KGB, through its Special Departments, serves as a means of exercising civilian (or party) control over the use of nuclear weapons.

The Soviets claim that their armed forces are continually being threatened by ideological sabotage, attempts by Western governments to subvert individuals by means of bourgeois propaganda aimed at weakening their political convictions and making them vulnerable to foreign espionage. Hence a key element of OO activities is political surveillance of the armed forces at all levels. Since World War II this surveillance function has taken precedence over other counter-intelligence and counterespionage activities.[52] The OOs carry out their political surveillance on both a formal and an informal level. Officially the OOs are empowered by law to conduct investigations of armed forces personnel for the same crimes that are under KGB purview for ordinary citizens. These include crimes defined in Articles 64–70, 75, 76, 78–79, 83–84, and 88 of the RSFSR Criminal Code. In addition, the KGB has the authority to investigate the military crimes defined in Article 259 (a, b, and c)—divulgence of a military secret or loss of a document containing a military secret. All other crimes committed by members of the armed forces are investigated by special military procurators (or prosecutors) of the USSR Military Procurator's Office, which is a branch of the USSR Supreme Court.[53]

In investigating cases under their purview, OO officers no longer have the arbitrary powers that their predecessors enjoyed. They are supposed to follow set rules of criminal procedure at all stages of the investigation. These regulations govern procedure for arrest and questioning of suspects, time limits on the confinement of those accused before trial, and various other aspects of the investigation.[54] Furthermore the OOs no longer have the right to conduct trials. Once the investigation has been completed the case is tried by special military tribunals under the USSR Military Procuracy. It is difficult to say whether the OOs actually operate according to these legal norms. The Military Procurator's office is formally responsible for ensuring that correct legal procedures are observed by all investigators, including those from the KGB, but it is doubtful that they actually enforce their supervisory powers with the latter. Soviet military law experts stress the

[263]

necessity of complete cooperation with investigations on the part of the military command and the political organs, in terms of providing information, witnesses, and so on.[55] Yet it appears that OO investigators are not required to cooperate in return. While armed forces personnel cannot be arrested by investigators from the Military Procuracy without the permission of their commander, such a restriction does not apply to OO investigators of crimes involving the military.[56]

In addition to criminal investigation, the Special Departments have extensive informal responsibilities for ensuring the political reliability of the armed forces. Soviet sources state explicitly that Special Departments are not only to uncover and investigate political crimes but also to prevent the emergence of such crimes by various "prophylactic methods."[57] Thus the OOs conduct daily educational work "to increase political vigilance and communist convictions" among the armed forces. Apparently the KGB's Special Departments have increasingly taken on this educative indoctrination function, which has usually been associated with the MPA. G. K. Tsinev, for example, noted in 1979 that "preventative activity" by the OOs had increased significantly and that a strong effort was under way to detect persons who manifest potential antistate tendencies and to deal with them through persuasion and education rather than arrest.[58] An example of this method appeared in Ostriakov's book on the Special Departments:

> News reached the OO that in a small, distant garrison two young soldiers were discussing Soviet foreign policy and taking the wrong position. The OO conducted several talks with these soldiers and their behavior became the subject of a stern, critical examination by their comrades at a meeting of soldiers.[59]

Another example was cited in a Western study based on interviews with former Soviet servicemen:

> Considerable efforts are made by the KGB to maintain "ideological purity" in the armed forces, to protect servicemen from "corrupting" Western influences. Thus, an officer who made a mistake of showing his precious possession, an old issue of *Playboy Magazine*, to several trusted friends was immediately summoned to the "special section," was ordered to produce the magazine there, and was threatened with "consequences" for having the "anti-Soviet" publication.[60]

Not surprisingly, telephone conversations and correspondence of military personnel are monitored by OO officers, ostensibly to ensure that military personnel are not violating security procedures or revealing state secrets. But such monitoring also gives the OOs an opportunity to detect any "incorrect" political attitudes and thereby to set personnel straight by means of "friendly chats."[61]

To uncover "political deviants" the OOs require a broad network of surveillance and rely heavily on informers. According to Aleksei Myagkov, recruiting informers is one of the most important tasks of an OO officer. Myagkov claims that on reporting for duty in East Germany he was told to enlist ten agents within two months. Once the potential informer was selected, Myagkov had little difficulty recruiting him: "In practice one rarely comes across a Soviet citizen who refuses to cooperate with the KGB. Everyone thinks about the consequences for his own future."[62] Informers are recruited from every category of the military, including high-ranking officers and civilians under military employment. They are not paid for their work but do it either voluntarily or because of provocation or blackmail. The earlier-mentioned study, based on interviews with former Soviet servicemen, confirms that the practice of using informers in the Soviet armed forces is widespread:

> An important part of the discipline-maintaining mechanism is the system of informers. There are informers who report any politically incautious word by other soldiers to the KGB representative of a unit, the head of the so-called "special section" (*spetsotdel*), or sometimes to a political officer. Although the KGB is practically unmentionable in the Soviet Union, everyone seems to know that keeping as far as possible from that institution is essential to one's wellbeing. A threat to send a guilty soldier to the "special section" is effective.[63]

Estimates of the number of OO informers among military personnel vary. The proportion has undoubtedly declined considerably since the estimated World War II level of 12 percent and probably depends on the service branch, functions, and location of a given military unit. One source claimed that about 3 percent of the strength of a rifle company are informers, while the percentage is higher among tank, technical, rocket, air defense, and air assault troops, particularly in the air forces. In the Navy the proportion of informers is only 1 to 2 percent because of the compact living conditions on ships and the limited opportunities for communicating with outsiders.[64] Among other assignments, informers are to report cases of drunkenness, insubordination, security violations, and anti-Soviet attitudes. Informers engage in political discussions to gauge the views of their colleagues and sometimes conduct deliberately provocative activities, such as planting secret documents to test the "vigilance" of military personnel. If a particular soldier or officer is considered suspect, several informers will likely be assigned to watch him closely for any unusual actions or statements.[65]

Relations with the MPA and GRU

The OOs work closely with the MPA, sending their representatives to monthly meetings at MPA headquarters in military districts to discuss the state of discipline among the troops and to consider measures to strengthen law and order. OO officers are also members of party commissions that exist in all military units for the purpose of reviewing decisions on admission to or expulsion from the party and to consider cases of misconduct within the military.[66] Like other employees of the Soviet state, OO officers must produce results—some tangible evidence that they are being productive. Thus according to one source, if real spies are not detected, anti-Soviets and enemies of the regime are occasionally "created" by the OO officer in order to make himself appear efficient and productive.[67] The *zampolits*, who bear the main responsibility for political indoctrination of the troops, no doubt resent this, as it reflects poorly on their own performance. But they have little recourse, given the OOs' awesome investigatory and punitive powers. In general the Special Departments are in a position of much greater authority than the MPA. First, the OOs themselves have officials within the MPA who monitor the activities of its personnel. Second, the OOs operate with more autonomy vis-à-vis the central party apparatus than does the MPA, which functions under the supervision of the Central Committee with the status of a Central Committee department.

A somewhat analogous situation exists between the Special Departments and the GRU (*Glavnoe Razvedyvatel'noe Upravlenie*), Main Intelligence Directorate, of the General Staff of the Ministry of Defense. Its main task is to collect strategic, technical, and tactical military intelligence. In addition, according to some sources, it has special units for engaging in guerrilla warfare and sabotage operations on foreign soil.[68] The GRU and KGB have overlapping responsibilities in some areas, such as the collection of scientific technology from the West. Both agencies carry out assignments for the Military Industrial Commission (VPK) of the Presidium of the Council of Ministers, which coordinates the development of Soviet weapons and the Soviet national-level program to acquire Western technology.[69] There have been reports of antagonism between the GRU and the KGB, particularly among residents in the Soviet embassies.[70]

Whatever antagonism exists between officers of these organizations, there is little doubt that the KGB is the more powerful institution of the two and would prevail in any jurisdictional dispute. Because the functions of the KGB are much broader than those of the GRU, it is a considerably larger institution with many more resources and manpower at its disposal, as well as greater political influence. As a USSR state committee, the KGB has the same status as the Ministry of Defense, whereas the GRU is merely an agency of this ministry. Consequently the KGB chairman is a full member of the Politburo, but GRU Chief Ivashutin is not even a member of the Central Committee. Barron's assertion that the GRU is an appendage of the KGB is doubtless exaggerated; but it should be noted that both Ivashutin and his predecessor, Ivan Serov, were former SMERSH officials. (Serov, in fact, was KGB chairman before being demoted to chief of the GRU in 1958.) Furthermore according to Barron, Ivashutin brought five senior KGB officers with him to the GRU.[71]

Equally significant is the fact that the KGB is empowered by law to investigate state crimes among GRU staff, as well as crimes involving military or state secrets. Whenever there is a question of the breach of security regulations in the GRU, the KGB becomes involved. Thus the claim of former GRU officer Viktor Suvorov that KGB Special Departments do not exist within the GRU is not likely to be true.[72] Given that the primary function of the Special Departments is to prevent the penetration of foreign intelligence agents into the Soviet armed forces and the consequent betrayal of military secrets, it seems logical that the GRU would be among the primary agencies of OO concentration. As Ostriakov states explicitly, it was the Special Departments that exposed the Penkovskiy case, in which Western intelligence agents had succeeded in obtaining GRU documents with the help of Penkovskiy.[73] Indeed, Barron notes that the GRU suffered a loss of independence as a result of the Penkovskiy case and the earlier (1958) KGB exposure of GRU Lt. Col. Iurii Popov as a CIA spy.[74]

Recent Trends

Toward the close of the Brezhnev era the Soviet press began to devote increasing attention to the KGB's military counterintelligence and political security functions. Numerous books and articles praising the activities of "military Chekists" and their historic achievements created the impression that the authority of the Special Departments was on the rise.[75] Calls for stronger "vigilance" in the armed forces have also become more frequent in past few years, with the implication that the services of the Special Departments are particularly important. The Soviets claim that the threat of Western espionage and subversion is increasing; hence vigilance in the military must be heightened and security measures intensified. Chebrikov pointedly noted in his speech to the Twenty-Seventh Party Congress:

> Our enemies have not renounced their intention of liquidating socialism as a social system. The special services of the U.S.A. and several NATO countries make persistent efforts to compromise the internal and external politics of the USSR and carry out actions directed at subverting the Soviet economy. They seek out our political, *military*, economic and scientific-technical secrets; they try to infiltrate government enterprises, *important defense installations and scientific research institutes*.[76]

Articles appear regularly in the press on the necessity for stricter observance of security measures in the Soviet armed forces. Examples of carelessness and loose talk are reported and it is claimed that efforts to educate men on the importance of tight security are insufficient. Thus observed one article in *Krasnaia zvezda*, "it is precisely the deficiencies in educational work that might explain, for example, the failure to eliminate cases of a negligent and careless attitude towards official documents and materials and violations of regulations in radio communications."[77] More recently, an editorial from this paper implied that the problem of insufficient vigilance existed at high levels within the armed forces. After citing "instances where information earmarked for a strictly limited circle of people is divulged at various conferences and meetings," the editorial went on to stress that "shortcomings associated with the organization of troop service and the protection of coded communications and the keeping of military and state secrets are largely conditioned, as an analysis of their causes show, by deficiencies in the training of commanders and other officials."[78] Marshal Sokolov himself, in a speech made shortly before his removal from the post of defense minister, admitted "flagrant violations of security measures" among military cadres.[79] While this was not stated explicitly, the implication was that greater political surveillance of the armed forces is necessary. It might be added that episodes such as that in which the West German plane managed to reach Red Square without being forced down sustain these arguments for greater vigilance.

Soviet sources have stressed that vigilance is not restricted to compliance with security regulations: "To be vigilant means ... to be capable of discerning the treacherous intrigues and any tricks by bourgeois propaganda, rebuffing views and morals which are alien to us and actively countering the class enemy's subversive activity."[80] One commentator, claiming that Western radio stations expend huge efforts at "ideological sabotage," went on to note: "Nor do they overlook members of the Soviet Armed Forces and other fraternal armies. Here they seek to distort the social nature and historical function of the socialist armies and the role of the communist and workers' parties in leading them, and to slander the Soviet servicemen's fulfillment of their internationalist duty in Afghanistan, the Cuban servicemen's fulfillment of this duty in Angola, and the Polish servicemen's fulfillment of their national patriotic duty."[81] With increasing problems of draft evasion and the general decline of morale in the armed forces, the KGB's role of combating ideological sabotage against the military gains in importance.[82]

According to *Krasnaia zvezda*, "vigilance" encompasses the struggle against all forms of deviant behavior in the military, including "egotism, careerism, mercenariness, carelessness, drunkenness, and immorality." In their subversive activities, the article notes, "our enemies count on people with these vices, since they are more easily led astray."[83] Linking such forms of misbehavior to the dangers of enemy subversion may provide a justification for KGB involvement in many facets of military life, including the struggle against corruption. The anticorruption campaign has not left the armed forces untouched. Numerous exposés of improper and illegal activity on the part of Soviet officers began to appear in the press after Andropov came to power, and criticism of the military for not enforcing law and order was intensified.[84] It is possible that the KGB was participating in this anticorruption effort within the military just as it took an active role in such efforts among the state and party bureaucracy.

Discussions of corruption in the armed forces decreased after Andropov's death, only to become more frequent as Gorbachev consolidated his power and introduced *glasnost'*. USSR Military Procurator B. S. Popov, writing in *Krasnaia zvezda* in April 1986, was highly critical of the state of law and order in the Soviet armed forces. Popov noted that many crimes committed by members of the military might not have occurred if commanders and officers were more careful about discipline. He claimed that commanders often turn a blind eye to violations of legality and that far from all of those who are guilty are held to account.[85]

Cases of misuse of official position for economic gain have been reported with increasing frequency. Several military officers have been exposed for stealing state property and diverting military funds for personal use since Gorbachev came to power.[86]

Public exposure of corruption in its ranks undoubtedly causes disquiet within the armed forces, particularly when combined with criticism for lack of discipline and insufficient vigilance. Like the KGB, the military has a large stake in maintaining its public prestige, and such attacks could diminish its influence in the Kremlin which has already declined considerably under Gorbachev. Although there is no indication that the KGB is responsible for this negative publicity, its Special Departments do serve as a means of gathering potentially damaging information against military personnel. Thus armed forces leaders may welcome KGB protection of military secrets and defense installations, as well as its efforts to indoctrinate soldiers. But the Special Departments probably arouse considerable resentment as well. The military, after all, has no similar apparatus within the KGB, and the Soviet Union is one of the few modern states to place military counterintelligence under civilian authority. The KGB's security role in the armed forces and the ensuing tensions between the KGB and the military serve the interests of the party leadership, which always faces the potential threat, no matter how remote, of a challenge from either of these coercive forces. The MPA may act as a restraint on the armed forces, but its authority is limited in that its purview does not extend beyond domestic military concerns and it does not have the punitive powers or the access to information enjoyed by the KGB's Special Departments. The KGB, not the MPA, is seen as the ultimate defense against efforts to subvert the military from both abroad and within. There are, of course, other factors, to be discussed further, that mitigate these tensions and create areas of common ground on which the views of the military and political police might converge. But it is above all the Special Departments, with their broad powers of surveillance and criminal investigation within the armed forces, that make the KGB such a crucial variable in civil-military relations.

Notes

1. According to a 1967 study by Roman Kolkowicz, the MPA has been "the Party's crucial instrument of control over the military," without which the party would not be able to rely on the military's obedience. Roman Kolkowicz, *The Soviet Military and the Communist Party* (Princeton: N.J.: Princeton University Press, 1967), p. 123.
2. Timothy J. Colton, *Commissars, Commanders and Civilian Authority: The Structure of*

Soviet Military Politics (Cambridge, Mass., and London: Harvard University Press, 1979), p. 279.

3. Amos Perlmutter and William LeoGrande, "The Party in Uniform: Towards a Theory of Civil-Military Relations in Communist Political Systems," *American Political Science Review* 76 (1982):778–789. William Odom's approach is similar in that he stresses a broad consensus between the party and the military on most important issues and sees factional conflicts as intraparty rather than party versus military. But he conceives of the relationship between the party and military as symbiotic rather than coalitional, as Perlmutter and LeoGrande see it. See William Odom, "The Party-Military Connection: A Critique," in *Civil-Military Relations in Communist Systems*, eds. Dale Herspring and Ivan Volgyes (Boulder, Colo.: Westview Press, 1978), pp. 27–52.

4. Perlmutter and LeoGrande, "The Party in Uniform," p. 786, acknowledge that the "ideological foundations of civilian control may well be buttressed by more practical sorts of political arrangements, for example, an internal security force or militia," but they view ideology as the "heart of the civilian control system." Colton, citing the absence of widespread arrests or apparent use of police violence, claims that the security police concentrate on genuine counterintelligence and play a small role in monitoring the activities of the armed forces. Colton, *Commissars*, pp. 226–227.

5. Barrington Moore, Jr., *Terror and Progress USSR: Some Sources of Change and Stability in the Soviet Dictatorship* (Cambridge, Mass.: Harvard University Press, 1954), p. 27.

6. Ibid.

7. Among the sources on the Cheka's Special Departments are S. Z. Ostriakov, *Voennye chekisty* (Moscow: Voenizdat, 1979): Iu. B. Dolgopolov, *Voina bez linii fronta* (Moscow: Voenizdat, 1981); "Osobye otdely," *SVE* 6 (1978):142–143; I. Ustinov and K. Kapitonov, "Polveka na boevom postu," *Voenno-istoricheskii zhurnal*, no. 1 (1969): 99–102; and George Leggett, *The Cheka: Lenin's Political Police* (Oxford: Clarendon Press, 1981) pp. 95–99, 205–208.

8. Leggett, *The Cheka*, p. 207. The total Vecheka budget for 1920 was 4,588,200,000 rubles.

9. Two Soviet histories of the Special Departments offer very different interpretations of this incident. One source (Ostriakov, *Voennye chekisty*, p. 41) attributes the dispute to an "incorrect attitude toward the army Chekists" on the part of the political commissar. The other source (Dolgopolov, *Voina*, pp. 66–67) blames the OO officer, who "misunderstood the leading role of local party organizations in relation to all other organs within their territory." That Soviet histories would attach such significance to this incident, offering strikingly different accounts, suggests that there may be an ongoing dispute today over the relationship between the Special Department on the one hand and the MPA and the party on the other.

10. Leggett, *The Cheka*, pp. 206–207; Dolgopolov, *Voina*, pp. 64–65.

11. Ostriakov, *Voennye chekisty*, pp. 87–123; V. S. Ivanov, *Chasovye sovetskikh granits*, 2d exp. ed. (Moscow: Politizdat, 1983), pp. 60–61. Ostriakov mistakenly gives November 1921 as the date when border protection was transferred to the Cheka; actually it was 24 November 1920. According to Ostriakov (pp. 104–105), OOs seem to have retained border control in certain republics after 1923. See chapter 7 for more details.

12. Ostriakov, *Voennye chekisty*, pp. 122–127.

13. John Erikson, *The Soviet High Command: A Military-Political History 1918–1941* (London: Macmillian, 1962), pp. 376–377.

14. A. Iu. Vedenin, *Gody i liudi* (Moscow: Politizdat, 1964), p. 56; P. Kruzhin, "Osobye otdely i Brezhnev," *RLRB* (in Russian) RS-1371/79, 20 September 1979.

15. Zbigniew K. Brzezinski, *The Permanent Purge: Politics in Soviet Totalitarianism* (Cambridge, Mass.: Harvard University Press, 1964), pp. 74–76. Also see Erikson, *The Soviet High Command*, pp. 404–473.

16. *Istoriia velikoi otechestvennoi voiny sovetskogo soiuza 1941–1945* (Moscow: Voenizdat 1965), 6:134–135. Ostriakov, *Voennye chekisty*, p. 132. For more information on Fedorchuk's career in the Special Departments, see Peter Deriabin and T. H. Bagley, "Fedorchuk, the

KGB, and the Soviet Succession," *ORBIS* 26, no. 3 (Fall, 1982): 611–635. Another person who joined the OOs at this time was D. P. Nosyrev, former chief of the KGB for Leningrad City and *Oblast*.

17. See Robert W. Stephan, "Death to Spies: The Story of SMERSH" (unpublished master's thesis, American University, 1984), p. 54, and "SMERSH: Soviet Military Counter-intelligence during the Second World War," *Journal of Contemporary History* 22 (1987): 585–613.

18. Ostriakov, *Voennye chekisty*, p. 149.

19. Ibid., p. 167. Also see D. P. Nosyrev, ed., *V poedinke s abverom: Dokumentalnyi ocherk o chekistakh Leningradskogo fronta 1941–45* (Moscow: Voenizdat, 1968), p. 28.

20. See *Survey of Soviet Intelligence and Counterintelligence* (Washington, D.C.: Intelligence Division, GSUSA, Department of the Army, 9 January 1948, declassified NND 770011), pp. 15, 30–31.

21. Dolgopolov, *Voina*, p. 113.

22. For a defector's account of Abakumov and SMERSH, see A. I. Romanov, *Nights Are Longest There: Smersh from the Inside*, trans. Gerald Brooke (London: Hutchinson, 1972). Military intelligence was conducted by a separate organization, the Main Intelligence Administration (GRU) of the General Staff. It concentrated on collecting technical, economic, and logistical information on foreign nations.

23. Ostriakov, *Voennye chekisty*, p. 178; Nosyrev, *V poedinke*, p. 106.

24. Dolgopolov, *Voina*, p. 145; N. N. Koshelev and B. O. Lebin, "Boitsy nezrimogo fronta," in *Slavnaia pobeda pod Leningradom* (Leningrad: Lenizdat, 1976), pp. 479–487.

25. *Survey of Soviet Intelligence*, p. 15.

26. See Aleksandr I. Solzhenitsyn, *The Gulag Archipelago, 1918–1956*, trans. Thomas P. Whitney (New York: Harper and Row, 1973), esp. pp. 15–23, 78–83; Simon Wolin and Robert Slusser, eds., *The Soviet Secret Police* (New York: Praeger, 1957), pp. 19–20; and Zbigniew Brzezinski, ed., *Political Controls in the Soviet Army* (New York: Research Program on the USSR, 1954), pp. 17–73, 78–83.

27. Brzezinski, *Political Controls*, p. 82.

28. S. G. Novikov, "Voennaia prokuratura na strazhe zakonnosti i pravoporiadka v periode velikoi otechestvennoi voiny," *Sovetskoe gosudarstvo i pravo*, no. 4 (April 1985): 54–61 (quotation, p. 56). Although the author assures us that supervision by the Procurator ensured adherence to the law by the state security organs and prevented excessively repressive punishments, this claim is doubtful in view of much other evidence to the contrary.

29. *Survey of Soviet Intelligence*, p. 11.

30. Ibid., pp. 51–52.

31. See A. G. Rytov, *Rytsari piatogo okeana* (Moscow: Voenizdat, 1970), pp. 145–149; K. F. Telegin, *Ne otdali Moskvy* (Moscow: Sovetskaia Rossiia, 1975), pp. 120–132. See also Solzhenitsyn, *Gulag*, pp. 18–19; Vladimir and Evdokia Petrov, *Empire of Fear* (New York: Praeger, 1956), pp. 98–99; and Brzezinski, *Political Controls*, pp. 80–83. For a fictionalized account of SMERSH, see a novel by V. Bogomolov, *V avguste sorok chetvertogo*, serialized in *Novyi Mir*, nos. 10–12 (1974). This novel is based on facts, and the author reproduces many of the original documents and communications, though with names changed and certain information omitted for security reasons.

32. Stephan, "Death to Spies," p. 114.

33. Ostriakov, *Voennye chekisty*, p. 205. Also see Novikov, "Voennaia prokuratura," p. 60, and V. Pirozhkov, "Nevidimyi front," *Agitator*, no. 23 (December 1984): 31–34.

34. Ostriakov, *Voennye chekisty*, p. 256. Also see Solzhenitsyn, *Gulag*, pp. 82–83, 237–251.

35. According to the International Institute for Strategic Studies in London, there are currently 10,000 MVD and KGB personnel in Afghanistan. See *The Military Balance*, 1986–87 (London: International Institute for Strategic Studies, 1986), p. 46.

36. Petrov, *Empire of Fear*, p. 99. After 1953 Zhukov was apparently urging that military victims of the purges be rehabilitated—a potential embarrassment to the KGB and

the Special Departments. See Michael J. Deane, *Political Control of the Soviet Armed Forces* (New York: Crane, Russak, 1977), pp. 60–61. Thus the latter in their turn probably supported Khrushchev in his dismissal of Zhukov in 1957.

37. See note 47 for evidence that this is now a chief directorate.

38. See Leonov's obituary in *KZ*, 14 January 1981, p. 4; *Ezhegodnik BSE*, 1971, p. 637; and Ostriakov, *Voennye chekisty*, pp. 272–273.

39. *Survey of Soviet Intelligence*, pp. 49–51.

40. John Barron, *The KGB: Secret Work of Soviet Secret Agents* (New York: Bantam Books, 1974), pp. 19–20.

41. Aleksei Myagkov, *Inside the KGB* (Surrey: Foreign Affairs Publishing House, 1976), pp. 53–54; N. I. Seredin et al., eds., *Armeiskie chekisty: Vospominaniia voennykh Kontrrazvedchikov Leningradskogo, Volkhovskogo i Karel'skogo fronta* (Leningrad: Lenizdat, 1985), p. 342 (where mention is made of the Special Department for the Leningrad MD). Also see Peter Deriabin and Frank Gibney, *The Secret World* (New York: Ballantine, 1982), p. 108. This is a reprint, with some revision, of a book originally published in 1959. Deriabin lists four main divisions for the Army, Navy, Air Force, and General Staff, but the number of divisions has no doubt increased.

42. V. P. Artemiev, "OKR: State Security in the Soviet Armed Forces," *Military Review* 43, no. 9 (September 1963):22; Brzezinskii, *Political Controls* , pp. 55–57.

43. Myagkov, *Inside the KGB*, p. 26; *The Military Balance*, 1986–87 p. 36.

44. Colton, *Commissars*, p. 15.

45. See Myagkov, *Inside the KGB*, pp. 44–48; Deriabin and Gibney, *Secret World*, p. 69; Barron, *KGB: Secret Work*, p. 99; and *Survey of Soviet Intelligence*, pp. 82, 160–161.

46. For details on these officials, see Knight, "The KGB's Special Departments."

47. See *CIA Directory of Soviet Officials*, vol. 1, *National Organizations* (November 1973), p. 202; Ostriakov, *Voennye chekisty*, p. 152; and *XXVII s'ezd KPSS. Stenograficheskii otchet* (Moscow: Politizdat, 1986), 3:417. The fact that Dushin was the only KGB official aside from Chebrikov to sign the obituary of USSR Military Procurator Gornyi (*Izvestiia*, 9 January 1986, p. 6) is further evidence to support this hypothesis. In 1981 at the Twenty-Sixth Party Congress, Dushin was referred to the head of a directorate rather than a chief directorate. This would indicate that the Third Directorate became a Chief Directorate sometime after 1981.

48. Ostriakov, *Voennye chekisty*, pp. 275, 300–301.

49. Ibid., p. 275.

50. See Barron, *KGB: Secret Work*, p. 13; and Stephen M. Meyer, "Soviet Nuclear Operations," in *Managing Nuclear Operations*, ed. Aston B. Carter, John D. Steinbruner, and Charles A. Zracket (Washington, D.C.: The Brookings Institution, 1987), pp. 487–491. According to Meyer, the change was probably motivated by technological and strategic developments rather than by political concerns.

51. Meyer, "Soviet Nuclear Operations," p. 492.

52. Artemiev, "OKR," p. 23.

53. A. G. Gornyi, ed., *Osnovy sovetskogo voennogo zakonodatel'stva* (Moscow: Voenizdat, 1966), pp. 311–320, 387–389; A. G. Gornyi et al., eds., *Voennoe zakonodatel'stvo i pravovoe vospitanie voinov* (Moscow, Voenizdat, 1983), pp. 117–123, 200.

54. Gornyi, *Osnovy*, pp. 380–419.

55. See, for example, A. G. Gornyi, ed., *Voennoe pravo* (Moscow: Voenizdat, 1985), pp. 268–269.

56. See Gornyi, *Osnovy*, where the requirement of obtaining a commander's permission for arrest is said to apply only to military crimes, not to crimes against the state investigated by the OOs.

57. See "Armeiskie chekisty," an interview with G. K. Tsinev, *Trud*, 7 March 1979, p. 4; and Ostriakov, *Voennye chekisty*, p. 312.

58. "Armeiskie chekisty," *Trud*.

59. Ostraikov, *Voennye chekisty*, p. 312.

60. Robert Bathurst and Michael Burger, *Controlling the Soviet Soldier: Some Eyewit-*

ness Accounts (College Station: Center for Strategic Technology, Texas A&M University System, April 1981), p. 22.

61. Ostriakov, *Voennye chekisty*, p. 299; Artemiev, "OKR," p. 30.

62. Myagkov, *Inside the KGB*, p. 65. Also see Sergei Zamascikov, *Political Organizations in the Soviet Armed Forces: The Role of the Party and Komsomol* (Falls Church, Va.: Delphic Association, 1982), p. 71.

63. Bathurst and Burger, *Controlling the Soviet Soldier*, p. 22. Special departments or sections are sometimes referred to as *"spetsodely"* rather than *"osobye otdely."*

64. *Survey of Soviet Intelligence*, p. 52; Artemiev, "OKR," pp. 28–29.

65. Brzezinski, *Political Controls*, p. 67.

66. M. P. Maliarov, ed., *Prokurorskii nadzor v SSSR* (Moscow: Iuridicheskaia Literatura, 1966), p. 300; Zamascikov, *Political Organizations*, pp. 31–36.

67. Myagkov, *Inside the KGB*, pp. 74–75.

68. Aleksei Myagkov, "The Soviet Union's Special Forces," *Soviet Analyst* 9, no. 1 (8 January 1980).

69. See *Soviet Acquisition of Militarily Significant Western Technology: An Update* (Washington, D.C.: U.S. Government Printing Office, September, 1985). Also see chapter 9 for further discussion of this intelligence-gathering effort.

70. According to former GRU officer Viktor Suvorov, "the GRU and KGB are ready at any moment to destroy each other. Between them exist exactly those mutual relations which suit the Party. The jealousy and mutual hatred between the GRU and KGB are familiar to the police of every country where the Soviet Union has an embassy." Viktor Suvorov, *Inside Soviet Military Intelligence* (New York: Macmillan, 1984), p. 47. It should be noted that Suvorov's credibility and the accuracy of his information is highly questionable, but Oleg Penkovskiy, the GRU officer caught as a spy in 1962, also commented on the hostility between the GRU and the KGB. Oleg Penkovskiy, *The Penkovskiy Papers*, trans. Peter Deriabin (New York: Doubleday, 1965), pp. 53, 267. A more recent account of such rivalry appears in the memoirs of a former Soviet diplomat, Nicolas Polianski, *M.I.D. 12 ans dans les services diplomatiques du Kremlin* (Paris: Pierre Belford, 1984).

71. Barron, *KGB: Secret Work*, pp. 463–465.

72. Suvorov, *Inside Soviet Military Intelligence*, p. 48. Suvorov (pp. 48–50) also makes the unlikely claim that the GRU's budget is many times greater than that of the KGB and relates a story of how Ivashutin refused to comply with a request from Andropov, who was then KGB chief. It is hard to believe that Ivashutin would not obey a request from a full Politburo member.

73. Ostriakov, *Voennye chekisty*, p. 283.

74. Barron, *KGB: Secret Work*, p. 464.

75. Among Soviet books on the OOs are Dolgolpolov, *Voina*; Ostriakov, *Voennye chekisty*, Nosyrev, *V poedinke*; Seredin, *Armeiskie chekisty*; M. A. Belousov, *Ob etom ne soobshchailos: Zapiski armeiskogo chekista* (Moscow: Voenizdat, 1978); Iu. I. Semenov, *Komissar gosbezopasnosti* (Moscow: Voenizdat, 1979); and G. K. Tsinev, ed., *Voennye kontrrazvedchiki* (Moscow: Voenizdat, 1979). For articles on the OOs, see Korovin, "Uchastie organov gosbezopasnosti v osushchestvlenii funktsii oborny strany," *Sovetskoe gosudarsvo i pravo*, no. 5 (1975):53–60; G. K. Tsinev, "Na strazhe interesov vooruzhennykh sil SSSR," *Kommunist vooruzhennykh sil*, no. 12 (December 1978):26–31; Tsinev in *Trud*, 7 March 1979; Iu. Stvolinskii, "Ofitser kontrrazvedki," *Leningradskaia pravda*, 22 December 1981, p. 3; and V. Seregin, "Proval eshche odnoi aktsii TsRU," *Pravda*, 13 December 1983, p. 4.

76. *Pravda*, 1 March 1986, p. 6, emphasis added.

77. *KZ*, 5 June 1984, p. 1. Also see *KZ*, 9 June 1984, p. 3; 8 March 1984, p. 2; 15 February 1986, p. 1.

78. *KZ*, 24 July 1987, p. 1. This editorial was unusually strongly worded, especially in its claims that the statutes on responsibility for military and state secrets are not explained sufficiently to military personnel. This criticism could be aimed at the special departments themselves, as well as at political officers.

79. See his speech delivered at a meeting of the party *aktiv* of the USSR Ministry of Defense, as reported in *KZ*, 18 March 1987, p. 2.

80. V. Builov, "Leninym zaveshchannaia bditel'nost'," *KZ*, 29 September 1983, pp. 2–3.

81. *KZ*, 27 November 1984, p. 2.

82. For a closer examination of these problems see Ellen Jones, "The Consequences of Social Change for Soviet Civil-Military Relations," in *The Soldier and the Soviet State*, ed. Timothy Colton and Thane Gustafson (forthcoming).

83. Builov, "Leninym zaveshchannaia bditel'nost'."

84. See, for example, *KZ*, 1 June 1983, p. 2; 14 June 1983, p. 2; 17 August 1983, p. 2; 19 August 1983, p. 2; and 25 August 1983, p. 2. See also Konstantin Simis, "An Officer and a Crook: Ripping Off the Red Army," *The Washington Post*, 8 January 1984.

85. V. Popov, "Komandir i zakon. bez pauz i kompromissov," *KZ*, 12 April 1986, p. 2.

86. See, for example, the following reports in *KZ*: 7 May 1985, p. 2; 19 May 1985, p. 2; 26 June 1985, p. 2; 6 August 1985, p. 2; 14 August 1985, p. 2; 22 August 1985, p. 2; 19 December 1985, p. 2; 22 December 1985, p. 2; 10 April 1986, p. 2; 12 October 1986, p. 2; 13 February 1987, p. 2; 31 March 1987, p. 2. Also see *Pravda*, 21 March 1987, p. 6; 25 April 1987, p. 3.

9

The KGB and Soviet Foreign Policy

Although this study is concerned primarily with the KGB's role in Soviet domestic politics and society, this role cannot be properly understood without taking into consideration the KGB's involvement in foreign affairs. Domestic and foreign issues are closely intertwined in the Soviet policy process, and developments in both areas have a significant impact on each other. The state of East-West relations, for example, appears to be a crucial factor in the determination of Soviet policy toward dissent. The close connection between domestic and foreign policy is exemplified by the fact that the KGB itself combines both internal security and foreign intelligence functions in one organization. In this respect Soviet practice differs from that of most Western governments, where these functions are usually assigned to separate agencies. Such a dual role stems from the ideological preconceptions of the Soviet regime, in particular its tendency to blur the distinction between internal and external security threats. The foreign and domestic functions of the KGB are, of course, executed by separate directorates whose personnel tend, with some exceptions, to follow career tracks that are distinct from one another. At the top level of the KGB hierarchy, however, these roles are combined in the person of the KGB chairman, who, in his current capacity as a full member of the Politburo, participates in the policy process as a coordinator of the KGB's domestic and foreign operations.

The KGB's multifarious foreign operations have drawn wide attention in the Western press and have been the subject of numerous

Western studies. Yet few, if any, attempts have been made to assess the KGB's influence on the foreign policy process. Is the KGB simply an instrument of the party leadership in implementing its objectives, or does it have a significant role in decision making? Does the KGB as an institution take a stand on various foreign policy issues that it brings to bear on policymaking? This chapter presents a general overview of the KGB's foreign activities and will then consider how these activities, taken together with the KGB's domestic role, affect the KGB's institutional perceptions and its ability to influence policy.

Organization of Foreign Operations

The organizational structure for the foreign operations of the political police has changed relatively little over the years. Although the Cheka engaged in limited espionage operations from its inception, it had no formal agency for operations abroad until December 1920, when a foreign department (*Inostrannyi otdel*, or INO) was first established under its auspices. The chief of the INO from 1921 to 1929 was M. A. Trilisser, who from 1926 onward was simultaneously second deputy chairman of the OGPU. The INO's functions during this time were straightforward: collecting political, military, and economic intelligence on foreign states; monitoring emigré groups abroad; and conducting surveillance of Soviet officials posted abroad. Cheka intelligence officers served under legal cover as members of Soviet diplomatic and commercial missions, often as second secretaries or attachés. Later, when operations of the INO expanded under the OGPU, illegal agents were sent abroad, functioning under deep cover with false identity papers.[1]

After the NKVD was formed in 1934 the INO, as a department of the Main Administration of State Security (GUGB), continued to expand its foreign network, devoting particular attention to operations against the different political groups and organizations of Russian emigrés abroad. The INO (which later became the INU, or foreign administration) was not the only organization responsible for espionage and covert foreign activities. Rather, it was part of a network of contiguous agencies that operated abroad and whose work was coordinated at the center by the Politburo.[2] Shortly before World War II these agencies included three additional departments of the GUGB: the Economic Department, responsible for counterespionage in Soviet industry and agriculture as well as for military and technical espionage abroad; the Secret Political

Department (SPO), responsible for political surveillance of the Communist party, intelligentsia, religious, and other groups; and the Counterintelligence Department (KRO), charged with detecting foreign agents within the Soviet Union. The latter two departments were active abroad only insofar as the ramifications of a case they were working on led them outside the country.

Among the other agencies executing foreign tasks for the Politburo were the Military Intelligence Administration of the General Staff, the All-Union Council of Trade Unions, the People's Commissariat of Foreign Affairs, the People's Commissariat of Foreign Trade, various other cultural and trade societies, and the Executive Committee of the COMINTERN. These agencies carried out their work separately, but all had the common purpose of furthering the Kremlin's foreign policy designs. As far as the specific tasks of the INU were concerned, they involved, broadly speaking, active counterintelligence (infiltration of foreign intelligence organizations); universal espionage—all-round detailed study of important free-world countries; covert propaganda and political work directed toward the establishment of a political situation favorable to the development of communism (including disinformation, forgeries, provoking internal conflicts, fomenting political discontent, etc.); and surveillance of Soviet citizens abroad.[3]

There were some changes in the postwar organization of security police foreign operations. According to some sources, INU operations were coordinated with those of military intelligence (GRU) in a so-called Committee of Information (KI), established in 1947–1948 and headed by a series of foreign ministry officials. But the GRU reverted to the control of the Ministry of Defense in 1948 and the KI was later dissolved.[4] Despite these changes, the tasks of the INU remained essentially the same during the war and postwar years and throughout the period of its transformation into the First Chief Directorate after the USSR KGB was created in 1954.

The First Chief Directorate of the USSR KGB is responsible for KGB operations abroad. According to John Barron, the First CD is composed of three separate directorates: Directorate S, which oversees illegal agents (those under deep cover) throughout the world; Directorate T, responsible for the collection of scientific and technological intelligence; and Directorate K, which carries out infiltration of foreign intelligence and security services and exercises surveillance over Soviet citizens abroad. In addition, the First CD has three important services: Service I, which analyzes and distributes intelligence collected by KGB foreign intelligence officers and agents, publishes a daily current events

[279]

summary for the Politburo, and makes forecasts of future world developments; Service A, which is responsible for planning and implementing so-called active measures; and Service R, which evaluates KGB operations abroad. The operational core of the First CD lies in its eleven geographical departments, which supervise KGB employees assigned to residencies abroad. These officers or *"rezidents"*, operating under legal cover, engage in intelligence collection, espionage, and active measures.[5] The head of the First CD is Col. Gen. V. A. Kriuchkov, who served under Andropov in the Soviet Embassy in Hungary and later was a leading official in the CC Department for Liaison with Ruling Communist Parties, again serving under Andropov. He followed Andropov to the KGB in 1967.[6]

While the overall tasks of the First CD are similar to those of its predecessors, its role has expanded considerably since Stalin died and particularly since the early 1970s. This is partly a result of the fact that the dimensions of Soviet foreign policy in general have expanded, with greater involvement in the Third World, foreign trade, arms control, and so on. Furthermore the Kremlin has placed increased emphasis on covert operations and intelligence gathering as a means of implementing Soviet foreign policy objectives. As greater manpower and resources have been devoted to this type of activity, the techniques and methods have become more sophisticated and effective.

Before turning to the KGB's operations abroad it should be noted that the Second CD plays an important support role in the regime's intelligence operations. First, it recruits agents for intelligence purposes from among foreigners stationed within the USSR—diplomats, journalists, businessmen, students, and tourists. Second, it engages in counterintelligence by uncovering attempts on the part of foreign intelligence services to recruit Soviet citizens.[7]

Intelligence, Counterintelligence, and Active Measures

The KGB's foreign activities can be divided roughly into two categories. The first involves intelligence collection, espionage, and so-called offensive counterintelligence and the second involves "active measures" (disinformation, propaganda, sabotage, etc.). Not surprisingly, there are no precise open-source estimates on the number of agents whom the First CD employs abroad, but most experts seem to agree that the KGB operates the world's largest and most far-reaching foreign intelligence apparatus. There was a marked increase in KGB intelligence gathering in the West after the era of détente began in 1972. Détente permitted a vast influx of Soviet and Eastern European diplomatic, cultural, and commercial officials into the United States and other Western countries. According to former FBI Director Clarence Kelly, between 1972 and 1977 the number of Communist bloc officials in the United States rose by 50 percent.[8] KGB officers and their Eastern European counterparts operate under various guises—diplomats, trade officials, journalists, scientists, and so on. The proportion of Soviet officials abroad who are engaged in intelligence gathering has been estimated to range from 30 to 40 percent in the United States to over 50 percent in some Third World countries. In addition, many Soviet representatives who are not intelligence officers are nevertheless given some sort of assignment by the KGB.[9]

Apparently the First CD has little trouble recruiting personnel for its foreign operations. The high salaries, military rank, access to foreign currency, and opportunity to live abroad offer attractive enticements to young people choosing a career. There is also the power and prestige associated with working for the KGB. According to the Soviet defector and former UN diplomat Arkady Shevchenko, KGB Chairman Andropov elevated KGB *rezidents* (who used to occupy junior or mid-level diplomatic rank as a cover) to more important administrative positions, with a corresponding increase in authority.[10] The First CD recruits are said to represent the "cream of the crop" among those setting out on a career. They are usually graduates of one of the more prestigious higher educational institutes and have knowledge of one or more foreign languages. The KGB has a two-year postgraduate training course for these recruits at its Higher Intelligence School located near Moscow. The curriculum includes the use of ciphers, arms, and sabotage training, Communist party and Marxist history, economics, law, and foreign languages.[11]

A former Czechoslovak intelligence officer, Ladislav Bittman, described the typical KGB foreign officers of the post-Stalin era:

> Chosen for their loyalty, appearance and family connections with party and agency officials, the new breed of KGB candidates includes graduates of Soviet universities and institutes, particularly the prestigious Institute for International Studies in Moscow. In addition to courses dealing with Marxist-Leninist doctrine, they study foreign history, culture, languages, and official diplomatic techniques. After joining the KGB, they are subjected to intensive schooling in methods and techniques employed by the intelligence service. When a KGB officer completes training in foreign policy and clandestine techniques and begins to operate in a foreign area, he radiates more self-confidence and

personality than a diplomat without the KGB connection. The mundane and boring Russian diplomats are not usually KGB members. A KGB official dresses more elegantly, entertains more freely and shows more individuality even in discussing sensitive foreign policy issues and Soviet politics.[12]

This impression is confirmed by the accounts of a former employee of the Soviet Ministry of Foreign Affairs, Nicolas Polianski, who described the KGB *resident* in Berne, Switzerland: "He was amiable, very courteous, whether feigned or not, he was well-dressed. He knew how to control himself without losing his vigor, he exuded a tranquil forcefulness, measured and confident."[13] Polianski also refers to the high salaries and numerous privileges enjoyed by KGB foreign intelligence officers.[14]

The KGB is the primary agency responsible for supplying the Kremlin with political intelligence. According to Shevchenko, Moscow cables out questions on a daily basis to KGB *residents* abroad to guide them in their tasks. Shevchenko's view of the quality of such KGB intelligence in the 1970s was not very high. He claims that too much emphasis was placed on producing large quantities of information rather than on quality: "It enabled the KGB to overwhelm the relatively smaller amount of data supplied by the Foreign Ministry and by military intelligence operations."[15] As noted earlier, raw intelligence is reportedly analyzed and disseminated to the Soviet leadership by KGB Service I. (In cases of especially important agent reports the Politburo is said to receive them in raw form.) Apparently Service I lacks the manpower to process the large amount of intelligence it receives, despite the fact that it expanded considerably during the 1970s. Nevertheless according to former KGB officer Stanislav Levchenko, Service I makes a well-informed and conscientious effort to provide an accurate and objective picture to the Politburo and other clients.[16]

In addition to political intelligence, KGB officers have concentrated increasingly on efforts to acquire advanced Western technology. A 1985 U.S. government publication on this subject reported that "the magnitude of the Soviets' collection effort and their ability to assimilate collected equipment and technology are far greater than was previously believed."[17] According to this report, the KGB acts as a collector of militarily significant Western technology (in the form of documents and hardware) on behalf of the Military Industrial Commission (VPK) of the Presidium of the Council of Ministers. This commission coordinates the development of all Soviet weapons systems along with the program to acquire Western technology. The VPK levies requirements among the

KGB, the GRU, and several other agencies, including those of Eastern European intelligence services. This collection program is judged in the West to be highly successful, lightening the burden on Soviet research and improving the technical performance of Soviet military equipment and weapons systems.

The VPK expands its collection requirements by approximately 15 percent annually. According to this U.S. government report, KGB Directorate T, which is responsible for technological collection, employs about 1000 officers, including 300 abroad. Most of these officers are professionally trained scientific specialists occupying cover posts as science attachés in Soviet embassies or as officials in Soviet trade missions. Interestingly the GRU, which has about 1500 officers abroad engaged in scientific collection, is judged to be more successful than the KGB in terms of fulfilling requirements: "The GRU probably is more successful because of its overall scientific orientation, its bolder operational style, its increased collection opportunities that reflect a wider variety of technology-related cover positions overseas and its clearer understanding of collection objectives."[18] Nevertheless the KGB collects slightly more of the acquisitions judged to be most significant for purposes of military research by the Soviets. Both the KGB and the GRU increased their technical collection efforts considerably in the early 1980s, when the average number of requirements levied on them by the VPK increased by about 50 percent.

It might be added that the Andropov era in the KGB saw a greater orientation toward electronic espionage—communications interception and satellites—to supplement intelligence gathered by agents. According to Robert Campbell, the USSR now deploys at least three satellites for intelligence collection.[19] Some of this intelligence may be strictly military and therefore collected by the GRU, but the KGB probably also makes use of these satellites. The relative weight of this type of intelligence may well increase in the future.

The increase in the use of so-called active measures as an element of Soviet foreign policy has attracted considerable attention—and alarm—in the West in recent years. This type of activity has long been employed by the Soviets abroad, but it has become more widespread and more effective since the late 1960s. A great deal of information has appeared in the West documenting the extensive use of active measures by the Soviets, so there is no need to present a detailed account here.[20] Active measures are clandestine operations the purpose of which is to further Soviet foreign policy goals and to extend Soviet influence throughout the world. Among these covert techniques is disinformation:

[283]

leaking of false information and rumors to the foreign media or the planting of forgeries in order to deceive the public or the political elite in a given country or countries.

A KGB training manual defines disinformation as follows:

> Strategic disinformation assists in the execution of state tasks and is directed at misleading the enemy concerning the basic questions of state policy, the military-economic status and the scientific-technical achievements of the Soviet Union; the policy of certain imperialist states with respect to each other and to other countries; and the specific counterintelligence tasks of the organs of state security. Tactical disinformation makes it possible to carry out the individual task of strategic disinformation and, in fact, comprises the principal disinformation work of the organs of state security.[21]

The United States is the prime target of disinformation, in particular forgery operations, which are designed to damage U.S. foreign and defense policies in a variety of ways. From 1976 to 1980 forgeries of U.S. government documents and communiqués were estimated to have appeared at a rate of four to five per year.[22]

The use of international front organizations and foreign Communist parties to expand the USSR's political influence and further its propaganda campaigns is another form of active measures. Front organizations such as the World Peace Council and World Federation of Trade Unions profess noncommunist goals but are funded and manipulated behind the scenes by the Soviets. The programs advocated by front organizations mirror Soviet programs and echo Soviet media themes. Together with the International Department of the Central Committee, the KGB funnels money to these organizations and recruits Soviet agents to serve on their administrative bodies. The KGB also assists the International Department in the use of foreign Communist parties to further Soviet aims by smuggling financial aid to these parties and by maintaining liaison with them.[23]

On the darker side of active measures are those involving support for terrorists and insurgents. Although there is no direct open-source evidence that the Soviets plan or orchestrate terrorist acts by groups from Western Europe or the Middle East, there is much indirect evidence to show that the Soviet Union does indeed support international terrorism. The Soviets maintain close relationships with a number of governments and organizations that are direct supporters of terrorist groups. Moscow sells large quantities of arms to Libya and Syria, for example, and also maintains a close alliance with the PLO, providing it with arms, monetary assistance, and paramilitary training. Moscow's surrogate, Cuba, plays a central role in Latin American terrorism by providing groups with training, arms, and sanctuary, and Moscow's European satellite states often serve as middlemen or subcontractors for channeling aid to terrorist groups. Although the KGB, not surprisingly, avoids direct involvement with terrorist operations, it plays an important role in diverting aid to these groups and providing the Soviet leadership with intelligence reports on their activities.[24]

The KGB also has been heavily involved in the support of "national wars of liberation" in the Third World. Together with satellite intelligence services, the KGB helps to organize military training and political indoctrination of leftist guerrillas, as well as the provision of arms and advisers. The manipulation of national wars of liberation enables the Soviets to influence the political future of the country in question and to make its new government more responsive to Soviet objectives. The Soviets concentrated mainly on African countries until the late 1970s but then extended their support for "national liberation movements" to Central America, where they have regularly employed the services of the Cubans.[25] There are indications that the Kremlin has recently been reassessing its Third World policy and may devote more resources to its own economy than to new revolutionary movements in economically backward countries. Nevertheless as one Western analyst has stressed, this does not mean an end to Soviet intervention in the Third World; rather, the Kremlin might be more selective in providing support to radical movements.[26]

The KGB relies heavily on the intelligence services of Soviet satellite countries in carrying out both its active measures and espionage operations. The East German, Czechoslovak, Polish, Hungarian, Bulgarian, and Cuban services, which have reportedly made great improvements in their operations in recent years, form an important adjunct to the KGB. While formally subordinated to their own governments, these satellite services are, according to most Western experts, heavily influenced by the KGB. As a former official in the Czechoslovak intelligence service states, "Soviet intelligence is informed about every major aspect of their activities, and Russian advisors (called liaison officers) participate in planning major operations and assessing the results."[27] As far back as the 1960s the KGB introduced a new element of coordination with the satellite services through the creation of departments for disinformation in East German, Czechoslovak and Hungarian services and the establishment of direct lines of communication from these departments to the KGB.

[285]

These changes augmented the KGB's covert operational capability considerably.[28]

According to Barron, the Eleventh Department of the KGB's First CD is responsible for liaison with satellite intelligence services, each of which performs a variety of tasks for the KGB. The Bulgarians, for example, engage in the direction of terrorist groups and the smuggling of drugs and arms; the East Germans conduct broad espionage efforts against West Germany; and the Cubans assist KGB operations in both the United States and the Third World.[29] Chebrikov himself made reference to the close working arrangements between the KGB and satellite intelligence services in his 1985 *Kommunist* article: "Soviet Chekists carry out their work against enemy subversive activities in close contact with security organs in other countries of the socialist community. . . . On the basis of corresponding agreements, ties among the state security organs of our fraternal countries are becoming stronger and the forms of their cooperation in the struggle against the class enemy are being improved."[30] The fact that Chebrikov makes frequent, publicized trips to satellite countries reinforces the impression of close ties between the KGB and satellite services.[31]

It is important to stress that Soviet active measures involve not only the KGB and satellite intelligence services but also several other Soviet agencies, which all participate in a coordinated effort to further Soviet policy objectives. In this sense the Kremlin has a distinct advantage over democratic regimes because the Communist party's monopoly over the political process enables it to control all Soviet organizations and agencies abroad and to employ their services for any given program of action. Aside from the KGB, the Central Committee's International Department (ID) takes a leading role in directing and implementing active measures. The ID, which is responsible for liaison with nonruling Communist parties, international front organizations, and national liberation movements, as well as for the operation of a number of clandestine radio stations, is one of the most important foreign policy bodies in the Soviet system. It is responsible for coordinating and reviewing information on foreign policy from a variety of sources and briefs the Politburo on key foreign policy issues.[32]

The chief of the ID and a CC secretary is Anatolii Dobrynin, former ambassador to Washington. Dobrynin, who replaced the long-time ID chief Boris Ponomarev in early 1986, is widely regarded as a skillful and experienced diplomat with extensive knowledge of foreign policy. His appointment signifies the importance of the ID to the Soviets.

Another key agency was the International Information Department

(IID), created in 1978 to improve the effectiveness of Soviet foreign propaganda by coordinating the efforts of the USSR's major propaganda channels.[33] Its formation reflected the leadership's desire to make the foreign propaganda network more responsive to the needs of policy makers, but sometime in late spring 1986 this department was abolished, apparently because it was not achieving this goal. Its chief, Leonid Zamiatin, was made ambassador to Great Britain.

The Soviet campaign against NATO's INF deployment offers one of the clearest examples of a coordinated active measures effort by Moscow. The campaign, which began in late 1979, mobilized the entire Soviet arsenal of active measures resources, as well as diplomatic efforts. As one Western analyst pointed out, Moscow's tactics involved a dual-track approach: a "campaign from above" to influence NATO's decision makers and a "campaign from below" to create mass opposition to the INF deployment by exploiting popular fears of nuclear weapons.[34] The campaign from above attempted to drive a wedge between the United States and its NATO allies by portraying the United States as an aggressive, villainous power that endangered the security interests of Western Europe. At the same time, the Soviet Union was presented as a benign, well-meaning neighbor anxious to reach a compromise and to achieve a security balance with the West. In the campaign from below the Soviets exploited the growing political disaffection and disillusion-ment in Western Europe arising from European government policies, as well as the distinct rise in anti-Americanism, particularly among the younger generation.

While making broad use of its vast foreign propaganda apparatus, the Kremlin enlisted the KGB to carry out numerous disinformation activities that enhanced the overt propaganda campaign. In addition, the KGB, the ID, and the IID worked with the various international front organizations and European Communist parties, which organized mass demonstrations, marches, and petitions to protest NATO's plans. The Soviet campaign did not succeed in blocking the INF deployment, but it did not fail completely. The campaign did much to promote the cause of the peace movement in Europe and to erode popular support for NATO's security objectives. As one Western scholar observed,

> Moscow's ability to mount a propaganda and "active measures"
> campaign of the magnitude of the "campaign from below" is quite
> impressive. It also demonstrates the effective work and coordination of
> the various Soviet fronts, whose important role in Soviet foreign political
> activities is often underestimated or even dismissed. The anti-INF
> campaign illustrated the parallel activities of and coordination among the

[287]

different elements that make up the means and instrumentalities of Soviet foreign political pursuits.[35]

The KGB and Foreign Policy Decision Making

The discussion thus far has illustrated the KGB's key role in implementing the Kremlin's foreign policy objectives, a role that appears to have grown in importance since the early 1970s. This brings us to the question raised at the beginning of the chapter. Is the KGB merely an executor of the Kremlin's directives or does it actually influence policy formulation in some significant way? In order to address this question effectively we must first consider the framework of the Soviet foreign policy process.

Western scholars have developed several different approaches to understanding this process. For example, Jiri Valenta, in his study of the Soviet invasion of Czechoslovakia, employs the bureaucratic politics model to conceptualize Soviet decision making.[36] This model postulates that Soviet foreign policy stems not from a single actor but rather from the political interaction of several actors who represent different bureaucratic elites. Valenta portrays Soviet foreign policy decision making as a process fraught with political maneuvering and conflicting interests. No single leader possesses sufficient power to decide all issues, so decisions are reached collectively only after considerable political bargaining and arduous debate:

> Despite the shared images of national security, senior Soviet decisionmakers differ on how various issues should be approached and resolved. As in Western societies, the Soviet decisionmaking process is political, not scientific. The decisionmakers are not necessarily cast in the same mold. Often their backgrounds and areas of bureaucratic experience contrast sharply and often they assume different administrative duties and bureaucratic responsibilities and have different domestic and personal interests.[37]

A rather different approach is taken by Hannes Adomeit, who sees a broad consensus among Soviet leaders about operational principles in foreign policy, particularly in international crises: "Soviet decisionmaking in international crises will typically demonstrate a 'rallying around the flag,' the concentration of decisions in the hands of a select executive committee, the restoration of important elements of centralization and a return to traditional reflexes and responses."[38] While Adomeit allows that some conflict affects foreign policy decision making, he sees this conflict as occurring within a relatively narrow framework.

What about the inclusion in 1973 of the chiefs of the KGB, the Foreign Ministry, and the Defense Ministry on the key policymaking body, the Politburo? This could be seen as strengthening the tendency toward bureaucratic coalition politics, or, as Adomeit suggests, it could be viewed as part of "a trend towards further integration of various interests into a broad consensus and hence a dilution of conflict."[39]

Although the consensus model does not deny the KGB's influence on decision making, it is probably more useful to examine how the KGB affects foreign policymaking by employing the bureaucratic politics paradigm. Valenta, for example, has offered insights into how the KGB, as a defender of its institutional interests, may have influenced Soviet behavior in the Czechoslovak crisis of 1968. Nevertheless neither the bureaucratic nor the consensus model distinguishes clearly between different levels of participation in the decision-making process, which in the case of the KGB is important in understanding its influence. The KGB participates in the foreign policy decision-making process at the highest level, the Politburo, where its chief, Chebrikov, is a member of the collective leadership. At the same time, it influences the formulation of foreign policy at a lower level as an executor of that policy, a provider of information, and a generator of ideas, solutions, and alternatives. It may well be that the consensus model accurately describes decision making at the highest level, while the bureaucratic model is better suited to understanding lower-level KGB influence.

It is also important to consider whether or not the KGB represents a united voice in the decision-making process. If we are looking at the Politburo, we can assume that Chebrikov has consolidated the various views and opinions of his staff and therefore presents a single KGB stance. Below that level, however, it is quite possible that a monolithic KGB viewpoint does not exist. Officials responsible for domestic security and those who work in foreign operations may well feel very differently on certain issues. Thus, for example, Brezhnev's policy of détente inaugurated in 1972 was probably welcomed by officials in the First Chief Directorate because it offered opportunities for the assignment of increased numbers of KGB officers to Western countries under legal cover. Yet for those in charge of internal security détente meant an increase in the number of foreigners visiting the USSR, widening of communications with the West, and relaxation of the crackdown on dissent—all of which made the KGB's job inside the USSR more difficult. Thus when we examine the KGB's influence on foreign policy and its probable stance on certain issues, we must look at both the domestic and foreign concerns of the KGB as well as the level of its policy input.

Evidence of KGB influence on foreign policy decisions, as a participant in high-level decision making, a provider of information, and an implementer of policy, is best considered on a case-by-case basis. The KGB's relatively low political status in the Khrushchev years meant that it was not represented as an institution on the key decision-making body, the Presidium (as the Politburo was then called). Indeed from 1961 to 1964 the KGB chairman did not even have full membership on the Central Committee. Furthermore before Andropov's 1967 appointment, KGB chairmen had little experience in foreign policy. Serov had served abroad as a police official in the Soviet Army, but this was primarily a security function. Both Shelepin and Semichastnyi had been involved entirely in the Komsomol and party apparatus before their appointments to the KGB.

Nonetheless these KGB chairmen presided over their organization's foreign operations and no doubt developed their own views on foreign policy. Judging from their public statements, both Shelepin and Semichastnyi were hard-liners who did not favor rapprochement with the West. Robert Slusser has offered considerable evidence to show that both men opposed Khrushchev's efforts in this direction. Shelepin, for example, found nothing positive to say about the West in his speech to the Twenty-Second Party Congress in 1961, preferring to discuss only the threat posed to the USSR by Western military and intelligence agencies. Semichastnyi revealed his intense hostility toward the United States (as well as his very negative assessment of Yugoslav revisionism) on several occasions.[40]

Without direct access to the Presidium, the KGB leadership apparently embarked on a few autonomous police initiatives to impede Khrushchev's efforts at limited détente, such as the arrest in 1963 of Yale Professor Frederick Barghoorn on trumped-up charges of spying. This deliberate KGB provocation, which ended when President Kennedy managed to obtain Barghoorn's release, was highly embarrassing to Khrushchev.[41] Even more detrimental to Khrushchev was a KGB mustard gas attack on a West German technician, Horst Schwirkmann, at precisely the time that Khrushchev was making an effort to conclude a major trade agreement with West Germany. The incident, which occurred in September 1964, shortly before Khrushchev's ouster, outraged Bonn and destroyed all possibilities for a trade agreement.[42] The KGB leadership, aware of the impending coup, probably realized that such an act could be committed with impunity.

By late 1965 the influence of the so-called Shelepintsy (the faction surrounding Aleksandr Shelepin and including Semichastnyi; former KGB deputy V. S. Tikunov; Dmitrii Goriunov, head of Tass; and N. G. Egorychev, first secretary of the Moscow *Gorkom*) had risen considerably. Shelepin himself, who continued to oversee police matters, had been a full Politburo member since 1964. His group apparently advocated greater Soviet involvement abroad and in 1967 urged a policy of belligerance toward Egypt, at the time a Soviet ally.[43] As far back as December 1964 Shelepin had travelled to Cairo to promise Soviet assistance in the struggle against imperialism, after which several diplomatic posts in the Middle East were gradually filled by Shelepintsy from the KGB. In spring 1967 Shelepin's protégé Egorychev also visited the Middle East. In addition to circulating false reports about Israeli plans to attack Syria, the KGB (and the GRU) seriously underestimated Israel's military potential, and their reports persuaded Nasser that the Arabs could defeat Israel. The Shelepintsy paid for their adventurist policies, however. Following a June 1967 CC plenum, Egorychev lost his post as head of the Moscow *Gorkom* and Shelepin was removed from the Secretariat (Semichastnyi had already been dismissed from his post as KGB chief in May 1967).[44]

According to Galia Golan, the KGB remained in the background during decision making over the October 1973 Yom Kippur War. The only evidence of high-level KGB involvement was a statement made by Sadat to the effect that Andropov, as a close friend of Egypt's former intelligence chief Ahmad Ismail, had voiced his willingness to intervene on Egypt's behalf. Andropov did participate in some meetings with the Egyptians, but, although he was by now a full member of the Politburo, there were no other signs of his influence. According to Golan, Andropov even "put off with feeble excuses an invitation from Sadat to go to Egypt."[45]

The KGB's role in providing intelligence during the Yom Kippur War was highly important, however. In contrast to their earlier intelligence failures, the KGB and the GRU were well informed about Arab plans. According to one source, "not only were the Russians aware of Egyptian-Syrian intentions at least ten days in advance, thanks to their antennae in Damascus, but having learned from their former disappointments, they decided to furnish Sadat with all the material assistance necessary for the realization of his objectives."[46] The same source adds that a KGB report presented at a meeting of the Politburo in 1974 was responsible for the Kremlin's decision to change its Middle East policy. The report is said to have recommended greater support for extremist and terrorist groups and concentration on penetrating the regions of the Persian Gulf and the Horn of Africa.[47]

The Soviet decision to invade Czechoslovakia in August 1968 offers a good illustration of the involvement of the KGB as an institution in foreign policy decision making. At this time KGB Chairman Andropov was only a candidate (nonvoting) member of the Politburo, but, having presided over the Soviet invasion of Hungary in 1956 and having served for over ten years as chief of the CC Department for Liaison with Ruling Communist Parties, he was a leading expert on Eastern Europe and was no doubt consulted extensively during the crisis. Andropov had accompanied Brezhnev on several "discipline trips" to Eastern European countries in 1966–1967, intended mainly to prevent their establishment of diplomatic relations with West Germany.[48]

Valenta has suggested that although the collective leadership decides the most important policy questions, not all leaders participate on a day-to-day basis, and most issues are decided upon by experts in the specific area of concern. Thus "players prominent in foreign affairs appear to be heavily represented in deciding issues where national security interests are at stake."[49] In the specific case of Czechoslovakia, Valenta found that the decision-making circle was broadened to include CC bureaucrats and party officials responsible for domestic affairs, presumably because the problem directly affected internal Soviet interests. Valenta also suggested that the decision-making circle is broadened whenever there is disagreement within the Politburo, which there appears to have been in the case of Czechoslovakia.[50] Given these circumstances, it is likely that Andropov, with both foreign and domestic responsibilities and a direct line of intelligence from Czechoslovakia, probably had a significant impact on the decision-making process.[51]

What were Andropov's views on the Czechoslovak problem? Judging from the few public remarks Andropov made in reference to Czechoslovakia, it appears that his views coincided with those of the interventionists. In December 1967 he warned of the dangers posed by foreign intelligence services that tried to "weaken the might of the socialist countries and shake their unity and cohesion with the forces of the workers' and national liberation movement."[52] After the invasion Andropov made the following comments in a speech to KGB Komsomol members:

> Today the correlation of forces has shifted in favor of socialism. Such a powerful factor as the community of socialist nations is standing in opposition to hostile intrigues. . . . The enemy gives direct and indirect support to counterrevolutionary elements, engages in ideological

sabotage, establishes all sorts of antisocialist, anti-Soviet and other hostile organizations and seeks to fan the flames of nationalism. Graphic confirmation of this is offered by the events in Czechoslovakia, where that country's working people, supported by the fraternal international assistance of the peoples of the nations of the socialist community, resolutely nipped in the bud an attempt by counterrevolutionaries to turn Czechoslovakia off the socialist path.[53]

Not surprisingly, statements made by other leading KGB officials indicate that Andropov's views reflected those of the KGB as a whole. USSR KGB Deputy Chairman A. N. Malygin voiced strong approval for the invasion in an early 1969 article in a Komsomol journal. He noted that the intervention in Czechoslovakia had successfully thwarted "imperialist" plans to weaken the socialist structure there.[54] V. V. Fedorchuk, at the time an official in the KGB's Third Directorate, also appeared to concur on the necessity for the invasion when he referred afterward to the grave threats that had been posed to Czechoslovakia by "imperialist" counterrevolutionary strategies.[55]

Valenta offers two strong reasons why the KGB, including those responsible for both domestic and foreign operations, probably favored the invasion. First was the threat posed to the USSR's internal stability by a possible spillover of unrest into the USSR. This anxiety was shared by Soviet bureaucrats in charge of ideological supervision and by republic party leaders such as Shelest in the Ukraine. Second was the effect of Prague reformism on the Czechoslovak intelligence service. In spring 1968 a new reformist minister of interior, Gen. Josef Pavel, was appointed in Prague. Pavel attempted to reorganize the state security apparatus and purge it of pro-Soviet Stalinists, on whom the KGB relied for cooperation. Furthermore when the investigation of Jan Masaryk's death was reopened in May 1968, it had potentially serious ramifications for the Czechoslovak security police. All of this jeopardized the operations of the KGB in Czechoslovakia.[56]

Although Andropov himself did not participate directly in the high-level negotiations with Czechoslovak leaders that took place in the months preceding the invasion, he was, as noted earlier, probably consulted frequently. Furthermore the KGB, as the main provider of intelligence estimates to the leadership, was in a position to influence decision making by screening and interpreting the information. Considerable evidence shows that the KGB, in order to bolster the prointerventionist position, used intelligence and covert action to produce proof of counterrevolution in Czechoslovakia. Ladislav Bittman, who was serving in the Czechoslovak intelligence service at the time, observed:

The active role of the Soviet intelligence service in the events of 1968 and 1969 in Czechoslovakia centered on the systematic implementation of political provocation, disinformation and propaganda campaigns aimed at influencing Czechoslovak public opinion, terrorizing a selected group of liberals and creating supportive arguments for the legitimation of the Soviet invasion.[57]

As Valenta points out, the invasion of Czechoslovakia enabled the KGB to restore its mission and intelligence capabilities there and also removed a potential threat to KGB officials responsible for Soviet political security at home. The organizational interests of the KGB made themselves felt and no doubt influenced the Kremlin's decision to invade.[58] In this case the KGB probably exerted its main influence by virtue of its role as executor of policy and provider of information. However, as Andropov's personal authority grew, particularly after he gained full membership in the Politburo in 1973, the KGB's involvement in leadership decision making increased.

Much has been made in the West of Andropov's so-called liberalism.[59] While it is difficult to reconcile such an image with Andropov's advocacy of the Czechoslovak invasion and with KGB treatment of political dissenters under his leadership, public statements made by Andropov in the 1970s revealed strong support for Brezhnev's policy of détente. In a speech delivered in late 1973 Andropov noted enthusiastically: "Never before has the foreign policy of the Soviet Union been so effective or produced such splendid results within so short a time. . . . The entire foreign policy of our party has led to the fact that the international situation is now being shaped to a great extent under the influence of the peace initiative of the Soviet Union."[60] Andropov continued to hail détente and the relaxation of international tensions throughout the 1970s. His enthusiasm for this trend and his optimism about the future of East-West relations contrasted noticeably with the views expressed by certain Politburo colleagues such as Minister of Defense Ustinov and Ukrainian Party Chief Shcherbitskii.[61]

Andropov's views on détente also appeared to differ from those expressed by other KGB officials, in particular First Deputy Chairman Semen Tsvigun. Judging from his statements, Tsvigun took a dim view of the Kremlin's efforts to improve relations with the West. In 1972, the year in which these efforts began, Tsvigun was still writing about the lessons to be learned from Czechoslovakia: "The events of 1968 in Czechoslovakia unequivocally confirm that the aim of imperialist politics of 'building bridges' was in fact a preparation for the restoration of capitalism in socialist countries."[62] Tsvigun had nothing positive to say about the West throughout the 1970s and continued to warn about the evil intentions of the "imperialists." In a 1977 article on Dzerzhinskii, Tsvigun took the opportunity to note that despite Brezhnev's policy of détente, "the confrontation of the two socioeconomic systems remains the leading trend in the development of the world." Indeed, according to Tsvigun, détente was providing imperialists with new opportunities for subversion against the Soviet Union.[63]

It may seem peculiar that Tsvigun did not always agree with the policies of his mentor and close relative, Brezhnev, but his distaste for détente and his hard-line attitude are understandable in view of his overall responsibility for the KGB's domestic security functions. Détente made the job of Tsvigun and other KGB officials working on the domestic side more difficult. By stressing the dangers of détente and discussing the increased budgets of Western intelligence services, Tsvigun was probably also lobbying for more money and resources for the KGB.

Andropov, by contrast, took a broader view, incorporating both domestic and foreign policy concerns. While supporting such policies as the invasion of Czechoslovakia, he did not necessarily advocate a hard-line stance toward the West, particularly if it was accompanied by military interventionism and a stepped-up arms race. Not only does increased defense spending enhance the domestic influence of the Soviet military, it also places greater strains on the economy, draining more resources from the already weak consumer sector. Food shortages and other failures to meet consumer needs could eventually create political unrest, just as they did in Poland. It might be added that Andropov was one of the first to question the Soviet policy of open-ended military and economic assistance to Third World clients, presumably because of the deleterious effects on East-West relations and the growing economic burden it placed on the Soviet Union.[64]

Nonmilitary solutions are no doubt seen as preferable by those implementing KGB operations abroad, particularly where there are opportunities for exploiting social and political factors to the benefit of the Soviet Union. This gives the KGB greater influence over Soviet global strategy. An aggressive Soviet military posture makes the ideological struggle more difficult, as it is not easy for the KGB to exploit social and political tensions in the West and influence the course of "liberation movements" when the Soviet Union has the image of an aggressor.

The Soviet invasion of Afghanistan, for example, created obstacles for the KGB in implementing the campaign against NATO's INF deployment. Indeed Andropov's remarks in his 1980 RSFSR Supreme Soviet election speech indicate that he may have disagreed with the

Soviet decision to send a large-scale military force into Afghanistan, or at least that he was not happy about the result. He was the only Politburo member to express pessimism over the world situation after the invasion, noting that "it must be said frankly that there are real grounds for anxiety about the future and the destiny of détente and peace."[65] By contrast, Ustinov stated positively that "imperialism's opportunities for disposing of people's destinies as it sees fit have shrunk considerably. ... The relaxation of tension has become the dominant trend of world development."[66]

Other members of the KGB leadership may have viewed the Afghanistan invasion in a different light. In the opinion of most Western analysts there was little immediate threat to the USSR's internal stability from Muslim insurgency in Afghanistan in 1979.[67] Unlike the case of Czechoslovakia, where the spirit of reform threatened to spill over into the Ukraine and other Soviet republics, the likelihood of repercussions for Soviet Central Asia or the Caucasus from Muslim fundamentalism or Amin's nationalism was small. Nevertheless KGB officials on the domestic side, particularly those serving in areas near Afghanistan, may have favored the invasion because they worried about the long-term effects of the Muslim movement. Writing in the press a year later, Azerbaidzhan KGB Chief Iusif-Zade expressed such concern: "In view of the situation in Iran and Afghanistan, the U.S. special services are trying to exploit the Islamic religion, especially in areas where the Muslim population lives, as one factor influencing the political situation in our country."[68]

It is difficult to speculate on how KGB officials viewed the Polish crisis of 1980–1981. Andropov himself spoke very little on the problem. Presumably although they were gravely concerned about the possible political ramifications of events in Poland, they did not want to see the USSR resort to military intervention. Again, from the point of view of those dealing with KGB foreign operations, such intervention would have had negative consequences. In particular the USSR's international image would have declined precisely when the KGB, the International Department, and the International Information Department were working hard, by means of a vast propaganda and active measures campaign, to mobilize Western European public opinion against NATO's INF plans. Furthermore an invasion of Poland would have signified Soviet inability to curb political unrest there by peaceful means and thus would have enhanced the Soviet military's role in solving foreign policy problems.

As an expert on Eastern Europe, the head of the agency responsible for providing political intelligence on events in Poland, and a full member of the Politburo, Andropov no doubt greatly influenced the decision to refrain from military intervention in Poland—a decision that may even have run up against opposition from some of Brezhnev's marshals and generals.[69] The strategy of quelling disturbances in Poland by using internal Polish forces instead of Soviet troops meant an important role for the KGB in coordinating these efforts. The success of this strategy can, in part at least, be attributed to Andropov, whose political star began to rise in the Kremlin at this time.

While the internal political system has been in continuous flux since Brezhnev's death, Andropov's KGB successors have not faced foreign policy crises like those discussed earlier. This is fortuitous because neither Fedorchuk nor Chebrikov had foreign policy expertise when each took up his post. After twelve years of suppressing dissent in the Ukraine before assuming the KGB chairmanship, Fedorchuk was especially virulent in his criticisms of the West and evinced no favorable inclinations toward the idea of détente. Not surprisingly, when he served as KGB chairman in the Ukraine Fedorchuk had expressed grave concern about events in Poland and had been a strong advocate of the suppression of solidarity. In 1981 he declared: "Today the enemies of peace and socialism are linking their insidious designs with growing political and economic pressure on the socialist community; this can be clearly seen from the example of Poland." Fedorchuk went on to point out how events in Poland proved that "any kind of belittling of Marxist and Communist ideology, any mistake, shortcoming or violations of the economic laws of socialism and relaxation of ideological and political education of the masses backfires."[70] Such a highly orthodox and rigid approach no doubt made Fedorchuk an effective KGB chief in the Ukraine but hardly suited the demands of the job of chairman of the KGB.

Chebrikov's admission into the Politburo as a full member in April 1985 gave him a voice in foreign policy at the highest level. In addition, most Western experts believe that the KGB chairman serves on the Defense Council, an important collegial decision-making body that provides top-level coordination for defense-related activities of the Soviet government.[71] Given that he has served in the KGB for almost twenty years, it might be assumed that Chebrikov, like Andropov, represents the institutional interests of the KGB in this decision-making capacity. Although Chebrikov lacks Andropov's foreign policy expertise, his numerous trips to Eastern Europe since he became head of the KGB indicate that he is now very much involved in KGB operations beyond Soviet borders and is encouraging cooperative efforts with satellite intelligence agencies. Furthermore his forceful advocacy of Soviet "counter-propaganda" efforts abroad implies a commitment to a strong foreign policy role for the KGB.

Chebrikov made few public statements before he became chairman of the KGB in December 1982. In one article, which appeared in a Komsomol journal in 1981, Chebrikov expressed his concern about the Polish situation by mentioning the dangers of nationalist and separatist tendencies, as well as "revisionism," but in general was much less alarmist than Fedorchuk.[72] In his speeches and articles since taking over the KGB Chebrikov expressed concern about the internal political effects of the "communications revolution" and such Western technological innovations as videos and computers. His continual warnings about "ideological sabotage" suggest that he is not a strong advocate of expanding ties with the West. Furthermore, if we assume that Chebrikov's views influenced the handling of the Daniloff affair and the Mathias Rust case, which were under the investigative purview of the KGB, then it seems clear that he considers security concerns to be more important than smooth relations with the West.[73]

Chebrikov voiced considerable optimism about prospects for the 1985 Geneva summit between Reagan and Gorbachev. In his speech to commemorate the October Revolution in autumn 1985, Chebrikov noted,

> As is known, the Soviet-U.S. summit meeting in Geneva is due to be held very soon. The CPSU Central Committee and the government of the USSR attach great importance to it and are doing everything to ensure that it yields tangible results. We believe that if political courage is manifested and if we meet each other halfway it will still be possible to put a lot of things right.[74]

His more recent comments, however, have been more negative. In particular, his speech on 11 September 1987 suggested that he is opposed to Gorbachev's arms control initiatives.[75]

Chebrikov and his colleagues may welcome the arms control process as a means of curbing military spending, but they may be uneasy about the thorny problem of verification of arms control agreements. Considering that the KGB is responsible for protecting nuclear secrets, its officials probably do not welcome the idea of allowing Western representatives access to Soviet defense installations. In a speech delivered in 1984, for example, Chebrikov accused the United States of making an artificial issue out of verification as a means of dragging out negotiations.[76]

What will be the future impact of the KGB on foreign policy? Given the Kremlin's apparent inclination to avoid high-risk military intervention as a means of furthering its international objectives, a greater emphasis has been placed on diplomacy and active measures in recent years. This trend, which has resulted in a significant expansion of KGB operations abroad, is likely to continue even if the Soviet Union reduces support for new radical movements in the Third World. There is every indication that the Gorbachev leadership, while curtailing the more repressive internal functions of the KGB, will depend heavily on the foreign activities of this institution.

The conduct of foreign policy under Gorbachev has revealed more tactical flexibility and pragmatism than that of the Brezhnev era. Gorbachev has assembled a forward-looking national security team that places strong emphasis on public relations and dynamic approaches to international problems.[77] Despite the apparent discrepancies between the views of Chebrikov and Gorbachev, the KGB's foreign intelligence officers, who represent a sophisticated, well-educated elite, should fit well into this mold and provide useful expertise to further Soviet objectives abroad. Indeed, for a long time KGB officials have worked closely with the International Department and "think tanks" such as the Institute on the United States and Canada, which are said to be taking a greater role in foreign policy decision making. Andropov himself was reportedly on close terms with officials such as Georgii Arbatov and Aleksandr Bovin, who have emerged as influential figures in the foreign policy realm. We can probably assume that Andropov's protégés who remain in the KGB, V. A. Kriuchkov in particular, have retained this connection. Thus whatever the personal authority of the KGB chairman at any given time, as a provider of information and an executor of policy the KGB will continue to have a strong impact on foreign policy.

Notes

1. George Leggett, *The Cheka: Lenin's Political Police* (Oxford: Clarendon Press, 1981), pp. 231–232, 298–299; *Soviet Intelligence and Counterintelligence* (Washington, D.C.: Foreign Documents Branch, Central Intelligence Group, no. 84, 31 July 1947; declassified 6/10/83), pp. 1–10.

2. *Espionage Activities of the USSR* (Ms. No. P-137, Historical Division, Headquarters U.S. Army Europe, 1952).

3. Ibid.; Simon Wolin and Robert Slusser, eds., *The Soviet Secret Police* (New York: Praeger, 1957), pp. 138–142.

4. Wolin and Slusser, *Soviet Secret Police*, pp. 25–26; Robert Conquest, *The Soviet Police System* (New York: Praeger, 1968), p. 91.

5. John Barron, *KGB Today: The Hidden Hand* (New York: Readers Digest Press,

1983), pp. 444–449. Also see Cord Meyer, *Facing Reality: From World Federalism to the C.I.A.* (New York: Harper & Row, 1980), pp. 315–329.

6. For further details on Kriuchkov see chapter 4, pp. 122–123.

7. John Barron, *The KGB: Secret Work of Soviet Secret Agents* (New York: Bantam Books, 1974), pp. 113–117.

8. As cited in Ladislav Bittman, *The KGB and Soviet Disinformation: An Insider's View* (Washington, N.Y.: Pergamon-Brassey's, 1985), p. 25.

9. Ibid., pp. 25–27; *The Washington Post*, 25 April 1983, p. 20.

10. Arkady N. Shevchenko, *Breaking with Moscow* (New York: Ballantine, 1985), p. 315. Apparently it was not so easy for the KGB to recruit well-educated personnel for its foreign operations in the late 1950s. First, there was a dearth of graduates with foreign language training, and second, the disclosures about the security police after Stalin's death did significant damage to its image. Later, however, the number of students at Moscow's foreign language and area studies programs expanded and more students from worker and peasant families were admitted, which alleviated the KGB's recruitment problem. In addition, the KGB's professional image began to improve significantly. See a paper prepared by a Soviet foreign language graduate and Intourist guide who defected in 1974: "KGB Procedures and Problems in Recruiting Foreign Language Personnel," *Radio Liberty Background Report*, no. 1-75, 20 January 1975.

11. See Rose E. Gottemoeller and Paul F. Langer, *Foreign Area Studies in the USSR: Training and Employment of Specialists* (Santa Monica, Calif.: Rand Corp., 1983), pp. 47, 98–101.

12. Bittman, *The KGB and Soviet Disinformation*, p. 15.

13. Nicolas Polianski, *M.I.D. 12 ans dans les services diplomatiques du Kremlin* (Paris: Pierre Belfond, 1984), p. 106. This impression is not universally held, however. Shevchenko characterized the KGB *rezident* in New York during the 1970s, Boris Solomatin, as "cynical, boorish and a drunk." Shevchenko, *Breaking with Moscow*, p. 57.

14. According to Polianski, for example, KGB officers receive salaries that are one and a half to two times higher than those for corresponding ranks in other ministries. *M.I.D.*, p. 308.

15. Shevchenko, *Breaking with Moscow*, pp. 325–326.

16. Barron, *KGB Today*, pp. 446–447. In his earlier book (*KGB: Secret Work*, pp. 107–109) Barron stated that Service I distributed raw intelligence to party leaders but provided no analysis. Presumably on the basis of new information such as the testimony of Stanislav Levchenko, Barron's more recent book states that Service I does in fact analyze and interpret the intelligence and only sends the occasional report in raw form to the Politburo.

17. *Soviet Acquisition of Militarily Significant Western Technology: An Update*, (Washington, D.C., September 1985), p. 1.

18. Ibid., p. 16. Also see Philip Hansen, "Soviet Industrial Espionage," *Bulletin of the Atomic Scientists* 43 (April 1987):25–29.

19. Robert W. Campbell, "Satellite Communications in the USSR," *Soviet Economy* 1, no. 4 (October–December 1985):330.

20. Among the Western open-source publications on this subject are U.S. Congress, House Permanent Select Committee on Intelligence, *Soviet Covert Action (The Forgery Offensive)* (Washington, D.C.: U.S. Government Printing Office, 1980); U.S. Congress, House Permanent Select Committee on Intelligence, *Soviet Active Measures* (Washington, D.C.: U.S. Government Printing Office, 1982); U.S. State Department Special Report No. 110, *Soviet Active Measures* (September 1983); Richard H. Shultz and Roy Godson, *Dezinformatsia. Active Measures in Soviet Strategy* (Washington, N.Y.: Pergamon-Brassey's, 1984); Bittman, *The KGB and Soviet Disinformation*; and Brian D. Dailey and Patrick J. Parker, eds., *Soviet Strategic Deception* (Stanford, Calif.: Hoover Institution Press, 1987).

21. U.S. Congress, *Soviet Covert Action*, p. 63.

22. Ibid., p. 66.

23. Ibid., pp. 79–81; U.S. Department of State, "The World Peace Council's Peace

Assemblies," *Foreign Affairs Note*, May 1983; U.S. Department of State, "World Federation of Trade Unions: Soviet Foreign Policy Tool," *Foreign Affairs Note*, August 1983.

24. See U.S. Senate Committee on the Judiciary, Subcommittee on Security and Terrorism, *Terrorism: The Role of Moscow and Its Subcontractors* (Washington, D.C.: U.S. Government Printing Office, 1982); "Patterns of International Terrorism: 1980" (CIA Research Paper, June 1981); U.S. Department of State, "Patterns of Global Terrorism: 1984," November 1985.

25. Bittman, *The KGB and Soviet Disinformation*, pp. 140–143; U.S. Congress, *Soviet Covert Action*, pp. 85–86.

26. See Francis Fukuyama, "Gorbachev and the Third World," *Foreign Affairs* (Spring 1986):715–731. As Fukuyama points out, it was Andropov who first began questioning the expediency of extensive Soviet activities in the Third World. See the discussion later in this chapter.

27. Bittman, *The KGB and Soviet Disinformation*, p. 29.

28. Ladislav Bittman, *The Deception Game: Czechoslovak Intelligence in Soviet Political Warfare* (Syracuse, N.Y.: Syracuse University Research Corp., 1972), pp. 16–17. For a general discussion of the satellite intelligence services see Jeffrey T. Richelson, *Sword and Shield: Soviet Intelligence and Security Apparatus* (Cambridge, Mass.: Ballinger, 1986), pp. 205–208.

29. Barron, *KGB Today*, p. 449.

30. Chebrikov, "Sverias s Leninym, rukovodstvuias trebovaniem partii," *Kommunist*, no. 9 (June 1985), pp. 52–53.

31. In May 1983 it was reported that Chebrikov flew to Bulgaria, which naturally aroused further speculation about the KGB connection with the assassination attempt on the pope (see *Pravda*, 19 May 1983, p. 4). He was reported as visiting Warsaw in late November 1983 (*Izvestiia*, 26 November 1983, p. 4), and in May 1984 his visit to East Germany was announced (*Pravda*, 23 May 1984, p. 4). More recently he visited Hungary in April 1986, Yugoslavia in December 1986, and Cuba in April 1987. See *FBIS. Daily Report, Soviet Union* 3, no. 078 (23 April 1986): F3; *Izvestiia*, 6 December 1986, p. 4; and *Pravda*, 5 April 1987, p. 4.

32. See Leonard Schapiro, "The International Department of the CPSU: Key to Soviet Policy," *International Journal* 32 (Winter 1976–77):41–55; Robert W. Kitrinos, "International Department of the CPSU," *POC* 33 (September–October 1984):59–69; and Lilita Dzirkals, Thane Gustafson, and A. Ross Johnson, *The Media and Intra-Elite Communication in the USSR* (Santa Monica, Calif.: Rand Corp., 1982), pp. 20–23.

33. See Shultz and Godson, *Dezinformatsia*, pp. 21–31; Dzirkals et al., *The Media and Intra-Elite Communication*, p. 23.

34. Alex R. Alexiev, "The Soviet Campaign against INF: Strategy, Tactics and Means," *ORBIS* 29, no. 2 (Summer 1985):319–350. Also see Wynfred Joshua, "Soviet Manipulation of the European Peace Movement," *Strategic Review* 11, no. 1 (Winter 1983): 9–18; and *Soviet Covert Action*, pp. 70–75.

35. Alexiev, "The Soviet Campaign against INF," pp. 348–349.

36. Jiri Valenta, *Soviet Intervention in Czechoslovakia, 1968: Anatomy of a Decision* (Baltimore and London: Johns Hopkins University Press, 1979).

37. Ibid., p. 5.

38. Hannes Adomeit, "Consensus versus Conflict: The Dimension of Foreign Policy," in *The Domestic Context of Soviet Foreign Policy*, ed. Seweryn Bialer (Boulder, Colo.: Westview Press, 1981), pp. 49–86 (quotation, p. 49). Also see Hannes Adomeit, *Soviet Risk-Taking and Crisis Behavior: A Theoretical and Empirical Analysis* (London: Allen & Unwin, 1982).

39. Adomeit, "Consensus versus Conflict," p. 72.

40. See Slusser's articles on Shelepin and Semichastnyi in George W. Simmonds, ed., *Soviet Leaders* (New York: Thomas Y. Crowell, 1967); and Slusser, "America, China and the Hydra-Headed Opposition," in *Soviet Policy-Making: Studies of Communism in Transition*, ed. Peter H. Juviler and Henry W. Morton (London: Pall Mall Press, 1967).

41. For a firsthand account of this incident see Barghoorn, "The Soviet Security

Police," in *Interest Groups in Soviet Politics*, ed. H. Gordon Skilling and Franklyn Griffiths (Princeton, N.J.: Princeton University Press 1971).

42. Barron, *KGB: Secret Work*, pp. 10–11; Slusser, "America, China and the Hydra-Headed Opposition," p. 259.

43. Alexander Dallin placed Shelepin in the camp of the "action-oriented, know nothing, anti-Western, anti-intellectual elements." See Alexander Dallin, "The Domestic Sources of Soviet Foreign Policy," in Bialer, *The Domestic Context of Soviet Foreign Policy*, pp. 335–408.

44. See *Der Spiegel*, 4 December 1967, pp. 162–164; Jacques Derogy and Hesi Carmel, *The Untold History of Israel* (New York: Grove Press, 1979), pp. 208–220; and Barron, *KGB: Secret Work*, pp. 11–12.

45. Galia Golan, "Soviet Decisionmaking in the Yom Kippur War," in *Soviet Decisionmaking for National Security*, ed. Jiri Valenta and William C. Potter (London: Allen & Unwin, 1984), pp. 185–217 (quotation, p. 194).

46. Derogy and Carmel, *Untold History of Israel*, pp. 294–295.

47. Ibid., pp. 296–297.

48. See Valenta, "Soviet Decisionmaking and the Czechoslovak Crisis of 1968," *Studies in Comparative Communism* 8, nos. 1–2 (Spring-Summer 1975):155–156.

49. Valenta, *Soviet Intervention in Czechoslovakia*, p. 10.

50. Ibid., pp. 10–11, 58–63.

51. Karen Dawisha, in her study entitled *The Kremlin and the Prague Spring* (Berkeley, Los Angeles, London: University of California Press, 1984) concluded that because Andropov was silent in pubic about Czechoslovakia and absent from negotiations, the KGB had little influence over the decision to invade (pp. 361–362), but the evidence discussed below counters this impression.

52. *Pravda*, 21 December 1967, p. 3.

53. See his 23 October 1968 speech, reprinted in Iv. V. Andropov, *Izbrannye rechi i stat'ei* (Moscow: Politizdat, 1983), pp. 120–125 (quotation, p. 121).

54. A. Malygin, "V bitve idei net kompromisov," *Molodoi Kommunist*, no. 1, 1969, pp. 49–62.

55. V. V. Fedorchuk and S. A. Stepanov, "Otravlennoe oruzhie imperialistov," *Vestnik protivovozdushnoi oborony*, no. 2 (1969):86–89.

56. Valenta, *Soviet Intervention in Czechoslovakia*, p. 23; Bittman, *The Deception Game*, pp. 186–190; Josef Frolik, *The Frolik Defection* (London: Leo Cooper, 1975), pp. 147–152; and Dawisha, *Kremlin and the Prague Spring*, pp. 52–54.

57. Bittman, *The Deception Game*, pp. 187–196.

58. Valenta, *Soviet Intervention in Czechoslovakia*, p. 107.

59. The first suggestion that Andropov was a "liberal" came from a former CC adviser and member of the USSR Academy of Sciences, Boris Rabbot. See *New York Times Magazine*, 6 November 1977, p. 3.

60. From an Estonian Radio broadcast on 27 December 1973, translated in *FBIS. Daily Report, Soviet Union*, 3 (2 January 1974):R6.

61. See, for example, Andropov, *Izbrannye rechi i stat'ei*, pp. 119–134, 135–149. Also see A. Knight, "The Powers of the Soviet KGB," *Survey* 25, no. 3 (112) (Summer 1980): 150–151.

62. Tsvigun, "Ideologicheskaia diversiia orudie imperialisticheskoi reactsii," *Kommunist*, no. 5 (March 1972) p. 110.

63. S. Tsvigun, "Nash Feliks," *Znamia*, no. 12 (1977):199–211 (quotation, p. 210).

64. On this point see Fukuyama, "Gorbachev and the Third World." Fukuyama notes that "Andropov was the first senior political leader to revive the dictum of Lenin and Khrushchev that the Soviet Union's chief influence in the world revolutionary movement comes about less through direct economic assistance than as a result of the force of its example as a socialist society" (p. 719).

65. *Pravda*, 12 February 1980, p. 2.

66. *Pravda*, 14 February 1980, p. 2.

67. See, for example, Jiri Valenta, "Decisionmaking in Afghanistan, 1979," in Valenta and Potter, *Soviet Decisionmaking*, pp. 218–236.

68. *Bakiinskii rabochii*, 19 December 1980, p. 3.

69. On the role of the Soviet high command in the Polish crisis and their efforts to push for military intervention, see Richard D. Anderson, Jr., "Soviet Decision-making and Poland," *POC* 31, no. 2 (March-April 1982):22–36.

70. From an article in the Ukrainian journal *Pid praporom leninizmu*, no. 19 (October 1981):10–17. As quoted in Roman Solchanyk, "Ukrainian KGB Chief Warns of Ideological Sabotage," *RLRB*, RL 422/81, 22 October 1981.

71. On the defense council see Ellen Jones, *Red Army and Society: A Sociology of the Soviet Military* (Winchester, Mass.: Allen & Unwin, 1985), pp. 6–10; and Jan Sejna and Joseph D. Douglass, Jr., *Decision-making in Communist Countries: An Inside View* (Cambridge, Mass., and Washington, D.C.: Institution for Foreign Policy Analysis, 1986), pp. 30–39.

72. V. M. Chebrikov, "Vigilance—A Well-Tried Weapon," *Molodoi Kommunist*, no. 4 (April 1981):28–34. Translated in *FBIS. Daily Report, Soviet Union* 3 (11 June 1981), USSR Annex. Sidney Ploss, in his study of the Polish crisis, concludes from statements such as those by Fedorchuk and Chebrikov that the KGB as an institution favored military intervention. See Sidney I. Ploss, *Moscow and the Polish Crisis: An Interpretation of Soviet Policies and Intentions* (Boulder, Colo., and London: Westview Press, 1986), pp. 94–95. There is no indication, however, that Andropov, as KGB chief, advocated military intervention.

73. Rust was tried in Moscow in early September 1987 and received a sentence of four years in a general regime labor camp under Articles 83 (unlawful entry into the Soviet Union), 84 (violation of rules of international flights), and 206 (hooliganism) of the RSFSR Criminal Code.

74. *Pravda*, 7 November 1985, p. 2.

75. *Pravda*, 11 September 1987, p. 3. Chebrikov made a pointed reference to the opposition of Dzerzhinskii, the first Soviet security chief, to the treaty of Brest-Litovsk in 1918, and later noted that many of Dzerzhinskii's assessments "sound topical today." Furthermore, he went out of his way to stress that the West was attempting to use democratization in the Soviet Union for its own subversive goals.

76. See his speech delivered in honor of the fortieth anniversary of the "liberation" of Estonia, printed in *Sovetskaia estoniia*, 23 September 1984, pp. 2–3.

77. For a good overview of Gorbachev's foreign policy see Roderic Lyne, "Making Waves: Mr. Gorbachev's Public Diplomacy, 1985–6," *International Affairs* 63, no. 2 (Spring 1987):205–224.

10
Conclusion

The various models and theories that Western scholars have offered to explain the Soviet system present a contradictory picture of the KGB's political role. It has been variously referred to as "the party's obedient instrument," a "national security bureaucracy," and one of "the pillars of the Soviet system." The Soviet regime itself has been portrayed in terms ranging from "pluralistic" and "oligarchic" to Seweryn Bialer's recent description: "an authoritative and intimidating police state."[1] This apparent lack of consensus on the role definition of the political police can be explained partly by the fact that little academic research has been devoted to the KGB and partly by the changes that the Soviet system has undergone since the Stalin era. Now, with Gorbachev attempting to introduce substantial reforms, it is especially important to identify the underlying factors that determine the KGB's role and affect its powers. Thus the primary aim of this study has been to provide a conceptual framework for understanding the KGB as a political institution by describing its activities and assessing its influence.

This conceptual framework hinges on three closely related issues. First is the question of the KGB's basic purpose as determined by the Soviet leadership. What are the key functions carried out by the KGB on behalf of the regime, and what continuities can be observed as these functions have evolved? The second issue concerns the KGB's institutional identity: to what extent does the KGB act as a organization with its own point of view and distinct interests? Do KGB officials perceive themselves first and foremost as representatives of the party or as security policemen? Finally, there is the question of the KGB's power. Does the KGB have any power in its own right, or is it simply a "loyal arm of the party," as Soviet officials claim? What factors have an impact on the KGB's authority in relation to other political institutions, the party in particular?

The most effective way to address these issues has been by considering them in historical perspective. The security police has a long tradition in Russian and Soviet history, which sheds much light on its operations today. The political police, tsarist and Soviet, has always been the ultimate symbol of repression, and the degree of repression at any given time has been a useful gauge for measuring the apparent powers of the police. As this study has stressed, the tsarist political police, while intrusive and unscrupulous, was not that efficient in its attempts to stem the tide of the revolutionary movement. The Soviet political police more than made up for the failings of its predecessors, gradually evolving into one of the most ruthless police systems in the world. What made the Vecheka so effective was that it was established for the sole purpose of buttressing a regime that lacked any popular support for its rule. The Russian monarchy, even as it became discredited in the eyes of the people, always had a certain legitimacy based on the autocratic tradition and the Orthodox Church. The Bolsheviks had no legitimacy whatsoever and were threatened on all sides by opposition. It was thus essential to the Bolsheviks' survival that the political police have unrestrained coercive powers over the population.

As was seen in the discussion of the Stalin period, the political police evolved into an institution that went far beyond what Lenin could have imagined in the terror it inflicted on Soviet society. But in looking for the roots of this terror we are brought back to Lenin and his failure to establish any formal, institutionalized party, or state controls on the police. He relied on personal relationships to maintain party authority, and whatever the facade of legality, there were always enough loopholes in the law to enable the political police to act in an arbitrary manner in suppressing political discontent. In a sense, therefore, the vast powers of the NKVD/NKGB acquired subsequently were really a matter of degree because they did not signify an essential change in the basic purpose of the political police as it had existed under Lenin: to ensure society's compliance with the demands of a regime that was illegitimate. The difference under Stalin was that the party leadership eventually turned against itself and drew the political police into its factional disputes. This made individual members of the regime vulnerable to the very terror they had allowed the police to inflict on opposition that existed outside the party.

The disavowal of terror by the post-Stalin leadership deprived the police of a key weapon. It also meant that members of the political elite no longer faced violent police reprisals for voicing dissenting views, which placed a distinct limit on the power of the party leader. Furthermore, of course, the population at large could express disagreements with the regime without being shot. While these reforms resulted in a distinctly more open society, with fewer restrictions on communications and artistic expression, the pendulum began to swing back toward Stalinism by the mid-1960s, when the regime enlisted the KGB to crack down on public dissent. Not surprisingly, this development was accompanied by a noticeable increase in the public stature of the political police—a trend that continued throughout the Brezhnev era.

Why did such a reversal occur? The answer lies in the fact that the Khrushchev leadership, while collectively placing a taboo on terror and making numerous legal changes to reduce the powers of the political police, did not place definite limits on the KGB's authority to persecute dissenters. As before the loopholes in the law remained, and the KGB was gradually encouraged to flout the legal norms whenever the party leadership deemed it politically expedient. The 1954 statute supposedly governing the KGB by setting forth its tasks and the parameters of its authority remains unpublished to this day; and the party has never clarified the question of how it exercises control over the police. Thus it is not surprising that the apparent powers of the political police would wax and wane with changes in the Kremlin policy.

There can be little doubt that the dismantlement of Beria's vast police apparatus in 1953, accompanied by the reforms of the legal codes and the process of de-Stalinization, seriously damaged both the collective morale and the public prestige of the political police. Yet as this study has shown, the post-Stalin purge of the police apparatus affected mainly its top layers and did not extend to the rank-and-file personnel. Many of the younger Stalinist police officers remained in their posts and rose in the hierarchy to leading KGB positions during the 1960s and 1970s. Furthermore the party leadership has not replenished the ranks of the KGB with party officials on an extensive, consistent basis. Except at the very highest levels outsiders have rarely been brought into the KGB, and its employees have developed experience and expertise through security of tenure. With the increasing public prestige accorded to them, KGB employees have developed a strong sense of professionalism and esprit de corps. Thus like the military, the KGB has become a closed, highly specialized bureaucracy whose personnel (with the exception of possible cleavages between domestic and foreign cadres) share homogeneity of background and career experience. No evidence has yet emerged that Gorbachev has tried to undermine this professionalism by bringing in large numbers of party apparatchiki to serve in the KGB.

Some have argued that such institutional cohesion, which might invite parochialism, has been offset by the practice of appointing party officials to the KGB chairmanship. Just as Lenin depended on Dzerzhinskii, the loyal party man, to ensure that the Cheka would act in the party's interests, recent Kremlin leaders have appointed trusted apparatchiki such as Andropov and Chebrikov to control the KGB. Yet although both were party men when they joined the KGB, we cannot assume that they did not come to to identify more with the institution they headed than with the party. As Barrington Moore observed, "In general, there is a tendency for the Party man to be absorbed by the organization in which he works. This happens because he faces the choice of doing a good job within or for the organization, or remaining ineffective as a man of words."[2] That Andropov probably developed a certain amount of loyalty to the KGB while serving as its chief for fifteen years is attested to by the fact that his tenure there led to a marked increase in the KGB's professionalism, effectiveness, and political status. Although it is still too early to assess Chebrikov's influence on the KGB, can we really consider him first and foremost a party man after he has been a leading KGB official for almost twenty years?

This question is of crucial importance because of the vague, ad hoc nature of other means of party control over the political police. As Soviet sources attest, the KGB is a rigidly hierarchical structure with strong centralized management. It is doubtful that local party officials enjoy significant authority over the KGB; even republic party leaders appear to have little direct control over republic KGB organs. This brings us to the central party apparatus in Moscow. Our examination of the Administrative Organs Department of the CPSU Secretariat, which is the only secretarial department concerned with police affairs, has not yielded sufficient evidence to conclude that this body exercises strong controls over the KGB. Although the AO Department takes part in the formulation of legislation affecting the KGB and possibly vets certain KGB personnel appointments, there is no indication that it involves itself with KGB operations or issues directives to the KGB. Presumably, then, the real controls over the KGB are exercised by the Politburo.

Politburo membership, however, is not restricted to representatives from the party apparatus but often includes those from other Soviet institutions, such as the Ministry of Foreign Affairs, the economic apparatus, the Ministry of Defense (from 1973 to 1984), and the KGB. Some scholars do not even consider the Politburo to represent the highest organization of the party. According to Dmitri Simes, for example, the Secretariat is the leading party body and the Politburo is the "top executive-legislative committee of the Soviet elite as a whole, not just that of the party apparatus."[3] While this contention is arguable, the important point is that the KGB executes Politburo decisions and is subjected to Politburo authority, but it is also represented on this body and hence is integrated into the decision-making process. The fact that KGB officials are now serving in leading party organizations at all levels in the CPSU from the republic down suggests that this process of integration has been implemented throughout the system.

It has been suggested that nonparty institutions such as the KGB may not necessarily be in conflict with the party over important issues. Karen Dawisha, in her criticism of the bureaucratic politics model of the Soviet Union, argued that although there may be conflicting views among members of the leadership, the stands taken by individuals are not necessarily determined by the institutions they represent or the positions they hold.[4] Adherence to a common ideology, Dawisha notes, promotes consensus among Soviet leaders. This argument may have some validity as it applies to the KGB, particularly in view of the fact that party leaders from Brezhnev onward have gone out of their way to accommodate the needs and interests of the security police. By all accounts the latter enjoys a privileged status in Soviet society: excellent pay, substantial perquisites, security of tenure and favorable publicity in the press. (Since July 1984 over 250 books have been published to commemorate the upcoming seventieth anniversary of the Security police.[5]) Thus on the face of things the KGB has had, until recently, little cause to enter into conflict with the party. Furthermore party leaders have at times cultivated bases of support within the KGB, which may have led to some inter-KGB factionalism and thereby reduced the tendency to act as a united institution.

Yet in examining the question of power we need not necessarily look for observable conflict within the leadership and try to establish who or what institution prevails in decision making. Power can be exercised in other, less overt ways—by means of influence or subtle forms of manipulation. One political theorist, Stephen Lukes, has suggested that power can involve "control over the agenda of politics and of the ways in which potential issues are kept out of the political process."[6] As the purveyor of information to the Kremlin on all sorts of domestic and foreign issues, the KGB is clearly in a position to influence the policy agenda. Indeed, this study has offered evidence that in supplying information to the Kremlin, the KGB has had an impact on some high-level decisions. Furthermore a good case can be made to show that the KGB has affected policy as an executor of Kremlin directives, largely because of the degree of autonomy it has enjoyed in carrying out its tasks. As Alexander Dallin observed, "in general, the concern among Western scholars with the decision-making process may well have contributed to a neglect of the extent to which a policy can be subverted in the process of its implementation."[7]

Even if we assume that Chebrikov agrees with most policies decided in the Kremlin (which is doubtful), it is difficult to accept that other KGB officials do not have views that are determined by their institutional affiliations, the nature of the tasks they perform, and their interactions with members of other institutions. The antagonism that exists between KGB and GRU officers abroad, for example, as well as tensions caused by the presence of the KGB's Special Departments in the armed forces may well create animosity between the KGB and the military. Jurisdictional competition probably also arises between the KGB and other organizations, such as the Ministry of Foreign Affairs and the Ministry of Internal Affairs. In addition to possible disagreements over policy, MFA officials resent the KGB's extensive surveillance of their diplomats and its use of MFA employees abroad for intelligence gathering. The fact that the KGB is free to intervene in MVD cases and to enlist its cooperation at any time provokes considerable resentment within the MVD, which is no doubt aggravated further by KGB members' higher pay and more privileged status.

These antagonisms may well contribute to institutional parochialism within the KGB at higher levels, where policies can be subverted by decisions made about the type of information to be released or about the way in which policy directives are carried out. In sum, although KGB officials no doubt share common values and goals with officials from the party and other institutions, they also have their own views on certain issues, such as defense spending, détente, or criminal policy.

What, then, are the KGB's assets as a political institution with its own interests to promote? Again, looking at events from a historical perspective, we see that the political police weathered the vicissitudes of Khrushchev's reforms and de-Stalinization by accommodating itself to changing circumstances. Terror was no longer available as a weapon, but, largely thanks to Andropov's astute leadership, the KGB developed techniques to ensure political stability at home that were just as effective as those used by its Stalinist predecessors. To put it simply, the political police moved from coercion to manipulation.

KGB officials have become more sophisticated, employing subtler psychological techniques to subdue manifestations of political dissent and increasing their role in the political socialization process. Although coercion is still used, the KGB operates under the guise of socialist legality and has sought to *prevent* dissent occurring rather than to punish it. KGB foreign activities have reflected this change in method with a growing emphasis on propaganda and "public relations" on behalf of the USSR. In a sense such stress on manipulation rather than on coercion, which involves a keen awareness of both the Kremlin's image and that of the KGB specifically, confers an even greater authority on the KGB. As Stephen Lukes observed, "is it not the supreme and most insidious exercise of power to prevent people, to whatever degree, from having grievances by shaping their perceptions, cognitions, and preferences in such a way that they accept their role in the existing order of things?"[8]

To be sure, the KGB has not been so successful in its propaganda that it is perceived by all Soviet citizens as a benevolent institution. As Soviet emigrés have indicated, political compliance on the part of many people is often ensured by the *fear* of KGB coercion. But this is still in the realm of prophylaxis rather than punishment. The widely held perception of the KGB as an efficient organization and the fact that political dissent has been confined to such a small minority of the population without the use of terror attests to the KGB's effectiveness. It might be added that the KGB has, by and large, proved to be highly dependable as a defender of the regime's interests. There have, of course, been defections by KGB foreign intelligence officers, but there is only one known case of a domestic KGB officer turning against his employer.[9]

Another asset for the KGB has been its involvement in the campaign against official corruption. Our discussion of Andropov's accession to the party leadership and the subsequent succession struggles after his death have demonstrated how potent a weapon KGB information on official malfeasance can be. Not only Andropov but also Gorbachev relied on the KGB for help in purging opponents on charges of corruption.

Both of these assets, however, are contingent on the regime's monopoly over communications. Political socialization and propaganda begin to lose their effectiveness when controls on the media are relaxed to permit the expression of alternative viewpoints; and the use of politically damaging information against officials becomes more difficult when channels of communication are opened.

[311]

Gorbachev's policy of *glasnost'* threatens to undercut this monopoly, as well as to make the KGB itself vulnerable to public criticism. Yet "openness" has not been extended to sensitive political topics or to criticism of the Communist party. Indeed, with a few exceptions, such as the exposure of the scandal involving the KGB, this process has gone no further than it did under Khrushchev and could be curtailed at any time if a new leader were to take power.

Another factor that has contributed to the KGB's powers has been its broad prerogatives to persecute dissent both legally and extralegally. Changes in the laws have been gradually introduced since the early 1960s to give the KGB more latitude as an investigatory organ while at the same time the party has allowed the KGB to circumvent the laws completely in many cases. Again, Gorbachev's proposed legal reforms may diminish this asset. But it is highly unlikely that the legal loopholes will be eliminated altogether. This would be inconsistent with the basic purpose of the political police as it has existed since 1917: to ensure the political, economic, and social domination of the Communist party. As Leonard Schapiro observed, the law has been and always will be "the acid test of a free society."[10] In the case of the Soviet Union, whatever legal constraints are placed on the security police is not for the Soviet people to decide. The extent and nature of these constraints will be determined by the party leadership, whose preservation still depends on the KGB.

Other considerations might also inhibit Gorbachev and his colleagues in their efforts to limit the powers of the KGB. There are, for example, considerable risks associated with the program of economic decentralization that is being implemented. Indeed the party may have a difficult time maintaining its political control while at the same time promoting economic freedom. This might lead in the longer term to more reliance on the KGB to ensure that the stimulus of economic reform does not get out of hand. It is worth recalling that during the period of the New Economic Policy in the 1920s the party increased its dependence on the political police and broadened police powers. A similar point might be made with regard to *glasnost'*. If this process were to gain momentum of its own, going beyond the limits that the regime can tolerate without being politically threatened, then the KGB would presumably be enlisted to crack down on the excesses. Also important is the technological revolution in communications and the use of personal computers and videocassettes, which offer Soviet citizens an alternative means of transmitting information and ideas. While this presents a serious challenge to the KGB, it could also mean that its services will be seen by the regime as essential to countering this threat.

This brings us to one of the most significant assets of the KGB—the fact that it combines both domestic security functions and those of intelligence and counterintelligence. The KGB is a key institution for furthering Soviet foreign policy objectives abroad and protecting the state from subversive activities by foreign governments. Unlike Western democracies, the Soviet Union has never distinguished clearly between external and internal enemies, which is probably why, for example, the KGB's military counterintelligence functions include extensive political surveillance of the armed forces. The traditional view that domestic political discontent is foreign-inspired has served as an ideological justification for a strong internal police apparatus and an obstacle to those who seek to extend individual rights. This may be what Sakharov meant when he warned a group of American officials visiting the Soviet Union in spring 1987 to remember that the Soviet Union was a "multilayered, contradictory" society. According to one member of the group, "we heard of one such contradiction while we were in the USSR, when a request to allow Naum Meiman, a refusnik, to visit his dying wife in Washington was turned down. We were told this eighty-year-old man might still have state security secrets, even though he had not been exposed to such secrets for over thirty years. His wife died without seeing her husband."[11]

In the final analysis, then, Gorbachev is not presiding over a full-scale "police state," but the KGB clearly has power and authority in its own right. The security police may have to modify its methods and curtail its repressive activities in deference to larger goals that party leaders such as Gorbachev are pursuing, but few members of the *nomenklatura* that runs the country would ever question the need for its existence. The latter are well aware that their own positions depend on the internal political stability that is preserved by the KGB. It is, of course, highly unlikely that the KGB would ever become powerful enough to seriously threaten the interests of the party, particularly if Gorbachev's reforms prove successful. At the same time, however, Gorbachev's policies have aroused considerable opposition by established interests. Not only the KGB and entrenched party and state bureaucrats but also members of the military establishment probably have good reason to feel threatened by the proposed changes. Judging from the precedent of Khrushchev, it is always possible that Gorbachev's political opponents would appeal to the KGB and the military for support in challenging him. Or perhaps Gorbachev's own awareness of this possibility will eventually cause him to slow the pace of his reforms. Whatever the case may be, Soviet leaders will continue to face the

[313]

difficult challenge of reconciling the interests of political security with pressures for reform.

Notes

1. Seweryn Bialer, *The Soviet Paradox: External Expansion, Internal Decline* (New York: Alfred A. Knopf, 1986), p. 20.

2. Barrington Moore, Jr., *Terror and Progress USSR. Some Sources of Change and Stability in the Soviet Dictatorship* (Cambridge, Mass.: Harvard University Press, 1954), p. 27.

3. Dmitri K. Simes, "The Military and Militarism in Soviet Society," *International Security* 6, no. 3 (Winter 1981–1982):123–143 (quotation, p. 133).

4. Karen Dawisha, "The Limits of the Bureaucratic Model: Observations on the Soviet Case," *Studies in Comparative Communism* 8, no. 4 (Winter 1980):300–346.

5. These publications are part of a three-year national competition for the best books, motion pictures, and television films on the Chekisty, see p. 94 and *Literaturnaia Rossiia*, 24 July 1987, p. 3.

6. Stephen Lukes, *Power: A Radical View* (London: Macmillan, 1974), p. 21.

7. Alexander Dallin, "Domestic Factors Influencing Soviet Foreign Policy," in *The USSR and the Middle East*, ed. Michael Confino and Shimon Shamir (New Brunswick, NJ: Transaction Books, 1973), pp. 31–58 (quotation, p. 38).

8. Lukes, *Power*, p. 24.

9. This was KGB Capt. Viktor Orekhov, who some time during the 1970s warned dissidents about impending searches and arrests. He was reportedly caught and sentenced to twelve years' imprisonment. See Viktor Fainberg, "Mark Morozov and Captain Orekhov," *RLRB*, RL 350/86, 15 September 1986.

10. Leonard Schapiro, *Russian Studies*, ed. Ellen Dahrendorf with an introduction by Harry Willetts (London: Collins Harvill, 1986), p. 38.

11. Peter G. Peterson, "Gorbachev's Bottom Line," *New York Review of Books* 34, no. 11 (25 June 1987):29.

Appendix A:
The Soviet Security Police 1917–1987

PERIOD	NAME
20 Dec. 1917–6 Feb. 1922	Vecheka (All-Russian Extraordinary Commission for Combating Counterrevolution and Sabotage)
6 Feb. 1922–15 Nov. 1923	GPU (State Political Administration)
15 Nov. 1923–10 July 1934	OGPU (United State Political Administration)
10 July 1934– 3 Feb. 1941	GUGB (Main Administration of State Security) of the NKVD (People's Commissariat of Internal Affairs)
3 Feb. 1941–20 July 1941	NKGB (People's Commissariat of State Security)
20 July 1941–14 Apr. 1943	GUGB of the NKVD
14 Apr. 1943–19 Mar. 1946	NKGB
19 Mar. 1946–7 Mar. 1953	MGB (Ministry of State Security)
7 Mar. 1953–13 Mar. 1954	GUGB of the MVD (Ministry of Internal Affairs)
13 Mar. 1954–5 July 1978	KGB (Committee of State Security) attached to the USSR Council of Ministers
5 July 1978–present	KGB of the USSR

Appendix B:
Crimes under the Investigative
Purview of the KGB[1]

The 1960 RSFSR Criminal Code

ESPECIALLY DANGEROUS CRIMES AGAINST THE STATE:

Article 64. Treason. "An act intentionally committed by a citizen of the USSR to the detriment of the state independence, the territorial inviolability or the military might of the USSR; going over to the side of the enemy, espionage, transmission of a state or military secret to a foreign state, flight abroad or refusal to return from abroad to the USSR, rendering aid to a foreign state in carrying on hostile activity against the USSR or a conspiracy for the purpose of seizing power."

Punishment. Ten to fifteen years' deprivation of freedom with confiscation of property, with or without additional exile from two to five years; or death with confiscation of property.

In comparison with the Stalinist law on "Counterrevolutionary Crimes," Article 58, the new law eliminated the criminal responsibility of family members of the offender, who previously could be punished even if they had no knowledge of the treasonous act. Transmission of a military or state secret was no longer deemed a treasonous crime, unless the secret was actually passed to a foreign government. Otherwise divulging such a secret was a separate crime (Article 75), restricted to persons entrusted with these secrets because of their work, and was

[317]

temporarily (until 1961) removed from the purview of the state security organs. Added to Article 64, however, was the clause "rendering aid to a foreign state in carrying on hostile activity against the USSR or conspiracy for the purpose of seizing power," which had not been included in the earlier definition.

Article 65. Espionage. "The transfer, or the stealing or collection for purpose of transfer to a foreign state or foreign organization or its secret service, of information constituting a state or military secret, or the transfer or collection on assignment from a foreign intelligence service of any other information for use to the detriment of the interests of the USSR, if espionage is committed by a foreigner or a person without citizenship."

Punishment. Seven to fifteen years' deprivation of freedom with confiscation of property, with or without exile for two to five years, or death with confiscation of property.

Article 66. Terrorism. "Killing or inflicting grave bodily harm on a state or social figure or representative of authority, committed in connection with his state or social activity, for the purpose of subverting or weakening the Soviet regime."

Punishment. Ten to fifteen years' deprivation of freedom with confiscation of property with or without exile for two to five years, or death with confiscation of property for murder. Eight to fifteen years' deprivation of freedom with confiscation of property, with or without additional exile from two to five years for causing grave bodily harm.

This article was similar to the Stalinist law on state crimes except that acts committed against family members of such persons were excluded, and the definition of "state or social figures" and "representatives of authority" was narrowed considerably. Previously almost all rank-and-file workers could be included in this classification, resulting in a situation in which ordinary murders were often treated as terrorism. In addition, whereas previously "the encroachment on the property" of a state or social figure had been defined as terrorism, this was no longer so.

Article 67. Terrorism against a Representative of a Foreign State. "The killing of or causing grave bodily harm to a representative of a foreign state for the purpose of provoking war or international complications."

Punishment. Ten to fifteen years' deprivation of freedom with con-

[318]

fiscation of property with or without exile for two to five years, or death with confiscation of property for murder. Eight to fifteen years' deprivation of freedom with confiscation of property, with or without additional exile from two to five years for causing grave bodily harm.

Article 68. Sabotage (diversiia). "The destruction or damage, by explosion, arson, or other means, of enterprises, structures, transportation routes, means of communication, or other state or social property, or the commission of mass poisoning and the spreading of epidemics or epizootics, for the purpose of weakening the Soviet state."

Punishment. Eight to fifteen years' deprivation of freedom with confiscation of property, with or without exile for two to five years, or death with confiscation of property.

This article was similar to the earlier Stalinist law except that "commission of mass poisoning or spreading of epidemics or epizootics" was added.

Article 69. Wrecking. "An action or omission to act directed toward the subversion of industry, transport, agriculture, the monetary system, trade, or other branches of the national economy, or the activity of state agencies or social organizations, for the purpose of weakening the Soviet state, if such act is committed by making use of state social institutions, enterprises, or organizations, or by obstructing their normal work."

Punishment. Eight to fifteen years' deprivation of freedom with confiscation of property and with exile for two to five years or without exile.

The new RSFSR Code did not include under state crimes a separate article for sabotage in the form of deliberate failure to carry out tasks or negligence with the aim of weakening the economic structure (Article 58-14 of the Stalinist law on state crimes). Rather, this crime was incorporated into Article 69, which encompasses not only an action directed toward the subversion of the economy but also the failure to act. Under the Stalinist codes wrecking or "economic counterrevolution" had covered a wide gambit of offenses, which had served as the basis for the notorious trials of bourgeois economic specialists in the early 1930s. While the new code narrowed the definition of "wrecking" by excluding the phrase "using state institutions or enterprises or obstructing their activity, in the interests of former owners or interested capitalist organizations," it specified that wrecking need not actually be carried out, as was stated in the earlier law, but rather that the *aim* of wrecking ("an act directed toward") was sufficient to be considered a crime.

Article 70. Anti-Soviet Agitation and Propaganda. "Agitation or propaganda carried on for the purpose of subverting or weakening the Soviet regime or of committing particular, especially dangerous crimes against the state, or the circulation or preparation or keeping, for the same purpose, of literature of such content."

Punishment. Six months' to seven years' deprivation of freedom with or without exile for two to five years or exile for two to five years. If committed by a person previously convicted of an especially dangerous state crime or committed during wartime, deprivation of freedom for three to ten years, with or without exile for two to five years.

This was similar to the earlier definition of the crime "counter-revolutionary agitation and propaganda" except that "the circulation of slanderous fabrications which defame the Soviet state and social system" was added to the definition of the crime under the new law, thus broadening its scope. Article 71 (propagandizing of war) was similar in content to the earlier definitions under Article 58 but was not placed under the investigative purview of the state security organs.

Article 72. Organizational Activity Directed to Commission of Especially Dangerous Crimes against the State and Also Participation in Anti-Soviet Organization. "To be punished in accordance with Articles 64–71."

Article 73. Especially Dangerous Crimes against the State Committed against Another Working People's State. "To be punished in accordance with Articles 64–72."

OTHER CRIMES AGAINST THE STATE

Article 79. Mass Disorders. "Organization of mass disorders accompanied by pogroms, acts of destruction, arson, and other similar actions, or the direct commission of the aforementioned crimes by participants in them, or the offering by such persons of armed resistance to authority."

Punishment. Two to five years' deprivation of freedom.

[320]

This differs from the Stalinist definition of mass disorders in that it does not include "other participants in the disorders" as liable to criminal prosecution, only the organizers and those who actively commit destruction, arson, or similar actions.

Post-1960 Additions to KGB's Investigatory Purview and Amendments to Existing Codes

JUNE 1961

Article 75. Divulgence of a State Secret. "Divulgence of information constituting a state secret by a person to whom such information has been entrusted or has become known because of his position or work without treason or espionage."

Punishment. Two to five years' deprivation of freedom, or if grave consequences are entailed, five to eight years' deprivation of freedom.

Article 76. Loss of Documents Containing State Secrets. "Loss of documents containing state secrets or articles of information concerning which constitutes a state secret, by a person to whom they have been entrusted, if the loss is a result of violation of the rules established for handling the aforementioned documents or articles."

Punishment. One to three years' deprivation of freedom, or if grave consequences are entailed, three to eight years' deprivation of freedom.

Article 78. Smuggling. "The illegal transfer of goods or other valuables across the state border of the USSR, committed by concealment of articles in special containers or by fraudulent utilization of customs or other documents or on a large scale, or by a group of persons organized for smuggling or by an official by utilization of official position or the smuggling of explosives, narcotics, virulent and poisonous substances, arms and military equipment."

Punishment. Three to ten years' deprivation of freedom with confiscation of property, with or without exile from two to five years.

[321]

Article 83. Illegal Exit Abroad and Illegal Entry into the USSR. "Exit abroad, entry into the USSR or crossing the border without the requisite passport or the permission of the proper authorities."
Punishment. One to three years' deprivation of freedom.

Article 84. Violation of Rules for International Flights. "Flying into or out of the USSR without the requisite permit, nonobservance of the routes, landing places, air gateways, or altitude of flights indicated on the permit, or any other violation of rules of international flights."
Punishment. One to ten years' deprivation of freedom or a fine of up to 1000 rubles with or without confiscation of aircraft.

Article 88. Violation of Rules for Currency Transactions. "Violations of rules for currency transactions or speculation in currency or securities."
Punishment. Three to eight years' deprivation of freedom with or without confiscation of property with obligatory confiscation of currency on securities, with or without exile for two to five years. For speculation on a large scale or by persons previously convicted of this crime, five to fifteen years' deprivation of freedom with confiscation of property, with or without exile for two to five years, or death with confiscation of property.

Article 259 (subsections "a," "b," and "c"). Divulgence of a Military Secret or Loss of Documents Containing a Military Secret.
Punishment. Ranges from one to ten years' deprivation of freedom.

JULY 1962

Article 88-1. Failure to Report Crimes against the State. "Failure to report crimes against the state that are known to be in preparation or to have been committed provided for by Articles 64–69, 72."
Punishment. One to three years' deprivation of freedom or corrective labor for six months to one year.

Article 88-2. Concealment of Crimes against the State. "When not

[322]

promised in advance, the concealment of crimes against the state provided for by Articles 64–69, 72, 78, 88.''

Punishment. One to five years' deprivation of freedom with or without exile from two to five years, or exile for five years.

Before July 1962 the KGB was given authority to investigate failure to report state crimes and concealment of state crimes that fell under Articles 189 and 190 of the Criminal Code.

DECEMBER 1965

Article 92. Stealing of State or Social Property, Committed by Appropriation or Embezzlement or by Abuse of Official Position.

Punishment. Up to four years' deprivation of freedom or corrective labor for one year or loss of official position. For previous offenders, seven years' deprivation with or without loss of official position. If acts entail grave harm to the state or public organizations, six to fifteen years' deprivation of freedom with or without confiscation of property and with loss of official position.

Article 93-1. Stealing of State or Social Property on an Especially Large Scale.

Punishment. Eight to fifteen years' deprivation of freedom with confiscation of property, with or without exile, or death with confiscation of property.

JANUARY 1984

Article 64. The words "to the detriment of the state independence, territorial inviolability or military might of the USSR" replaced by the words "to the detriment of the sovereignty, territorial inviolability or state security and defense capability of the USSR."

Article 68. Broadened to include any act *"aimed* at the mass destruction of people, the causing of bodily harm or any other harm to health" (emphasis added).

[323]

Article 70. Part 1: The words "of literature of such content" replaced by the words "of works of such content in written, printed or other form."

Part 2: paragraph 1, reworded as follows: "These same actions committed by a person previously convicted of especially dangerous crimes against the state or committed in wartime" changed to "these same actions, if committed with the use of money or other material values received from foreign organizations or persons acting in the interests of these organizations, or by a person previously convicted of especially dangerous state crimes, or committed during wartime."

New Article

Article 76-1. The Transmission of Information Constituting a Work-Related Secret to Foreign Organizations. "The passing or gathering for the purpose of passing to foreign organizations or their representatives of economic, scientific, technical or other information constituting an official secret by a person to whom this information has been entrusted in his official capacity or work or has become known through other means."

Punishment. Up to three years' deprivation of freedom or corrective labor for up to two years. Up to eight years' deprivation of freedom if acts cause major property damage or other grave consequences.

Notes

1. Translations are taken from Harold J. Berman *Soviet Criminal Law and Procedure. The RSFSR Codes*, 2d ed. (Cambridge, MA: Harvard University Press, 1972), and various issues of *Current Digest of the Soviet Press*. In addition, some were translated directly by this author from the *Vedomosti VS SSSR* and *RSFSR*.

The KGB shares concurrent jurisdiction with the Procuracy for investigating crimes defined in all of the articles listed here and also with the Internal Affairs apparatus for investigating crimes set forth in Articles 88, 92, and 93-1.

Appendix C:
KGB Central Apparatus 1954–1987

CHAIRMEN	FIRST DEPUTY CHAIRMEN	DEPUTY CHAIRMEN	
I. A. Serov (Apr. 1954–Dec. 1958)	K. F. Lunev (1959)	K. F. Lunev (1954–1958)	V. I. Ustinov (1954–1957)
		S. S. Belchenko (Dec. 1957–?)	P. I. Ivashutin (Dec. 1957–Oct. 1961)
A. S. Shelepin (Dec. 1958–Oct. 1961)		V. S. Tikunov (1959–1961)	
V. E. Semichastnyi (Oct. 1961–May 1967)	P. I. Ivashutin (Oct. 1961–Jul. 1963)	A. I. Perepelitsyn (1962–1967)	S. G. Bannikov (1966–1967)
	N. S. Zakharov (1963–Dec. 1967)	N. S. Zakharov (1962–1963)	L. I. Pankratov (1963–1971)
Iu. V. Andropov (May 1967–May 1982)	S. K. Tsvigun (12/67–1/82)	V. M. Chebrikov (1968–1982)	A. N. Malygin (1968–1972)
		G. K. Tsinev (1970–1982)	V. P. Pirozhkov (1971–)
		N. P. Emokhonov (1971–1983)	V. A. Matrosov (1984–)
		V. A. Lezhepekov (1979–1983)	M. I. Ermakov (1974–)
	G. K. Tsinev (Feb. 1982–Dec. 1985)	S. N. Antonov (1981–?)	V. A. Kriuchkov (1978–)
V. V. Fedorchuk (May 1982–Dec. 1982)	V. M. Chebrikov (Jan. 1982–Dec. 1982)	V. V. Fedorchuk (1982)	G. F. Girgorenko (1981–?)
V. M. Chebrikov (Dec. 1982–)	N. P. Emokhonov (May 1983)	F. D. Bobkov (1983–1986)	G. E. Ageev (1983–)
	F. D. Bobkov (Dec. 1985–)	I. A. Markelov (Mar. 1986–)	V. A. Ponomarev (Mar. 1986–)

DIRECTORATES

First CD	*Second CD*	*Third CD*
A. M. Sakharovskii	O. M. Gribanov	D. S. Leonov
(id. 1966–1971)	(1961–1966)	(1954–1959)
V. A. Kriuchkov	G. F. Grigorenko (?)	G. K. Tsinnev
(1976–)	(1976–1981)	(1959–?)
		V. V. Fedorchuk
Fifth CD		(1967–1970)
F. D. Bobkov (?)		I. A. Fadeikin
(1970s–)		(early 1970s)
		N. A. Dushin
Seventh Dir.	*Eighth CD*	(1981–)
V. I. Alidin	S. N. Lialin	
(id. 1967)	(?–1967)	*Ninth Dir.*
	N. P. Emokhonov(?)	V. I. Ustinov
Border Guards	(1968–)	(1954–1957)
P. I. Zyrianov		N. S. Zakharov
(1954–1972)		(1957–1961)
V. A. Matrosov		S. N. Antonov(?)
(1972–pres.)		(1970s)

Party Committee
Secretaries: S. S. Marfunin (1961–?)   *Personnel Dept.*
          G. I. Vlasenko (id. Mar. 1966)   V. M. Chebrikov
          P. P. Laptev (1971–1976)   (1967–?)
          G. E. Ageev (1976–1982)   *Secretariat*
          A. N. Suplatov (id. Aug. 1984)   V. A. Kriuchkov
                                             (1967–?)

          Administration Dept.   *Archives*
          Finance Dept.   *Technical Support*

Appendix D:
Leading KGB Cadres: 1958–1962; 1980–1984

1958–1962*

NAME	POSITION(S)	BIRTH DATE	NATIONALITY	DATE OF CP MEMBERSHIP	EDUCATION	DATE OF JOINING STATE SECURITY
Aksenov, Aleksandr Nikiforovich	Dep. Chm., KGB Belorussia	1924	Belorussian	1945	Higher Party School	1959
Alizade, Mamed Ali Sadykovich	Dep. Chm., KGB Azerbaidzhan	1919	Azerbaidzhan	–	higher	1938
Arstanbekov, Aubakir Abraimovich	Dep. Chm., Chm. KGB Kazakhstan	1908	Kazakh	1931	higher	1930
Azimov, Ilias Azimovich	Oblast KGB Chief; Dep. Chm. KGB Uzbekistan	1920	Uzbek	1948	higher	1943
Badamiants, Georgii Artashesovich	Chm., KGB Armenia	1910	Armenian	1941	higher technical	1948
Bel'chenko, Sergei Savovich	Dep. Chm. USSR KGB	1902	Belorussian	–		before 1940
Beschastnov, Aleksei Dmitrievich	Central KGB apparatus	1913	Russian	1932	unfinished higher	1937
Byzov, Aleksei Petrovich	Chm., KGB Uzbekistan	1904	Russian	1923	middle	1920
Evdokimenko, Georgii Stepanovich	Central KGB apparatus	1914	Russian	1940	higher technical (agriculture)	1939
Galkin, Lev Fedorovich	Chief, Krai KGB	1908	Russian	1927	?	1932
Gubin, Vladimir Vladimirovich	Chm., KGB Kazakhstan	?	Russian	1927	?	1925
Iakiaev, Khaidar Khalikovich	Chief, Surkhandarinsk Oblast KGB	1927	Uzbek	1948	higher	1945
Inauri, Aleksei Nikolaevich	Chm., KGB Georgia	1908	Georgian	1932	higher military	1954
Ivashutin, Petr Ivanovich	Dep. Chm., USSR KGB	1909	Russian	1930	middle	1939
Kardashev, Aleksandr Vasilevich	Chm., KGB Azerbaidzhan	1917	Russian	1940	Higher Party School	1952

NAME	POSITION(s)	BIRTH DATE	NATIONALITY	DATE OF CP MEMBERSHIP	EDUCATION	DATE OF JOINING STATE SECURITY
Kiselev, Sergei Ivanovich	Central KGB	1920	Russian	1944	higher technical (chemical)	1948
Kopylov, Fedor Ivanovich	Dep. Chief, Belogorodsk Oblast KGB; Chm., KGB Azerbaidzhan	1910	Russian	1932	higher technical	1956
Korotkov, Aleksandr Mikhailovich	USSR KGB apparatus	1909	Russian	?	?	1928
Kutmanaliev, Adzhike Ashubaevich	Chief, Oblast KGB; Dep. Chm., KGB Kirgizia	1919	Kirgiz	?	technical (agricultural)	1944
Leonov, Dmitrii Sergeevich	Central KGB apparatus	1899	Russian	1918	higher military	1953
Liakishev, Mikhail Andreevich	Dep. Chm., KGB Georgia	1917	Russian	?	naval aviation school	1941
Liadus, Kazimir Frantsevich	Chm., KGB Lithuania	1901	Lithuanian	1925	middle	1954
Lukshin, Vasilii Andreevich	USSR KGB apparatus	1912	Russian	1932	higher; Higher Party School	1954
Mamedov, Aivaz Abdurkhmanovich	Dep. Chm., KGB Azerbaidzhan	1921	Azerbaidzhan	1942	higher	1944
Mironov, Nikolai Romanovich	Chief, KGB Leningrad	1913	Russian	1940	higher	1951
Naymushin, Georgii Fedorovich	Chm., KGB Uzbekistan	1913	Russian	1940	Higher Party School	1954
Nikitchenko, Vitalii Fedorovich	Chm., KGB Ukraine	1908	Ukrainian	1940	higher technical	1954
Palkin, Aleksei Petrovich	Dep. Chm., KGB Latvia	1916	Russian	1939	?	1935
Perepelitsyn, Aleksandr Ivanovich	Chm., KGB Belorussia; Dep. Chm., USSR KGB	1912	Russian	1938	?	1952
Petrov, Vasilii Ivanovich	Chm., KGB Belorussia	1918	Russian	1940	higher	1946
Pishulin, Dmitrii Ivanovich	Chm., KGB Turkmenistan	1923	Russian	1943	middle	1943
Pork, Avgust Petrovich	Chm., KGB Estonia	1917	Estonian	1943	higher legal	1950
Randakiavichius, Alfonsas Bernardovich	Chm., KGB Lithuania	1919	Lithuanian	?	Higher Party School	1956
Rudak, Arkadii Denisovich	Dep. Chm., KGB Belorussia	1911	Belorussian	1939	?	1960
Sakharovskii, Aleksandr Mikhailovich	Chief of Main Admin., USSR KGB	1909	Russian	1930	?	1939
Savchenko, Ivan Tikhonovich	Chm., KGB Moldavia	1908	Ukrainian	1939	?	?
Semichastnyi, Vladimir Efimovich	Chm., USSR KGB	1924	Ukrainian	1944	middle	1958
Serov, Ivan Aleksandrovich	Chm., USSR KGB	1905	Russian	1926	higher military	1939
Shaginian, Aikaz Srapionovich	Dep. Chm., KGB Armenia	1924	Armenian	1944	higher	1951
Shelepin, Aleksandr Nikolaevich	Chm., USSR KGB	1918	Russian	1940	higher (history and philosophy)	1958
Shul'zhenko, Boris Sergeevich	Dep. Chm., KGB Ukraine	1919	Ukrainian	1943	higher	1941
Shumilov, Vasilii Timofeevich	Chief, KGB, Leningrad City and Oblast	1924	Russian	1946	?	1960
Smirnov, Dmitrii Mikhailovich	KGB apparatus, Belorussia	1902	Russian	?	primary	1919

NAME	POSITION(S)	BIRTH DATE	NATIONALITY	DATE OF CP MEMBERSHIP	EDUCATION	DATE OF JOINING STATE SECURITY
Tikunov, Vadim Stepanovich	Dep. Chm., USSR KGB	1921	Russian	1942	higher legal	1959
Tleuliev, Abdymanap	1st Dep. Chm., KGB Kazakhstan	1913	Kazakh	1939	Higher Party School	1954
Tsinev, Georgii Karpovich	Chief, 3d Dir., USSR KGB	1907	Ukrainian	1932	higher technical military	1953
Tsvigun, Semion Kuzmich	Chm., KGB Tadzhikistan	1916	Ukrainian	1940	higher pedagogical	1939
Vaskin, Vasilii Timofeevich	Chief of KGB Admin., Saratov Oblast	?	Russian	1939	?	?
Vevers, Ian Ianovich	Chm., KGB Latvia	1899	Latvian	1919	?	1922
Zakharov, Nikolai Stepanovich	Dep. Chm., USSR KGB	1909	Russian	1932	Higher Party School	1940
1980–1984**						
Ageev, Genii Evgen'evich	Dep. Chm., USSR KGB	1929	Russian	1952	?	1965
Alidin, Viktor Ivanovich	Chief, KGB for Moscow City and Oblast	1911	Russian	1932	?	?
Andropov, Iurii Vladimirovich	Chm., USSR KGB	1914	Russian	1939	unfinished higher	1967
Antonov, Sergei Nikolaevich	Dep. Chm., USSR KGB	1922	Russian	?	?	1945
Avdukevich, Longin Ivanovich	Chm., KGB Latvia	1916	Belorussian	1940	Higher Party School	1955
Baluev, Veniamin Georgievich	Chm., KGB Belorussia	1927	Russian	1949	higher pedagogical	1949
Bobkov, Filipp Denisovich	Dep. Chm., USSR KGB	1925	Russian	1944	?	1945
Boiko, Aleksei Sergeevich	Chm., KGB Turkmenistan	1925	Russian	1946	higher pedagogical	1943
Chebrikov, Viktor Mikhailovich	Chm., USSR KGB	1923	Russian	1944	higher technical	1967
Chechurin, Lev Anatolevich	Chief, Karagandinsk Oblast KGB	1935	Russian	1960	higher agricultural	1970
Chirikov, Lev Nikolaevich	Chm., Baskir KGB; Central KGB apparatus	1923	Russian	1944	?	1943
Dushin, Nikolai Alekseevich	Central KGB apparatus	?	Russian	?	?	1942
Emokhonov, Nikolai Pavlovich	1st Dep. Chm., USSR KGB	1921	Russian	1947	higher military/technical	1968
Fedorchuk, Vitalii Vasilevich	Chm., Ukrainian KGB; Chm., USSR KGB	1918	Ukrainian	1940	KGB Higher School	1939
Glotov, Boris Aleksandrovich	1st Dep. Chm., KGB Armenia	1925	Russian	1952	higher legal	1951
Golovin, Vladimir Aleksandrovich	Chm., KGB Uzbekistan	1922	Russian	1944	higher legal	1942
Gorbatenko, Aleksei Mikhalovich	Central KGB apparatus	1916	?	1940	?	1939
Grebeniuk Grigorii Pavlovich	Central KGB apparatus	1921	Ukrainian	1943	?	1972
Inauri, Aleksei Nikolaevich	Chm., KGB Georgia	1908	Georgian	1932	higher military	1954
Iusif-Zade, Ziia Mamemievich	Chm., KGB Azerbaidzhan	1929	Azerbaidzhan	1955	higher pedagogical	1956
Iuzbashian, Marius Abramovich	Chm., KGB Armenia	1924	Armenian	1948	higher	1943
Kamalidenov, Zakash Kamalidenovich	Chm., KGB Kazakhstan	1936	Kazakh	1960	higher technical, Higher Party School	1979

NAME	POSITION(s)	BIRTH DATE	NATIONALITY	DATE OF CP MEMBERSHIP	EDUCATION	DATE OF JOINING STATE SECURITY
Khlestkov, Aleksei Aleksandrovich	Chief, Rostov Oblast KGB	1920	Russian	1941	?	1965
Kortelainen, Karl Efremovich	Chm., KGB Estonia	1930	Estonian	1953	higher military	1951
Krasilnikov, Vitalii Sergeevich	Chm., KGB Azerbaidzhan	1920	Russian	1943	higher technical	1952
Kriuchkov, Vladimir Aleksandrovich	Dep. Chm., USSR KGB	1924	Russian	1944	higher legal	1967
Laptev, Pavil Pavlovich	Asst. to KGB Chm.	1928	Russian	1951	higher legal	1979
Lomov, Nikolai Petrovich	Chm., KGB Kirgizia	1925	Russian	1947	Higher Party School	1964
Manuilov, Sergei Evgen'evich	Dep. Chm., Leningrad KGB	1923	Russian	?	higher	1942
Melkumov, Levon Nikolaevich	Chm., KGB Uzbekistan	1924	Armenian	1944	higher (economic)	1950
Nikulin, Iakov Prokoplevich	Chm., KGB Belorussia	1913	Russian	1941	middle	1940
Nosyrev, Daniel Pavlovich	Chief, KGB Leningrad City & Oblast	1915	Russian	?	higher technical	1940
Mukha, Stefan Nesterovich	Chm., KGB Ukraine	1930	Ukrainian	1955	higher technical	1975
Perventsev, Evgenii Ivanovich	Chm., KGB Tadzhikistan	1926	Russian	1950	Higher Party School	1950
Petkiavichius, Iuozas Iuozovich	Chm., KGB Lithuania	1924	Lithuanian	1947	Higher Party School	1960
Pirozhkov, Vladimir Petrovich	Dep. Chm., USSR KGB	?	Russian	1946	?	1966
Pork, Avgust Petrovich	Chm., KGB Estonia	1917	Estonian	1943	higher legal	1950
Poryvkin, Veniamin Efimovich	1st Dep. Chm., KGB Estonia	1924	Russian	1948	higher	1971
Pugo, Boris Karlovich	Chm., KGB Latvia	1937	Latvian	1963	higher technical	1977
Pulatov, Kamil P.	1st Dep. Chm., KGB Tadzhikistan	1936	Tadzhik	?	?	1976
Shemiakin, Nikolai Nestorovich	Central KGB apparatus	1927	Russian	1952	?	1961
Shevchenko, Vasilii Tarasovich	Chm., KGB Kazakhstan	1921	Ukrainian	1941	higher legal	1943
Shornikov, Sergei Semenovich	Central KGB apparatus	?	Russian	?	Frunze Military Academy	1952
Tardzhimanov, Mkrtich Oganesovich	Chief Oblast KGB	1927	Azerbaidzhan	?	higher technical	1955
Tleuliev, Abdumanap	1st Dep. Chm., KGB Kazakhstan	1913	Kazakh	1939	Higher Party School	1954
Tsinev, Georgii Karpovich	Dep., First Dep. Chm., USSR KGB	1907	Ukrainian	1932	higher military	1953
Tsvigun, Semen Kuz'mich	First Dep. Chm., USSR KGB	1916	Ukrainian	1940	higher pedogogical	1939
Vinokurov, Boris Andreevich	Dep. Chm., KGB Turkmenistan	1924	Russian	1948	middle	1950
Volkov, Gavriel Moiseevich	Chm., KGB Moldavia	1920	Russian	1945	KGB higher school	1942
Zvezdenkov, Valentin Vladimirovich	1st Dep. Chm., KGB Lithuania	1920	Russian	1942	middle	1938

SOURCES: See those listed in note 1, chapter 5.

* Includes individuals holding leading KGB posts at any time between 1958 and 1962.

** Includes individuals holding leading KGB posts at any time between 1980 and 1984.

Appendix E:
Key KGB Posts in Non-Russian Republics, Moscow and Leningrad, 1954–1987

1. ARMENIAN SSR

Chairmen

G. A. Badamiants
1954–Nov. 1972
A. P. Ragozin
Nov. 1972–Nov. 1975
G. A. Mikhaelian
Nov. 1975–June 1978
M. A. Iuzbashian
June 1978–

First Dep. Chm.*

M. O. Tardzhimanov
1971–1973
G. A. Mikhaelian
id. Mar. 1975
B. A. Glotov
1979–Dec. 1981
Ia. I. Oloviannikov
Dec. 1981–

2. AZERBAIDZHAN SSR

Chairmen

A. M. Guskov
1954–Oct. 1956

F. I. Kopylov
Oct. 1956–Sept. 1959
A. V. Kardashev
Sept. 1959–Oct. 1963
S. K. Tsvigun
Oct. 1963–June 1967
G. A. Aliev
June 1967–Oct. 1969
V. S. Krasilnikov
Oct. 1969–June 1980
Z. M. Iusif-Zade
June 1980–

First Dep. Chm.

G. A. Aliev
id. March 1967
Z. M. Iusif-Zade
1977–1980
F. D. Kudashkin
id. Dec. 1982

3. BELORUSSIAN SSR

Chairmen

A. I. Perepelitsyn
1954–Nov. 1959
V. I. Petrov

Nov. 1959–Aug. 1970
Ia. P. Nikulkin
Aug. 1970–Aug. 1980
V. G. Baluev
Aug. 1980–

First Dep. Chm.

A. D. Rudak
1963–1969
V. V. Buevich
id. Feb. 1980
L. I. Gostevskii
id. Feb. 1985

4. ESTONIAN SSR

Chairmen

I. P. Karpov
1955–June 1961
A. P. Pork
June 1961–June 1982
K. E. Kortelainen
June 1982–

First Dep. Chm.

V. E. Porkyvkin
1977–

5. GEORGIAN SSR

Chairmen

A. N. Inauri
1954–

First Dep. Chm.

F. S. Piliugin
Jan. 1976–Mar. 1978
A. I. Arkhipov
Mar. 1978–1985
L. G. Kazmin
id. Feb. 1985

6. KAZAKHSTAN SSR

Chairmen

V. V. Gubin
1954–Oct. 1959
K. F. Lunev
Oct. 1959–Sep. 1960
A. A. Arstanbekov
Sep. 1960–Nov. 1963
G. S. Evdokimenko
Nov. 1963–Nov. 1975
V. T. Shevchenko
Nov. 1975–Feb. 1982
Z. K. Kamalidenov
Feb. 1982–Jan. 1986
V. M. Miroshnik
Jan. 1986–

First Dep. Chm.

A. T. Tleuliev
1971–1975
V. F. Kukhliev
id. Feb. 1985

7. KIRGIZ SSR

Chairmen

A. V. Tereshchenko
1954–Feb. 1956
N. G. Ermolov
Feb. 1956–July 1961

P. V. Chvertko
July 1961–Mar. 1967
D. Asankulov
Mar. 1967–Apr. 1978
N. P. Lomov
Apr. 1978–Dec. 1985
V. A. Riabokon
Dec. 1985–

First Dep. Chm.

T. S. Aitbaev
id. Feb. 1985

8. LATVIAN SSR

Chairmen

Ia. Ia. Vevers
1954–Jan. 1963
L. A. Avdiukevich
Jan. 1963–Nov. 1980
B. K. Pugo
Nov. 1980–May 1984
S. V. Zukul
May 1984–

First Dep. Chm.

B. K. Pugo
1977–Nov. 1980
S. V. Gulin
id. Feb. 1985

9. LITHUANIAN SSR

Chairmen

K. F. Liaudis
1954–Nov. 1959
A. B. Randakiavichius
Nov. 1959–Jan. 1967
Iu. Iu. Petkiavichius
Jan. 1967–May 1987
E. Eismontas
May 1987–

First Dep. Chm.

Ia. F. Sinitsyn

id. Mar. 1955
P. A. Voroshilov
Feb. 1978–1980
V. V. Zvezdenkov
id. Feb. 1985

10. MOLDAVIAN SSR

Chairmen

I. L. Mordovets
1954–Apr. 1955
A. V. Prokopenko
Apr. 1955–Sep. 1959
I. T. Savchenko
Sep. 1959–Mar. 1967
P. V. Chvertko
Mar. 1967–Dec. 1975
A. P. Ragozin
Dec. 1975–Jan. 1979
G. M. Volkov
Jan. 1979–

First Dep. Chm.

G. I. Lavranchuk
1972–1981

11. TADZHIK SSR

Chairmen

D. K. Vishnevskii
1954–Apr. 1955
D. D. Kochetov
Apr. 1955–Apr. 1957
S. K. Tsvigun
Apr. 1957–Oct. 1963
M. M. Miliutin
Oct. 1963–May 1968
S. G. Sazonov
May 1968–Nov. 1970
V. T. Shevchenko
Nov. 1970–Oct. 1975
E. I. Perventsev
Oct. 1975–Jan. 1985
V. V. Petkel'
Jan. 1985–

[332]

First Dep. Chm.

K. P. Pulatov
Jan. 1980–Jan. 1986

12. TURKMEN SSR

Chairmen

V. V. Vaskin
1954–Aug. 1956
S. G. Bannikov
Aug. 1956–Sep. 1959
D. I. Pishulin
Sep. 1959–Feb. 1965
L. I. Korobov
Feb. 1965–Jan. 1974
Ia. P. Kiselev
Jan. 1974–Dec. 1978
A. S. Boiko
Jan. 1979–

First Dep. Chm.

N. A. Obezov
1980–1984
S. Iusupov
id. Feb. 1985

13 UKRAINIAN SSR

Chairmen

V. F. Nikitchenko
1954–July 1970
V. V. Fedorchuk
July 1970–May 1982

S. N. Mukha
June 1982–May 1987
N. M. Golushko
May 1987–

First Dep. Chm.

B. S. Shulzhenko
1963–1970
S. I. Krikun
1971–1975
S. N. Mukha
June 1975–June 1982

14. UZBEK SSR

Chairmen

A. P. Byzov
1954–1960
G. F. Naymushin
1960–Dec. 1963
S. I. Kiselev
Dec. 1963–Nov. 1969
A. D. Beschastnov
Nov. 1969–Oct. 1974
E. B. Nordman
Oct. 1974–Mar. 1978
L. N. Melkumov
Mar. 1978–Sep. 1983
V. A. Golovin
Sep. 1983–

First Dep. Chm.

K. Ruzmetov
1963–1967

V. I. Shibalin
Jan. 1979–1985
Kh. Tashkhodzhaev
id. Feb. 1985

MOSCOW CITY AND OBLAST

Chiefs

N. I. Krainov
1955–Feb. 1957
M. P. Svetlichnyi
Feb. 1957–Dec. 1967
S. N. Lialin
Dec. 1967–June 1971
V. I. Alidin
June 1971–Jan. 1986
N. E. Chelnokov
Jan. 1986–

LENINGRAD OBLAST

Chiefs

S. S. Belchenko
Jan. 1955–1957
N. R. Mironov
1957–1959
V. T. Shumilov
Jan. 1960–Jan. 1971
D. P. Nosyrev
Jan. 1971–May 1987
V. M. Prilukov
May 1987–

---

* Dates for first deputy chairmen are approximate, based on identification in the Soviet press, which is rare for these officials. In several cases no information could be found.

Suggestions for Further Reading

Bibliography

On the political police in the tsarist period see Edward Ellis Smith, *"The Okhrana":* *The Russian Department of Police: A Bibliography* (Stanford, Calif.: Stanford University Press, 1967). On the Cheka see a Soviet bibliography by N. S. Aksenova and M. V. Vasil'eva, *Soldaty Dzerzhinskogo Soiuz beregut. Rekomendatel'nyi ukazatel' literatury o chekistakh* (Moscow: Izdatel'stvo "Kniga," 1972); and a comprehensive bibliographical essay by A. L. Litvin (Kazan'), "VChk v sovetskoi istoricheskoi literature," *Voprosy istorii*, no. 5 (May 1986):96–102.

For Western bibliographies of the Cheka and its successor organizations (including the KGB) see *Soviet Intelligence and Security Services: A Selected Bibliography of Soviet Publications* Congressional Research Service, Library of Congress, vol. 1 covering 1964–1970 and vol. 2 covering 1971–1972 (Washington D.C.: U.S. Government Printing Office, 1972, 1975); Robert M. Slusser, "Recent Soviet Books on the History of the Secret Police," *Slavic Review* 24, no. 2 (March 1965): 90–98; and an excellent compilation by Raymond G. Rocca and John J. Dziak, *Bibliography on Soviet Intelligence and Security Services* (Boulder, Colo., and London: Westview Press, 1984). There is also a good bibliography of *samizdat* writings, many of which contain useful descriptions of the KGB's treatment of internal dissent: Josephine Woll in collaboration with Vladimir Treml, *Soviet Dissident Literature: A Critical Guide* (Boston: G. K. Hall, 1983).

History

There is one general English-language history of the police in the tsarist and Soviet periods: Ronald Hingley, *The Russian Police: Muscovite, Imperial Russian and Soviet Security Operations, 1565–1970* (London: Hutchinson, 1970). For a study of the Third Section see Sidney Monas, *The Third Section* (Cambridge, Mass.:

Harvard University Press, 1961). To my knowledge there are no Soviet histories of the tsarist political police. The only sources in Russian are the memoirs of tsarist police officials, cited in chapter 1. For the post-1917 period there is an excellent, comprehensive scholarly study of the Vecheka in English by George Leggett, which was first published in 1981 and has recently appeared in a paperback edition: George Leggett, *The Cheka: Lenin's Political Police* (Oxford: Clarendon Press, 1986). Leggett's book is based on a vast number of primary and secondary Soviet sources, thus providing further avenues for research. In addition, the Soviets have produced numerous histories of the Cheka and collections of documents on this period, which Leggett cites in his book.

For Western histories on the post-Cheka police see an unpublished study by Gary Waxmonsky, *Police and Politics in Soviet Society, 1921–29* (Unpublished Ph.D. dissertation, Princeton University, 1982); Simon Wolin and Robert Slusser, eds., *The Soviet Secret Police* (New York: Praeger, 1957), which examines the political police from 1917 to the post-Stalin era; Boris Levytsky, *The Uses of Terror: The Soviet Secret Police, 1917–1970*, trans. H. A. Piehler (New York: Coward, McCann & Geoghegan, 1972); and two studies by Robert Conquest: *The Great Terror: Stalin's Purge of the Thirties*, rev. ed. (New York: Collier, 1973), and *Inside Stalin's Secret Police: NKVD Politics 1936–39* (Stanford, Calif.: Hoover Institution Press, 1985). Although they do not deal specifically with the political police, the numerous studies of Stalin and Stalinism, cited in chapter 1, and the memoir literature on this period offer the scholar a rich source of information for much-needed research on the role of the police under Stalin.

Soviet historians are less than forthcoming about the activities of the Stalinist police. The numerous Soviet histories of the political police (some of which are mentioned here in the section on career data) are often fictionalized or anecdotal in content and focus more on the Cheka than on its successors. They do not tell us much about police operations, but they do offer some useful biographical information. The Soviets have provided numerous studies of the institutional evolution of the Soviet state and the Soviet legal system, which have been exploited here for the purpose of understanding the formal bases upon which the Stalinist police apparatus rested. Some of these are cited in chapter 1. Among them are K. A. Sofronenko, ed., *Istoriia gosudarstva i prava SSSR*. Pt. 2: *Istoriia sovetskogo gosudarstva i prava* (Moscow: Gosizdat, 1962); and E. A. Skripilev, ed., *Istoriia sovetskogo gosudarstva i prava*, Vol. 2: *Sovetskoe gosudarstvo v periode stroitel'stva sotsializma (1921–35 gg.)* (Moscow: Gosizdat, 1968). In addition, the journal *Sovetskoe gosudarstvo i pravo* has published several articles on the Stalinist legal system and other aspects of Soviet police history. Numerous legal textbooks are also available that were published in the Stalin period and describe the system of criminal procedure for state crimes as well as the investigative purview of the political police. Among them are M. S. Strogovich, *Ugolovnyi protsess* (Moscow: Iuridicheskoe Izdatel'stvo, 1946); and S. S. Studenikin, *Sovetskoe administrativnoe pravo* (Moscow: Gosizdat Iuridicheskoi Literatury, 1949).

The Political Police and the Post-Stalin Legal System

Among the more useful Western sources is a three-volume collection on Soviet law under various editorships and published in the Law in Eastern Europe Series by the Documentation Office for East European Law, *Soviet Law after Stalin* (Leiden: A. W. Sijthoff, 1977–1979). Also important and used extensively for this book is H. J. Berman, *Soviet Criminal Law and Procedure: The RSFSR Codes*, 2d ed. (Cambridge, Mass.: Harvard University Press, 1972). This includes a full English translation of the legal and procedural codes, as well as a lengthy discussion of the changes since the Stalin era. The Soviets themselves have provided many useful sources on the legal system as it relates to crimes under the purview of the KGB. In addition to articles in legal journals, such as *Sovetskoe gosudarstvo i pravo*, *Pravovedenie*, and *Sotsialisticheskaia zakonnost'*, are legal textbooks dealing with this subject. Among them are V. I. Kurliandskii and M. P. Mikhailov, eds., *Osobo opasnye gosudarstvennye prestupleniia* (Moscow: Gosizdat Iuridicheskaia Literatura, 1963); V. A. Stremovskii, *Uchastniki predvaritel'nogo sledstviia v sovetskom ugolovnom protsesse* (Rostov: Izdatel'stvo Rostovskogo universiteta, 1966); A. M. Rekunkov and A. K. Orlov, *Kommentarii k ugolovnoprotsessual'nomu kodeksu RSFSR* (Moscow, Iuridicheskaia Literatura 1985) and, for documentation of changes in the legal codes, various issues of *Vedomosti VS SSSR*, as cited in this book.

Institutional Status and Structure of the KGB

A variety of administrative law textbooks published in the Soviet Union since 1953 discuss the formal role and status of the KGB. Among the more comprehensive are V. M. Manokhin ed., *Sovetskoe administrativnoe pravo* (Moscow: Iuridicheskaia Literatura, 1977) and Iu. M. Kozlov et al., eds., *Sovetskoe administrativnoe pravo. Upravlenie v oblasti administrativno-politicheskoi deiatel'nosti* (Moscow: Iuridicheskaia Literatura, 1979). These sources offer little information on the internal organization of the KGB, however. On this question the only open-source information available comes from Western accounts based mainly on defectors' reports. Of the numerous Western books published on the KGB in recent years, the best and more authoritative are two by John Barron: *KGB: Secret Work of Soviet Secret Agents* (New York: Bantam Books, 1974) and *KGB Today: The Hidden Hand* (New York: Readers Digest Press, 1983). Aside from some discussion of the KGB's internal organization, the main focus of these books is on the KGB's foreign espionage activities.

KGB Career Data

The best source of biographical and career information on KGB officials is the Soviet press. A discussion of the specific periodicals, encyclopedias, and dictionaries consulted appears in chapter 5, note 1, along with references to various . English-language sources. It should also be noted that *Krasnaia zvezda* publishes obituaries of leading KGB officials, while republic newspapers provide obituaries of republic-level KGB officials. These often give information that is new and valuable. In addition, the various regional histories of the state security organs that have appeared in the past twenty years frequently offer biographical data. These histories are referred to in notes throughout this book. Among the more useful ones are L. A. Plotnikova, ed., *Chekisty* (Leningrad: Lenizdat, 1982); Z. M. Iusif-Zade, ed., *Chekisty Azerbaidzhana. Dokumenty, ocherki, rasskazy* (Baku: Azerneskr, 1981); *Rytsari dolga: vospominaniia chekistov* (Donetsk: Donbass, 1982); N. I. Milovanov, ed., *Ne zhaleia zhizni* (Alma Ata: Izdatel'stvo "Kazakhstan," 1977); N. Sh. Maisuradze, ed., *Bez lini fronta. Nevydumannye rasskazy o geroicheskoi bor'be Chekistov gruzii* (Tbilisi: "Merani," 1981); V. V. Kryzhanovskii, ed., *Chekisty Karelii* (Petrozavodsk: "Kareliia," 1982); and a series of six volumes on the Moscow security police, *Chekisty rasskazyvaiut* (Moscow: Sovetskaia Rossiia, 1970–1983).

The *Radio Liberty Research Bulletin* is an invaluable source of biographical and career information on KGB officials. Also useful are the CIA *Directory of Soviet Officials*, published periodically in separate volumes for republic and national-level officials, and two volumes entitled *Leaders of the Soviet Republics*, produced by the Australian National University, Canberra, Australia. The first covering the years 1955–1972 and published in 1973, was compiled by Grey Hodnett and Val Ogareff. The second, covering 1971–1980, was published in 1981 and compiled by Val Ogareff.

The KGB and Party Politics

Again, the major source used here is the Soviet press—the major newspapers and journals that report on political developments. Also very useful for following and analyzing political events is the *Radio Liberty Research Bulletin*. Additional insights are offered by books written by those with some access to unreported information on Kremlin politics, such as Michael Voslensky, *Nomenklatura: Anatomy of the Soviet Ruling Class*, trans. Eric Mosbacher (London: The Bodley Head, 1984); Roy Medvedev, *Khrushchev*, trans. Brian Pearce (New York: Anchor Press, 1983); and Zhores Medvedev, *Andropov* (New York: W. W. Norton, 1983). On the KGB as an interest group see Frederick Barghoorn, "The Security Police," in *Interest Groups in Soviet Politics*, ed. H. Gordon Skilling and Franklyn Griffiths (Princeton, N.J.: Princeton University Press, 1971).

[338]

The KGB and Internal Dissent

For following developments on a regular basis the best sources are *Vesti iz SSSR* (*USSR News Brief*), a bimonthly newsletter on the Soviet human rights movement produced in Munich, Germany, since the early 1980s; *A Chronicle of Current Events*, the *samizdat* journal that has appeared since 1968 and is published in English by Amnesty International Publications; and the Radio Liberty *Arkhiv Samizdata*. For insights into how the KGB interacts with dissidents and the latter's perceptions of the KGB, there are many excellent firsthand accounts by dissidents and emigrés. Among them are Vladimir Bukovsky, *To Build a Castle— My Life as a Dissenter*, trans. Michael Scammell (New York: Viking, 1978), Andrei Amalrik, *Notes of a Revolutionary*, trans. Guy Daniels (New York: Alfred A. Knopf, 1982); Petro Grigorenko, *Memoirs*, trans. Thomas P. Whitney (London and New York: W. W. Norton, 1982); Dina Kaminskaya, *Final Judgement: My Life as a Soviet Defense Attorney*, trans. Michael Glenny (New York: Simon and Schuster, 1982); and Viktor Krasin, *Sud* (New York: Chalidze Publications, 1983). There are numerous Western studies of the dissident movement per se. For a consideration of the factors involved in determining Kremlin policy toward dissent see the various writings by Peter Reddaway, cited in chapter 6, in particular *Soviet Policies on Dissent and Emigration: The Radical Change of Course since 1979*. (Colloquium Paper No. 192, Kennan Institute for Advanced Russian Studies, Washington, D.C., 28 August 1984).

KGB Troops and Special Departments in the Armed Forces

With the exception of a few defectors' accounts published in the West, the main sources on this subject are Soviet. In addition to the national and republic press, the *Soviet Military Encyclopedia* and other reference works, the numerous Soviet histories of the internal troops, border troops, and Special Departments are valuable sources of information on both the past and present operations of these institutions. Among the more useful on the special and border troops are I. G. Belikov et al., eds., *Imeni Dzerzhinskogo: Boevoi put'ordena Lenina krasnoznamenoi divizii im. F. E. Dzerzhinskogo* (Moscow: Voenizdat, 1976); N. Zubov, *Oni okhraniali Lenina* (Moscow: Molodaia gvardiia, 1984); V. S. Ivanov et al., *Chasovye sovetskikh granits: kratkii ocherk istorii pogranichnykh voisk SSSR* (Moscow: Politizdat, 1983); P. I. Zyrianov et al., eds., *Pogranichnye voiska SSSR 1918–1928: Sbornik dokumentov i materialov* (Moscow: Nauka 1973); and several volumes of documents on the border troops in World War II, *Pogranichnye voiska SSSR v velikoi otechestvennoi voine*, published in Moscow by the USSR Academy of Sciences in 1975–1976. Also see a study in English by James Reitz, "The Soviet Security Troops—The Kremlin's Other Armies," in *Soviet Armed Forces Review Annual*, vol. 6, ed. David Jones (Gulf Breeze, Fla.: Academic International Press, 1982). There are several good Soviet histories on the special departments.

Among them are S. Z. Ostriakov, *Voennye chekisty* (Moscow: Voenizdat, 1979); Iu. B. Dolgopolov, *Voina bez linii fronta* (Moscow: Voenizdat, 1981); and V. P. Nosyrev, ed., *V poedinke s Abverom: Dokumental'nyi ocherk o chekistakh Leningradskogo fronta, 1941–45* (Moscow: Voenizdat, 1968). Also see an account by a former employee of the KGB's Third Directorate: Aleksei Myagkov, *Inside the KGB* (Richmond, England: Foreign Affairs Publishing, 1976).

KGB Foreign Activities

Most of the numerous Western writings on the KGB's foreign intelligence activities are journalistic in nature. John Barron's two books on the KGB, cited earlier, are the most authoritative. Also very informative are three recent books on the subject of KGB "active measures": Ladislav Bittman, *The KGB and Soviet Disinformation. An Insider's View* (Washington, N.Y.: Pergamon-Brassey's, 1985); Richard H. Shultz and Roy Godson, *Dezinformatsia: Active Measures in Soviet Strategy* (Washington, N.Y.: Pergamon-Brassey's, 1984); and Brian D. Dailey and Patrick J. Parker, eds., *Soviet Strategic Deception* (Stanford, Calif.: Hoover Institution Press, 1987). In addition, several U.S. government publications offer reliable and useful information on the KGB abroad. Among them are two publications by the U.S. Congress, House Permanent Select Committee on Intelligence: *Soviet Covert Action (The Forgery Offensive)* (Washington, D.C.: U.S. Government Printing Office, 1980), and *Soviet Active Measure* (Washington, D.C.: U.S. Government Printing Office, 1982); and a more recent U.S. government publication: *Soviet Acquisition of Militarily Significant Western Technology: An Update* (September, 1985).

Two excellent books by former members of the Soviet diplomatic corps provide good insights about KGB employees abroad: Arkady N. Shevchenko, *Breaking with Moscow* (New York: Ballantine, 1985); and Nicolas Polianski, *M.I.D. 12 ans dans les services diplomatiques du Kremlin* (Paris: Pierre Belfond, 1984). No studies have appeared in the West of the specific role of the KGB in decisonmaking. Information for this book was gleaned from various general Western studies on the subject, including Jiri Valenta, *Soviet Intervention in Czechoslovakia, 1968: Anatomy of a Decision* (Baltimore and London: Johns Hopkins University Press, 1979); Seweryn Bialer, ed., *The Domestic Context of Soviet Foreign Policy* (Boulder, Colo.: Westview Press, 1981); and Jiri Valenta and William C. Potter, eds., *Soviet Decisionmaking for National Security* (London: Allen & Unwin, 1984).

Theoretical Issues

Brian Chapman's *Police State* (London: Pall Mall Press, 1970) provides an excellent theoretical background for examining the Soviet political police as an institution. Chapman discusses the general concept of a police state and describes the evolution of different types of police states up to the modern age. Also valuable is Alexander Dallin and George Breslauer, *Political Terror in Communist Systems* (Stanford, Calif.: Stanford University Press, 1970); Barrington Moore, Jr., *Terror and Progress USSR: Some Sources of Change and Stablility in the Soviet Dictatorship* (Cambridge, Mass.: Harvard University Press, 1954); and Stephen Schafer, *The Political Criminal* (New York: Free Press, 1974). The literature on totalitarianism, discussed in chapter 1, offers a good theoretical framework for understanding the Stalinist police apparatus, as does the recent interpretive literature on Stalinism. Highly recommended is the collection edited by Robert C. Tucker, *Stalinism: Essays in Historical Interpretation* (New York: W. W. Norton, 1977).

Index